GLOBALISATION AND THE MARGINALISED

GLOBALISATION AND THE MARGINALISED

Issues and Concerns for Development

Editors
M.C. Behera
Jumyir Basar

Commonwealth

Globalisation and the Marginalised

Edition : 2027

ISBN : 978-81-311-0302-9

Published by :
COMMONWEALTH PUBLISHERS (P) LTD.
4831/24, Govind Lane,
Ansari Road, Darya Ganj,
New Delhi - 110002
Ph. : 23242541, 23272541
e-mail : commonwealthpublishers2016@gmail.com

Distributed by :
ARJUN PUBLISHING HOUSE
4831/24, Govind Lane,
Ansari Road, Darya Ganj,
New Delhi - 110002
Ph. : 23242541, 23272541
e-mail : arjunbooks2001@gmail.com
arjunpubhouse@gmail.com

Laser Typesetting by :
Dimple Computers
Delhi

Printed at :
Milan Enterprises
Delhi

Preface

The arguments, discussions and opinions expressed in the papers included in this volume are those of respective authors. The editors in no way are responsible for this. However, the editors express their deep sense of gratitude to the contributors of papers. The papers included in this volume were invited from individual scholars and a few of them were presented in the seminar on Encountering Globalisation: Tribal Communities in India and Development Issues held on 27th and 28th February, 2009. The seminar was sponsored by ICSSR, New Delhi. The editors are grateful to ICSSR, New Delhi, and collegues at Arunachal Institute of Tribal Studies, its Director, Prof. Tamo Mibang and Prof. K.C. Belliappa, Vice Chancellor, Rajiv Gandhi University, Itanagar.

The editors are grateful to Commonwealth Publishers, New Delhi for its timely publication.

M.C. Behera
Jumyir Basar

Contents

Chapters		Pages

Contributors

A. Ibotombi Singh: Ph.D, Senior Lecturer in Economics, D. N. Government College, Itanagar – 795113, e-mail: singh_ai@yahoo.co.in

A.K. Agarwal: Ph.D, Professor, Department of Economics, Mizoram University, Tanhril, Aizawl - 796009 , Mizoram. akg_49 @yahoo.co.in

A. Rajmani Singh, Ph.D, Associate Professor, Dept of Commerce, Manipur University, rajaheibam@rediffmail.com,rajaheibam2@gmail.com, Ph.09863145171.

Aditya Joshi : MBA, North Eastern Regional Institute of Science and Technology, Nirjuli- 791 109, Arunachal Pradesh.

Ambrish Gautam: Faculty, P.G. Dept. of Sociology, Ranchi University, Ranchi–834008, Contact No:- +919835142785, E–mail: *amb_admn05@yahoo.co.in*

Amitav Mitra: Ph.D, Professor of Economics, Rajiv Gandhi University, Rono Hills, Itanagar, e-mail: amitraau@rediffmail.com

Eswarappa Kasi: Ph.D, Guest Faculty, Department of Anthropology, University of Hyderabad, Hyderabad-500 046, Andhra Pradesh, kasieswar@gmail.com

Jayanta Choudhury: Ph.D. Asst. Professor, Rural Development, Tripura University, Agartala, Tripura. E-mail: jayantard@gmail.com

Jumyir Basar: Asst. Professor, Arunachal Institute of Tribal Studies, Rajiv Gandhi University, Itanagar-791112, E-mail: jumyir@yahoo.com, Ph.09436055264.

K. Haloi: Sr. Faculty, National Institute of Rural Development, North-Eastern Regional Centre, Khanapara, Guwahati-22, Assam, kh_nirdnerc@rediffmail.com, Ph. 09435556900.

Kashinath Jena: Ph.D, Associate Professor, Department of Political Science, Tripura University, Agartala, Tripura, e-mail : nanpur@rediffmail.com, Ph.09856346477.

Krishna Chandra Pradhan: Ph.D, Sr. Lecturer in Economics, Khemundi College, Digapahandi, Ganjam (Orissa)–761012, kcpradhan66@gmail.com

Kumari Sweta: P.G. Dept. of Sociology, Ranchi University, Ranchi–834008.

M.A. Salam: Reader, Department of Economics, Government College, Bomdila, masalam005@rediffmail.com, Ph.9436057826.

M.C. Behera: Associate Professor, Arunachal Institute of Tribal Studies, Rajiv Gandhi University, Itanagar. E-mail : mcbehera1959@gmail.com, Ph. 09436252229.

Maila Lama: Asst. Professor, Department of Economics, Rajiv Gandhi University, Rono Hills:Doimukh, Itanagar-791112, Arunachal Pradesh.

Mihin Dollo: Research Scholar, G.B. Pant Institute of Himalayan Environment and Development, North East Unit, Vivek Vihar, Itanagar-791113, Arunachal Pradesh, Ph. No. 0360 2211773.

Millo Mamung: Research Scholar, Arunachal Institute of Tribal Studies, Rajiv Gandhi University, Rono Hills, Itanagar-791112.

P.K. Kar : Ph. D, Senior Reader and Head, Department of Sociology, F.M. (Autonomous) College, Balasore-756001, Orissa.

Prasanna K. Samal: Ph.D, Scientist In-charge, G.B. Pant Institute of Himalayan Environment and Development, North East Unit, Vivek Vihar, Itanagar-791113, Arunachal Pradesh, e-mail: prasannasamal@rediffmail.com

Priyanka Priyadarshini : Ph.D, Assistant Professor in Economics, JN College, Pasighat, East Siang, Arunachal Pradesh.

R.M. Pant: Ph.D, Professor & Head, Centre for Management Studies, North Eastern Regional Institute of Science and Technology, Nirjuli-791109, Itanagar, Arunachal Pradesh, e-mail: rajive_nerist@yahoo.com

Rajesh Chatterjee: Ph.D. Asst. Professor, Rural Development, Tripura University, Agartala, Tripura, e-mail: rajeshscholar@yahoo.co.in

Ram Krishna Mandal, Associate Prof. in Economics, Dera Natung Govt. College, Itanagar, Arunachal Pradesh, Phone No. 0360-2292088, 9436633120, E-mail: rkm_1966@yahoo.co.in

S.K. Panda: Ph.D, Watershed Development Team Member, (Social Science Faculty), District Watershed Mission, Baripada-757 001, Mayurbhanj (Orissa).

Sib Ranjan Misra: Ph.D, Professor & Head, Department of Economics and Politics, Visva-Bharati University, Santiniketan-731235, West Bengal, Phone: +91 (03463)261699, rmisra1@rediffmail.com, srmeco@gmail.com

Sujit K. Dutta, Ph.D., Dy Director, National Institute of Rural Development, North-Eastern Regional Centre, Khanapara, Guwahati-22, Assam.

Surjyanarayan Tripathy: Ph.D, Professor, Centre for Study of Social Exclusion and Inclusive Policy, Gokhale Institute of Politics and Economics, BMCC Road, Pune, Maharashtra- 411004.

Introduction

M.C. Behera and Jumyir Basar

Marginalisation is multidimensional concept and it is more often inherent in the social structure (Mullaley, 2005) and development process. (Cernea, 1995, 2000; Mandal and Behera, 2005; Basar, 2008 and Behera and Basar, 2009). Development induced displacement is an example of marginalisation in the process of development. In rural-urban divide, an offshoot in the process of development, the rural people are generally marginalised. In social structure marginalisation manifests in social categories like scheduled caste, scheduled tribe, backward caste and along gender divide placing the female population in marginal category. No doubt, they are designated as weaker sections in Indian Constitution[1]. Inequality, backwardness, deprivation, displacement and exclusion are some indicators of and at the same time synonyms for marginalisation.

Marginalisation displays both inter and intra-dimensionality. When tribal communities are situated in relation to non-tribal communities in general, the point of reference is inter-category marginalisation; the tribal communities are generally marginalised communities. (GoI, 2006). In the same vein, women as a category are marginalised group as compared to men and rural people are generally a marginalised group as compared to their urban counterparts. However, reference to this type of inter group marginalisation has only general classificatory significance, for within the rural people there are divisions on

1. Constitution of India, Allahabad, Allahabad Law Agency, 1977 edition.

the basis of caste. The scheduled castes or backward castes in a village community form into marginalised section as compared to general castes, and from among general castes the women as a category comprise the marginalised group. Further, women in general do not display marginalisation in an exclusive sense, for women of marginalised groups are likely to be more marginalised (Nath, 2008) more marginal as compared to women of general (non-marginalised) groups. We cannot deny of the comparable possibility of cross-section marginalisation between tribal and non-tribal communities. The non-tribal rural people or a section of them in remote areas can be found marginalised in terms of their economic status as compared to a section of people in many tribal communities of North East India[2].

Poverty in terms of livelihoods insecurity is an indicator of marginalisation and more often it is a causative factor of migration. We will find a number of people from general caste migrate from Orissa and Bihar to other states of the country while there is no such migration from among the tribes of Arunachal Pradesh or Nagaland or Mizoram in North-East India. The caste based rural communities are far backward than the Mina tribe of Rajasthan. What is important here is that our understanding of marginalisation in terms of social category has a weak base especially in India in the present context where government is committed to general welfare of all sections of people through development interventions. Moreover, the development philosophy has another aspect along with the welfare commitments. It is wed to the principle of efficiency and growth within the frame of competition and market mechanism. Naturally, the inequality emerges within the social category itself.

This logic however does not ignore the fact that the non-marginalised groups do not have an edge over the marginalised ones in the process of development. Those who were advanced are now more advanced, and those who were marginalised have become more marginalised. But from among the marginalised

2. One of the authors have witnessed the differences between a number of remote villages in Orissa and a section of people in a number of tribal communities in Arunachal Pradesh over a period of two decades.

groups there are people who are more advanced not only in their respective groups but in comparison to many sections of people in the former advanced social category. Needless to say, marginalisation emerges in itself as a category across the caste, tribe and gender; and consolidates along the axes of inequality, deprivation, displacement, and exclusion consequent upon the development process. The papers included in this volume point to the issues of marginalisation from the above perspectives.

Thematic Perspectives

Thematically, we have organised the papers into four sections. *The first section, namely Comprehending Marginalisation,* includes four papers. These papers broadly present different dimensions of marginalisation, precisely in terms of exclusion and migration. The second section namely, *Issues and Concerns* includes four papers. These papers have discussed various issues existing in contemporary marginalised communities and the challenges they pose for further inclusive and sustainable development. As marginalised communities have been exposed to development process since long, the papers, though implicit, relate to the emerging issues and concerns to the past experience with development of the marginalised groups. The third section includes six papers under the theme of *Managing Development.* A common thread that runs through these papers is the institutional intervention in the process of development of the marginalised people, whether they are tribals or general rural people. The final section, i.e. the fourth section includes six papers under the theme *Mapping Development Dynamics which generally focus on* various aspects of development of the marginalised people. In fact the papers list achievements and working of various developmental programmes.

Comprehending Marginalisation

Marginalisation has different dimensions. The papers under the theme of comprehending marginalisation, however, shed light on the nature of marginalisation in the process of development of the marginalised people especially the tribals. These papers essentially focus on exclusion and migration as dimensions of marginalisation. In their joint paper entitled

Formal Education in Arunachal Pradesh: Issues of Exclusion, M.C. Behera and Jumyir Basar have tried to comprehend marginalisation in the form of exclusion. They argue that exclusion and interventions go together. The authors have analysed literacy rates across the gender and districts to study exclusion in the process of implementation of formal education. Drawing on empirical evidences relating to implementation of formal education in Arunachal Pradesh after Independence, Behera and Basar find exclusion of people both in absolute and relative terms. Before Independence, there was no formal system of education in the tribal communities. But after the introduction of it some people are found illiterate, 45.26 per cent as per 2001 census, thereby pointing to their absolute exclusion from the formal system. Further, a section of people are found having education up to primary level while others having higher level of education in general, technical and professional fronts. Less number of institutions at higher level of education indicates deprivation of all the aspiring youths from such education[3]. There are inter-district variations ranging between 40.64 per cent in East Kameng to 69.43 in Papum Pare districts, and gender gap in literacy rates which is noted19.83 percentage point as per 2001 census. Temporal variations in terms of gradual increase in number of schools from 7 in 1947 to 2025 in 2005 and spatial disparity in establishing schools over a period of 59 years have resulted in, among other factors, such variations. Regional disparity is evident from inter-district variations in schools. Data, which the authors have presented, show that former Dibang Valley district had 2.90 per cent of primary schools in the state as against 13.42 per cent in the former Lohit district in 2001. The literacy gaps across gender and region, and gaps at the levels of education, as the authors have argued, measure exclusion in relative sense.

Surjyanarayan Tripathy, in his paper entitled *Distress Migration in Tribal Orissa: a Study in KBK Districts*, focuses on distress migration as a dimension of marginalisation, for the

3. During the year 2007-08, number of middle schools was recorded 664, secondary schools 163 and higher secondary schools 97. Total institutions providing technical and general education at under graduation level were recorded 13 in the state.

poverty stricken tribals and scheduled caste people in KBK districts of Orissa seasonally migrate in search of their livelihoods. For many years, poverty was seen as a root causes of unwanted migration, and development or a reduction in poverty as the solution to it. With more than 60 years of experience in tribal development in general and in the present KBK districts in particular still the tribals and other marginalised people migrate to improve their livelihoods. No doubt, in itself, it is an indication of the existence of poverty and marginalisation of the STs and SCs in the general process of development. Marginalisation relating to poverty and associated migration has a self perpetuating tendency due to indebtedness, loss of access to common property resources and the migration itself. Tripathy, therefore, is of the opinion that poverty induces people to migrate in order to improve their livelihoods but in turn migration results in them becoming further impoverished, vulnerable and marginalised in more than one ways, for migrants fall prey to exploiting contractors, social isolation and identity crisis. He records 118 households (65.56) reported to have remitted annually Rs. +1000-2000 to their native places. Tripathy also relates distress migration to the lapses in development process as he views the phenomenon of rural-urban migration in the light of prevailing rural conditions of poverty, inequality and unemployment. His argument draws on empirical evidences that the Government policies for rural development could not mitigate these conditions; he attributes the reasons to leakages of funds, misappropriation and other factors promoting corruption.

The paper entitled *Dynamics of Tribal Development: Encountering ground reality in "KBK" Districts of Orissa* by Krishna Chandra Pradhan supplements to the arguments presented in the papers of Tripathy, and Behera and Basar. He presents gender and regional disparity in literacy level drawing on field data. The gaps measure the extent of exclusion of the people in terms of illiteracy and thus are indicative of marginalisation. What is important is the point that the gaps emerged in the process of development itself. Further it supports to the argument of Tripathy who relates distress migration to poverty and marginalisation. Literacy gap and low level of education in themselves are indicators of marginalisation. Ambrish Gautam and Kumari Sweta in their joint paper entitled *Opportunities and Challenges for Tribes in Ranchi City* have outlined the status of tribals, who have entered into job markets contrary to their reciprocal life and groundings in resource base, in Ranchi city. They have voiced the decline of traditional technology of the tribals and insecurity in the present livelihood options. The paper has touched upon the aspects of migration of tribals to the city, their displacement from their natural habitat consequent upon industrialisation and urbanisation, exposure to conspicuous consumption in the city and largely of the conditions of backwardness in their earlier habitats.

Issues and Concerns

The papers included in this section present a macro picture of various issues and challenges which have emerged in the process of development of marginalised people in general and tribal people in particular. Broadly, the issues relate to inadequacies in the process to realise the objectives of developing the marginalised people and it is very much evident from their categorisation as 'marginalised'. The concerns, on the other hand, are the challenges to address the development issues in the present context. The presentation of A.K. Agarwal, in his paper entitled Globalisation, Policies, Programmes and Potential Areas of Development of North-East Economy: An Analysis, well substantiates to the point. He has tried to locate developing countries with reference to India in relation to developed countries in the context of globalisation. He mentions that the extent of India's globalisation is one of the lowest in the world sharing a meagre 0.7 per cent or so in the world trade. In terms of international capital inflows into India, particularly foreign direct investment (FDI), it is 3-4 billion constituting about 0.3 - 0.4 per cent of the total. Foreign institutional investment is also relatively small - about 10 per cent of BSE market capitalization. *India is undoubtedly marginalised in its share of FDI. He argues that* North east India despite its inherent advantages like fertile land, abundant natural resources, a fairly homogeneous and literate population has been unable to keep pace with the economic and industrial development as recorded elsewhere in the country. Agarwal outlines absence of essential infrastructural facilities, inadequate skilled human resource, and insufficient enterprise and inefficient management of state finances in absence of adequate resource mobilisation to meet their own needs as indicators of marginalisation. As a consequence of marginalisation at different levels insurgency has cropped up in the North East. The issues and challenges of development are obvious when the region is exposed to the forces of globalisation. So Agarwal recommends some measures to address these issues for the development of North-East India. Though the objective of discussion has its own context, the relational nature of marginalisation permeates Agarwal's entire analysis which presents India's marginalisation in comparison to other countries and North East's marginalisation as compared to other parts of the country.

The same concern is raised in the paper of Sib Ranjan Misra relating to tribal communities of the country. *The major problems faced by the tribals, as Misra presents* in his paper entitled *Tribal Communities in India: Some Emerging Issues in the Light of Globalization*, are land alienation, restrictions over their use of forests, entry into labour market and displacement by some kind of development programmes. Added to these, there are large scale deprivations, uncertainty, non-percolation of the benefits of developments to the lower strata of the tribals and exploitation as products of globalisation. The values, beliefs, ideas, ethics and artefacts of the occidental culture sneak into their territory through different media and produce cultural hybridization. Youths are socialised into a set of sub-cultural ambiences rather than a single cultural environment. Obviously, the tribal people are at a critical point in their history. They are losing command over resources at a very fast rate. They are facing at the same time social disintegration. There is an intensive interplay between the tribal ethnicity, state and class. In the process of their integration with national and international ethos, it is difficult to retain the core of their ethnic identity. The forces of globalization and localization, precisely the conflicting forces of homogeneity and heterogeneity, are exerting tremendous pressure on individuals. In fact the tribals face a situation of conflicting interests which Misra summarises as : (i) the livelihood interests of the tribal communities, (ii) commercial interests of government and contractors, and (iii) interventions from environmental protectionists.

Amitava Mitra and Maila Lama, in their joint paper, which is titled *The Potentiality and Challenges of Developing Ecotourism in Arunachal Pradesh: An Empirical Study*, have identified the challenges of development in the tribal dominated state of Arunachal Pradesh and accordingly have suggested ecotourism as a strategy of development. However, their concern is obvious when they outline challenges to be addressed in order to create pre-conditions to develop ecotourism. The challenges are not specific to ecotourism only, but these are general in nature and are constraints for sustainable development of the marginalised tribal communities. In spite of more than 60 years experimentation with plan programmes in the state the challenges still persist and pose problems for launching any development strategy keeping in line with the present development discourse. *Kashinath Jena and Rajesh Chatterjee, in their joint paper entitled Emerging Issues in Tribal Communities of Tripura: An Overview, also have raised the issue of marginalisation of tribal women in the process of development in Tripura. They have recorded a rise in the percentage of agricultural labourers of tribal women from 2.81 per cent in 1961 to 36.65 per cent in 1991.* They have also found that the tribal household industry has been dying out under the impact of market forces, changing taste and preferences of the people and of course, increasing price of yarns. It has impacted the livelihood sources of tribal women. In 1961, it was 10.96 per cent female workers involved in household industry, but it has declined to 0.52 per cent in 1991.

Managing Development

The process of development of marginalised people and communities in India happens to be exogenous in nature given the frame of top-down approach to planning. (Behera, 1994; Jha, 1985). Of course, there is a reversal in approach in recent years with decentralisation and devolution of powers to local institutions and thus to people. Though stress is laid on empowerment of people, there is still the predominance of bureaucracy in the whole process starting from conception to implementation of the programmes and schemes. (Behera, 2006, particularly introduction). For all practical purposes, people involve in their development by following the path which is laid before them. Some times the new paths either contradict or complement to the traditional ones. Often traditional ways are found vigorous than the new ones so that they are not replaced with the new ones. This is quite evident in the joint paper of Mihin Dollo and Prasanna K. Samal which is entitled *Managing Natural Resources by Traditional Communities: The Case of Apatani Tribe for Sustainable Development in Arunachal Pradesh.* The authors have evaluated the traditional knowledge and the expertise of the Apatani community in the management of natural resources such as forest, land and water. In their analysis, socio-cultural cohesiveness is evident in community's practice of resource use and management. The community has distinct traditional landuse practices and rich traditional ecological knowledge of natural resources management and conservation, which was acquired over the centuries through informal experimentation. Forest is judiciously guarded coupled with exceedingly managed bamboo garden. Nearly 158 plant species used in ethnomedicine are sustainably extracted from the forest and periphery of the settlement. Richness of forest is maintained through traditional ecological knowledge by means of selective harvesting, as well as by conserving the potential, ritualistic and socio-culturally valued species. There has been efficient management of irrigation for paddy-cum-fish culture by informal farmer groups. Unlike other tribal communities in north-east India, who mainly practise shifting cultivation, the Apatanis depend mainly on perennial wet-rice cultivation. Dollo and Samal have found that Apatanis successfully grow 16 varieties of rice in the waterlogged paddy fields by means of organic farming and appropriate use of diverse natural resources. The traditional wet-rice farming system is functional even today and is being modified by the community as and when required. Landuse and management practice of the Apatani is based on well tried traditional land law systems, and land is classified into 10 major categories on the basis of traditional uses. The authors have addressed the above issues by highlighting the practices of traditional forest resource management, irrigation and of agriculture.

P. K. Kar and S.K. Panda have outlined a mixed result from various developmental activities launched in tribal areas of Mayurbhanj district in Orissa in their joint paper entitled *Intervening Programmes and Schemes for Development in Mayurbhanj District of Orissa.* Development programmes such as TSP, TRYFED, NSFDS, NRHM, AYUSH, ASHA have, no doubt, ameliorated the socio-economic conditions of the tribals. But the developmental programmes during different plan periods have not been completely successful in raising their socio-economic situation. It is quite clear from available data, as presented by the authors, on the achievements recorded from various schemes. They find that development is managed (mismanaged?) without a favourable condition resulting from lack of education and awareness, stronghold of tradition with the culture of accumulation of assets and rigid attitude to change, inadequacy of representation in Government and Non Government services, increased landlessness, steady decline in fund allocation since the late eighties and allocation mismatching the need of the target groups. A similar paper entitled *Fighting Drought in the Era of Globalisation: Programmes and Schemes in Anantapur District of Andhra Pradesh* is presented Eswarappa Kasi in which he has discussed various poverty alleviation programmes implemented in the drought prone area of Andhra Pradesh. The programmes aim at eliminating the severity of drought and securing sustainable livelihoods of the farmers who are made marginalised due to frequent occurrences of drought. In his paper entitled, Eswarappa has focused on the role of donor agencies and the State to address the interface between the poverty reduction strategies and the goal of sustainable development by managing natural resource base in drought prone villages.

A.Rajmani Singh, in his paper entitled *International Fund for Agricultural Development (IFAD) and Poverty Alleviation in Hilly Areas of Manipur*, has also focused on the role of the International Fund for Agricultural Development (IFAD) in eradicating poverty especially in hill districts of Manipur with

Senapati and Ukhrul districts as case study. While working in close partnership with the Government of India and other donors, IFAD funds different projects with the objective of improving economic, education and health conditions of rural and tribal people. IFAD also funds projects for women's empowerment and natural resources management. Since 1979, the organization has financed 22 programmes and projects, releasing a total amount of US $ 595.3 million approximately. The IFAD also funded North Eastern Region Community Resource Management Project for Upland Areas (NERCORMP) and helped reorganize land use and resource management in six districts across the states of Meghalaya, Manipur and Assam. He finds from the analysis of data that IFAD funded projects have improved productivity and ensured the sustainability of farming and harvesting practices, and more than 230,000 rural people in the project area have seen dramatic improvements in their living conditions. They now have substantially higher incomes and regular, more nutritious meals, and their children are healthier and better educated. But, this process of development of tribal economy has not affected their long traditional way of living, culture and indigenous knowledge system.

Decentralised planning is a strategy of people's development. Broadly, it is inclusive in principle and thus a measure to uplift the socio-economic conditions of rural and other marginalised people. Jayanta Choudhury in his paper entitled *Decentralized Planning in Tripura* has outlined the functioning of decentralised planning in Tripura for rural development. However, he finds the institutionalised process of implementation of decentralised planning more of a political manoeuvring than articulation of people's needs in general. Official formalities like paper works are more visible than real works and functionaries of line departments, with their respective departmental targets and planning, do not show much interest in Panchayat activities. In Arunachal Pradesh, however, the situation is different. The line departments work according to the guidelines of national planning, but in most cases with respect to traditional rights on land and forests. This is a situation where development objectives can not be fulfilled meaningfully. For example land can not be used as collateral to obtain bank finance for development projects in the absence of cadastral survey, land reforms and land records. This issue is highlighted in the paper of K. Haloi, entitled *System of Land Management in Arunachal Pradesh,* in which he has discussed the land management system in Arunachal Pradesh and changing practices in the process of development.

Mapping Development Dynamics

After World War-II, the present developing nations began to experience 'development discourse' (see Esteva, 1992 and Akhter, 2006). Needless to say, development policies and programmes are not new phenomena. In the process of development, quite a number of objectives have been achieved and at the same time new challenges have emerged. As a result there are shifts in development paradigm and hence approaches to development. (Behera, 2006; Chambers, 1983, 1993, 2005). However, the papers included under this section highlight the development scenario in a general perspective. A. Ibotombi Singh and Amitava Mitra, in their joint paper entitled *Growth of Services Sector in Arunachal Pradesh: A Post Reform Experience*, have presented the trend of growth of services sector in the tribal state of Arunachal Pradesh. Over the past decades, particularly since the beginning of economic reforms and acceleration in the rate of growth in 1990s, the Arunachal Economy has followed a growth pattern which is different from the historical as well as the contemporary development processes. So they have attempted at an analysis of the process of transition in Arunachal Pradesh with the empirical evidences. Basically the authors have examined the relationship between the growth of services sector and economic development of Arunachal Pradesh for its longer term development strategy and policy perspectives. Particularly, they have reviewed the developments in the services sector, discussed the sectoral contribution to NSDP and changes in the occupational structure and have investigated the relationship between the District Domestic Product and factors affecting the demand for services like the level of education, urbanization and the per capita district income. Priyanka Priyadarshini & Millo Mamung, on the other hand, have investigated the transformation of rural economy with reference to changing livelihoods options. In their joint paper entitled *Economic Diversification in Selected Tribal Villages of Arunachal Pradesh and Livelihood Options* the authors have presented micro situations.

Before the introduction of plan programmes in Arunachal Pradesh, the tribal communities living here had limited livelihood options, ranging between foregoing and subsistence agriculture, mostly of shifting mode and little of the permanent cultivation. (see Haimendorf, 1946, 1962; Elwin, 1959; Jha, 1985; Behera, 1994 and NCAER, 1967). In other words, primary sector activities like fishing, hunting, collection and limited domestication of animals and agricultural activities were the domain of livelihood options. But, after independence, development programmes and schemes pertaining to sectoral activities were introduced (Behera, 1997) thereby enlarging the sources of livelihood of tribespersons. Needless to say, the tribal communities got exposed to sources of livelihood not only in primary sector activities but also in secondary and tertiary sector activities. In their paper Priyanka Priyadarshini and Millo Mamung have examined the existing livelihood options in four villages - two from Apatani and two from Khampti communities. They have addressed the research issue with reference to economic diversification and concomitant work participation, intergenerational change in occupation and various livelihood sources available. They find that development interventions have unequally impacted rural economy.

Sujit K. Dutta has highlighted the functioning of both traditional and newly introduced institutions in the process of empowering tribal communities *in* his paper entitled *Local Governance in Tribal Areas of North East.* He has enumerated conflicts between the two in Meghalaya and success story in Nagaland and Arunachal Pradesh. Ram Krishna Mandal in his paper, under the title of *Panchayati Raj Institutions, Women Empowerment and Economic Development*, has focused on issues of women empowerment in Arunachal Pradesh through PRIs. Women in tribal societies of Arunachal Pradesh are not allowed traditionally to participate in tribal village councils. (Talukdar,

1987; Danggen, 2003 and Karlo, 2005). Thus, the traditional village councils are male dominated institutions. But the introduction of Panchayat Raj at grassroots and Parliamentary democracy at upper layer has armed the women with political rights on the equal footing of their male counterparts. Nevertheless, women empowerment in rural area, as Mandal finds, is limited by their traditional status role. (Behera, 1999, 2001) Further, he finds that the normal process of working of the PRI right from 1969 has not ensured the participation of women; it is rather reservation policy and various acts which have ensured their participation in PRIs. R.M. Pant and Aditya Joshi in their joint paper entitled *Education and Development in Arunachal Pradesh* have presented the pioneering efforts made in the development of education in the state of Arunachal Pradesh and its impact, though limited, in the process of empowerment of tribal people. The last paper by M.A. Salam, in his paper entitled *The Economy of Arunachal Pradesh: A Note on Transformation*, has critically presented the process of transformation in Arunachal economy in response to different phases of political and territorial evolution in the state. Besides he has also viewed changes with reference to changing development perspectives at large. Salam has essentially focused on monetisation and institutional changes relating to organisation of production during the plan periods.

In Conclusion Still Marginalised

The marginalised groups, whether STs or SCs or OBCs or rural people have been benefited from development programmes, but their marginal status remain as such in relation to people of urban and industrialised regions. Marginalisation further manifests at the level of education, employment, access to common property resources or at the level of general achievements. Even from among the marginalised groups a section becomes further marginalised. Those tribals who are displaced due to industrialisation or mega dams are neo-marginalised people within the tribal group who are otherwise marginalised. Marginalisation, whether across region or groups seems to be an unending process. Rural-urban divide remains a reality and the process of development causes inequality, displacement, migration and various forms of deprivation at different levels.

REFERENCES

Agarwal, A.K.1985 : *North-East India: An Economic Perspective*, Allahabad: Chugh Publications.

Akhter, Farida 2006: 'Rural development in the Era of Globalisation-Fragmented realities' in M.C. Behera (ed.) *Globalising Rural Development-Competing Paradigms and Emerging Realities*, Sage, New Delhi.

Basar, Jumyir 2008: Development of Marginalised Groups and Different Dimensions of Marginalisation in Tribal Communities of Arunachal Pradesh (India): A Preliminary Inquiry, paper presented at The 38th World Congress of the International Institute of Sociology, Budapest, Hungary, June 26-30, 2008.

Behera, M.C. 1994:*Planning and Socio-Economic Development of the Tribals*, Commonwealth Publishers, New Delhi.

Behera, M.C. 1997 : 'Planning process and implementation of plan measures in Arunachal Pradesh during early plan periods', *Arunachal Review*, IV (18).

Behera, M.C. 1999: Impact of Orange Cultivation on Traditional Role of Galo Women (Minor Project of UGC).

Behera, M.C. 2001: 'Sex-based Division of Labour, Responsibility and Accountability: A Case Study of Traditional Role Set of Galo Women' in *South East Asian Anthropologist*, New Series, Vol. I. (2001).

Behera, M.C. and Basar, Jumyir 2009: 'Conceptualising Social Exclusion in the Context of Tribal Communities in Arunahcal Pradesh', Presented by Co-author at *30th NEIHA Conference* at Nagaon, Assam held from 5th to 7th November, 2009.

Behera, M.C.(ed.) 2006: *Globalising Rural Development-Competing Paradigms and Emerging Realities*, Sage, New Delhi.

Cernea, M. M. 1995 : 'Understanding and preventing impoverishment from displacement: Reflections on the state of knowledge'. *Journal of Refugee Studies 8* (3).

Cernea, M. M. 2000 : 'Risks, safeguards and reconstruction: A model for population displacement and resettlement', in M. M. Cernea and Christopher McDowell, (Eds.), *Risks and reconstruction: Experiences of resettlers and refugees* (pp.11-55). Washington DC: World Bank.

Chambers, Robert 1983: *Rural Development: Putting the Last First*, Longman and Scientific Technical with John Wiley and Sons Inc., New York.

Chambers, Robert 1993: *Challenging the Professions - Frontiers for rural development*, Intermediate Technology Publications, London.

Chambers, Robert 2005: *Ideas for Development*, Earth Scan, London.

Danggen, Bani 2003: *The Kebang*, Himalayan Publishers, Itanagar.

Elwin, V. 1959/1988: *A Philosophy for NEFA*, Directorate of Research, Itanagar.

Esteva, Gustavo 1992: 'Development', in Wolfgang Sachs (ed.), *Development Dictionary*, Zed Books, London.

GOI : Censuses of 1961, 1971, 1981, 1991 and 2001.

GOI, 2006 : 'The National Tribal Policy (A Policy for the Scheduled Tribes of India)', *Draft*, Ministry of Tribal Affairs, Government of India, New Delhi.

GOI, 1986-87 : *Report of the Commissioner for Scheduled Castes and Scheduled Tribes*, 28th Report, New Delhi.

Haimendorf, C. Von. Furer 1946 /1950 : *Ethnographic Notes on the Tribes of the Subansiri Region*, Assam Government Press, Shillong.

Haimendorf, C. Von. Furer 1962 : *The Apatanis and their neighbours (A Primitive Civilization of the Eastern Himalayas)*, Routledge and Kegan Paul, London.

Jha, S.D. 1985 : *The Wealth of Arunachal Pradesh*, Mittal Publications New Delhi.

Karlo, Rejir 2005: *Emerging Pattern of Tribal Leadership in Arunachal Pradesh*, Commonwealth Publishers, New Delhi.

Mandal, P.K. and Behera, M.C. 2005: 'Socio-Economic Portents of Displacement of indigenous Peoples in Arunachal Pradesh: A Preliminary Inquiry', in S. Dutta, P.K. Mandal and T. Showren (eds), *The Problems of Internally Displaced Persons and Refugees in the North East India*, Himalayan Publishers, Itanagar. Also reproduced under the title 'Socio-Economic Portents of Displacement of Indigenous Peoples', in Samir Kumar Das (ed), 2008: *Blisters on their feet: Tales of Internally Displaced Persons in India's North East*, Sage, New Delhi.

Mullaly, B. 2007: 'Oppression: The Focus of Structural Social Work', in B. Mullaly (ed), *The New Structural Social Work*, Oxford University Press, Don Mills.

Nath, Daisy 2008: The Impact of Globalisation on Tribal Women in the North East with Special Reference to Angami Women: An Overview, paper presented at the National Seminar on *Encountering Globalisation: Tribal Communities in India and Development Issues*, Itanagar, 27-28 February, 2009.

NCAER, 1967 : *Techno-Economic Survey of Arunachal Pradesh*, NCAER, New Delhi.

Talukdar, A.C. 1987: *Political Transition in the Grassroots in Tribal India,* Omsons, Gauhati.

I

Comprehending Marginalisation

1

Formal Education in Arunachal Pradesh : Issues of Exclusion[1]

M.C.Behera and Jumyir Basar

The present study is an attempt to understand the issue of exclusion consequent upon introduction of formal system of education in Arunachal Pradesh. Literacy rate is taken as a measure to study exclusion in the process of formal education.

Before Independence of our country the system of education in tribal communities of Arunachal Pradesh was informal in nature. The skill and knowledge requirement was basically culture determined along gender axis of division of labour. Nevertheless, there existed inter-individual skill and knowledge differences in each gender category. All male members were, for example, engaged in forest activities, but they differed in individual capabilities of doing a specific work. One could be a good hunter than others; one could be an efficient elephant trapper than his fellow villagers/kinsmen. Similarly, a young man might not be having the expertise of wood carving or basket making and all working male members in a community could

1. This is the revised version of the paper presented in the national seminar on *Development of Tribal People in Arunachal Pradesh*, 20-22 November, 2009, Dera Natung Government College, Itanagar.

not be skilled in smith works. The skill differences were natural along gender divide and there was no institutional system which denied opportunities to any member of the community from accessing to skill learning in order to secure livelihoods.

Roughly, in the process of informal education for skill development, there happened to be such stages as observation, imitation, participation and finally, learning of skill, which were open to all. (Basar and Tok, 2004; Begi, 2007 : 24-27; Perme, 2008 : 25-33 and also see Pertin, 2009). Further, knowledge of the members of a community about history, deliverance of justice, social norms, etc. was transmitted through words of mouth in the living house near fire place (Basar, 2006), in *mushup* (Perme, *op. cit.*) and during festivals and dances[2]. Participation in such occasions was open and inclusive across the gender. Needless to say, there were no such restrictions as age, specialisation, previous experience or education as they exist in formal system of education to exclude a section of population or restrict their access to informal system of education in the community.

Interventions and Beginning of Formal Education

The tribal communities of Arunachal Pradesh were very much tradition bound before independence. (see Haimendorf, 1946, 1962; Elwin, 1959; Jha, 1985.; Behera, 1994 and NCAER,1967). Precisely, the economy was operating at subsistence level in between the stages of food gathering and food production. The system of education was informal as is discussed above. However, a few schools, 7 in number as Begi (2007) reports, existed in the present state of Arunachal Pradesh before Independence. These schools were established through both private and government initiatives. Surprisingly, all these schools did not exist during Independence except two government schools as reported in the Techno-Economic Survey of North-East Frontier Agency (*op. cit*). Perhaps these two schools were established in 1947 itself. Practically, real beginning was made in the field of formal education with the opening of 9

2. During festivals and dances, it is the usual practice among the Tani group of tribes to narrate the creation of universe to describe the origin of a particular dance or festival or ritual.

schools and appointment of Mrs. Indira Miri as Education Officer at Sadiya in the year 1947. It is noteworthy that the efforts in this regard were solely government initiatives through plan interventions which were later followed by private ventures.

Growth of Formal Education

School Education

The growth of formal education in the state has been studied with reference to school education and higher and technical levels of education as well. It is to be mentioned that at each level there are both governmental and non-governmental initiatives. A systematic presentation of year-wise and district-wise data on establishment of schools is made in Appendix-1. But the information is basically about the opening of a school, especially the primary school. Obviously, it lacks in full information on elementary and secondary levels of institutions. However, records available with the Department of Economics and Statistics, Government of Arunachal Pradesh and various census reports shed light in this regard. After 2001 census, the growth of schools at elementary levels over a period of six years is presented in Appendix-2. The appendix of reference also shows distribution of schools in the districts and villages covered by a school on an average.

During the period from 1947-48 to 1950-51 only one middle school and 63 Junior Basic schools were established raising the total number of educational institutions to 68. (GoAP, 1997:2)[3]. Needless to say, there was no middle school prior to it and no secondary or higher secondary schools by that time in the territory. However, during the First Five Year Plan, the period

3. By the end of 1950 there were only 37 schools and at the end of 1951 there were 43 schools including 7 schools mentioned before Independence. (Appendix-1). Begi (as presented in Appendix-4 in his book, Begi, 2007) has collected number of schools established year - wise and district - wise from the monthly progress reports of schools submitted to Deputy Director of School Education (DDSE). From interview with first generation of students and consulting historical records, he has estimated number of schools before 1947. (per.com). Hence there is a mismatch between statistical data in government records and actual field data.

between 1951-52 and 1955-56, three secondary schools were established. During the same period also 14 middle schools and 28 Junior Basic/Primary schools were established. (*ibid.*: 4).

During the Second Five Year Plan, the period between 1956-57 and 1960-61, 2 (two) Sec/Hr. Secondary schools were added by upgrading 2 middle schools. But there was a total reduction of 23 Junior Basic schools due to upgradation of some schools to middle level and for some other reasons which are yet to be established. That is why Junior Basic schools recorded at 152 earlier were reduced to 129 in 1961. (GoAP, nd[1].5). But subsequently the institutions increased to 567 during the decade covered by the 1971 Census. In 1972, there were 572 educational institutions in total in the state. Further, during 1980-81, there were 49 pre-primary, 845 primary, 117 middle and 44 secondary/ higher secondary schools in the state. The census report 1991 records 284 pre-primary, 1,144 primary, 73 secondary and 48 higher secondary schools.

Census 2001 records 3863 rural habitations and 17 urban centres in the state. In 3863 rural habitations there are 1263 primary, 309 upper primary, 109 secondary and 47 higher secondary schools. On the other hand, in 17 urban centres there are 74 primary, 51 upper primary, 23 secondary and 25 higher secondary schools. During the year 2007-08, there are 1561 primary, 664 upper primary, 163 secondary and 97 higher secondary schools, both aided and unaided, recorded in the state. Out of them there are 126 primary, 51 secondary and 12 higher secondary schools under private sector. This leaves 1435 primary, 565 upper primary, 112 secondary and 85 higher secondary schools in government sector including one Kendriya Vidyalaya (KV) and three Jawahar Navodaya Vidyalayas (JNV) at upper primary level, four Kendriya Vidyalayas and seven Jawahar Navodaya Vidyalayas at secondary level, and seven Kendriya Vidyalayas and six Jawahar Navodaya Vidyalayas at higher secondary level.[4]

4. Directorate of School Education, Government of Arunachal Pradesh, Itanagar.

Table 1
Growth of Schools through Private Initiatives

Year/Schools	*Hr. Sec*	*Sec/High/ Post-Basic*	*Middle*	*Primary*	*Pre-Primary*	*Physically Handi-capped*
1994-1996	5	3	9	26	—	1
1998	6	10	21	20	16	1
1999	6	12	27	54	20	1
2001	13	25	36	74	28	1
2002	14	28	51	75	—	1
2003	14	36	49	82	—	1
2006	19	49	65	117	—	1
2007	24	52	87	127	—	1

Source : Computed from Statistical Abstracts of 1994, 1995, 1996, 1998, 1999, 2001, 2002, 2003, 2006 and 2007. Directorate of Economics and Statistics, Government of Arunachal Pradesh, Itanagar.

As has been said the spread of formal education in Arunachal Pradesh is a state- sponsored exercise in the beginning. Later, private initiatives followed with the establishment of Rama Krishna Mission Schools in 1960s. During 1990s schools in private sector became a profit earning enterprise (Behera and Mantaw, 1998 : 221) and it is so even now. During the first part of the first decade of this century, private institutes in the fields of higher and technical education came up. Though data before 1994 are not available, it is still evident from Table1 that establishment of educational institutions under private initiatives practically started from 1990s excluding R. K. Mission schools, Sharada Mission Schools, Vivekananda Kendra Vidyalayas, Donyi-Polo Vidya Bhawan and Boum Kakir Mission schools which started in 1960s, 1970s and in 1980s. It is Donyi-Polo Mission which has started Donyi-Polo Vidya Bhawan and one school for hearing impaired students. The schools show erratic trend at various levels. For example, the number of primary schools has dropped from 26 in 1994-1996 to 20 in 1998. This is due to the reason of upgradation of primary sections to middle level. Of course, with upgradation there is new establishment of schools. From field observation, it can be stated that private schools have been established in administrative headquarters with more concentration at district headquarters and state capital. As it transpires from Table 1, by 2007, there are 24 schools at higher secondary level, 52 at secondary, 87 at middle and 127 at primary levels.

Higher and Technical Education

The growth of institutes of higher and technical education under government management is shown in Table 2. At the level

Table 2
Institutions of Higher and Technical Education under Government Management

Programmes	*No. of Institution*	*No. of Institutions in*				*Remarks*
		Capital Complex	*District Hqs*	*SDO/ Circle HQs*	*Year of Establishment*	
General UG	8	1	4	3	1964, 1979, 1986, 1988, 1996, 1996, 1997, 2007	
General PG	1	1	—	—	1984	Converted to Central University on 8-4-2007
Technical Diploma	1	1	—	—	2002	
Technical PG	1	1	—	—	1984 (NERIST)	Deemed University
Professional UG	1	—	1	—	2001	College of Horti-culture and Forestry under Central Agriculture University, Imphal.

Source : Basic Information on Institutions of Higher and Technical Education, Arunachal Pradesh, 2008-09, Directorate of Higher Education, Govt. of A.P. Itanagar.

of higher education, the first degree college was established in 1964 followed by the second one in 1979 after an interval of 15 years. Except NERIST, technical education at diploma level started in 2002. Till date there are two such institutions in the state. The University which was established in 1984 has been converted to a Central University in 2007. Surprisingly, government initiatives in opening up institutions for technical and professional courses have been very late. However, in 1984 the first institute, namely North-Eastern Regional Institute of Science and Technology (NERIST), was established to cater to the needs of all the states in the region. There is only one technical institute, namely Rajiv Gandhi Polytechnic, which was established in 2002 with the initiatives of the state government. The College of Horticulture and Forestry at Pasighat, which was established in 2001 is a campus of Central Agriculture University, Imphal. Needless to say, the initiative of the state government

Table 3
Institutions of Higher and Technical Education under Private Management

Programmes	*No. of Institutions*	*No. of Institutions in*				*Remarks*
		Capital Complex	*District Hqs*	*SDO/ Circle HQs*	*Year of Establishment*	
General UG	4	1	3	—	2002, 2003, 2004, 2007	3 colleges by missionaries, 1 by trust.
Technical Diploma	1	—	—	1	2006	Polytechnic at Basar
Professional UG	3	—	3	—	2002-medical 2006-B.Ed 2007-Law	1-Medical 1-Law 1-B.Ed
Total	20	5	11	4	—	

Source: Basic Information on Institutions of Higher and Technical Education, Arunachal Pradesh, 2008-09, Directorate of Higher Education, Govt. of A.P., Itanagar.

to introduce diverse and need based courses by establishing professional and technical institutes.

Initiatives from private sector to establish institutes of higher and technical education in the state are also not encouraging. It transpires from Table 3 that there are only 4 degree colleges of general education; the first on, namely Don Bosco College, began only in 2002 in capital complex. All the degree colleges are run by missionaries and trust. The only technical institute providing diploma course was established in 2006 in Basar of West Siang district. The professional institutes include only medical, law and B.Ed courses. The medical institution, established in 2002 in Itanagar, provides degree in homoeopathy. The B.Ed course also started late and still late is the course in law. However, Department of Education, Rajiv Gandhi University has been providing B.Ed degree since 1988.

Table 4
Enrolment of Arunachalee Students, 2007-08

Educational institutions		*Boys*	*Girls*	*Total*	*Average*
Primary schools		77782	69494	147276	29456
Upper Primary		27917	24219	52136	26068
Secondary schools		12238	10741	22979	114895
Hr. Secondary schools		6662	5082	11744	5872
Colleges (general)		4771	3908	8674	2891
University (PG)		393	408	801	400
Technical and NERIST		121(777)	38(259)	159(1036)	—
Professio-	Law	84	10	94	47
nal	B.Ed	26	31	57	57
	BHMS	16(30)	39(59)	55(89)	11
	Horti. and Agri.	13(64)	12 (44)	25 (108)	12
	Technical(Dip.)	382(111)	163(73)	545(181)	182

Source : Government of Arunachal Pradesh (2008-09).

Note : Data relating to College/University pertain to the year 2008-09.

The growth of formal education can be appreciated from

the rising enrolments. Though there is no authentic data it is mentioned in various sources that the enrolment in 1947 was less than 100. In census 1961, it was recorded 4,443 which increased to 33,000 in 1971 census over a span of one decade. (Begi, *op. cit.* 80). No doubt, the student population consisted of Arunachalees and non-Arunachalees studying at various levels of education. In 2004-05 there were 2,85,862 students enrolled at elementary level of education in the state out of which 2,06,255 were Arunachalee tribals. (*ibid.*, 82). It is to be mentioned that there were 44 college students on the roll in 1966 which increased to 106 in 1972 and to 1100 in 1987 (GoAP, nd[1]:82). In Table 4 enrolment of students at various levels of education is presented for the year 2007-08 under both government and private managements.

Selection of Students to Educational Institutions Outside the State

With a view to create human resource from among the tribal people themselves and enable them to shoulder the responsibility of their own development, the government used to nominate students to different courses outside the state for study. There was no entrance examination up to 1970s for selection of students to medical or engineering courses. Those who passed in science subject and mathematics at secondary level were nominated to diploma courses. Further science students after higher secondary were nominated to medical and engineering courses.

In recent years, Directorate of Higher and Technical Education, Government of Arunachal Pradesh conducts joint entrance examination for medical, engineering and other technical courses and nominates candidates to institutes outside the state. These students are also provided with stipend, book grants, etc. During the current session (2009-10), the Government has sponsored and allotted 281 seats to Arunachalee students to diploma engineering course, 110 seats to degree engineering course, 35 to MBBS, 13 to B.Sc. (Agri.), 8 to B.Pharma, 12 to BHMS, 2 to B.Sc. (Fisheries), 5 to B.Sc. (Forestry), 6 to B.Sc.(Nurshing) and 2 to BVSC course[5].

---

5. Directorate of Higher and Technical Education, Government of Arunachal Pradesh, Itanagar.

The government on the basis of entrance examination also nominates students to Vanastahli at Rajasthan[6], Sainik School at Imphal, Bhubaneswar and Goalpara, Jawahar Navodaya Vidyalay, Kendriya Vidyalaya in Gaziabad, Vishesh Kendriya Vidyalaya in Delhi, etc.

Impact of Interventions

The impact of formal education is apparent in rising literacy rate. Table 5 shows that the literacy rate in Arunachal Pradesh has increased from 7.23 per cent in 1961 to 54.74 per cent in 2001. Correspondingly, the male literacy rate has increased from 12.24 per cent to 64.07 per cent and female literacy from 1.24 per cent to 44.24 per cent during the same period. It is to be mentioned that Arunachal Pradesh is a tribal state. Hence, the literacy rate of tribal population has significance in terms of the impact of formal education as the tribal people did not have formal system of education before independence. It transpires from Table 5 that the literacy rate of ST population has increased from 2.51 to 49.6 per cent during the period from 1961 to 2001. During the period the ST male literacy rate has increased from 4.62 per cent to 58.8 per cent and ST female literacy from almost negligible (0.41%) to 40.6 per cent.

The objective of formal education in the state has been to develop human resource so that the people participate in the process of their own development. It is to be mentioned that during initial periods of the planning the human resource came from outside Arunachal Pradesh to undertake development activities introduced through plan programmes. Even there was a situation when the allotted money could not be spent because of shortage of human resource. (Chowdhury, 1982:244). But in course of time, the human resource developed from among the people of Arunachal Pradesh who have been participating in the process of development of the state. It is evident from Table 6. The percentage composition of ST employees in government sector is on the rise from 24.12 per cent in 1981 to 48.45 per cent in 2001. The rate of growth of ST employees is

6. During 1966 seven girl students from Arunachal Pradesh were studying in Vanasthali Vidyalaya, Rajasthan. (NEFA Information, 1966, 1(1), p.17; 1(5), p. 22).

more than the rate of growth of total employees during the period except in 1994 due to phenomenal growth in previous year. Further, there is a decline in the rate of growth of total employees in 2001 over the previous year of reference, but the rate of growth of ST employees has registered an increase by 27.26 per cent during the same period. But this does not ensure that all the educated Arunachlees are employed. As on 31-3.2007 (GoAP, 2007), a number of 25648 jobseekers are listed in the live register implying that they are excluded till date.

Table 5
Growth of Literacy Rate

Year	*Arunachal Pradesh*			*ST Population*		
	Persons	*Male*	*Female*	*Persons*	*Male*	*Female*
1961	7.23	12.24	1.42	2.51	4.62	0.41
1971	11.29	17.82	3.71	5.20	8.72	1.70
1981	20.09	27.98	11.02	10.77	16.40	5.14
1991	41.59	51.45	29.69	26.86	34.20	19.51
2001	54.74	64.07	44.24	49.6	58.8	40.6

Source : Census reports of 1961, 1971, 1981, 1991 and 2001.

The rate was estimated for population of 4+ age groups in 1961 and 1971, and for 6+ age groups in 1981 and 1991.

Nature of Interventions: Analysis of Emerging Realities

Interventions have not been uniform. Consequently, the nature of growth of formal education in the state has not been uniform. All the districts did not have access to school education simultaneously because of gradual establishment of schools as can be seen from Appendix-1. Out of 59 years of record available there are districts like Dibang Valley, Anjaw and Lower Dibang Valley in which no school was opened up for 46, 32 and 30 years respectively. It is a surprise that Lower Dibang Valley district, in which there were two schools during the period between 1940 and 1945, did not have any school for 30 years out of 59 years. In 1947 nine schools were opened only in five districts with three each in West Siang and East Siang districts. Districts like East Kameng and Upper Subansiri had the first school only in 1953 while Dibang Valley and Kurung Kumey opened their accounts only in 1954 and 1958 respectively. Even by 2007-08, all the

Table 6
Census of Government Employees in Arunachal Pradesh (1981-1995)

Particulars	1981	1988	1992	1994	1995	2001
Govt. Total no. of Employees	19113	30187	36173	39819	41399	38945
ST Employees	4610 (24.12)	8899 (29.48)	95869 (26.56)	10827 (27.19)	14828 (35.82)	18870 (48.45)
Rate of growth of total employees	—	57.94	19.83	10.08	3.97	- 5.92
Rate of growth ST Employees	—	93.04	977.30	–88.71	36.95	27.26

Source: Computed from Begi, 200, Table No. 4.6, p. 83 and GoAP, 2007, p. 84.

villages are not covered with schools; on an average a school covers more than one village as can be seen from Appendix-2. In some districts like former Lower Subansiri (now Lower Subansiri and Kurung Kumey) and former Dibang Valley (now Dibang Valley and Lower Dibang Valley) a school is recorded covering more than three villages. It is to be further mentioned that there is a school in the state in every 50 kms on an average ranging between as low as 16 kms in Tirap and as high as 228 kms in former Dibang Valley district.

The unequal distribution of schools is also calculated with reference to population as can be seen in Table 7. For example, rural ST population in Tawang district is less than total population in the district by 0.04 percentage point but the rural primary schools are less than total in the state by 0.30 percentage point. Though this is a crude measure still it is indicative of the fact that there are more schools in administrative headquarters declared as urban centres. In other words, the schools have urban bias in terms of covering the population. In general, the population and number of schools are not proportionally related. This uneven distribution of schools over the years, across the districts and disproportional to population, among other things, could be the reason of inter-district literacy differences as can be seen in Table 7. Literacy percentage is comparatively higher in districts like Papum Pare, West Kameng, West Siang and East

Table 7
Percentage Distribution of Population and Primary Schools in the Districts [1]

Districts	*Literacy %*	*% of population in the District*	*% of Rural ST to total Population[2]*	*% of Primary Schools to total in the state*	*% of Primary Schools in rural areas to total in the state**
Tawang	47.32	3.55	3.51 (-0.04)	4.33	4.03 (-0.30)
West Kameng	60.76	6.79	7.80 (+1.01)	8.37	7.38(-0.99)
East Kameng	40.64	5.21	4.85 (-0.36)	8.37	8.21(-0.16)
Papum Pare	69.32	11.11	6.89 (-4.22)	5.55	4.94 (-0.61)
Lower Subansiri/ Kurung Kumey	44.79 (L.S-59.39 ; KK-25.74)	8.95	9.87 (+0.92)	8.97	8.21(-0.76)
Upper Subansiri	50.35	5.04	4.55 (-0.49)	7.30	7.30 (-0.00)
West Siang	59.47	9.46	9.52 (+0.06)	12.93	12.40 (-0.53)
East Siang	60.73	7.96	7.52 (-0.44)	8.14	7.45 (-0.69)
Upper Siang	49.78	3.04	3.83 (+0.79)	3.88	3.73 (-0.15)
Changlang	51.32	11.42	12.99 (+1.57)	10.34	10.27 (-0.07)
Lohit and Anjaw	56.07 (L-58.70; A-38.40)	13.07	13.42 (+0.35)	9.58	9.13 (-0.45)
Dibang and Lower Dibang Valley	58.89 (D-52.96; LD-59.76)	5.26	5.47 (+0.21)	2.90	2.59 (-0.31)
Tirap	41.73	9.14	9.77 (+0.63)	9.28	8.67 (-0.61)

Source: GoAP 2002: Statistical Abstract of Arunachal Pradesh.

Notes: 1. Population figure corresponds to Census, 2001 and primary schools to 2001-02.

2. Figures in the parentheses show percentage point variations of ST population and rural primary schools over the district.

Includes only Arunachal Pradesh Government Schools. There are no data available on the basis of rural-urban classification. Primary schools, numbering 75 under private sector, have been taken as urban schools. There are about 30 government primary schools in 20 urban centres, including the state capital. Similarly, there are also some Vivekananda Kendra Vidyalayas, recorded under private sector, in rural areas. Considering the above facts and non-availability of data on rural-urban basis, primary schools under government sector have been considered rural schools for the convenience of substantiating to the fact that there is inequality in the distribution of primary schools in the state which is an indicator of the nature of exclusion in the process of implementation of plan programmes for the growth of education.

Siang in which there is more evenness in temporal distribution of schools than in districts like East Kameng, Lower Subansiri/Kurung Kumey with lower literacy percentage. However, there are exceptions like Tirap and Dibang/Lower Dibang Valley. In Tirap the distribution of schools is more even than it is in Dibang and Lower Dibang Valley districts; but the literacy percentage is comparatively less in it.

Needless to say, there are other factors besides uneven distribution of schools over time and space which have influenced inter-district variations in literacy level. The other factors are population size, existence of urban centres, remoteness of areas in a district, social structure like chiefdom and adaptable tribal dynamics. For example, in Lower Subansiri and Kurung Kumey the combined literacy rate is 44.79 per cent; separately, the rate is 59.39 for the former and 25.74 for the later. Kurung Kumey is a remote hilly region with a density of 5 persons per square km without any urban centre. On the other hand, Lower Subansiri has a density of 42 persons per square km. with an urban centre. So is the case with Lohit and Anjaw. Further, Anjaw is sparsely populated; only 1.68 per cent of population (density figure is not available) live in it as compared to 13.62 in Lohit. In Lohit there are two urban centres, Tezu and Namsai. The tribal dynamics in this context is used to mean a community's acceptance to education in general. In this regard Khamptis, Monpas, Apatanis, Galos and Adis distinctly stand out. That is why Dibang Valley districts have a comparatively higher literacy rate in spite of spatial and temporal unevenness in the distribution of schools. This district is also inhabited by Adis. Further, a higher percentage of non-Arunachalee population is found in this district. Economic diversification requires human resource which is not sufficient, and so there is dependence on outside labour force. This is evident from 56.42 per cent of non-ST population in the district. The same picture is found in Lohit district where non- ST population is 67.59 per cent. On the other hand, non-ST population is 2.11 per cent and 22.72 per cent in Kurung Kumey and Anjaw districts respectively. In Lower Subansiri, West Siang and East Siang districts non-ST population stands at15.85 per cent, 18.28 per cent and 30.87 per cent respectively. It is to be mentioned that these districts are inhabited by Apatani, Galo and Adi tribes respectively who have generally accepted formal education right from the beginning. It is to be further mentioned that non-ST population are found in administrative and urban centres of the district. In Tirap, it is the social inequality due to chieftainship that has resulted in lower literacy percentage.

It follows that more than one factor have influenced the literacy rate in the districts. But what stands out is the unevenness in the distribution of schools. We can infer that tribal dynamism is due to the exposure to external dynamics through introduction of educational institutions and other measures in the area in the beginning. Urbanisation, existence of non-ST population etc. could be interpreted due to earlier exposure to development interventions in one form or the other.

The analysis not only presents the picture of inter-district literacy gap (Table 8), unequal distribution and urban bias of schools, it also presents gender bias in terms of literacy gap as can be seen from Table 5 and enrolment as can be seen from Table 4. The gender gap and rural urban gap can also be seen from Table 8. Associated with uneven distribution and gradual introduction of schools is inadequacy in number of schools and facilities at higher levels of education. Table 4 shows that there is a gradual decline in enrolments at successive higher levels of education. Due to non-availability of comparable time series data for analysis, average student per class is calculated for each level. At primary level the average enrolment per class is 29456 which has dropped to 5872 at higher secondary level. The difference in enrolments in successive higher level of education marks the extent of exclusion which might have also occurred due to stagnation or dropouts[7] or retention. But the fact that number of schools at higher secondary level is less as compared to primary level is indicative of inadequate opportunities available at higher level of education. This is also true when there is only one law college or a homoeopathy college in the state. For technical education at PG and UG levels there are only 159 ST students enrolled which constitutes 15.35 per cent of total enrolment in NERIST. This figure refers to total ST students of NE states and so the ST students of Arunachal Pradesh pursuing technical education at NERIST are still less. The reservation quota restricts opportunities to a greater extent. Fewer opportunities in general and expensive opportunities in private sector in particular deprive many aspiring candidates from accessing to technical education. Obviously, lack of opportunities is an important causative factor of exclusion.

It is to be mentioned that formal education began with a zero base. But gradual introduction and selection of students to study outside amounted to *unequal treatment to equals*. In response to unequal treatment to equals in the process of establishing educational institutions in a phased manner and nomination of children to various educational institutions outside, a selected few got initial exposure to education. There emerged an elite class from among these selected few in course of time in undifferentiated tribal communities in the state. People of this section undoubtedly were the first group to participate in the development process of the state. This class reasonably understood the importance of education and had the capability - in terms of awareness, information, nearness to power and money – to provide quality education to their children.

---

7. At primary stage the dropout rate has been recorded 64.85 %-boys 45.86% and girls 48.01%- for the year 2004-05. This rate has increased to 62.63%- boys 63.22 and girls 61.90% at elementary level (Begi, 2007:171). For the years 2007-08 and 2008-09 the Directorate of School Education has recorded Cohort dropout at 5.69 and 9.0 respectively within the age group of 6-11 and 7.06 and 5.6 for age group of 11-14 during the same period.

Table 8

Rural-Urban and Sex-wise Distribution of Literacy Percentage in the Districts of Arunachal Pradesh

Sl. No.	Name of District	Literacy			Rural Literacy			Urban Literacy		
		Male	Female	Total	Male	Female	Total	Male	Female	Total
1.	Tawang	60.3	30.0	47.3	44.9	25.0	35.1	93.1	66.6	87.2
2.	West Kameng	70.3	47.5	60.8	69.0	44.8	58.9	84.2	71.3	78.3
3.	East Kameng	52.4	28.6	40.6	41.8	20.8	31.3	79.9	52.7	67.4
4.	Papum Pare	77.3	60.4	69.3	68.3	49.0	59.0	85.4	71.3	78.9
5.	Lower Subansiri and Kurung Kumey	53.4	36.0	44.8	48.7	31.3	40.1	83.6	69.8	77.1
6.	Upper Subansiri	59.5	40.7	50.3	50.5	32.5	41.5	80.5	63.0	72.5
7.	Weat Siang	66.6	51.6	59.5	60.7	46.7	53.9	86.7	73.0	80.9
8.	East Siang	68.4	52.4	60.7	63.5	47.5	55.7	81.9	67.2	75.1
9.	Upper Siang	58.7	38.8	49.8	58.7	38.8	49.8	-	-	-
10.	Changlang	62.1	39.2	51.3	58.7	35.4	47.6	89.0	75.4	83.2
11.	Lohit and Anjaw	65.7	44.5	56.1	61.3	38.8	51.0	83.4	69.3	72.2
12.	L/Dibang Valley and Dibang Valley	67.2	48.7	58.9	62.0	42.5	53.1	89.3	78.1	84.5
13.	Tirap	53.4	28.8	41.7	46.2	21.2	34.2	87.9	73.1	81.4
	Arunachal Pradesh	63.8	43.5	54.3	57.7	·36.9	47.8	85.2	69.5	78.3

Source : Directorate of School Education, Government of Arunachal Pradesh, Itanagar.

Not only they sent their children to good private schools both inside and out side the state, they also managed to avail opportunities from the process of selection to government quota to good educational institutes. A casual researcher can find that almost all the Arunachalee children studying in good schools and later in technical institutions belong to the first generation or subsequently emerged elite class in the state[8].

The differences in literacy rates and educational institutions across the districts mark the extent by which a district is excluded from the other in this field. Besides, differences also exist between rural and urban areas. Across the gender the literacy gap is quite visible. These differences are the measures of exclusion both in absolute and relative terms[9]. Social exclusion, or simply exclusion, is considered to be the outcome of "the process through which groups are wholly or partially restricted from full participation in the economic, educational, and social membership. Exclusion involves both the act of restricting access *intentionally or otherwise* and the consequences that follow,..." (Throat and Newman, 2007: 2) (emphasis added). So it refers to

---

8. One of the authors had conducted a preliminary survey in December, 2007 in connection with a project under distance mode of education. He found that during 2006-07 academic session 98 per cent of female learners and 87 per cent of male learners from among the Arunachalee students pursuing PG courses in Rajiv Gandhi University belonged to at least second generation of the elite families. The elite families belonged to the families in which at least one of the parents is in government job, or in contract/ business or in direct politics.

9. Exclusion is embedded in inequality and the extent of deviation from the 100 per cent achievements. The literacy rate less than 100 per cent means that the per cent of illiterate people belongs to the excluded group. Similarly, if the rate of literacy in one district is more as compared to another district, it means that the difference between the literacy rates is the extent of exclusion in the field. The exclusion is evident between urban-rural achievements and between general and ST categories. Obviously, the exclusion has both absolute and relative dimensions. The deviation from 100 per cent marks the extent of absolute exclusion, while the difference of percentage points between the districts or categories relative exclusion. (Ref. Table 7).

"the accumulation of disadvantages, which isolate people from integrated social and physical human development" (Berman and Phillips, 2000; and Alber, Gershoff and Brooks-Gunn, 2002) and prevents them "from participating in education or training and gaining access to services and citizenship activities. (Alber, Gershoff and Brooks-Gunn, 2002; and Bohnke, 2001). This understanding of the term exclusion is what follows from Rene Lenoir's book *Les Exclus* (1974, quoted in Guha, *op.cit.*) in which he has attempted an explanation of the situation that existed in France as a result of ever increasing crisis of industrial capitalism in the context of a welfare state. Primarily, social exclusion emerged as a policy concept and academic research in Europe in the 1980s in response to the growing social divides that resulted from new labour market conditions and the inadequacy of existing social welfare provisions to meet the changing needs of more diverse population. Unemployment was visible among people in the industrialised nations who could not participate in the normal activities of the society. (Guha, *op. cit*: 287).

Comprehending Exclusion and its Dimensions

Education has a societal purpose and takes care of societal needs. It is a common place of understanding that formal system of education, whether general or technical or professional, develops human resource and ensures participation in development process. The participation ordinarily has two implications: first, to maintain the system that works for development and second, by doing so, to secure one's livelihood. For example, a clerk working in an office helps maintain the system that is internal to development process either directly or indirectly. Direct participation can be viewed in terms of facilitating creation of infrastructure, actual creation of infrastructure, formulation of policies, implementation of programmes, production and exchange of commodities and the like. Participation in maintaining law and order, security to life and protection of life and property from external threats may be the indirect participation; both direct and indirect participation necessarily defines development process in its totality.

Education provides knowledge and develops skills of population; precisely it develops human resource of a community or/and a nation. It is the responsibility of the government committed to general welfare of people to provide education to its citizens directly through state agencies or by facilitating private initiatives. Normally, private ventures operate within state policy frame and hence provision of education is basically a state intervention.

As has been said when people participate in the process of development, they also secure their livelihoods. But the crux of the problem is that all the people may not have the education that can ensure equal level of livelihoods. A techie or a manager may earn many times the earnings of a clerk. It is because the techie has the education different from that of a clerk. Needless to say, it is the difference in education that excludes a clerk from participating in development process like the techie.

Further a mismatch can be apprehended both in principle and in practice between production of number of technocrats in the system of education and nation's requirement of their services in the process of development. In other words, all the equally skilled techies may not get opportunity to equal level of livelihoods or income; some may even work below their eligibility and capability. It is not difficult in Arunachal Pradesh to find diploma and degree holders in engineering course working in the post of a general school teacher or a clerk. By doing so, they are, on one hand, deprived of the equal opportunity which a few from their category got accesses to, and on the other, deprive just eligible candidates to the post.

This type of mismatch is a characteristic feature of formal system of education that excludes equally skilled people from equal level of participation in market linked development process. Further, higher skilled persons also exclude less but just skilled ones for a job in competition.

Besides the above types of exclusion, there are some other types of exclusion which are quite evident in our study of the growth of formal system of education in Arunachal Pradesh through government interventions.

It is evident from our discussion that ST female literacy is less than ST male literacy and all the students enrolled at primary level do not get access to higher and technical education due to shortage of these institutions. Further, all the districts did not have equal access to education at the same time due to gradual establishment of schools. No doubt, the early educated people had the opportunity of participation in development process while uneducated ones in formal system were excluded from it. The urban bias of institutes of higher and technical education and absence of colleges in 50 per cent of the districts do restrict equal access to all aspiring population of the state to higher and technical education. Exclusion from the facility of education is a cumulative process of exclusion from livelihood sources in different degrees. Those who are employed are not all those who have equal level of education. Obviously, a section of equally educated persons have been excluded from government jobs. Moreover, those who are not educated in formal system of education are totally excluded. Partial exclusion of a section of people is the result of availability of limited avenues and competition while total exclusion of another section of people is the result of their being uneducated in formal system in its conspicuous absence consequent upon gradual nature of opening schools in all districts and villages. Associated with it is the restricted access to opportunities due to limited and urban centred institutes of higher and technical education.

Conclusion

As we have stated, during the period of informal system of education, the incidence of exclusion due to inadequacy of institutional arrangement or non-availability of facility did not exist. Exclusion of deprivational or marginal type also could not be found resulting from the mismatch between available skilled persons and access to source of livelihood in the community in which informal system existed. But after the introduction of formal system of education institutional factors are found promoting inequality at the level of literacy and thus creating exclusion in the process of development in terms of accessing to education. Further, the emerging exclusion has cumulative impacts as a section of people with eligible qualification is found seeking jobs in the job market. Human resources developed through formal education to participate in development process remain outside its domain. It holds the premise that exclusion is contained in development intervention itself.

Appendix–1
District-wise and Year-wise Distribution of Number of Schools Established in Arunachal Pradesh Since 1947

Year	*District*																
	Tawang	*West Kameng*	*East Kam eng*	*PopumPare*	*Kurung Kumey*	*Lower Subansiri*	*Upper Subansiri*	*West Siang*	*East Siang*	*Upper Siang*	*Dibang Valley*	*Lower Dibang Valley*	*Lohit*	*Anjaw*	*Changlang*	*Tirap*	*Total*
1	2	3	4	5	6	7	8	9	10	11	12	13	14	15	16	17	18
Before 1947									(1918, 1940, 1946) 3			(1940 1945) 2	(1934) 1			(1839) 1	7
1947		1						3	3	1			1				9
1948				1				2	2	1			2			2	10
1949		2							1						1	1	5
1950		1						1	1	1		1		1			6
1951		1				1			2						1	1	6
1952	1							1		1			1		2	1	7
1953	1	3	2			4	1	2	3	1		1	2			2	22

Appendix–1 (Contd. . . .)

1	2	3	4	5	6	7	8	9	10	11	12	13	14	15	16	17	18
1954		4						2			1	1			2	4	14
1955								2	2						1		5
1956		1		1			1	1	1				2		1		8
1957															2		2
1958	1				2			2		1			1		1	3	11
1959									1	1			1	1			4
1960								3		1					1		9
1961				1	1			2	1	2				1		2	10
1962	1	1	2	1		2		4	4			1	1	1	1	3	23
1963				1	2	2	4	5	2	1		2	2		2	2	25
1964	2	1	1	2		1	1	3	6	1		1	2		7	4	32
1965	1	2	1		1	3	1	4	8	2			4	1	4	11	43
1966	1	3	2		2	2	2	12	4	5	3	-	2	1	1	4	44
1967	1		2		1	1	5	3	10	6		2	5		10	10	56
1968	-	1			1		1	1	1	1			2		2		10
1969	2	3	5	3	1	1	1	9	6		1		3		3	3	41

Appendix–1 (Contd. . . .)

1	2	3	4	5	6	7	8	9	10	11	12	13	14	15	16	17	18
1970		5			2	1	2	2	1			1	1		1	2	18
1971	4	4		3	1	2		5	1				1		5	1	27
1972		1		2	1	1	4	6	7	2	1		1		4	4	34
1973	1	3		1	1	1		6	1			1	1			4	20
1974	1	8	4	3	2	1	1	1	3		1	1	3	2	2	2	35
1975	3	5	6	4	4	3	4	12	7	2	1	2	3	1	7	5	69
1976	2	5	2	3	3		2	8	3	2	1	1	1	2	8	3	46
1977	6	1	3	3	1	4		5	6	2		3	4	6	7	1	52
1978	3	4	8	6	2	4	4	5	3	2	2	4	6	1	2	1	57
1979	4	4	7	1	5	4	12	8	5	3	1	2	5	2	7	4	74
1980	1	2	4	5		1	3	11	1			1	2		2	2	35
1981	1	4	11	2	2		5	8				3	7	2	4	4	53
1982	1	1	5	2	3		9	4	2	1			1	1	4	7	41
1983	1	2	5	4	4	1	3	4	3	1			1	1	3	3	36
1984	3		5	2	5		7	1	2	3	1		1	2	2	4	38
1985		2	6	5	8	4	4	5	2			1	2		12		51

Appendix–1 (Contd. . . .)

1	2	3	4	5	6	7	8	9	10	11	12	13	14	15	16	17	18
1986	5		9	4	2	1	6	7	4	5			3	1	7	4	58
1987	2	9	10	4	3	4	6	4		1		1	1	2	10	3	60
1988	1	4	6	2	5	1	7	1	2	5	1	3	7	2	5	3	55
1989	3	8	5	7	2	4	6	9	2	2			1	2	4	9	64
1990	4	1	6	3	6	2	1	6	1			1	2		3	2	38
1991		4		3	5	2		3		1		4	4	1	1	5	33
1992	5	4	4	5	3	7	4	6	2		1		3	1	5	4	54
1993	4	1	1	6	4	4	3	5	4			4	1	1	3	4	45
1994	3	9	6	3	1	1	5	5	1	1	1		1	1	5	3	46
1995		5	1	8	2	3		4	1	1			3	1	6	1	36
1996	1	5	2	4	1	3	4	3	4	2		4	2		1	3	39
1997		3	4	3	1	6		1	1				1		4		24
1998	3	4	4	3	2	2	2	3	6	3			3	1	2	4	42
1999		2	5	6	2	3	1		2	1		3	3		7		35
2000	2	2	2	2	3	4	2	1	5			1	1		6	1	32
2001	2	2	3	3	1	5	2	1	6	1		2	2		4		34

Appendix–1 (Contd. . . .)

1	2	3	4	5	6	7	8	9	10	11	12	13	14	15	16	17	18
2002	2			3	1			2	1	2		3			2	1	17
2003	2	1	6	13	1	2	5	3	6	2			1		1	4	47
2004	5	2	5	3	4	4	1	6	3						2	3	38
2005		1				1			1	1			5	3			12
No. of schools, year of estt. Not available	1	6		6	3	2	19	34	6				21	2	2	19	121
Total Schools in the Districts	87	149	161	147	107	107	151	257	167	72	16	57	137	44	192	174	2025
No. of Years School not established	22	13	21	19	17	17	22	6	7	21	46	30	10	32	8	13	

Source: Begi, 2007:213-217.

Appendix–2
Distribution and Coverage of Schools in the Districts of Arunachal Pradesh

District	Area in Sq Km	No. of inhabited villages	No. of Schools at elementary level 2001			Average no. of villages covered by a School (Rural)	Area covered by one in Sq. Km	No. of schools at elementary level, 2007-08			% of growth over 6 years	Average no. of village covered by a school (Rural)
			A.P. Govt.	Other then A.P. Govt.	Total			A.P. Govt.	Other then A.P. Govt.	Total		
Tawang	2172	181	66	7	73	2.74	29.753	81	7	88	22.73	2.00
West Kameng	7422	212	105	17	132	2.01	56.227	129	23	152	22.86	1.643
East Kameng	4134	310	131	4	135	2.37	30.622	155	8	163	18.32	2.00
Papum Pare	2875	267	81	16	97	3.30	29.639	157	17	174	93.83	1.70
Lower Subansiri/ Kurung Kumey	10135	652	140	20	160	4.66	63.344	177	32	209	26.43	3.68
Upper Subansiri	7032	398	123	1	124	3.24	56.710	137	9	146	11.38	2.91
West Siang	7643	398	209	12	221	1.90	34.584	225	22	247	7.66	1.77
East Siang	4687	144	123	12	135	1.17	34.719	134	16	150	8.94	1.07
Upper Siang	6188	92	59	3	62	1.56	99.810	71	3	74	20.34	1.30
Changlang	4662	336	158	5	161	2.13	28.957	171	16	187	8.23	1.97
Lohit & Anjaw	11402	493	145	14	159	3.40	71.711	180	18	198	24.14	2.74
Dibang Valley and Lower Dibang Valley	13029	213	52	03	57	4.10	228.579	64	09	73	23.08	3.33
Tirap	2362	167	134	12	146	1.25	16.178	146	19	165	08.96	1.14
Total	83,743	3863	1526	126	1662	2.53	50.387	1827	199	2026	19.72	2.11

Source : GoAP: Statistical Abstracts of 2002 and 2007-08.

REFERENCES

Agarwal, A.K.1985. *North-East India: An Economic Perspective*, Allahabad: Chugh Publications.

Alber, J.L.; E.T. Gershoff and J. Brooks-Gunn 2002. "Social Exclusion of Children in the US: identifying potential indicators". In A. J. Khan, S.B. Khamerman (eds), *Beyond Child Poverty: The Social Exclusion of Children*. New York: Columbia University Press, pp. 245-286.

Basar, Jumyir and Boa Rina Tok 2004. "Traditional System of Informal Education in Tribal Communities in Arunachal Pradesh–an overview". Presented in the national seminar on *Indigenous Educating Process among various Tribes of Arunachal Pradesh*. October 29-30, 2004, Itanagar: Arunachal University (presently Rajiv Gandhi University).

Basar, Jumyir 2006. "Galo House as a Cultural Space". Resarun, Vol. 32. Itanagar: Directorate of Research, pp.105-118.

Begi, Joram 2007. *Education in Arunachal Pradesh since 1947 (Constraints, Opportunities, Initiatives and Needs)*, New Delhi:Mittal Publications.

Behera, M.C. 1991. "Education in Cultural Perspective", *Arunachal Times*, July, 7-8, 1991.

———— 1994. *Planning and Socio-Economic Development of the Tribals*, New Delhi: Commonwealth Publishers.

———— 2006.'Contextualising Human Resource Development in Arunachal Pradesh: Open and Distance Learning (ODL) at Perspective'. Paper presented at 2nd Biennial Conference and National Seminar on *Challenges of Higher Education in the Present Perspective and Role of Distance Mode*, 3rd-4th November, 2006, Tripura University, Agartala.

———— and Helina Mantaw 1998. "Growth of Entrepreneurship in Arunachal Pradesh: Problems and Prospects – A Study with reference to the Khampti Tribe". In B. Datta Ray and Prabin Baishya (eds), 1998. *Sociological Constraints to Industrial Development in North East India*. New Delhi:Concept.

Berman, Y. and D. Phillips 2000. "Indicators of Social Quality and Social Exclusion at National and Community Level". In *Soc Indic Res*, Vol. 3, pp. 329-350.

Bohnke, P. 2001. *Nothing Left to Lose? Poverty and Social Exclusion in Comparison: Empirical Evidence in Germany*. Berlin: Social Science Research Centre, pp.1-35.

Chowdhury, J. N., 1982. *Arunachal though the Ages*, Shillong.

Deori, R.K. 1982. *The Sulungs*, Shillong: Research Department, Government of Arunachal Pradesh.

Elwin,V. (ed.). 1959. *India's North East Frontier in the Nineteenth Century*, London: Oxford University Press.

GOI, 1986-87. *Report of the Commissioner for Scheduled Castes and Scheduled Tribes*, 28th Report, New Delhi.

_______________. Censuses of 1961, 1971, 1981, 1991 and 2001.

Government of Arunachal Pradesh, 1981. *Twenty Years' Development Activities of Arunachal Pradesh since 1960-61 to 1979-80*. Itanagar: Directorate of Economics and Statistics, Government of Arunachal Pradesh.

Government of Arunachal Pradesh (nd[1]). Basic Statistics of Arunachal Pradesh (1950-51 to 1986-87), Itanagar : Directorate of Economics and Statistics.

_______________. 1991, 1994,1995, 1996,1998,1999, 2001, 2002, 2003, 2002, 2006, 2007. *Statistical Abstract*. Itanagar: Directorate of Economics and Statistics, Government of Arunachal Pradesh.

_______________.1997. *50 Years Space of Development in Arunachal Pradesh (1947 to 1997)*, Itanagar: Directorate of Economics and Statistics, Government of Arunachal Pradesh.

_______________.2000. *Economic Review of Arunachal Pradesh*, Itanagar: Directorate of Economics and Statistics, Government of Arunachal Pradesh.

_______________.2005. *Report of Provisional Statistics, Arunachal Pradesh, Seventh All India School Education Survey*, Itanagar: Department of Education.

_______________2008-09. Basic *Information on Institutions of Higher and Technical Education, Arunachal Pradesh*. Itanagar: Directorate Higher and Technical Education.

Guha, Abhijit. 2007. "'Social Exclusion': A Sceptical View", *Jr. of Indian Anthropological Society*, Vol. 42, pp. 287-292.

Haimendorf, C.Von.Furer 1946 /1950. *Ethnographic Notes on the Tribes of the Subansiri Region*, Shillong: Assam Government Press.

_______________1962. *The Apatanis and their Neighbours (A Primitive Civilization of the Eastern Himalayas)*. London: Routledge and Kegan Paul.

Jha, S.D. 1985. *The Wealth of Arunachal Pradesh*. New Delhi: Mittal Publications.

NCAER, 1967. *Techno-Economic Survey of Arunachal Pradesh*. New Delhi:NCAER.

NEFA Information. 1966 1(1), 1(2),1(5); 1967 II(2). Itanagar: DIPR.

Nehru, J. 1958. "Forward to the second edition". In Verrier Elwin, 1959 (1988 reprint). *A Philosophy for NEFA*. Itanagar: Directorate of Research.

Perme, Onong 2008. "A Study on the Culture and Process of Education in Arunachal Pradesh with the Adis of East Siang as Case Study". *M.Phil Dissertation*. Itanagar: Arunachal Institute of Tribal Studies, Rajiv Gandhi University.

Pertin, Otem 2009. *Rethinking Tribal Institutions*, New Delhi: Commonwealth.

Throat, Sukhadeo and Katherine S. Newman. 2007. "Caste and Economic Discrimination: Causes, Consequences and Remedies", *Labour Market Discrimination and Urban Sector, Research Series, Social Exclusion*,1(1), New Delhi/New Jersey: Indian Institute of Dalit Studies/ Princeton University, pp. 1-7.

2

Distress Migration in Tribal Orissa : A Study in KBK Districts

Surjyanarayan Tripathy

The history of migration is replete with instances of people's struggle to survive and to prosper, to escape insecurity and poverty, and to move in response to opportunity. Migration can be understood as both a cause and a consequence of poverty for those who stay put and for those who move. Thus, there are no a priori factors which cause people to migrate and which lead to a particular set of consequences (Amin, 1995). For many years, poverty was seen as a root cause of migration, and development or a reduction in poverty was seen as the solution for unwanted migration. Thus, attacking the "root causes" of migration was widely believed to be the crucial method to reduce illegal and unwanted migration.

The economic theory of migration has its historical roots in models of development (Lewis, 1954). According to this theory rural-urban migration is caused by geographic differences in the supply and demand for labour. Migration is possible due to assumptions of wage differentials between rural and urban areas, a reserve army of 'underemployed' labour in agriculture, full unemployment, zero transfer costs and reinvestment of urban enterprise profits into production. Lewis model, especially the assumption of full employment, the Harris-Todaro model

(1970) and its extensions have been crucial in modelling rural-to-urban migration in less developed countries. The underlying micro-foundation of these models is that expected wage in urban areas is the driving force of rural migrants. Since the Harris-Todaro model many other researchers have extended the model by incorporating new factors that will increase the choices of individuals to migrate.

In the Harris-Todaro model, labour migration is modelled in the context of inter-sectoral (rural-urban) wage inequality. Migration decisions are made by rational self-interested individuals looking for higher paid work in urban areas and migration occurs if the economic benefits in terms of expected wages at urban destination - accounting for risk of initial spell of unemployment – exceed economic costs of moving and foregone wages at rural origin (Lucas, 1997). Generally, individuals with better education, skills and labour market experience have a comparative advantage in job search at destination labour markets, and therefore are more likely to migrate. Thus, migration is seen as a selective, rather than random, process, and whilst migrants 'self select' in this way, the same logic of rationality implies that non-migrants do not move because their comparative advantage lies in staying (Tunali, 2000). Consequently, it can be derived that other things being equal, migrants are more likely to be from *ex ante* better-off groups, who are more likely to be better educated and skilled, and non-migrants from worse-off groups. Furthermore, because poorer households face tighter financial constraints, migration costs limit the set of available destination choices, and therefore, the potential benefits which might discourage mobility. The negative impacts of financial or asset poverty are likely to be compounded in low income countries by incomplete financial markets.

Distress migration of male-members, *inter alia*, results in increase in female-headed households; feminization of poverty; impact on reproduction and population growth in sending areas; no formal entitlements to land or ownership; dependent on irregular and insufficient remittances; loss of social and other support networks; not enough labour to work the land and limited political participation The elderly are likely to be more dependent on family and 'community' networks which may decline through the out-migration of others. Increased dependence on government services and social welfare mechanisms, loss of young people and subsequent decline in the agricultural sector, consequences of an ageing population and undermined social security systems result from such migrations. (Tripathy, 2005).

A short-term strategy which through various mechanisms becomes a long-term process like temporary, contractual and seasonal nature of employment; forms of 'bonded' labour, exploitative working conditions; negative effects of 'migration pressure'; poor housing and other social services; neglect of rural production; increasing inequality, wealth and other differentials between sending and non-sending households; insecure employment through casual labour resulting in the inability to accumulate. Remittances can create opportunities for investment in land, education and other assets, savings and local development (see Brown and Connell, 1994).

A study of migration evidently exposes social, economic and political inequalities and these are often exacerbated by various international and national policies based as they are on particular understandings of the reasons for, and impact of, migration. Migration is a significant livelihood strategy for poor households. Nevertheless, the role of migration in supporting or moving out of chronic poverty is largely shaped by the social, cultural, geographical and economic exclusions experienced by the poor. Thus, research into chronic poverty needs to be able to identify when, where and for whom migration is a key livelihood strategy and the ways in which migration plays a role in accepting chronic poverty in diverse societies and for diverse groups within them.

It is enormously difficult to separate cause and effect when analyzing links between poverty and migration due to the impact that migration can have on improving or deteriorating welfare for migrants and non-migrants at destination and source over time. Poverty may induce people to migrate in order to improve their livelihoods but may in turn result in them becoming further impoverished and more vulnerable. Rural out-migration is often perceived to be the result of poverty, particularly in the case of seasonal migration, in which the poor migrate in search of alternative livelihoods in response to the detrimental effects of, for instance, the dry season on agricultural production and livelihoods, impairing home production and increasing vulnerability.

Causes of Labour Migration in Orissa

Labour migration in Orissa can be understood with reference to the general perspectives affecting migration. Migration is a process through which people move from one place of residence to another. The change in residence results in redistribution of population, both at its origin and at the destination. As such migration is one of the three components of population change. Thus, migration is a complex and dynamic process. Migratory movements are considered as physical events shaped by environmental forces. Labour migration may be defined as a form of labour mobility towards districts or states or outside where industry and employment are expanding. In other words, migration may be the phenomenon of the flow of the people over shorter or longer distances from one origin to a destination either for temporary or permanent settlement. Migratory movements are the results of pressure on land due to rapid growth of population, decline in the rural industries and handicrafts, lack of employment and livelihood, etc. Thus, migration is one of the dynamic constituents of population change and a vital component of development.

Normally, migration of labourers from rural to urban areas has been viewed as an economic phenomenon, even though non-economic factors have some bearing. Primarily due to lack of employment in their area of origin, migration occurs in order to provide better scope to the migrants elsewhere. With the growth of urbanization and industrialization, the trend of migration within the country has increased significantly.

Out-migration of Rural Workmen from the Tribal Districts of Orissa

A large segment of migrant labourers in Orissa belong to the category of landless agricultural labourers and very often from tribal, backward or scheduled castes. In few cases those who have limited land didn't possess the needed resource to develop the same and as a result, the barren land is left uncultivated for years. Therefore, they are compelled to work as agricultural labourers in the land of the big landlords or Zamidars of the same village or adjourning villages. The employment being seasonal and the wages being low, they find it hard to make both ends meet. Thus, the insufficiency of such labourers' income to cover the living expenses even on a subsistence level seems to be the basic underlying factor of their indebtedness leading to mass migration in search of employment. Moreover, due to deforestation, pressure on land, recurring drought, poverty and unemployment, the tribals of the study area migrate outside the districts and states along their wives and children for a period of 6 months to eke out their livelihood. (Tripathy and Das, 1997).

With regard to Orissa, the poorest state in India, 46 per cent of people lived below the poverty line in 1999-2000, as against 26 per cent for the entire country. Tribals constitute about 23 per cent of total population who are the backward, marginalized and poverty stricken population and KBK[1] districts account for 19.72 per cent population over 30.59 per cent geographical area of the State and tribals constitute 38.72 per cent. Several socio-economic indicators highlight the backwardness of KBK region, which is one of the poorest regions in the country. The tribals in Orissa continued to remain socially, economically and educationally backward, and are languishing at the bottom of the socio-economic ladder. The low level of income in KBK region, large scale unemployment, under employment, poverty and lower growth rate in agricultural sector lead ultimately to distress migration of tribals. Such migrant tribals fall prey to exploitative contractors and suffer bondage, social isolation and identity crisis. (Tripathy, 1989).

---

1. KBK districts basically refer to the undivided districts such as Kalahandi, Bolangir and Koraput and newly organized eight districts of Orissa namely, (i) Kalahandi. (ii) Nuapara (iii) Bolangir (iv) Sonepur (v) Koraput (vi) Nawarangpur (vii) Malkanagiri and (viii) Rayagada, which are among the most backward districts of India.

   Total population: 63,20,468 (19.96% to total state population)

   S.T. population: 24,48,301(38.73% to total KBK population)
   S.C. population: 10,00,840 (15.83% to total KBK population)

Their geographical isolation and improvised economy coupled with chronic poverty, illiteracy, made them vulnerable and they fail to withstand the forces and ultimately become the prey to all types of exploitation. There are also evidences which enlighten that because of deforestation, restrictions imposed by the Government for the use of forests, pressure on land, recurring drought, unemployment and chronic poverty- the tribals of KBK migrate to outside the state in search of employment and livelihoods in construction projects and brick-kiln and other manual works (Tripathy, 2006: 17). It must be kept in view that migration being the movement of human beings in the pursuit of certain cherished objects like better employment, batter wages and better quality of life, there is apparently nothing wrong. However, the problem is of serious magnitude when such migration leads to human misery and exploitation.

Vulnerability of Tribals and Factors Contributing to their Distressed Migration

General backwardness of tribal communities, illiteracy and lack of awareness, lack of social mobility, inefficient planning, planning not addressed to the felt needs of the local tribes, are some of the factors responsible for marginalization of the tribal community. The tribals reside in forests and inaccessible hill areas and have been maintaining their survival oriented culture. The agents of the new order represented by traders, money lenders, and contractors entered to the tribal regions and exploited them. They provided money lending and took away their fertile lands as a result of which, the tribal proceeded to interior parts of forest. Tribal deprivation has been the reality and in the process, their traditions of community ownership of resources, their dependence on forests and their practice of shifting cultivation have all suffered. With the thrust on industrialization and higher productivity, the resource rich regions of the tribals have been naturally sucked into the plans for national development. In fact, development projects, industries, irrigation schemes built on large dams have displaced the tribals and transformed them into landless migrant labour.

Entry of non-tribals into their traditional homelands and the non-acceptance of their traditional patterns of land ownership (based on an oral pattern) by those who cherish the written document system leads to their alienation from land. Impoverishment, indebtedness, land alienation and bondage are then the natural result of the process. Unfortunately, the story has been repeated number of times all over India where there is a substantial tribal population. Within the tribals, women are the worst victims of this development. Constraints on her access to forests and its resources directly affect her traditional housework and in the formal economy, she loses her status and control over community resources.

It has been observed that non-recognition of tribes over resources and restrictions on their use, alienation tribes from the means of production, denial of due entitlement of labour, distress payment of wages, and misappropriation of funds, have kept the tribal labour in the web of misery and starvation. In tribal dominated states in India, the life support system of the local tribes has been snatched away by non-tribals and state institutions. As a result, tribal movement originated in fierce struggle of their rights (Tripathy, 2000).

The phenomenon of rural-urban migration must be viewed in the light of prevailing rural conditions of poverty, inequality, unemployment which the Government policy of rural development could not mitigate due to leakages of funds, misappropriation and other factors. Thus, the problem of rural-urban migration has its ramification in the totality of the problem of poverty and unemployment.

In the absence of a detailed study, the present study has been claimed to be the first study ever attempted confined to Kalahandi, and Bolangir - the drought prone, tribal dominated and backward districts of Orissa. The study in general and the regional analysis in particular, provide a necessary base for further research into the underlying reasons of tribal migration and its socio-economic consequences.

The present study has been undertaken to focus on the nature of poverty, their causes and consequences prevailing in tribal concentrated sample villages of Kalahandi and Bolangir districts of Orissa. In this regard it attempts at examining the socio-economic profile of the tribal migrants in the study area with reference to their living standards. Needless to say, the paper essentially has policy implications at large.

The present study has been mainly confined to migrants of tribal concentrated sample villages of Kalahandi and Bolangir - the poverty stricken and drought ravaged tribal dominated districts of Orissa. These two districts have been purposively selected, as these districts are the most backward districts in the country known as KBK districts. However, though the filed analysis has been based on the sample tribal dominated villages of these districts, but the overall work has been developed on the basis of general framework and in-depth study of various issues relating to rural-urban migration in the State of Orissa with the help of both primary and secondary sources of available data.

Keeping in view the constraints of time and cost, it was decided to collect field data from 4 blocks on the basis of random sampling method for the purpose of field study. Two blocks from each sample district have been randomly selected for the purpose of field study. First of all a list of the blocks falling in the selected districts has been prepared. From among the blocks, two blocks named Kesinga and Dharamgarh blocks in Kalahandi district, Belpara and Turekala block in Bolangir district have been selected on the basis of their tribal concentration, migration potentiality and accessibility. Mostly, the head of the returned migrant household was interviewed to fill up the questionnaire. It was found that usually the migrant households migrate to different place within the state and outside the state to work in the brick - kiln industries mostly in case of Bolangir district and in case of Kalahandi to Raipur, Bastar and other places of Madhya Pradesh during the month of November. After the list of tribal villages has been prepared, 3 villages in each block have been selected through random sampling method. Thus, all total twelve villages have been covered under this study.

Data were collected from the migrant households of sample villages with the help of personal interview method through pre-tested schedules and questionnaires. The questionnaire was specifically designed to collect data. The returned migrant respondents in their native village were identified through village survey at different intervals during May 2005 to June 2006. Table 1 presents a picture about the demographic and literacy position of KBK districts (Orissa).

Table 1
Demographic and Literacy Indicators in the KBK Districts: 2001

District	*Population Density*	*Population Indicators*					*Literacy Rate*	
		Total (000)	*Female (%)*	*Rural (%)*	*ST* (%)*	*SC* (%)*	*Total (%)*	*Female (%)*
1	2	3	4	5	6	7	8	9
1. Koraput	134	1,178	49.96	83.18	50.67	13.41	36.20	24.81
2. Malkangiri	83	480	49.91	92.79	58.36	19.96	31.26	21.28
3. Nawrangpur	192	1,018	49.81	94.18	55.27	15.09	34.26	21.02
4. Rayagada	116	823	50.71	85.98	56.04	14.28	35.61	24.31
5. Bolangir	203	1,336	49.56	88.45	22.06	15.39	54.91	39.27
6. Sonepur	231	541	49.13	92.59	22.11	9.50	64.07	47.28
7. Kalahandi	168	1,334	50.00	92.49	28.88	17.01	46.20	29.56
8. Nuapada	138	531	50.15	94.34	35.59	13.09	42.29	26.01
KBK Districts	152	7,241	49.91	89.89	38.72	16.63	36.58	24.72
Orissa	236	36,707	49.29	85.03	22.21	16.20	63.61	50.97

Source : Census of India-2001, District Statistical Hand Book.
* As per 1991 Census

Table 2
SC and ST Population of the Sample Blocks in the Study Area

Name of the district	*Name of the block*	*Percentage of SC population*	*Percentage of ST population*
Kalahandi	Kesinga	15.9	23.5
	Dharamgada	16.7	17.4
Bolangir	Belpara	14.4	31.2
	Turekala	15.8	39.5

Source: Same as Table 1.

Table 2 depicts that among the sample blocks in the selected districts Dharamgada has the highest percentage of SC population (16.7%), followed by Kesinga (15.9%) and Turekala (15.8). Similarly, Turekala block has also the distinction of highest percentage of ST population (39.5), followed by Belpara (31.2) and Kesinga (23.5).

Table 3
SC and ST Population and Sex-ratio of the Sample Villages in the Study Area

Name of the district	*Name of the block*	*Name of the sample villages*	*% of SC population to total population*	*% of ST population to total population*	*Sex-ratio*
Kalahandi	(1) Kesinga	(1) Tansir	330 (19.6)	184 (10.9)	972
		(2) Titkela	318 (30.8)	143 (13.8)	975
		(3) Godtola	12 (2.4)	91 (17.9)	1028
	(2) Dharamgada	(1) Golmunda	433 (9.7)	2076 (46.3)	918
		(2) Kadalimunda	301 (14.33)	73 (3.5)	942
		(3) Dharamgada	19912(16.7)	20728(17.4)	982
Bolangir	(1) Belpara	(1) Bahabal	119 (14.4)	247 (29.9)	995
		(2) Kapani	118 (9.8)	399 (28.6)	997
		(3) Juba	220 (21.4)	433 (42.0)	1012
	(2) Turekala	(1) Barala	46 (8.0)	69 (11.1)	1032
		(2) Kadalipali	29 (18.6)	56 (35.9)	1026
		(3) Patimal	91 (29.1)	1 (0.3)	929

Source: Same as Table 1 .

Table 4
Number of Migrant Houses Surveyed from the List of Households

Name of the block	*Name of the sample villages*	*Sample Migrant households*
(1) Kesinga	(1) Tansir	15
	(2) Titkela	10
	(3) Godtola	5
(2) Dharamgada	(1) Golmunda	30
	(2) Kadalimunda	5
	(3) Dharamgada	40
(1) Belpara	(1) Bahabal	30
	(2) Kapani	15
	(3) Juba	15
(2) Turekala	(1) Barala	5
	(2) Kadalipali	5
	(3) Patimal	5
Total		180

Source : Field study.

Table -3 unfolds that among the sample villages in the selected blocks, Titkela village in Kesinga block has the highest percentage of SC population (30.8%), followed by Patimal village (29.1%) in Turekala block. Similarly, Golmunda village has also the distinction of highest percentage of ST population (46.3%), followed by Juba (42.0%) in Belpara block. It is found that the villages like Godtola, Juba, Barala and Kadalipali manifested more females per thousand of males. The village Golmunda exhibited the lowest sex-ratio (918:1000) among the villages.

Table 4 presents the list of households from which sample households were selected for the study. There are 180 sample households from 12 villages.

It is found from the Table 5 that most of the migrant households were dependent on agriculture. In most of the households there are no authentic records with regard to the possession of their land, size of holdings, etc. The area of land holding by the migrant household is not only extremely limited but also barren, scattered and rain-fed and as such the income from the agriculture is inadequate.

Table 5
Occupation-wise Distribution of Migrant Households at the Place of Origin

Sl. No.	*Occupation*	*Migrants*	*%*	*Av. monthly income per worker*
1.	Agricultural work	68	37.77	200
2.	Non-agricultural workers	23	12.77	350
3.	Leaf-plate making	12	6.67	400
4.	Bidi making	4	2.22	200
5.	Date mattress	5	2.78	180
6.	Rope making	3	1.67	200
7.	Bamboo basket weaving	7	3.89	400
8.	Hill broom collection	3	1.67	300
9.	Collection of sabai grass	3	1.67	150
10.	Wine production	10	5.56	500
11.	Kendu leaf plucking	15	8.33	600
12.	Preparation of stone-chips	27	15	450
Total		180	100.00	327

Source: Field study.

It is pertinent to conceive the nature of employment available to the migrant households at the place of destination. It is evident that the migrants are employed in a wide range of employments but mostly in brick-kiln industry and road lying works. Scattered nature of work place, distress and discriminatory wages are the reality of migrant workers leading to proionged poverty.

Table 6
Occupation-wise Distribution of Migrant Households at the Place of Destination

Sl. No.	*Different Occupation*	*Migrants Households*	*%*	*Average per worker monthly income (in Rs.)*
1.	Brick-kiln industry	104	57.78	1500
2.	Road laying, earth work and other	30	16.67	1600
3.	Construction works, hotels/ commercial establishments	10	5.55	800
4.	Manual works	16	8.89	1000
5.	Rickshaw pulling	12	6.67	1600
6.	Chips making	8	4.44	800
	Total	180	100.00	1409

Source: Field study.

Table 7
Distribution of Migrant Households According to their Sources of Debt

Sources of debt	*Migrant households*	*%*
Money lender	128	71.11
Regional rural bank	10	5.56
Commercial bank	4	2.22
Co-operatives	2	1.11
Self-help group	8	4.44
Friends, relatives	26	14.45
Others	2	1.11
Total	180	100.00

Source: Field study.

Despite vast expansion of the formal credit system in India, the dependence of rural poor on money lenders continues in some areas particularly in tribal regions of the state. In our analysis, the money lenders dominate the credit market as about 72 per cent of migrant households are dependent on them. For

Table 8
Distribution of Households According to the Level of Annual Income and Cash Remittance (in Rs.).

Level of income	*No. of migrant households*	*%*	*Cash-remittance*	*No. of migrant households*	*%*
5,000-10,000	5	2.78	0-1000	22	12.22
+10,000-15,000	38	21.11	+1000-2000	118	65.56
+15,000-20,000	86	47.78	+2000-3000	32	17.78
+20,000-25,000	38	21.00	+3000-4000	8	4.44
+25,000-30,000	13	7.22			
Total	180	100.00		180	100.00

Source: Field study

various reasons the credit flow to these sections of the population for meeting their credit requirements could not be institutionalized. This was due to the factors like inadequate supply of credit, demand-supply gap, improper identification of beneficiaries and unhealthy competition from informal credit agencies. Cumbersome and time consuming banking procedure, failure to supply credit at the time of need and rigid collateral requirement are the major stumbling blocks causing poor access to formal credit institutions. The crop loss due to natural calamities and unproductive utilization of borrowed funds resulted in rising default rate and delayed loan payments. The credit market has not been developed in the district to cater to the needs of the poor tribals. (Sarap, 1991; Swain, 2001; and Tripathy, 2006). Indebtedness leads to bondage and a type of contractual labour agreement between the labour contractor or agents; bondage in turn, reinforces exploitation and distress payment of wages

Table 8 exhibits the data relating to the level of income and cash remittance of the migrant households. It is revealed that 86 households (47.78) have the annual income in the range of +15,000-20,000 whereas only 7.22 per cent of households have their income in the range of +25,000-30,000. On the contrary, the cash remittance of the households shows that 118 households (65.56) reported to have remitted annually Rs. +1000-2000 to their native place, which is extremely low.

Observations

Migration based work and earnings are the major source of survival for the communities of this poverty stricken and low endowment regions of Bolangir and Kalahandi districts of Orissa. Though migration is an irreversible reality for the majority of those who depend on it, and indeed for many it is the single major outlet from rural poverty, it is an act fraught with immense hardship and insecurity. There are several reasons for this - skill levels are low, connections and networks are scarce, services are absent and above all, labour and remuneration practices in industries and markets that employ seasonal migrants tend to be callous and exploitative. Legal protection for this category of workers is often missing.

As has been observed from the study the most important reasons for failure of economic development and removal of poverty in the tribal dominated sample villages of Kalahandi and Bolangir districts of Orissa are corruption which is rampant causing 'leakages' in the amounts earmarked for rural employment generating schemes[2] (OREGS) Survey (CEFS), New

2. Press Release about OREGS Survey, Participatory Loot in Orissa's Rural Employment Guarantee Scheme, Centre for Environment and Food Security (CEFS), New Delhi (2007).

   The Centre for Environment and Food Security (CEFS) has completed a rapid survey to evaluate and assess the performance of the National Rural Employment Guarantee Scheme in the state of Orissa. The rapid survey was conducted in 100 villages spread over six districts of KBK (Kalahandi-Koraput-Balangir) region of Orissa. The Survey conducted during May-June 2007 covered six districts, namely; Balangir, Nuapada, Kalahandi, Koraput, Nabarangpur and Rayagada districts. The preliminary findings of this rapid survey are shocking, scandalous and outrageous. The National Rural Employment Guarantee Scheme, which is projected as the biggest anti-poverty programme in the history of Independent India, has been hijacked by officials responsible for implementing this scheme. Our survey findings have revealed that there is participatory loot, plunder and pillage in Orissa's Rural Employment Guarantee Scheme (OREGS). There is open loot of taxpayers' money, there is plunder of Poor's right to guaranteed employment and there is pillage of every single norm of democratic governance and administrative accountability. Widespread hunger, abject poverty and dehumanizing deprivation in KBK villages are

Delhi (2007). When this happens the investments do not create the employment opportunities as contemplated at their initiation, nor do they result in goods and services being provided in proportion to the investments made.

It has also been observed that PDS has not delivered essential commodities to meet the minimum food needs of the drought-hit villages of sample villages of Kalahandi and Bolangir districts of Orissa. A considerable amount of food grains and essential goods are supplied to the urban centre and sold directly to the businessmen by the dealers in a close nexus with the corrupt officials of the supply department. Thus, corruption has obstructed the noble objectives to deliver the essential food and other items to the rural poor. An inevitable sequel to the insensitivity and absurdity of the food security system is distress migration from the drought - hit villages of sample villages of Kalahandi and Bolangir districts to the urban areas.

As a result of which there is a vicious circle of poverty, unemployment, indebtedness and migration in the district of Kalahandi and Bolangir. Lack of employment and distressed condition of living compels the tribal migrants to take advance from the contractors resulting in migration. Whatever paltry amount they save is insufficient to pay back the loan amount borrowed from the money lenders as the rate of interest is exorbitantly high. The cycle of poverty originates from the sordid reality of crop loss, unemployment inducing to food insecurity, vulnerability to health hazards and ultimately, indebtedness and chronic poverty. The vicious circle continues unabated for decades in the sample district as the planned measures could not percolate down benefits in the rural regions of the districts.

---

worse than Sub-Saharan Africa. On Human Development Index, Ruwanda and Ethiopia would fare better than most of KBK villages. Hunger and abject poverty is wide spread in all the 100 villages of KBK region we visited. Our interactions and interviews with villagers suggest that about 99% of the Adivasis and Dalits living in KBK villages are suffering from chronic hunger and malnutrition. Large number of children in these villages is suffering from severe malnutrition. Hunger and abject poverty is so apparent and writ large on the hollowed cheeks, sunken eyes, distended bellies of children, skeleton figures, listlessness and despair in their looks.

Suggestions

The challenge to policy makers is to facilitate the progress of movement that is most likely to lead to an alleviation of poverty while protecting migrants from abuse, exploitation, bondage and poverty.

Social protection and public services for the chronically poor with effective delivery mechanism can spearhead the assault on chronic poverty. Together with these the policy paradigms are anti-discrimination and gender empowerment, building individual and collective assets and strategic urbanization and migration. Collectively, these policy packages can alleviate poverty directly and ensure just social compact that will underpin long-term efforts to eradicate chronic poverty.

In order to halt the process of migration which entails exploitation of marginalized tribal migrants in the KBK districts of Orissa, infrastructure development through irrigation, watershed management, road construction, coupled with agro-processing, rural industries, food processing industries, rural manufacturing, provisions of social s·curities, development of social sector like education and health services, proper implementation of employment programmes, stringent action against corruption, are some of possible alternatives.

REFERENCES

Amin, S. (1995): "Migrations in Contemporary Africa", in Baker, J. and T.A. Aina (eds.), *The Migration Experience in Africa*, 1995, Sweden: The Nordic Africa Institute.

Brown, R.P.C. and J. Connell, (1994): "Migrants' Remittances, savings and investment", in *The South Pacific International Labour Review*, 133(3), 347-67.

Harris, John and Michael Todaro, 1970 : "Migration, Unemployment and Development: A Two Sector Analysis", *American Economic Review*, 60: 126-142.

Hulme, D., K. Moore and A. Shepherd, (2001): "Chronic Poverty: meanings and analytical frameworks", *CPRC Working Paper 2*, IDPM: University of Manchester.

Lewis, W. Arthur, (1954): "Economic Development with Unlimited Supplies of Labor", *The Manchester School of Economic and Social Studies*, 22: 139-191.

Lucas, R. E. (1997): "Internal Migration in Developing Countries", in M. Rosenzweig and O. Stark (eds.), *Handbook of Population and Family Economics*, Vol. 1B, Amsterdam: Elsevier Science Publishing.

OREGS Survey, (2007): *Participatory Loot in Orissa's Rural Employment Guarantee Scheme*, Centre for Environment and Food Security (CEFS), New Delhi.

Sarap, K. (1991): *Interlinked Agrarian Markets in Rural India*, Sage, New Delhi.

Swain, M. (2001): "Rural Indebtedness and usurious interest rates in Eastern India: Some Micro Evidences", *Journal of Social and Economic Development*, Vol.3, No. 1, 122-143.

Tunali, I. (2000): 'Rationality of Migration', in *International Economic Review*, 41 (4): 893-920.

Tripathy, S.N. (1989): *Bonded Labour in India*, Discovery Publishing House, New Delhi.

Tripathy, S.N. and C.R. Das (1997): *Migrant Labour in India*, Discovery Publishing House, New Delhi.

Tripathy, S.N. (2000): *Glimpses on Tribal Development*, Discovery Publishing House, New Delhi.

Tripathy, S.N. (2005): *Female Headed Households in India*, Sonali Publications, New Delhi.

Tripathy, S.N. (2006): *Dynamics of Tribal Migration*, Sonali Publications, New Delhi.

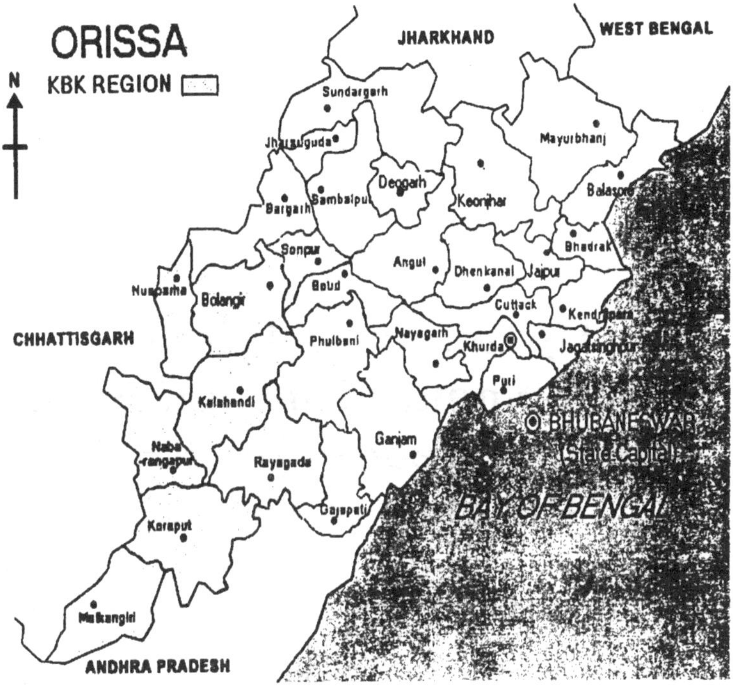
ORISSA
KBK REGION
N
JHARKHAND
WEST BENGAL
CHHATTISGARH
ANDHRA PRADESH
Sundargarh
Mayurbhanj
Deogarh
Sambalpur
Bargarh
Keonjhar
Balasore
Bhadrak
Sonpur
Angul
Dhenkanal
Boud
Bolangir
Cuttack
Phulbani
Nayagarh
Khurda
Kalahandi
Puri
Ganjam
Rayagada
Gajapati
Koraput
BHUBANESWAR
(State Capital)
BAY OF BENGAL
ANDHRA PRADESH

3

Dynamics of Tribal Development : Encountering Ground Reality in "KBK" Districts of Orissa

Krishna Chandra Pradhan

There are some 85 million Indians who are officially classified as "Scheduled Tribes". Of these, about 16 million live in the states of North-Eastern India, and the rest live in the heart of India, in a more-or-less contiguous hill and forest belt that extends across the states of Gujarat, Rajastan, Maharastra, Madhya Pradesh, Chhatisgarh, Jharkhand, Andhra Pradesh, Orissa, Bihar and West Bengal.

The Tribes of the north-east differ from their counterparts in other parts of India in several respects. The substantial one is their exposition to modern English education. As a result, their literacy and hence the chances of being advantageously absorbed in the modern economy are much higher than that of their counterparts elsewhere in India. Second, unlike the tribals of the mainland they have been largely free from the trauma caused by dispossession.

Orissa figures predominately in the list of underdeveloped states in India and has been a victim of some ill thought-out development strategy. Despite being a rich state in terms of its mines and minerals and natural resources, Orissa has not made any real progress as for as the development of the state and its people are concerned.

The tribal population constitutes 8.8 per cent of the total population in India. Next to Madhya Pradesh, Orissa has the largest concentration of tribal population in India. In the context of Orissa, the tribes constitute 22.21 per cent of the total population; they live in abject poverty having been segregated from the mainstream life. They are educationally, socially and economically far backward than other social groups. Despite planned effort there has been wide disparity in the distribution of income and wealth, gains of development disproportionately percolating to the tribal concentrated backward regions. The rural-urban dichotomy and a structure of dualistic economy continued unabated making this lop-sided development and regional imbalance more acute especially in the era of Globalization.

Over dependence on subsistence and uncertain agriculture, absence of rural non-farm employment, increasing deforestation and recurring droughts have resulted in abject poverty in the tribal dominated districts of Kalahandi, Bolangir and Koraput (KBK). Especially there are repeated cases of sale of child, bonded labour, starvation death, frequent outbreak of diseases, mass dropouts, migration, etc. in KBK districts. (Tripathy, 1989). It has been observed that the development of economic infrastructure like irrigation, electrification, banking, communication, which could have generated direct economic benefit to the people for sustainable form of livelihood in these districts has not been followed up in a right perspective.

Globalization and Tribals

Of the numerous ways the globalization has impacted upon the Indian economy, labour is an important dimension. In the process of globalization, livelihood security has assumed paramount importance. A large number of occupations and livelihoods are imposing insecurities and vulnerability due to lack of rights and statutary protection. There is wide spread concern that the acceleration in GDP growth in the post reforms period has not been accompanied by a commensurate expansion in employment. Because of withdrawals from the public sector, there has been slow expansion of employment leading to a rise in unemployment rates.

In the era of globalization, labour is disempowered in several dimensions. There has been numerical decline of work force and weakening trade unions. There has been also the shrinking of organized sector, increase of labour in which labour eke out a living unprotected by a regular salary and job security and inadequacy of social security nets. Workers in the informal economy can be persons working at home, or on premises of his/ her choice other than the employer's, to produce goods or services on a contract or order for a specific employer or contractor, independent wageworkers are attached to only one employer and providing service to individuals, households and enterprises, e.g. servants and watchmen working for households.

Globalization unleashes the forces of competition and marginalizes those who are unable to compete, thus, making the market forces the supreme arbiter of success or failures. Globalization of the economy also supposes an unregulated labour regime, which not only keeps labour costs at a minimum, but also statuary protection and union activities are discouraged.

Needless to mention that Indian economy has been plagued with the problems of acute unemployment and underdevelopment, particularly in the tribal concentrated rural areas. This is manifested in low or static standards of living of the people. The case of India is quite typical of this phenomenon where underdevelopment and unemployment are endemic among the rural population, leading to their migration in search of employment.

It is well known that Orissa is one of the poverty stricken states of India, where the magnitude of rural poverty has been the highest all along. The poverty ratio of different states for rural and urban areas in the year 1973-74, 1977-78 , 1993-94, 1999-2000 reveal that Orissa was always at higher stage of poverty ratios compared to the national average as well as most of the other states in India (Orissa Development Report: 267). It is also remarkable to note that the incidence of poverty is the highest among the tribal population in Orissa, which is as high as 80 per cent in some parts of the state.

In remote forest areas tribes mostly adopt shifting cultivation as a method of agriculture. The extreme poverty compelled many tribals to sell or mortgage their lands to the people of the plains. As a result, the tribals of the region were driven to inaccessible forests and hill areas where they maintained their survival-oriented culture. The agents of the 'new order' represented by traders, moneylenders and contractors didn't leave them there either. The outcome of this oppressive 'new order' was that the 'tribal poor' have found themselves exceedingly indebted and alienated from most of their land except for a few pieces of eroded land strips. (Tripathy, 1998: 35-36).

Thus, the tribals from time to time were deprived of their fertile lands and were subjected to ruthless exploitation by the invading people which have resulted in the hill men's flying in greater and greater wilderness. The infiltration of people from the plains continues resulting in depriving the hill men of the good lands they reclaimed. (Tripathy, 1998: 232).

The larger segment of migrant labourers in Orissa belongs to the category of landless agricultural labourers and often from scheduled and backward castes. In few cases those who have limited land did not possess the needed resources to develop the same and as a result, the barren land is left uncultivated for years.

Therefore, they are compelled to work as agricultural labourers in the land of the big landlords or Zamindars of the same village or adjourning villages. The employment being seasonal and the wages being low, they find it hard to make both ends meet. Thus, the insufficiency of such labourers' income to cover the living expenses even on a subsistence level seems to the basic underlying factor of their indebtedness leading to mass migration in search of employment. (Tripathy and Das, 1997).

Moreover, due to deforestation, pressure on land, recurring drought, poverty and unemployment, the tribals of the study area migrate outside the districts and states along their wives and children for a period of 6 months to eke out their livelihood.

As has been observed the most important reasons for failure of economic development and removal of poverty in the tribal dominated villages of Kalahandi, Bolangir and Malkangiri is corruption, which is rampant, causing "leakages" in the amounts earmarked for rural employment generating schemes. When this happens the investments do not create the employment opportunities as contemplated at their initiation, nor do they result in goods and services being provided in population to the investments made. (Tripathy, 2005).

A large section of tribal population remained away from mainstream of development mainly due to seclusion of their habitats in dispersed areas, closed circle cultural movements, traditional ways of understanding and limitation of knowledge. The gains of investment oriented planning followed in the country during the five year plans by and large went in the favour of advantageous groups of people standing at the comparatively upper strata. Plan outlays covered the popular prime areas associated with secondary and tertiary activities of investment; the planning strategy was diverted to classical approach adopting a resolute decision for more concentration on area development with specific target group coverage. This opened a new vista of action programme in the planning process.

Exploitation of the Tribals

The tribals who constitute about 8.8 per cent of country's total population are concentrated in more than 21 states and five union territories. They are the most vulnerable among the weaker sections of the community. The tribals exchange their little forest produce for other goods and services with the help of businessmen of nearby villages and towns. Because of their abject poverty, ignorance, simplicity and illiteracy, the middlemen, traders and contractors exploit the tribals. The moneylenders have been charging exorbitant rates of interest from them. Traders have been buying their produce at rock bottom prices and selling it at very high rates, thus, exploiting them in both ways. The contractors have been paying them very low wages.

Two things are of greater importance to tribals, *i.e.* land and forest. The tribal people are either hunters or food gatherers, settled or hill cultivators, shepherds or craftsmen. They cultivate the lands by means of traditional methods and thus get very low returns. As a result, these people live in a bare subsistence economy. But there is something inherent in the tribal philosophy, which has kept these people, contend with fulfilment of their necessities. Economic exploitation of tribals have resulted in heavy migrations, value adulterations, increased bonded labourers and subversive activities.

Thus, the tribals of Orissa continued to remain in the grip of socio-economic backwardness and poverty. The powerful exogenous forces of moneylenders, contractors, officials having their nexus with political leaders and police could exert dominant control over the tribes and exploit them.

Role of Education in the Development of Tribals

For a long time it was believed that development of a nation mainly depends upon exploration and exploitation of natural resources. But later on it was conceived that economic development could be accelerated only when its human resources are developed. Thus, education has been considered as a critical input for economic and social development. It is crucial for building human capabilities and widening the horizon of opportunities. Education and literacy empower disadvantaged groups with increased efficiency and ability to protect their interest, raise voice against oppression and make them politically conscious. Education is the pre-requisite factor, which improves human capabilities, enhances increased participation of people in production and thus, establishes synergic relationship between economic development and social development.

Schultz in his book, "The Economics of being poor", highlights that economic growth is not only a function of special formation but also of investment in human capital. South Asian countries like Sri Lanka, Singapore, Hong Kong, Malaysia and Korea, etc. have made remarkable success in eradicating human deprivation and creating human capabilities through appropriate policy paradigms. These countries underwent social transition because of noteworthy progress in the sphere of education, health, sanitation and water supply.

Keeping pace with the constitutional declaration, the country has adopted several policies and implemented various programmes and schemes for literacy development among the masses. But it has been observed that the tribals in general lag much behind their non-tribal counterparts in literacy status. Therefore, special schemes and programmes were introduced for them. But the programmes benefited the tribal males more than tribal females. Consequently, the former remained far ahead of the latter in literacy achievement. It is evident from census records. In 1991 census, tribal female literacy is 8.29 per cent as against the tribal male literacy which is recorded 27.93 per cent. Thus, there exists a wide gap of 19.64 percentage points between male tribal literacy rate and female tribal literacy rate.

Therefore, in order to improve the literacy position of tribal females the Government implemented 'Total Literacy Campaign' (TLC) from 1989 onwards in tribal dominated areas. To ensure Primary education to all, the Education Guarantee Scheme (EGC) was launched in 2001.

Moreover, human development calls for educating of both boys and girls at least, up to primary school level to begin with. But unfortunately, despite the provision of free and compulsory education to all in the Directive Principles of State Policy, this objective could not be achieved.

Development of Literacy : (Rural-Urban Divide)

It has been remarked that poverty and economic compulsions are the factors responsible for high dropouts of girls, as poverty stricken parents do not possess adequate income to support their daughters to continue their education. The girls are engaged in attending younger siblings, which enables their mothers to go out for wage earning and employment in the informal sector. Thus, the literacy levels among tribals in general and tribal girls in particular are abysmally low (Tripathy, 2005).

It is revealed from the Table 1 that the districts in the Group–A are comparatively advanced both economically and also in terms of literacy than the tribal dominated backward districts, which has been exhibited in the Group–B.

This clearly demonstrates the rural-urban disparity in terms of development of education.

It is found from the Table 2 that the literacy rate among the ST population was the lowest compared to General and SC category in all India level. As per 1991 census, the female literacy among ST population was 18.19 whereas the male literacy was 40.65. Thus, there existed a gender gap of 21.46 percentage points among the tribal females in India.

Table 1
Imbalance in the Development of Literacy in Orissa

Sl. No.	*District (Group–A) Non-Tribal Districts*	*Rate of Literacy (In %)*
1.	Khurda	80.19
2.	Jagatsinghpur	79.61
3.	Puri	78.40
4.	Kendrapada	77.33
5.	Cuttack	76.13
6.	Bhadrak	74.64
7.	Jharsuguda	71.47
8.	Dhenkanal	70.11
	Average= 76.2 %	
	District (Group–B), Tribal Districts	*Rate of Literacy, (in %)*
1.	Malkangiri	31.26
2.	Nawarangpur	34.26
3.	Rayagada	35.61
4.	Koraput	36.20
5.	Gajapati	41.73
6.	Kalahandi	46.20
7.	Nuapada	42.29
8.	Bolingir	54.29
Average= 40 %		

Source: 2001 Census Report.

Table 2
Literacy Rate of India

Census	*Total*			*S.T.*			*S.C.*		
year	*Male*	*Female*	*Person*	*Male*	*Female*	*Person*	*Male*	*Female*	*Person*
1961	34.37	12.90	23.95	13.04	2.89	7.98	16.77	3.14	10.10
1971	39.52	18.70	29.48	17.09	4.58	10.89	22.21	7.64	15.17
1981	46.89	24.82	36.23	24.52	8.04	16.35	31.12	10.93	21.38
1991	64.13	39.29	52.21	40.65	19.19	29.60	49.91	23.76	37.41
2001	75.85	54.16	65.38						

Source: Census of India, 2001.

Table 3
Literacy by Sex and Gender Gap in Literacy Rate

Districts	*Rural/Urban*	*Literacy Rate*		*Gender Gap*
		Male	*Female*	
	Total	71.7	39.5	32.2
	Rural	69.5	35.8	33.8
Bolingir	Urban	87.1	68.2	18.9
Kalahandi	Total	62.7	29.3	33.4
	Rural	60.7	26.5	34.2
	Urban	84.6	63.4	21.2
Malkangiri	Total	40.1	20.9	19.2
	Rural	37.4	18.4	19.0
	Urban	74.9	54.9	20.0

Source: Census of India, 2001.

In the context of KBK districts in Orissa, as per census data demonstrated in the Table 3, Bolangir district has the lowest male literacy. The gender gap in percentage points between the male and female literacy is the highest in Kalahandi (33.4) followed by Bolangir (32.2).

Table 4
S.C. and S.T. Population in the Selected Area

Blocks		*S.C. Population*	*%*	*S.T. Population*	*%*
1	*2*	*3*	*4*	*5*	*6*
Belpara	Total	9794	14.4	21293	31.2
	Rural	9794	14.4	21293	31.2
	Urban	0	0.0	0	0.0
Turekela	Total	6373	15.8	13917	39.5
	Rural	6373	15.8	13917	39.5
	Urban	0	0.0	0	0.0
Kesinga	Total	19150	15.9	28337	23.5
	Rural	16267	15.7	28337	25.4
	Urban	2883	17.0	1978	11.7
Dharmgada	Total	19912	16.7	20728	17.4
	Rural	19912	16.7	20728	17.4
	Urban	0	0.0	0	0.0

1	2	3	4	5	6
Kalimela	Total	25604	29.9	43121	48.7
	Rural	25604	29.9	43121	48.7
	Urban	0	0.0	0	0
Kudumu-	Total	398	18.2	266	10.3
luguma	Rural	398	18.2	266	10.3
	Urban	0	0.0	0	0.0

Source: Census of India, 2001.

Table 4 depicts that among the sample blocks in the selected districts, Kalimela has the highest percentage (28.9%) of SC population, followed by Kudumuluguma block of Malkangiri district. Similarly, Kalimela block has also the distinction of highest percentage of ST population (48.7%), fallowed by Turekela block (39.5%).

Table 5
Literacy Rate and Gender Gap in Sample Blocks

Block		*Literacy Rate*		*Gender Gap*
		Male	*Female*	
Belpara	Total	69.4	33.5	35.9
	Rural	69.4	33.5	35.9
	Urban	0.0	0.0	0.0
Turekela	Total	61.0	23.2	37.7
	Rural	61.0	23.2	37.7
	Urban	0.0	0.0	0.0
Kesinga	Total	72.6	39.7	32.8
	Rural	71.9	37.9	34.0
	Urban	76.6	51.3	25.4
Dharmgada	Total	59.8	24.0	35.8
	Rural	59.8	24.0	35.8
	Urban	0.0	0.0	0.0
Kalimela	Total	40.8	22.8	18.1
	Rural	40.8	22.8	18.1
	Urban	0.0	0.0	0.0
Kudumu-	Total	85.5	66.6	18.9
luguma	Rural	85.5	66.6	18.9
	Urban	0.0	0.0	0.0

Source: Census of India, 2001.

Table 5 depicts the literacy rate and gender gap in the selected blocks of KBK districts. It is found that female literacy is the lowest in Kalimela block (22.8%), followed by Turekela (23.2%). The gender gap in literacy is the highest in Turekela (37.7%).

It is found that there has been glaring disparity in the development of primary education in Orissa, particularly in KBK districts. Most of the tribal villages are located in inaccessible areas, on hill terrains, which created problems in the development of literacy. At the present rate of economic growth and considering the extremely low share of the poor in the total national income, absolute poverty in India may not be eliminated if this rural-urban gap is not minimized and the divide is not bridged up.

Deprived children are also the victims of teacher's stereotyped and negative views of their educability. The children often hear teachers cast remarks on their supposed poor genetic inheritance. The prejudiced views of the teachers serve the teacher's own self interest; that help teachers to be totally unaccountable for their own performance. The teachers too often join the ignorants in our society in blaming the victims instead of comprehending that the poor performance of tribal children is most often the result of lifelong discriminations against them. The excuses teachers repeat about the supported lack of capacity of tribal children to learn merely serves as an additional means for teachers to cover up their poor ability to teach and the poor functioning of the educational systems.

Primary education produces a literate population that can deal with problems at home and work, particularly in traditionally disadvantaged groups, *i.e.* rural, female and poor. It helps them to gain independent income to meet household basis needs at family level and raises productivity and growth potential at community and national level.

For females, it helps to increase their social mobility, status and autonomy. Private and social returns to primary education investments are for greater than the returns to secondary and higher education.

Despite high social returns to primary education, a large number of children are out of schools. Nearly two-thirds of those who enrol does not complete basic schooling in the KBK districts of Orissa.

The main hindrances in children's completing basic schooling include a variety of socio-economic, political and cultural factors. These include poor quality of teaching, high pupil-teacher ratio, lack of classroom facilities, nature of curriculum, high direct and opportunity costs. These factors create stumbling block and dissuade children from continuing their education.

It has been observed that there are large numbers of single teacher schools in the interior tribal pockets. The teacher never attends the school and the supervisor never supervises. The teacher bribes the officials and receives salary in the KBK districts. Due to lack of communication and awareness tribal children help their parents in income generating activities.

Hence, it is suggested that the teachers should have sincerity of purpose and dedicated attitude to serve the tribal students. Corruption must be minimized if not eliminated to accelerate tribal education in KBK districts, which will act as catalyst to minimize the rural-urban divide.

REFERENCES

Pradhan, K.C. (2006): "Tribal Development and Provisions of PESA", in S.N.Tripathy (ed) *Rural Development for Social Change*, Sonali Publications, New Delhi.

Pradhan, K.C. and Panigrahy, P.C.(2008) : "Development Driven Displacement –its impact on Tribals", in S. Padhy and B. Padhy (ed), *Trends and Issues in Tribal Studies*, Abhijeet Publications, New Delhi.

Pradhan, K.C. (2008): *Rural Women–Issues and Options*, Sonali Publications, New Delhi.

Tripathy, S.N. (2005): *Female Headed Households in India*, Sonali Publications, New Delhi.

Tripathy, S.N. (1998): *Shifting Cultivation in Tribal Orissa*, in self-edited "Tribals in India: the Changing Scenario", Discovery Publishing House, New Delhi.

Tripathy, S.N. (2005): *Dynamics of Tribal Migration*, Sonali Publications, New Delhi.

Tripathy, S.N. and C.R. Das (1997) : *Migrant Labour in India*, Discovery Publishing House, New Delhi.

Tripathy S.N. (1989) : *Bonded Labour in India*, Discovery Publishing House, New Delhi.

4

Opportunities and Challenges for Tribes in Ranchi City

Ambrish Gautam and Kumari Sweta

'Liberalizing trade without facilitation is like freeing the prisoner but with handcuffs on'.

Ali and Isse

Globalisation is the name for the process of increasing the connectivity and interdependence of the world markets and businesses. This process has sped up dramatically in the last two decades as technological advances make it easier for people to travel, communicate, and do business internationally. Two major recent driving forces in this regard are advances in telecommunication infrastructure and the rise of the Internet. In general, as economies become more inter-connected, opportunities have increased and so also competition. Thus, as globalization becomes a more and more common feature of world economics, powerful pro-globalization and anti-globalization lobbies have arisen. The pro-globalization lobby argues that globalization brings about much increased opportunities for almost everyone and increased competition is a good thing since it makes agents of production more efficient. The two most prominent pro-globalization organizations are the World Trade Organization and the World Economic Forum. The world formulates a set of rules to govern global trade and capital flows through the process of member consensus, and to supervise their member countries to ensure that the rules are being followed. The World Economic Forum, a private foundation, does not have decision-making power but enjoys a great deal of importance. The anti-globalization group argues that certain groups of people who are deprived in terms of resources are not currently capable of functioning within the increased competitive pressure that will be brought about by allowing their economies to be more connected to the rest of the world. Important anti-globalization organizations include environmental groups like Friends of the Earth and Green Peace, International aid organizations like Oxfam, Third world government organizations like the G77, business organizations and trade unions whose competitiveness is threatened by globalization like the U.S. Textiles and European farm lobby, as well as the Australian and U.S. trade union movements (www. Research Article Investor Guide.com University).

As we talk about the term globalization, this is not new to the world. It has been around before Great Britain ruled the waves and waived the rules to conquer. We can distinguish the whole process of globalisation broadly into three phases. During phase I (1860-1914) world income nearly tripled while trade grew by 4.5 times. Low, stable and non-discriminatory tariffs were the contributory factors. Phase II (1920-1939) reversed the reductions in tariffs, etc. Tariffs, quotas, licensing controls and exchange controls - all discriminatory import restrictions-proliferated. During this phase both world income and trade increased by 40 per cent only. During phase III (1950-2001) stable trade arrangements under General Agreement on Trade and Tariffs (GATT) and World Trade Organization (WTO) provided a set of rules and institutional structure that encouraged gradual reduction in trade barriers (Ali and Isse, 2003: 449-466). As a result, world income grew by five times and trade by eleven times (Altinger and Enders, 1996: 307-332).

Looking at the historical and economic background of the globalization Mathur (2003) observes that expansion in trade, capital flows and consistently high economic growth as embodied in GDP, have not led to any acceleration in the overall urban growth or growth of large cities. Globalization has not resulted in any expansion of overall employment opportunities. It has selectively led to expansion of opportunities in retail trade, communications, and financial, banking and real estate services. Globalization has meant an increased demand for residential, office and commercial space. On a limited scale, residential space has been converted into commercial malls; new shopping plazas have sprung up, and townships with quality infrastructure have been developed around major cities to accommodate the branch offices of multinational and domestic companies. It has influenced the city level productivity. An overall assessment of city level changes is that these are few and limited. City transformation has not occurred. With the exception of new physical development and some special restructuring, no land mark shifts have occurred in urban development; more over changes appear to be isolated and add-on rather than signalling a structural shift in the economy of cities. The basic postulate that major improvements in infrastructure services can occur only if they are undertaken within the context of city economies is still in an infant stage. Business process outsourcing and call centres that flourished in Indian metropolises in the last few years run in the nights to coincide with the daytime office hours in the west. This working at nights requires adjusting the biological clock and social practices to a different time, which is turning out to be a major cause for health related and social problems. Noticeable changes are occurring in family structure, especially in the urban centres, and fertility is falling due to a weakening of traditional family controls and a declining value given to procreation. Marriage is being considered as economic transaction, leading to serious threat to young women. The declining value of their procreative power puts women at the mercy of impersonal, market driven economic forces with which they are ill equipped to deal (Mathur, 2003).

The tribal population is found in almost all parts of the world. Tribes are called variously in different countries. For instance in the USA they are known as *Red Indian,* in Australia *Aboriginals*, in the European countries *Gypsys* and in the African and Asian countries *tribals.* India has the second largest concentration of tribal population after that of African continent. The Indian tribes are the autochthonous people of the land who are believed to be the earliest settlers in Indian peninsula. In India, they are generally called *'adivasis'* implying original inhabitants. However under the Constitution of India people belongings to various tribes have been specified as *'ST'* (Roseline, 2006:17-19).

The 67.7 million people belonging to 'Scheduled Tribe' in India are generally considered to be 'Adivasis', literally meaning 'indigenous people' or 'original inhabitants' though the term 'ST' is not coterminous with the term 'Adivasis'. ST is an administrative term used for purposes of 'administering' certain specific Constitutional privileges, protection and benefits for specific sections of peoples considered historically disadvantaged and backward. This administrative term does not exactly match all the people called adivasis. Over centuries, the adivasis have evolved an intricate convivial custodial mode of living. The predominant external caste based religion sanctioned and practised a rigid and highly discriminatory hierarchical ordering with a strong cultural mooring. Relegating the adivasis to the lowest rung in the social ladder was but natural and formed the basis of making social and political decision by the largely upper caste controlled mainstream (Makwan, 2006: 20-23).

Consisting of 461 groups the tribes constitute about 8 per cent of the total population of India. Among them about 80 per cent lives in the 'central belt', extending from Gujrat and Rajasthan in the west to west Bengal and Tripura in the east, and across the states of Maharastra, Madhya Pradesh, Chhatishgarh, Jharkhand and Orissa. Most of the remaining 20 per cent of tribal population lives in the North Eastern states of Meghalaya, Mizoram, Nagaland, Arunachal Pradesh and Sikkim and in the island Union Territories of Dadra and Nagar Haveli, etc. (Singh, 2007 : 12-15).

In the Ranchi district total tribal population is 1164624 (according to census 2001). Out of this rural ST population is 964242 and urban 200382. As the term globalization is centred on the integration of international market for goods, services, technology, finance and labour, so also the tribal economy around community life. The economy is an important constituent of the tribal community life and plays a deciding role in the formation of the cultural and social structure of society. Every community has its own way to meet its basic needs for the existence of its members failing which they are threatened with extinction. Nature here comes forward and joins hands with them to fulfill their needs, fashioned of course in their way depending on their customs, tradition, demographic structure, etc. Owing to this, people with the same natural surroundings have developed different economic processes to meet their needs (*ibid.*, 28-31).

The socio-economic structure in tribal communities is markedly different from that of the non-tribal or advanced groups of people. They have a very simple technology which fits well with their ecological surroundings and traditional outlook of subsistence nature. A tribe is usually considered an economically independent group of people having their own specific economy and thus having a living pattern of labour, division of labour and specialization, gift and ceremonial exchange, trade and barter, credit and value, wealth, consumption norms, capital formation, land tenure and good-tangible and intangible economic status. The basic characteristics of tribal economy is small economy *i.e.* transactions of goods and services take place within a small geographical area and within a community of persons; simple technology *i.e.* tools are either made by the user himself or are acquired for a fee from a craftsman or from a manufacturing group; cultural isolation; barter and exchange. The profit motive in economic dealings is generally absent, co-operative and collective endeavours are strongly developed, and rate of innovation is low. The manufacturer of consumer rather than capital goods is common. Nothing is being saved or invested. Specialization based on specially acquired specific technical ability is absent but the division of labour is based on sex division. The basket maker *mahlis* get the bamboo as raw material from the forest they inhabit. Other than this exchange exists as part of social relationship among the tribes. Gift giving and hospitality to social intimates is an important part of their economy (Vidyarthi, 1985: 33-39).

The market is important to tribal life from social, cultural and economic points of view. In the market two kinds of commodities enter, *i.e.* general purpose commodities primarily produced inside the region and special purpose commodities brought from outside the region (Jha, 2001: 9-12). Among the former, mention may be made of rice, corn, oil, earthenware, baskets, leaf mats, vegetables, ropes etc. The later include mill clothes, tailored garments, mirrors, cosmetics, branded clothes and many more things which are available in the market. There are nucleated villages of agriculturist Oraons and Mundas, the Hindus living together and partly agricultural communities of *Lohar* (blacksmiths), *Kumhar* (potters), *chick-baraik* (weaver) and *bania* (traders). Tribals have changed their livelihood options and most of them have started agriculture with advanced technique using the fertilizers. (Oraon, 2004: 39-42).

The non-agricultural tribal labourers are mostly engaged in different industries like HEC. It is believed that the non-agricultural labour type is the result of increase in the pressure on land due to population growth and opening of different mines and industries in tribal areas (*ibid.*, 40-42). The tribes have been in prolonged contact to this global life and responded to this. As a result of these factors many of them go out as seasonal migrants to work as labourers in railway and road construction, forestry construction work, civil work in emerging factories, houses, dams, bridges, etc. They move to the working place in bands, which include males and females (*ibid.*, 49-52). Some individuals or families of tribal communities of the region are working for their livelihood in different offices, hospitals, factories and business enterprises. Some of them are engaged in commercial trade of their own. Apart from their initiation, the seat reservation in different services as laid down in the Constitution has helped a lot in creating this type of economic life among the tribes (Singh, *op. cit.* 42-45).

As the globalization is not only economic phenomena but it is also a factor of socio-cultural change *i.e.* it expands the scope and speed of cultural interactions across societal boundaries; the incidence of migration and emergence of cultural diaspora bring about intense cultural social and economic interactions. Its impact has also been felt on natural resources management and on the culture of the community. Globalization of culture is the world wide dissemination of certain cultural norms and social institutions because of colonialism, trade, missionary activity, technological change and the incorporation of tribal people into state and large scale system of exchange. It intends to bring homogeneous and uniform environment of management with number of specialized institutions for corresponding functions whereas in small scale societies, single cultural institution performs multiple social functions (Kofman and Youngs, 2003: 261-272).

There is a difference in approach to manage resources between the tribals and non-tribals. There exist substantial autonomy among the principles of social organization, political system governed by an independent secular unit and the religious traditions and the value system controlled by a priest and local communities. The priest enjoys the freedom to pronounce upon matter related to rituals, customary rites and ceremonies. Tribal communities use normative or evaluative principles based on the super rational values in the community management as well as in resources management. These societies mostly own and use natural resources collectively. It divides natural resources into sacred and profane planes. The sacred resources are allocated to the supernatural power associated with village population in the village eco-system. The sacred natural resources are commonly used and managed by a village priest. But due to the adoption of bureaucracy as element of management of its affairs, state activities influence the traditional sphere of management, since the mega system, *i.e.* state administration gradually started imposing its order on the micro system (Madan and Mazumdar, 2002:18-22).

This new process has created several opportunities for the tribals of this city. Through this, due to attachment with the modern society their literacy rate has gone up and they are interested to live together with the other community people. Tribals are getting married with other caste and community. They are getting high profile jobs like administrators, police officers, doctors, etc. With the influence of global economic system tribals are getting connected with their products to the global market. They are producing the vegetables, grains seeds not for the personal and community use but also for the sale and purchase at a bargainable price. They are getting aware about their rights which are provided by the constitution and enjoying its benefits. The global economic system and the increase in the demand of the natural resources have made the tribes important. It is because natural resources like iron ore, bauxite, copper ore, coal deposits are located in their territory. Traditional school where the knowledge of the village social system was transmitted and embedded in holistic pattern have been converted to modern schools. Generally the modern tribal people know their utility in the global era.

Changes relating to globalisation have generated several problems for the tribals. The land which traditionally belonged to the tribes is presently occupied by MNCs and other companies. The compensation given to the tribes do not have long run benefit. They are displaced. Due to poor quality of human resource they also do not get good jobs in these companies. Added to it is competition from quality human resource. Resulting problems emerge in their life like land alienation, labour migration, landlessness, poverty and indebtedness. The tribals become forest labour and work for the forest lord, more often becoming bonded labour. They also face housing problem, displacement problem, unemployment, health and sanitation problem, malnutrition. The process of liberalization and the current upsurge in industrial production have increased the hunger for land among investors and entrepreneurs. Land was first shifted to the concurrent list of the Constitution and then forests were made the exclusive domain of the centre. The state didn't register any protest perhaps because the far-reaching implications of that move did not dawn on it; or may be it was because their politicians had already sided with contractors and timber merchants to ravage their land or the appearance of bigger all India mafia made them beat a hasty retreat.

The process of globalization has posed very serious questions by challenging the deficits in transnational governance and by raising the need for an individual in capitalist democracy. Formal equality of free individuals in capitalist democracy has its international counterpart in the sovereign equality of independent states and both only make sense in purely political terms and in the face of economic globalization which is a complex trend, including globalization of production processes, global capital, mobility, neo-liberal development agenda, and finally globalization of subcontracting and informal labour. It is difficult to limit the agenda of democracy and distributive justice within the state. The state is no longer the main framework for economic policy-making and governments have been forced to accommodate outside pressures adversely affecting the living standards of ordinary citizens. Even though gender discrimination influences deeply the status of women and children in the community, the attitudes towards women pregnancy, nutrition, and early childcare have a great impact on the status of maternal and child health.

The tribal people have their institution of barter and the tribal periodical markets in their respective areas. Earlier they do not have permanent markets but now they have permanent market. Each of the tribal villages falling in a radius of about 5 to 10 km has a separate weekly market place. In the tribal areas, weekly markets play an important role in the life of the people. All their outer and inner-group economics are channelized through these markets. The markets bring together people from different ethnic groups for not only economic but also secular and religious activities in the tribal region. Tribesman and caste men from a region meet on fixed days at the market place or another place to transact their socio-economic business. The impact of weekly markets on their traditional life too has shown an attitude of accepting innovation. The market is the most powerful channel of communication in the tribal region. Monetary economy has percolated through the market. Also the weekly market has obtained a place in the social organization of the tribals. Any announcement of community interest may be broadcast here and it will get relayed all over the area immediately. This tribal market maintains a network of socio-cultural ties among the people of its hinterland and gives them a common base for regional ethnology. All the people who come to the market chew betel or smoke cigarettes or biris which is considered both a luxury and good fun. Vanishing and cold cream, fountain pens, paper, note books, etc. attract the attention of the tribes. Women are easily attracted towards the trinkets, glass bangles, beads and other items of decoration. The Munda people sell here paddy, pulses, mahua and lac. Some lower Hindu castes bring clothes, mats and baskets for sale. Vegetables are sold here broadly because this help tribe to improve their economic condition.

Besides the governments of the countries concerned, several nternational agencies NGO and voluntary organization have come forward to develop the tribal. All such governmental and non-governmental efforts have definitely brought some positive impact on tribal life. But there are still many things to be done for their development. The problems of contact, acculturation, de-tribalisation, displacement, rehabilitation, etc. among the tribals have become manifold.

In Ranchi city due to impact of globalization several changes can be seen. The facilities, which can be seen only in metropolitan cities, are now available in Ranchi. The fashion is changing. Every youth wants to wear those clothes which were earlier available only in metropolitan cities. Girls are wearing small tops. Many modern shops have been opened here, which are making various new items available. Once upon a time only countable beauty parlours were available in this city where only girls of high families were visiting. But now-a-days, in every market complex, areas, beauty parlours have been opened where not only the girls of the rich family but of a lower and lower middle class or tribal families are visiting. We can see several modern and global quality restaurants opened in this city. Tribals working in the city and earning a money income have been exposed to restaurant culture, though other members in the family remain half starved.

Standard of living of the people of a city can be seen in shopping malls and complexes. Various shopping malls have been opened in Ranchi where every facility and goods are available for sale. Branded showrooms have also been opened like Church complex, Panchwati plaza, Hari Om tower, Gopal complex, etc. A few tribal youths are found part time job, working in companies, banks, restaurants, etc.

It may be noticed frequently that if all those facilities are available in this city then tribal will not be left untouched, because this city is basically tribal dominated and they all are much aware about all global development. Now internet is available at very cheap rate and phone, mobile phones are available easily at a very low investment. Cable televisions from CNN to MTV satellite channel are available at a low monthly rate. Only Indian made watches, cars and scooters were readily available but by economic liberalization it produces shelves stocked with Barbie Dall, cellular phones; and global brands like Nike, Benetton and DKNY are available readily. Western icons like tennis player Anna Kounikova and Pete Sampras, pop singer Mariah Carey and many others appeared on posters celebrating western products like Reebok Shoes. City has encountered always transnational flows, tourists from around the world had long been visiting the city and tourist places around. Music shops used to sell pirated cassette of tapes Madona and Michael Jackson and pirated videocassettes of holly wood films. But the volume and speed of transnational connections increased markedly over the course of 1990s. Just a decade later, dozens of cable channels was available and nearly 70 per cent of the non-elite, non English speaking people including tribals had at least some access to cable TV. Indeed, Hollywood productions and the Hindi films that are influenced by them have celebrated consumerism, individualism and greater freedom for women, which would be unacceptable by older standards of morality. Valentine day celebrations grew in popularity because of cable music channels such as MTV, Channel V even though various political parties oppose it.

Basically in this city globalization has increased consumerism and layered new meanings on top of the old ones that Indians continue to use to understand class and gender hierarchies. But despite new media messages about family life, globalization has failed to transform the gender and family arrangements of the ordinary middle class families in this city, who have been unable to take off with the global economy.

The question is how far the tribals are benefited from this? Is there transformation for a better life with sustainability? Or are they more marginalised, displace and confused?

REFERENCES

Ali, A.M., and H.S. Isse, 2003: "Determinants of Corruption: A Cross-Country Comparison", *Cato Journal* (Winter 2003),Vol.-22.

Altinger, L., and A.Enders, 1996: "The Scope and Depth of GATS Commitments" , *The World Economy* (May 1996).

Jha, Avinash, 2001: *Background to Globalisation*, CED, Bombay.

Census of India 2001.

Kofman, Eleonore and Gillian Youngs, 2003: Globalisation Theory and Practices, Continuum Publications.

Vidyarthi, L.P., and B.K. Rai, 1985: *Tribal Culture of India*, Concept, New Delhi.

Tipru, Makwan, 2006: "Journal the Rally XISS Publication" May 2006.

Mathur, O.P., 2003: "Impact of Globalization on Cities and City-Related Policies in India" Occasional Paper No. 4, Urban Partnerships Foundation, Inc.

P.C.Oraon, 2004: *Land and People of Jharkhand*, TRI Publications.

Sr. Roseline, 2006. "Journal the Rally, XISS Publication", May 2006 pp. 17-19.

Singh, Sunil Kumar, 2007: *Inside Jharkhand*, Crown Publication, Ranchi.

T.N. Madan and D.N. Mazumdar, 2002: *An Introduction to Social Anthropology*, Rajkamal Publicaton, New Delhi.

www. Research Article Investor Guide.com University.

II

Issues and Concerns

5

Globalisation, Policies, Programmes and Potential Areas of Development of North-East Economy : An Analysis

A.K. Agarwal

Globalisation is the process by which the events, decisions and activities in one part of the world have significant consequences for other parts of the globe. It represents closer integration of the world economy resulting from increase in trade, investment, finance and multi-country production networks of MNCs. It extends beyond economic interdependence to include dilution of time and space dimensions as a result of spread of information technology (Yousuf and Stiglitz, 2000). Technological developments in computing and telecommunications have reduced transaction costs and these costs continue falling further. This has made globalisation a supra-national phenomenon, which transcends national frontiers. This has far-reaching economic, social, political, cultural, environmental and technological consequences. Global forces play much greater role in the determination of cropping pattern, investment level and pattern, price structure, quality of production, occupational structure and direction of economic activities. Increased market access, reduction and removal of tariff and non-tariff barriers, investment measures, intellectual property rights, etc., have tremendous bearing on the economies of all the countries. It has the potential of raising employment levels, improving living standards, increasing consumers' product choice, expanding exchange opportunities and raising national income levels. It results in greater international division of labour and more efficient allocation of resources, thereby making economies of scale and specialization available to the producers of the world. Consumers enjoy wide range of products at the cheapest rate. Globalisation provides new opportunities to developing countries to derive benefits from FDI. Further, the efficiency of banking and financial sectors has also improved with opening of these sectors to foreign competition. Globalisation has improved efficiency in domestic economy of a number of countries due to increase in competition and cost-consciousness. On the other hand, there is long history of strong hostility towards international trade and investment. The backwash effects, unequal exchange, secular deterioration of terms of trade and neo-protectionism are the well known arguments put forward against free trade since long. The protests against globalization have become louder and louder (Bawa, 2002:3).

Globalisation and the economic progress that goes with it have proceeded unevenly in time and in space. The rise in income per head has differed widely between countries and regions (Streeten, 2000). The integration of the world economy over the past twenty years has been dramatic. The experience of the post 1980s globalisers shows that the process can have great benefits contributing to rising incomes and falling poverty and enabling some of the poorest countries in the world to catch up with the richer countries. The real losers from globalization are those developing countries that have not been able to seize the opportunities to participate in this process (Dollar and Kraay, 2001).

Globalisation has led to the need of firms to compete internationally, and international competition has reinforced globalisation. Cost reductions, greater efficiency and higher incomes have been achieved at the cost of uncertainty, unemployment and inequality. The application of capital-intensive technology which is more productive and relieves enterprises from labour conflicts is making it difficult to hold in least the growing volume of unemployment. Shedding of surplus of labour, which the remodelling of economy entails, makes markets reforms unacceptable to labour unions, particularly in the public sector which is heavily overstaffed. Add to this the increasing growth of labour force in itself a problem caused by rising population to which the policy makers have not addressed themselves in any meaningful sense. Under the circumstances globalisation has reduced the ability of national governments both to maintain full employment and to look after the victims of competitive struggle.

In a society where expectations have been sharpened by literacy and awareness, population growth is testing on growth and employment, equity and environmental sustainability. Poor are less victims of environmental degradation, but more a cause of it (Basu, 2000). Therefore, control of population growth will be a major step for ensuring benefits of globalisation. It will help in reducing unemployment, poverty and inequalities, and increased female participation in labour force. International institutions will have to join hands with the developing countries to eliminate the root cause of the economic, social and environmental ills (Bawa, 2002:5).

Efficiency gains depend on the degree to which a country liberalises its markets. Sharp tariff cuts give rise to increased access to cheaper imported goods and generate gains in consumption as well as improvements in the efficiency of use of domestic resources. Basing on this agriculture liberalization (especially movement towards eliminating export subsidies) may increase world prices of food products and thus have a negative effect on developing countries net food imports. However, any such impact would be offset to some degree by the increase in domestic supply that higher prices would stimulate. Current policies result in large global price swings that are highly detrimental to developing countries, and farmers in many developing countries suffer from a significant anti-agricultural policy bias.

Mechanisms are needed to ensure that any price increasing effects of reforms do not reduce the real income/consumption of the poorest in the society. Such social safety nets may not exist or may not function adequately in many countries. Multilateral trade liberalization generally takes a long time to negotiate and implement. Thus provides an opportunity for governments to develop and/or strengthen safety net programmes and complementary policies to maintain the real incomes of the poorest in the society. It should be emphasized here that the need for such mechanisms is quite general and not specific to agricultural reforms. All types of policy reforms that are beneficial for the economy as a whole, as well as exogenous shocks of various kinds, may have detrimental consequences for the poor. Mechanisms to offset the negative impact of shocks should therefore be broad in scope and not conditional in changes in trade policies only (Bernard and Martin, 2002:116-120).

Jobless growth is a matter of concern to the developing countries too. The causes of unemployment are global competition, lack of skills in an age of high and rapidly advancing technologies, slow growth and imports from low wage countries. Even though the percentage of these imports is small, they occur in the labour-intensive sectors, and firms often displace labour by capital in order to remain competitive. As a remedy the suggested measures include education and training programmes for workers, both to achieve higher productivity and to reduce unemployment, income support for low-paid workers, tax policies that create jobs and prevent environmental degradation, population controls, and social safety nets. But experience has shown that not-so-bright and not committed to the work ethic they have reinforced a sense of failure. The new technologies in information and communication and their global spread have brought with them learning-ability-related inequality. The new underclass should be our concern from viewpoint of social solidarity, control of rising crimes and drug use in the society.

The other set of unemployment belongs to the structural unemployment, arises due to lack of learning ability or self-confidence or self-discipline which render the labourers unemployed and perhaps unemployable. It is said that global competition and corporate restructuring would keep prices down while productivity gains would let growth flourish. A higher level of effective demand supported through public investment and buttressed with an income policy to keep inflation under control would surely make a contribution to reducing such type of unemployment to a certain extent. At the same time efforts should be made to create new job opportunities in the area of health, sanitation, protection and restoration of environment and other social services sectors which do not need the high and scarce skills demanded by modern technology and whose services cannot be replaced by either computers or imported low-cost goods from low-income countries using low-cost labour. We need to change valuation of such work and should guarantee minimum standards of reward for them/service providers.

The policies must be designed to mobilize the energies of the small-scale firms, and to make use of their lower costs, more labour-intensive techniques, greater employment creation, and wider dispersion of technology, without, on the one hand, sacrificing efficiency and innovation, and on the other, depriving the informal sector, by underpricing outputs, or overpricing inputs, of adequate rewards, and human working conditions. One does not have to accept the view of disappearance of the large firms to accept the growing role of these small enterprises. Indeed, the thesis propounded here is that the two should become complementary. All this holds out great productive and social promise for the informal sector, especially if supported by the right social policies (Streeten, 2000:32-33).

Globalisation and India

Before we look at our opportunities and challenges from globalisation, it is good to be certain of facts - where exactly India is in terms of globalisation. A most common measures of globalisation is openness to trade and a country's participation in trade. By this measure, the extent of India's globalisation is insignificant - it is one of the lowest in the world. India's share in the world trade is a meagre 0.7 per cent or so. A second commonly used measure of globalisation is a country's participation in international capital flows, particularly Doreign Direct Investment (FDI). Annual FDI inflows into India is 3-4 billion only or 0.3 - 0.4 per cent of the total. Foreign institutional investment is also relatively small - about 10 per cent or so as a proportion of BSE market capitalization. We are nowhere even close to being globalised in terms of any commonly used indicator of globalisation. In fact, we are still one of the least globalised among major countries - however we look at it (Jalan, 2002:9).

After independence India adopted the strategy of planned economic development rather than market-oriented development. During the first three decades of planned economic development, the main element of India's development strategy was import substitution led industrialization with an explicit focus on the public sector. The private sector was subjected to highly restrictive system of licensing and a variety of other discretionary controls eliminating the operational flexibility required for responding to the changing market conditions and the rapidly changing technology. Scarcity of capital and low domestic savings were considered to be as principal causes of the country's underdevelopment. The growth of real per capita income during the pre-liberation period of 1950-51 to 1985-86 turned out to be just 1.5 per cent as compared to the target of 3.5 per cent. It made difficult to achieve a significant reduction in the incidence of poverty (Dholak, 2002:30).

The reforms initiated in June 1991 sought to make the Indian economy a fast-growing one. We accepted globalisation as a price for worst ever financial crisis. At the outset there was growth of a large public sector bleeding the economy through supply of vital inputs such as water, power, fertilizer, and credit at highly subsidised rates to feudal and capitalist elements; rising level of unemployment and social disparities causing large scale unrest and disenchantment with the political system. The practice of uneconomic user charges for public utility services to appease interest groups became an accepted feature of the price tariff and substantially contributed to unsustainable fiscal deficit (Singh, 2000:24).

The reforms initiated with a hope to use resources more efficiently. For efficiency, both domestic and international competitions were considered essential. The system of industrial licensing and production controls has been dismantled. Trade has been liberalized considerably through measures like import of many goods under 'Open General Lincense', convertibility of rupee on the current account and dropping of tariff rates significantly. Interest rates have been partially freed. Private entry in banking has taken place. These measures have met with success on many fronts.

Dholakia (2002:30-31) observed that the pre-liberation period assigned a significant role to the non-agricultural public sector and simultaneously constrained the operation of the non-agricultural private sector in the Indian economy, while the post-liberalisation period envisaged a much greater role for the non-agricultural private sector and aimed at partially rolling back the non-agricultural public sector. During the post 1985 period, the agricultural sector has grown at an average rate of more than 3 per cent while the non-agricultural sector has grown at more than 7 per cent leading to an overall growth rate of around 6 per cent. Real per capita income has increased at an average rate of around 4 per cent during the 15 year period from 1985 to 2000.

It is generally observed that development is accompanied by a progressive diversification of employment structure, reflected to a fall in the share of the primary sector and rise in that of secondary and tertiary activities (Jegdish, 1995:682). The share of tertiary sector in GDP increased from 43.69 per cent in 1990-91 to 52.3 per cent in 1999-2000 while the share of primary sector decreased from 30.93 per cent to 25.5 per cent and of secondary sector from 25.38 per cent to 22.1 per cent during the period.

Jalan (2002:11) observed that earlier the manufacturing was given more importance and growth of services was a by-product of industrial development. The new reality is that the fastest growth in value added as well as productivity has been in the services sector. This change has been facilitated by unprecedented and unforeseen advances in computer and communication technology. As a result, the development of certain services is now regarded as one of the preconditions of economic growth, and not as one of its consequences. The boundary between goods and services is also disappearing. Another important aspect of the 'services revolution' is that geography and levels of industrialization are no longer the primary determinants of the location of facilities for production of services. As a result, the traditional role of developing countries is also changing - from mere recipients to important providers of long distance and high value services.

India has a tremendous advantage in the supply of knowledge based services such as, professional and technical services, because of a developed structure of technological and educational institutions and lower labour costs. The death of distance, the revolution of services and the mobility of capital, which characterize globalisation present unprecedented opportunities for India. But transition from a closed to a vibrant, open and a more globally dominant economy takes time and is not painless.

The negative dimensions of the era of globalisation are louder and clearer. There has been a decline in real public investment in agriculture including irrigation which continued to decline significantly in the post-reform period. This may have led to dampening effect on employment and wages in rural areas, especially in states where poverty is widespread, as is evident from a significant decline in non-agricultural rural employment in the immediate post-reform period (Dev, 1995:2085 - 88). It has been shown that the overall annual growth rate of agriculture declined to 3.6 per cent during the 1990s from 3.9 per cent during the1980s. The impact of reduction in public investment for agriculture can be evidenced in the form of continuation of structural retrogression, lower employment elasticity, continued volatility and regional differentiation, relative decline of foodgrains production *vis-à-vis* other crops, growing food insecurity despite huge piling up of unsold food stocks (Kabra, 2002:34).

Further it is observed that by not addressing the concerns of agriculturists, mainly small and marginal farmers and farm workers, concentrating all its attention on organized sector industry, trade, external sector and finance located in urban India, the concerns of the weaker sections, the poor, the unemployed and the worse-of were put on the back burner (Kabra, 2002:35). According to recently released official data the falling trend in organized sector employment in India has continued for the fourth consecutive year in 2000-01. The organized sector now accounts for just 8.9 per cent a decade back. In the last few years, the public sector has shed 4.2 lakh jobs. The private sector employment has remained steady during this period, raising its share in the organized sector employment to 31 per cent from 29 per cent in March 1995. The number of jobs in the organized sector declined from 28 million in March 2000 to 27.8 million in March 2001 - the fall of 1.7 lakh jobs in the year was the steepest decline in at least three decades (Economic Time : 28th January, 2003).

Bawa, (2002:6-7) has pointed out that the corporate sector of the country is under heavy competitive pressure and price in the country is getting aligned with those other countries. The financial market of the country is much more integrated with global finance today than a decade back. The volatile nature of private capital flows and developments elsewhere in the world have started impinging more on the economy of the country. The behaviour of the producers and consumers is changing fast. The strong winds of globalisation have made the Indian corporate sector feel shy of manufacturing sector and they are now attracted more towards service sector. Rate of industrial growth bas slowed down, and industrial sickness is on the rise. Fresh investment proposals in the manufacturing sector have sharply declined because as a panic reaction despite low interest rate prevailed now-a-days. The entrepreneurs are shy of investing in this sector. Small scale sector is virtually facing closure due to cheaper imports from China and other countries. There were more than 3 lakh sick SSI units in the country on March 31, 1999 and the number rapidly increased afterwards. There is a rapid deterioration in the provision of infrastructure. Education, health and other basic amenities are getting neglected due to increasing fiscal deficit. Current account deficit in trade is rising year after year. The commodity composition of exports at group and sub-group levels has virtually remained the same. Foreign Direct Investment has entered the country at highly favourable terms and involves large outflows. The country had to remove Quantitative Restrictions (QRs). Thus India has not gained much from WTO agreements. A large section of the India society is feeling insecure and a crisis of confidence is building up.

Notwithstanding the dismal performance of the economy in the post-liberalisation period, India has to continue with the pace of globalisation. No doubt the country was not prepared for globalisation with more than 100 crores population and the prevailing socio-political set up, but the foundation of social change cannot be laid in a short span of time and globalisation will continue without waiting for India to get ready to board the bus (Balasubramanyam, 2001). Under the circumstances there is need for generating credibility about the process of reforms so that the poor are not marginalized further. The government has to play a crucial role in building and strengthening institutions for rural, agricultural and industrial development in the country. There is need for more focussed role of the government in education, health, environment and infrastructure through different policies.

Another sector is the check on the consumption of well-off and upwardly mobile sections of the society through an appropriate fiscal policy if the market-driven growth has to have any meaning for the community as a whole. Distribution of income and ceiling on property in land need to be upgraded as equally important objectives. Public policies must aim at building an ethos of restraints rather than putting up with rank consumerism which is eroding values as well as resources. Strategies of development must strike a balance between development of material and non-material resources.

Globalisation and the North East Region

The north-eastern region also known as the land of seven sisters comprises the States of Arunachal Pradesh; Assam, Manipur, Meghalaya, Mizoram, Nagaland and Tripura (now included Sikkim). The region is known for its ethnic, linguistic, cultural, religious, physiographical diversity. The region is geographically isolated and is linked with the rest of the country through a narrow stretch of land near Sikkim in West Bengal. It covers 7.8 per cent of country's geographical area and accommodates about 3.8 per cent of India's population.

The North-Eastern region is cradled by five Asian Countries–China, Nepal, Bhutan, Myanmar and Bangladesh. Arunachal Pradesh, Manipur, Mizoram and Nagaland share a 1643 km long border with Myanmar, Assam, Meghalaya, Tripura and Mizoram share a 1880 km border with Bangladesh; Arunachal Pradesh, Assam and Sikkim share a 468 km with Bhutan, Arunachal Pradesh and Sikkim share a 1325 km border with Tibet Autonomous Region of the People's Republic of China. The region's difficulties as a loss of connectivity and access following partition in 1947 are well known. Today, however, benefitting from the new dynamic of regional cooperation, this enormous geographical proximity, alongwith shared culture and customs, provides the basis for considerable synergies (Mukherjee, 2007:25).

The states like Nagaland, Meghalaya and Mizoram were carved out from Assam. These states were created to fulfil certain ethnic aspirations of the people of these states. The region is most densely administered region of the country. The number of Districts has gone to 76 - including 4 Districts of Sikkim. Baring Assam (78438 sq km) and Arunachal Pradesh (83743 sq km) for their geographical size and baring Assam (266.38 lakh persons in 2001) for her population, all states of north east are small. The smallest in size is Tripura (10491 sq km) and lowest in population is Mizoram (8.9 lakh). Sikkim ranks smallest in size (2096 sq km) and accommodates 5.40 lakh persons only. The density of population varies from 13 in Arunachal Pradesh to 340 in Assam. Some of the broad features like geographical area, population, literacy, urbanization pattern and per capita income can be noted from Table 1.

Broadly the region consists of hills as well as plains and is inhabited by three distinct groups of people - the hill tribes, the plain tribes and the non-tribal population of plains. Geographically, apart from Brahmaputra, Barak (Assam) and Imphal (Manipur) Valleys and some flat lands in between the Hills of Meghalaya and Tripura the remaining two-third area of the region consists of hilly terrain. The most populous part is the Brahmaputra Valley. Tribal population is in majority in four hilly states namely Arunachal, Meghalaya, Mizoram and Nagaland.

Migration is one of the prime factors for high population growth in the region. Other demographic features of 2001 Census include high decennial growth rate of population, 64.41 per cent in Nagaland; relatively high literacy rate, 88.49 per cent in Mizoram; the second highest in the country, low urbanization, 15.46 per cent but exceptionally high in Mizoram (49.49%), and low population density of 151 persons per sq km. excluding Assam and Tripura (340 and 304 persons per sq km respectively). Sex ratio is low in Arunachal and Nagaland as compared to all India average of 933. Similarly, the percentage of population 0-

Table 1
North-Eastern Region - Some Basic Indicators

Sl. No.	*State*	*Area ('000 sq km)*	*Population (Persons in lakh) 2001*	*% of Indian population*	*Decadal growth rate (in %) (1991-2001)*
1	*2*	*3*	*4*	*5*	*6*
1.	Arunachal Pradesh	83.7	10.96	0.11	26.85
2.	Assam	78.4	266.38	2.59	18.85
3.	Manipur	22.3	23.88	0.23	30.02
4.	Meghalaya	22.4	23.06	0.22	29.18
5.	Mizoram	21.1	8.91	0.09	29.18
6.	Nagaland	16.6	19.89	0.19	64.41
7.	Tripura	10.5	31.91	0.31	15.74
8.	Sikkim	2.1	5.40	0.05	32.9
9.	N-E Region	257.1	390.39	3.81	22.18
10.	All India	3287.2	10252.51	100.00	21.34

Sl. No.	*Population Density (per sq km)*	*Sex Ratio*	*Literacy (in %)*	*Urbanisation (in %)*	*Per capita income (in Rs.)*	*Persons 0-6 Age group in (%)*
	7	8	9	10	11	12
1.	13	894	57.74	20.31	13424	21.12
2.	340	932	64.28	12.72	7335	19.73
3.	107	978	68.87	24.12	8194	16.69
4.	103	975	63.31	19.64	8474	22.18
5.	42	938	88.49	49.49	13360	18.60
6.	120	909	67.11	17.75	11174	17.75
7.	304	950	73.66	17.02	6200	18.03
8.	76	875	69.68	11.10	NA	18.37
9.	151	935	—	15.46	—	—
10.	324	933	65.38	27.80	11554	15.37

Source : Compiled from : N.E Newsletter Dec. 2000 and Jan. 2001, Census of India, Series I, Paper 1 of 2001, and Series 16, Paper 3 of 2001.

6 years of age group is quite high in all the constituent units of the region.

India's north-east is a kaleidoscope of ethnic and linguistic diversities harmonizing themselves into a large national identity. This region despite its inherent advantages like fertile land, abundant natural resources, a fairly homogeneous and literate population has been unable to keep pace with the economic and industrial development as recorded elsewhere in the country. This may be due to geographical disadvantages or absence of essential infrastructural facilities, inadequate skilled human resource, and insufficient enterprise. Besides the issue of efficient management of state finances in absence of adequate resource mobilisation to meet their own needs, another most important issue is of insurgency and extortion. The Union Government is assisting by reimbursing security-related expenditure. But this cannot compensate for the terrible price extracted by insurgents and extortionists at the expense of the region's development or the fear psychosis created by them among the people. As we are aware of the fact that the maintenance of law and order is essential for attracting capital and the skilled human resource from outside to be used for the development of regional economy.

The policy of the Government of India towards north east has undergone many changes. Now it remains firmly embedded in the development paradigm, according to which we need to bring development into the region. We need to develop the natural resources of the region, increase public investment in physical and social infrastructure, for which huge money is being poured by the centre. The announcements by the four Prime Ministers indicate the continuation of the policy of pouring in money without accountability and monitoring; thereby resulting in perpetuation of corruption, deprivation and insurgency (Nayar, 2008 :15-16). Many researchers have raised questions about where is this money going? Who is utilizing it? Jairam Ramesh (2008 : 24) opines that "it is my firm belief that this money is not going for development". Nayar further (2008:16) opines that "it is doubtful, if the leadership in North East has the capacity to respond to the demands of the liberalized market policies of the Government of India".

It may be noted here that the funds earmarked earlier for various schemes has not really gone into those schemes where it was intended. On the issue of policy so for adopted by the Central Government for economic development of the region Gulshan Sachdeva (1998:11) observed that "the state and sectoral plans of the Planning Commission have not been able to provide enough impetus for local development, which would have led to self-sustained growth. Instead of creating efficiency-oriented economic process, this policy framework resulted in the creation of a politically led distribution-oriented process. In the process, natural resources, profits, savings and the like are in fact, moving away from the region to other high productivity regions. Besides, the almost dependence on the centre's funds and planned direction has cultivated a trait of passiveness towards development. It has encouraged patronage and corruption. It has also created government monopoly in employment which has destroyed the work culture. Expectations rose very high, and they could not be fulfilled with centrally sponsored schemes". There are inter-state differences in regard to resource endowments, levels of industrialization as well as infrastructural facilities. In a nutshell the economies of the constituent states of the region are underdeveloped agrarian with very weak industrial base and inflated service sector mainly in government.

Agricultural activities dominate over industrial activities in the region with shifting cultivation being the common practice in tribal areas. However, the shift in work participation from the agricultural based activities to other workers category can be noticed in all the north-eastern states but it is more in Assam and Tripura during 1991-2001. The percentage share of cultivators and agricultural labourers has come down from 67.32 per cent to 52.65 per cent in Assam, from 63.20 to 50.91 in Tripura, and from 70.22 to 57.37 in Manipur during the same period. Another notable feature is female work participation rate confined mainly in agricultural activities including Manipur where female workers are heavily/engaged in handloom sector. The female work participation in agriculture ranges from 56.90 per cent in Assam, 79.66 per cent in Nagaland to 81.10 per cent in Arunachal Pradesh in 2001. The household industry could engage 3.44 per cent of total workforce in Assam and 9.16 per cent in Manipur – the highest in the region as compared to all India average of 4.07 per cent.

As economies develop the share of agricultural labour to total labour falls to 2 to 3 per cent. In that way off-farm migration helps the development of the rest of the economy. As more people leave agriculture, the economic base on non-agriculture increases, boosting migration rates. But as labour leaves agriculture, labour productivity in agriculture increases; income differentials fall and migration declines. So off-farm migration leads simultaneously to an increase of income in the rural sector and to development of non-agriculture. This process takes a long time, however. (Larson and Mundlak, 1995).

Poor level of input base and infrastructure, uneconomic holdings, absence of marketing facilities and lack of agricultural credit have kept agriculture as a subsistence sector and unremunerated to be taken up as a commercial venture. New technologies, seeds, fertilizers, etc., are fast becoming expensive. The traditional and time tested methods of farming do not provide the required competitive edge. Therefore, under the current discouraging experiences improvement in agricultural production and making it competitive seem to be an uphill task. Commercial profitable agriculture has remained a distant dream in tribal areas. Agricultural innovations have increased the cost of inputs and investment making small holdings unviable. With large venturing on using advanced technology, individual enterprises, such as coffee plantation, orchards, rubber plantation, etc., are not going to be viable and competitive.

The region characterized by a wide spectrum of agro-climates ranging from tropical humid and alpine temperature, and rich in biogenetic resources is congenial for multifarious agricultural development which ultimately depends on strengthening agricultural research and disseminating improved technologies through tightly managed extension services. The private sector should be allowed to supplement the activities like supply of inputs and marketing of output. Cropping intensity is feasible if more irrigation potential - through shallow tubewells, storage of water and its channelisation, is created in the region. Inter-cropping or mixed cropping will play a vital role in intensifying more production in the hill areas. Water harvesting through collection of run-off should be practiced on a wider scale. An integrated approach of agri-horti-silvipestoral system may lead to achieve the goal of increase in income of farmers which may include livestock as subsidiary source of income. The necessary marketing infrastructural support is also a pre-requisite for increasing the production of all alternative enterprises including crops, vegetables, dairy, poultry and fishery (Agarwal, 1997:14).

The agro-climatic conditions of the region are congenial for horticulture, plantation, floriculture, and spice cultivation, etc. The concept of 'contract farming' may be introduced under which the big companies like Hindustan Lever and Nestle, etc. may provide marketing, equipment, technical assistance, credit, fertilizer, and other inputs, as well as ancillary services, and small holders grow fruit and vegetable. In this way the activities best carried out on a large scale with modern techniques are done by these MNCs while the growing of crop is done by newly settled small holders, who in turn, acquire and assured market, credit and inputs at low costs (Agarwal, 2002).

This type of institutional arrangement can combine some of the advantages of plantation farming, such as quality control, coordination of interdependent stages of production and marketing, with those of small-holder production, such as autonomy, keener incentives and income generation for poor people. But the possibility of abuse of its monopolistic power by the private company against the small holders makes it necessary to have either small-holder organizations with counter-vailing power or independent public regulation.

Industrial investment in the region is one of the lowest in India mainly because of low income level of the people due to continuation of subsistence farming system and ploughing back the surpluses for industrialization, absence of investment from outside because of many well known factors like inadequate infrastructural facilities, extortions, insurgency and disliking by the local populace to the outsiders, and the absence of local entrepreneurship to take up the challenges and risks involved in production and marketing.

The Central and many state governments of the region are trying to attract capital from outside. Their efforts have not been fully successful so far. It has been observed that the capitalist entrepreneurs and multinational corporations are not very keen to set up the industries except a few proposals in Assam and Arunachal Pradesh. However, some efforts are still being made to boost up the industrialization by providing many incentives and concessions to the MNCs and budding entrepreneurs of present generation. The question of the marginalisation of the smaller ethnic groups residing in peripheral areas and the reckless and unsustainable exploitation of natural resources by the MNCs does not arise. As observed by Kumar (2002 : 67), the north east region of the country is going to ask for the foreign investment most, but there is no possibility of its smooth flow due to various well known reasons.

The failure of the government sponsored industrialisation in almost all the states of the region, as evident from the mounting losses of the PSUs particularly in Assam, Meghalaya, Mizoram, Nagaland and Tripura, have convinced us about need for a new approach. We must find ways to boost up the commodity-producing sectors of the north-eastern economy. Probably a renewed emphasis on agriculture and agriculture related industrialization may resolve the conflict between equity and efficiency in the region (Bhattacharjee, 2002 : 67).

The root causes of the problem in North East are deprivation (different in different areas), ethnic consciousness or resurgence, social and cultural insecurity. These are fed by people's sense of alienation and denial (Nayar, 2008 : 15). As noted rightly by Upadhyay (2008 : 97-98), "the educated youth among the hill peoples with their share in political power emerged as a new feudal class that changed the socio-economic scenario in the tribal society. Usurping the traditional right over land and forest of their own people and dividing the traditional society between rich and poor, they created class rivalry, which was unusual for tribal society". The solution probably lies in a shift towards ideal politics and economic common sense oriented to people's requirements. Jairam Ramesh (2008 : 25) suggests that "the political integration with the rest of India and economic integration with the rest of Asia, with East and South East Asia particularly, is certainly one direction that this region must be looking to as a new way of development".

In an increasingly integrated world economy, there is a good chance that the locational disadvantage of the north-east could be converted into an advantage through opening up of border trade with bordering countries, viz., Bangladesh, Bhutan, Myanmar and China. It may be pointed out here that Myanmar has border trade arrangements with China, Thailand and Bangladesh. Dipankar Banerjee (2008 : 43-44) noted that hundreds of quintals of sugar, edible oil, white oil, petrol, kerosene oil, paper, books, wood, branded cosmetics, cigarattes, and medicines are being smuggled out of India illegally to Bangladesh everyday by the border settlers. Similar is the case with Myanmar. Hence, most of the exported items from the region except coal, limestone, handicrafts, agro and forest based commodities do not originate from the north-eastern states and are produced elsewhere in India. Similarly, most of the imported items like iron and steel scrap, synthetic blankets, electronic and consumer goods are produced in China or elsewhere in other south-east countries, but not in Myanmar and Bangladesh which export them to Indian states. A number of consumable items-made in Korea, Japan and China, like blankets, textile, electronic gadgets, electrical goods and so on are readily available in markets of the north-eastern states. The estimated volume of unofficial trade is of about Rs. 1500 to Rs. 2000 crores annually at Moreh (Manipur) and Rs. 500 crores at Champhai (Mizoram). Estimates for unofficial trade at Tripura border with Bangladesh range between Rs. 500 crores to Rs. 1000 crores (Sachdeva, 1998: 115). The whole unauthorized border trade is a known phenomenon to the concerned authorities of the states as everybody involved in the system has its own share in the pie.

Under the circumstances emphasis should be laid on converting these unauthorized activities into authorised trade through bilateral trade agreements with the neighbouring countries, expansion of basic infrastructural facilities like roads, storage and warehouses, banking and townships in all border trading points. The Government of India is involved in a variety of cross border development projects with Myanmar, Bangladesh and Bhutan in diverse fields such as roads, railways, telecommunication, IT, science and technology, power etc. These initiatives are aimed at improving connectivity between NE India and other neighbouring countries.

It may be a good idea to declare certain areas of north-east as free trade areas officially, since for all practical purposes they are free trade areas, anyway. Since we are planning to move from SAPTA (South Asia Preferential Trading Arrangement) to SAFTA (South Asia Free Trade Areas) in a few years, beginning of free trade could be made from north-east. Further an aggressive strategy has to be worked out to create a growth quadrangle involving North East, Northern Myanmar, Yunnan Province of China, Northern Thailand and Bangladesh with the help of BIST-EC (Bangladesh-India-Sri Lanka-Thailand Economic Cooperation) agreement, this quadrangle could also become a reality (Sachdeva, 1998 : 120-125).

To take advantage of opening up of border trade the trade guidance is necessary for the entrepreneurs and exporters. The region should develop the capacity to produce the products of international quality at competitive prices. A high degree of professional and managerial competence is required for export promotion to these countries besides an effective control over the supply base as the main competitor is China known for cheap prices for their products. This cannot happen unless the region has strong linkages with the Indian Industry and Commerce. All types of barriers and restrictions in terms of Inner Line Permit System has to be removed.

Transfer of funds and devolution of Central resources through Planning Commission and Finance Commission has reached their optimum level. Thus the need for inviting investment cannot be over-emphasized. Private capital investment is badly required to generate productive employment, raise productivity and improve work culture. To attract private capital some fundamental policy initiatives are required to be taken by the state governments particularly in land and labour policies, extension of infrastructural facilities, maintenance of law and order, etc. Simultaneously efforts have to be made by the governments to increase the revenue earning capacity through widening of tax base, raising tax rates and imposition of new taxes leviable under Central Government jurisdiction, *i.e.* taxing income of tribals residing in the Sixth Schedule/Hill Areas of the region. While liberal funding and transfer of resources is expected from the centre the state citizens should also be ready to bear the additional burden of taxation to support the state resources to be used for the betterment of their own.

Conclusion

The globalisation and the economic policies adopted so far have not helped much to the north-eastern states. Even if by now the correct policies are adopted and pursued the region will be in a better position to improve the economy, which again depends on stability and level and quality of state administration in the region.

For economic development of NE Region, the development of the core sectors of infrastructure, power, communication, and human resource development is required besides flow of investment. The growth sectors for the north east in the coming years will be agriculture, horticulture, fish farming, handicrafts, and tourism, etc. having tremendous potential to generate employment opportunities outside the government.

The development of natural resources require greater attention in planning through survey and finding best ways of utilization of forest resources, development of industries derived from them and provision of related skills and market alongwith essential infrastructural facilities. Efforts should also be made to invest on linkage based industries and not those whose products have markets in the neighbouring countries like Myanmar and Bangladesh.

Tourism, if developed linking East Asian Countries will contribute to income and employment generation directly in tourism related sectors and indirectly in the well-developed labour intensive handloom and handicrafts sector. An integrated approach is required taking the advantage of greater women participation in economic activities, tradition of self-governance and liberal social outlook.

Improvement of existing infrastructural facilities and creation of new facilities like road and rail communication, exploitation of hydro energy generation potential to the extent of 31000 MW, gas based thermal energy and other industries based on natural gas will open new vistas of employment opportunities. Another area of prime concern is the expansion of service sector which include not only activities such as trade, finance, transport and communication but also housing and personal services-skilled and unskilled.

The high literacy base in the region is an advantage over many other states of the country and it should be fully exploited in this era of knowledge-based industrial revolution. This will generate not only resources but also employment potential for the educated youth. The revolution in information technology and the prospects of cross border trade will give a major thrust in economic development which must be effectively grasped. For this, concerted efforts are required to equip adequately for existing educational and technical institutions and build new institutions for generating marketable skills, on the one hand, and build the capability to adopt and absorb new technologies on the other.

Lastly, the government role cannot be ignored in providing social safety nets to the poor against the reform effects on price rise, employment structure, and so on. The state governments should continue to invest more and more in education, health, environment and infrastructure through different policies. There is need for strengthening institutions for rural, agricultural, and industrial development to accelerate the development process in the region.

REFERENCES

Agarwal, A.K., (1997) : "Agricultural Systems and Behaviour in North-Eastern States", in Behera, M.C. and Roy, N.C.(eds), *Trends in Agrarian Structure in the Hills of North-East India*, Commonwealth Publishers, New Delhi.

__________., (2002) : "Globalisation and its Relevance for the North-Eastern Region of India", paper presented in National Seminar on *Globalisation, Employment, Migration and Trade: Relevance for the North-Eastern Region of India*, November 22-23, 2002, NEHU, Shillong.

Balasubramanyam, V.N. (2001) : *Conversations with Indian Economists*, Macmillan India, Delhi.

Banerjee, Dipankar (2008) : "Demographic Movements 1905-2005 : Roots of Low Intensity Conflicts in North-East India", *North-East Quarterly*, Vol. 1. No. 3, April-June, 2008.

Basu, Kaushik., (2000):"On the Goals of Development", in Meier, G.M. and J.E. Stiglitz (ed)., *Frontiers of Economic Development*, Oxford University Press, New York.

Bawa, R.S., (2002): "Challenges and Opportunities of Globalisation - Implications for India", *The Indian Economic Journal*, Vol. 49, No. 3, January-March 2001-2002.

Bhattacharjee, P.R. (2002 : "The Problem of Ensuring Financial Efficiency) in the North-Eastern States", *Dialogue*, Vol. 4, No. 1, July-September.

Dev, S.M., (1995):"Economic Reforms and the Rural Poor", *Economic and Political Weekly*, Vol. 30, No. 33, August 19, pp. 2085-88.

Dholakia, Bakul H. (2002) "Sources of India's Accelerated Growth and the Vision of Indian Economy in 2020", *The Indian Economic Journal*, Vol. 49, No. 4, April-June, 2001-2002.

Dollar David and Kraay Aart., (2001) : "Trade, Growth and Poverty", Finance and development, Vol. 38, No. 3, September, pp. 17-19.

Jalan, Bimal, (2002) : "India and the Challenge of Globalisation", *The Indian Economic Journal*, Vol. 49, No. 3, January-March, 2001-2002, pp. 9-12.

Jegadish Gandhi, P., (1995) : "Services Sector in Tamil Nadu Economy", in Subrahmanya S. and Gowda Srinivasa M.V., (eds). Regional Economic Development in India, Deep and Deep publications, New Delhi.

Kabra, K.N., (2002) : "A Decade of Reforms : The Unfinished Agenda", The Theme Paper for Members Annual Conference of Indian Institute of Public Administration, New Delhi, 2002.

Kumar, B.B., (2002) : "Social Science Research in the N-E Region in the 21st Century", in Datta Ray B., (ed), Agenda for the North-East India, Concept, New Delhi.

Larson, Donald and Yair Mundlak, (1995) : "On the International Migration of Agricultural Labour", Policy Research Working Paper, 1425, World Bank International Economics Department, Washington, D.C., quoted in World Bank Policy and Research Bulletin, January-March, 1997, p. 2.

Mukherjee, Pranab, (2007) : "India's Look East Policy", Dialogue, Vol. 9, No.1, July-September, 2007.

Nayar, Gen. V.K.,(2008) : "Dealing with Conflicts", North East Quarterly Vol. 1, No. 2, January, 2008.

Ramesh, Jairam, (2008) : "North-East India in a New Asia", North-East Quarterly, Vol. 1, No. 2, January, 2008.

Sachdeva, Gulshan 1998: *Economic Situation in North-East [Draft (1998) Report]*, Centre for Policy Research, New Delhi.

Singh Manmohan, H.K. (2000) :"Rethinking Reforms : Back to the Middle Path", The Indian Economic Journal, Vol. 47, No. 3, January-March, 1999-2000, p. 24.

Streeten, Paul, (2000) : "Globalisation : International Integration and Disintegration", Political Economy Journal of India, Vol. 9, Nos. 3 and 4, pp. 1-37.

Thomas W. Hertel, Bernard M. Hoekman, Will Martin, (2002) : "Developing Countries and a New Round of WTO Negotiations", The World Bank Research Observer, Vol. 17, No.1, Spring, 2002.

Upadhyay, R.,(2008) : "North-East Violence – An Overall View", North-East Quarterly, Vol.1, No. 3, April-June, 2008.

Yusuf, Shahid and Stiglitz, J.E., (2000) : "Development Issues Settled and Open", in Meier, G.M. and J.E. Stiglitz (ed), *op. cit.* quoted in Bawa, R.S., *op. cit.*

6

Tribal Communities in India : Some Emerging Issues in the Light of Globalization

Sib Ranjan Misra

I

India occupies a unique place in the tribal world. It has the second largest concentration of tribal population, after that of African continent. A total number of 557 communities have been notified as scheduled tribes in the country consisting of 8.8 per cent of the country's population. The tribals have been occupying generally compact and isolated areas which are generally hilly and undulating. The Indian experiment of tribal development is often being considered as unique. In India, the tribals are recognized as full citizens. They have by and large maintained their identity. They have not been extinguished and they have maintained their demographic growth rate. At the same time, there are some issues which really agitate the minds of the social scientists and policy-makers. The problems like the non-percolation of the benefits of developments to the lower strata of the tribals, the pauperization, casualisation and psychological stresses and strains of a large section, the issues of livelihoods, and metamorphosis in the cultural environment are of serious concern. Against this backdrop, it is instructive to observe a few facts about globalization and reflect its implications particularly for the tribal communities in India.

This paper is organized into four sections. While section one introduces the tribal community and its features, section two discusses the issue of globalization. Section three dwells upon, in short, the problems of how globalization has impacted upon the communities. Section four deals with the summary and policy implications.

II

Globalization, as a concept, is used to describe the process by which the world is transformed into a single arena. It is not merely an economic phenomenon; rather, it covers all the aspects of modern life.

In other words, it can be defined as a process by which the world has been becoming increasingly inter-connected and unified, subject to homogeneous and uniform process of cultural, technological and economic unification. It recognizes the emergence of a globally inter-dependent economic, political, cultural, technological and communication system. It is a symbol of integration and harmony. We have become increasingly inter-connected into a global village[1] (which we have not yet visited). But as the 20th century has drawn to a close, we all use to feel the incredible and positive changes in the mind-set among people and nations on the one hand and the tale of tragedies, fear of identity and uncertainty on the other. It is true that our planet is one, but it is also a grim reality that on our planet '... 22 children die of starvation every minute... one million dollars are spent on arms every minute ... in the mean time, three children died and the arsenal of the instruments of murder in the hands of the adults grew by $ 150,000' (Dadayan, 1988 quoted in Dasgupta, 2004 : 16). It is looked upon as threatening

1. The phrase 'global village' was first used by Herber Marshall McLuhan in his two works, namely. *The Gutenberg Galaxy: The Making of Typographic Man* (1962) and *Understanding Media* (1964). He prophesized that "electronic interdependence" would replace the visual, individualistic print culture and make humankind to move from individualism and fragmentation to a collective identity, with a "tribal base." To this new social organization McLuhan gave the name global village. http://en.wikipedia.org/wiki/Marshall_McLuhan.

the loss of economic self-reliance and political sovereignty, erosion of democratic structures and damaging of plural cultural identities. Globalization is merely an extension of capitalism to cover more remote parts of the world - essentially, an expression of capitalist explosion (or implosion).

The tragedy of globalization is that it began with the aim of re-structuring and rebuilding civilizations. Yet the mission has produced discord, even more separatism and identity crisis. The global village, once a symbol of integration, unification and harmony now denotes difference, differentiation, demarcation, discrimination and dissonance. The world so compressed into a single economic, ecological, cultural and political system has never been so highly stratified. In terms of disparity, we remain parts rather than wholes.

It is easy to identify numerous contradictions (Thakur, 2007): progress along side of hunger, the blessings on hunger combined with the abomination of destitution, the pleasure of achievement along with the pains of failure and the slogan of equality linked to cries of disparity. Using data from the World Development Report, it can safely be concluded that severe poverty remains the main characteristics of the world's population as a whole. This is predominantly because of unbalanced policies of those who promote globalization. To them Stiglitz explains, "globalization (which typically is associated with accepting triumphant capitalism, American style) is progress; developing countries must accept it...But to many in the developing world "globalization has not brought the promised economic benefits." The damage includes ethnic conflict, economic collapse and identity crisis.

The Multinational Corporations (MNCs) have been investing in India for a variety of reasons like utilization of lucrative domestic market, availability of cheap raw materials and labour, and last but not the least, to avoid the stringent state regulations of the first world. The MNCs tend to explore the possibilities of investment in different sectors. The investment pattern is designed and engineered by market forces. Globalization has facilitated the penetration of increasing stream of new technology, unfettered market competition and weak and fractured social institutions. This is a kind of situation which has generated an anarchic environment of disorganized global capitalism. Because of asymmetric access to economic and social opportunities, the elites have abundant capability. This has stratified the society. The investment pattern has distorted consumption pattern, dampened employment elasticity and aggravated economic inequality and created perverted commodity structures. The MNCs have seriously disrupted traditional styles of living, behaviour patterns and consumption norms. They have created differences in social opportunities. This has led to diverse achievements in the quality of life of people of different strata in terms of economic performances.

It is argued that free trade and 'levelling of the global playing field' are illusions. Globalization is nothing more than making it easier for powerful, elite foreign companies to take control of a country's economy. For example, 70-75 per cent of world trade or over $ 2 trillion, is controlled by 100 multinational corporations and 40 per cent of global trading is intra-trading or trading between subsidiaries of the MNCs.

Globalization has been fuelling enormous inequality in wealth distribution leading to a rise in global poverty. This can be exemplified by the following statistics: 358 billionaires have combined assets worth $760 billion which is equivalent to the collective income of 2.5 billion poor people; income disparity between the rich and the poor has increased 100 per cent, whereby instead of a 30-fold disparity, the gap is now 60 fold; 20 per cent of the world's richest receive 82.7 per cent of the world income, while 20 per cent of the poorest receive just 1.4 per cent of the world income. (UNDP, 2002).

III

The term 'tribe'[2] originates from the Latin word 'tribus'. It means a socially cohesive unit, associated with a territory, the members of which regard themselves as autonomous. Often, a tribe possesses a distinct dialect and distinct cultural traits. The tribal social relations are dominated by kinship, a social relation of co-operation and non-violence. This society is based on a

2. The tribals and the Adivasis (dalits) are used here in a synonymous form. I will employ the term Dalits (literally oppressed) to refer to not only the seheduled castes but also the scheduled tribes as well as all other sections among the backward classes.

structure of closely knit personal relationships. The tribal society endeavours to protect themselves from the onslaughts (if any) from the advanced communities by maintaining isolation from the outside world. Isolation is often aimed at preserving their own culture and ensuring a certain degree of stability to their own value system.

There are some 85 million Indians who are officially classified as Scheduled Tribes (STs). Of these, about 16 million live in the states of North East India. There are many different endogamous communities - more than 500 – that come under the label 'STs." Despite certain internal differentiation, taken as a whole, the tribes of central and eastern India share certain attributes - cultural, social, economic and political - that allow one to treat them as a single segment. In everyday language, this commonality is conveyed in the term 'Adivasi'. All the Adivasis– Naga, Mizo, Korku, Bhil or Oraon are unified in the Indian imagination. In general, what they share is denoted in cultural terms namely, these Adivasis generally inhabit uplands or wooded areas, that they generally treat their women better than caste, that they have rich traditions, of music and dance, and they might occasionally worship some manifestations of Vishnu or Shiva and also that their rituals and religion centre around village gods and spirits.

The tribal communities generally represent a socially structured clan-based hierarchy. Villages normally consist of single community dominated inhabitants. They have their historically evolved social institutions. All these govern the entire socio-economic process and the pattern of social relations follows certain pre-conditions fixed by social institutions e.g. reciprocity, the pre-station (labour commoditization and services among the groups) and the movement of factors, which are compensated by return movements of goods in terms of barter trade, economic loans and social loans. In point of fact, it is to be noted that the stability of the agrarian structure may be attributed to the constraints on private initiative and enterprises that are imposed by traditional social institutions like matrilineal system of inheritance, the practice of 'ultra geniture' as well as the communal nature of land tenure, the state policy (which prevents non-tribals from acquiring land in the state) - all these help preserve the traditional social structure[3].

Even though the peasants and the tribals living in the country are independent and free to follow their profession, the process of social change today, if any, is not the result of internal dynamics of the society as a whole[4]. The change has been sometimes engineered by different forces like the state and to a large extent, motivated by the changed international economic order. This has caused the evolution of local social institutions in favour of a market economy, which is perceived as the modern instrument for bringing about the required transformation. (see Salam, 2006). The economy of the villages faces four constraints: indigenously evolved technical coalescence, a material flow that was designed and shaped by interlocking social behaviour, inadequate liquidity and the fragmented local markets, which could be removed only by the committed action of a government agency for accelerating the development process in the state. Hence, state intervention became inevitable and during the post-Independence period, helped in the commoditization of agriculture produce for different reasons like: the infusion of liquidity, development of the tertiary sector, price cliff, the backing of the government to increase the agricultural produce and the supportive role of the Agricultural Product Marketing

---

3. The tribals of North -east India differ from their counterparts in other parts of India in different ways. In the first place, they have, until recently, been more or less untouched by Hindu influence. Secondly, they have recently been exposed to modern or English education; as a consequence, their rates are higher than that of their counterparts elsewhere in India. Thirdly, unlike the tribals in the mainland, they have been largely exempted from the trauma by dispossession; their location on a corner of a country has inhibited dam builders and mine owners venturing near them.

4. It is sometimes argued that the Adivasis and the Tribals as a whole in India have gained least and lost most during the last six decades of democracy and development. The state has treated them with contempt and condescension. They are even more deprived than the Dalits, simply because they have been unable to effectively articulate their grievances through the democratic and electoral processes.

Committee (APMC). The main intention of the cultivation is to meet the market demand. Hence, crops are raised as per the market requirement; agricultural work is carried out mainly by labourers and the poor peasants prefer to earn money by selling their labour services rather than working on their small pieces of land, as a result of which they are categorized as agricultural labourers. (They joined the ranks of landless labourers but without any training, equipment and aptitude for any skilled or semi-skilled job.) The commoditization process first had an impact on the distribution aspect of agricultural produce and later on the production level by developing the labour market.

Hence, it is theorized that the market surplus of agricultural produce leads to peasant differentiation. In other words, the market surplus of agricultural produce causes the dissolution of peasant relationships among the peasant households.

The exogenous factors like the role of trade, the penetration of market and monetization have impacted on the dynamics of changes in pre-capitalist tribal societies. The exogenous factors of changes result from contact with the other economies. These are seen as important in breaking down the traditional mode of subsistence production and effecting a transition to a new mode characterized by the development of community agriculture and a changing agrarian structure. (see Nair,1987).

Of course, despite these exogenous factors, the mode of production continues largely to be tribal, *i.e.*, predominantly characterized by communal ownership of land and poorly developed productive forces with little differentiation of the peasantry and kinship as dominant in economic and social relations.

But a gradual move from shifting to more intensive methods of settled cultivation (because of a rising human-land ratio and the subsequent inability of Jhum cultivation to reproduce itself) has been taking place in recent times. This is a population – induced technical change. Private property ownership is seen to have emerged in areas where there is settled cultivation.

The pace of shift is rather slow because of the constraining influence of the system of land tenure and/or inheritance (communal ownership of land and the matrilineal system of inheritance).Traditional institutions continue perhaps to impede the momentum of change.

The recent technological advancement and unrivalled economic and political strength of global economic forces as agencies have created favourable conditions for the evasion and extraction of natural resources from the ecologically fragile territories of the tribal people. Thus, forced eviction of tribals to make way for mammoth capital-intensive development projects have become a distressingly routine and ever-increasing phenomenon. These projects are intrinsically associated with the predatory activities of international business houses and profit-seeking agencies, connected with an under-current of authoritarian and ethno-centric values and political institutions.

A critical review of the hydro–electric power generations projects reveals that India happens to be the second most (damned) dammed country in the world. It invested over Rs. 350 billion by 1999 and this figure has probably increased by now. The World Bank alone has directly provided funds for as many as 109 large scale dam projects in India as against only 62 for the whole of the African continent and 68 for Latin America. Between 1991 and 2000, the World Bank provided $10.5 billion for such projects in India, *i.e.* one-fifths of its total funding for 92 countries world over. Quite a major proportion of all major dam projects in India are intrinsically linked to world capital and its obedient stooges. Nearly 60 per cent of these large dams are located in central and western India where about 80 per cent of the tribals live.

The increased commercial extraction of timber, establishment of numerous forest-based industries and the so-called development projects have mutilated the forests, scared away the game, polluted water resources, depleted the fish resources and eventually, devastated the tribal livelihoods. Agribusiness, plantations, afforestations by mono-cultural species, high-way projects, bio-sphere reserves, game sanctuaries, national parks, reserved forests, etc. have displaced the tribals from their base.

With the gradual destruction of forests, the options are now reducing. Dwindling availability of forest produce – food, fuel, medicinal herbals etc. have deprived them of a supplementary source of both income and food. When these conditions persist, it implies women even travelling longer distances with heavy loads. Increasing number of labour migration (see Rao and Rana, 1997 for women labour migration) is a pointer towards the deterioration in traditional livelihoods. With erosion of traditional livelihoods strategy and few local options available, the tribals have been forced to enter market as migrant. Faced with a negative impact of schooling and health care, poor living and working conditions and constant fear of sexual abuse, the entry into the labour market of the tribal women in particular is nothing but a survival strategy since staying at home could mean starvation. The entry into the labour market by a large number of tribals is in itself a reflection of a society under siege, of a process of development that has displaced a large number of them from their traditional livelihoods without providing secure and sustainable options locally. It has been a slow death, a process of destruction of forests for commercial purposes and also for clearing for agriculture, by non-tribal immigrants, accompanied by the alienation of the tribal lands, primarily through loans and controls over capital by a few. What one has to guard against, however is the control of resources by a few, leading to exploitation of the assetless tribals by some amongst them. Their autonomy paradigm of community ownership has got lost somewhere along the way and replaced by individuals progress and fulfilment.

The tribal population's rights of forests are being minimized. The Tata Energy Research Institute (1997) reported that there was a net decline in availability of fresh water by two-thirds and net degraded land area rose by almost 80 million hectares between 1947 and 1997. The varieties and diversity of forest wealth gave way to mono-culture of select species.

Of course, it is indeed difficult to reconcile the three different interests: (i) the livelihood interests of the tribal communities, (ii) commercial interests of government and contractors, and (iii) environmental protectionists.

Indigenous conservation strategies evolved, modified and adopted by forest dwellers are often sustainable and well suited to the complex local ecological, socio-cultural and economic conditions. However, these strategies are not easily accessible to forest policy-makers.

In fact, traditional customary laws governing these tribals ensure resource conservation and management in the larger interests of the community. They also ensure inbuilt social security mechanisms addressing the needs of each member of the community. These mechanisms have helped nurture the community feeling to such an extent that individualistic traits favouring personal gain over larger community welfare are discouraged and rarely entertained.

Landownership system reflects the true community spirit of resource management and the inherent intuitive ecological understanding these communities have. Although the customary laws governing landownership and tenure vary with each tribe and even sometimes even within tribes and among villages, some fundamental principles are common. Some exceptions do exist, notably among the Semas of Nagaland, and the Khasis, Jaintias and Garos of Meghalaya. Landownership is vested with the Gaonbura (Chieftain) among the Semas, the Ang (Chief) among the Konyaks, the Syiems (King) among some Khasi groups. Even among these tribes, the spirit of community welfare is upheld in varying degrees ranging from that of a benevolent feudal overlordship to one closely resembling the community ownership reflected elsewhere and executed primarily through elaborate tenureship rights (Tiwari *et. al.*, 1995).

The continuing struggle of displaced tribals against the Sarobar Project (Oza, 1997) has to be seen in the context of the long history of their displacement and marginalization to make way for development project. It also became known that the tribals who were used to abundant source on the banks of the river Narmada - fish, plenty of fodder, fuel wood, timber, minor forest produce to support them; herbal medicines, a variety of crops that they grew - suddenly found themselves in an alien land, left to face market economy and hostile hosts at many places with a severely diminished resource base. The tribals who lived as a community were separated from their relatives and families and scattered here and there. Their families and communities broke severely affecting them socially, culturally and economically. There is no cognizance of the reality that there is a problem of social exclusion that is a much stronger manifestation of inequality due to deeper barriers. The incidence of poverty is among the SC and ST population is the highest. The incidence of poverty among SCs/STs is two and half times higher than for the other population. There are also a few other manifestations of exclusion. For example, the literacy rate among the SC/ST population as a percentage of the other population is only 74 per cent for the country as a whole. When the problem of gender bias and social exclusion are combined, the problem assumes yet another dimension that cannot be wished away since the affected category includes, by and large, the rural female population.

A recent survey conducted by the oustees themselves of 53 sites and 1,643 families reveal that 48 per cent of the oustees have been given uncultivable land, 40 per cent of the oustees were cheated in the land deals, 43 per cent allocated waterlogged land, 98 per cent of them have no facility of fuel and fodder, 61 per cent of the sites faced problems of drinking water and 85 per cent faced severe shortage for their cattle. With lack of amenities, poor land, breaking up of communities, hostile hosts at several places, a tough market to compete with and thrown to face cash economy, the process of marginalization and pauperization started.

The tribal employment in modern enterprises is negligible. Meanwhile, the tribals are forced to live in juxtaposition with alien capitalist relations and culture with traumatic results. They are forced onto the ever-expanding low-paid, insecure, transient and destitute labour market. It is often reported that quite a significant number of the tribals in central India supplement their income by participating in this distorted and over-exploitative capitalist sector. Besides, many more are slowly crushed into oblivion in their homeland or in urban slums. This is nothing short of ethnocide. At stake is their economic and cultural survival.

There are some social scientists who tend to argue whether survival of tribal culture is morally relevant. It is also argued that survival of any culture is less important than the individual's inherent human rights. This should be of primary moral concern.

Again it is mentioned that culture should not be freezed or disintegrated. They must continue to serve as a means by which some people make sense of their place in the world; however much of the content of their cultures change over time. If it does not survive then it is allowed to vanish.

It is true that we may not have the duty to preserve all the species that now exist in the world. Species may go and come as a part of natural course of evolution. But the relevant point of concern is that we should not be a cause of the destruction of a species which otherwise would survive.

So the proper focus of our moral concern is not the survival of culture as collective practices and traditions, but rather the political, civil and human rights of the individuals that constitute them. Our concern should be a moral concern to save the tribal culture but this moral concern should be a concern from the moral status and rights of the individual members of tribal cultures rather than for the cultures themselves (Mukherjee, 2004).

In fact, the inherent value thesis in favour of the preservation of the tribal culture is found to be unacceptable. It is argued that individual is the seat of rights. However, culture may be considered for preservation if they are compatible with development and on the basis of universal principles like mutual trusts (Miri, 2004).

Of course, development programmes like modernization or development are found very often to presuppose a moral superiority and hence suppress the cultural base of the people for whom they are meant. And eventually, the programmes fail because here the individuals' rights and freedom to choose have not been adequately taken care of.

Amid broad categories for social organizations, changing experiences of life e.g., the contact with neighbouring cultures, missionary activities, changes in agricultural pattern, political aspirations, education and health consciousness necessitates the emergence of new pattern.

The tribes all over the world witness world views. The community is found well-ordered, governed by law, behaving and thinking according to consistent principles, even though they appear chaotic and freakish, sensational, wild and unaccountable world of savages[5].

The tribal society has certain features. In the first place, it is shown by modern ethnologists that social institutions exhibit definite organization and are governed by authority, law and order in their public and personal relations. This is true of tribal society at large, with minor adjustment here and there. Secondly, rules and regulations are not formulated precisely and hardly reflected upon. They are to be learnt by each generation anew. Three, it is maintained that members of a tribe are under the control of extremely complex ties of kinship. And in the process, they are entangled in a mesh of duties, functions and privileges which correspond to an elaborate communal and kinship organization.

The concept of community is pertinent. Their belief and practices, their strenuous enterprises and activities, their art and crafts are regulated by their 'community feeling.' Community should be looked upon – as the close relational set-up of the members of the set-up regulated by the forces of triad, *e.g.*, the triad of the ancestral mother, ancestral father and the ancestral maternal uncle of a particular clan which constitutes the foundation of a society. They feel and think like members of a given community. In this capacity, their outer behaviour and mental states receive a certain stamp, becomes stereotyped by the institutions in which they live, circumscribed by the influence of tradition, of folklores and by the language they use.

It is unrealistic to impose any development plan on people from above. People's development can occur only when their ideas, habits, cultural and social constraints and their 'world view' are taken into consideration while formulating any development plan. Cultures of any society cannot be artificially or necessarily adjusted with requirements of a particular scheme of development. Culture can be changed under coercion or voluntarily. When it accepts the change voluntarily, the change is fine Development cannot occur in a vacuum, it occurs in a society which has a past heritage, values, norm, beliefs and

5. Savages, according to Mallinowski, refer to ideas of boundless liberty, irregularities of something extremely quaint.

habits. For launching a development plan, it requires that the planners should have the same desirability as the people of the society (tribal). It is necessary to have the knowledge of the community, their perception of development, their requirement as a community and the ethos of the culture of a specific region

In this connection, it may be noted that Vinobaji once made an enquiry from community development officials about their strategy for development. The officials were in a fix. Vinobaji asserted it is pertinent to organize the community first and then the organized community would develop itself. (Ramaswamy, 1992).

In sum, development projects are handed down without any concern for the cultural-historic and ecological complexities prevailing in the tribal region. Based upon anthropocentric premises of mutilation of nature, customary institutions and values, and imposition of individualism, static ideology and reductionist worldview, the development practices have wrecked the physical, cultural and cognitive survival of the large masses of the country, especially the tribals and the dalits. Development projects encompass a whole gamut of territorial resources taken away by the state, powerful individuals, private enterprises and multinational corporations, as well as displacement from one's own culture, creativity, community, power and knowledge systems through involuntary superimposition of the values and institutions of the globally and nationally dominant societies. The story of marginalization of the tribals continues in the name of development[6]. The situations of the tribals affected by different development projects is a part of the larger picture of the marginalization of tribals and the diversion of their resources to the elites at their expense throughout the country. The advent of the new economic policy and the mindless rush for industrialization has intensified the process. It is now clear through past and ongoing struggles around dams and many other

6. Some demographers maintain that on the basis of certain indicators of development, the Adivasis are even worse off than the Dalits (Maharatna, 2005). It is sometimes argued that what has united the Adivasis is not their cultural or ecological distinctiveness, but their economic and social disadvantages (Guha, 2007). The tribals in India share less of the prosperity due to institutional barriers and cultural reasons.

development projects that the present model of development not only ignores the tribals but is based on their resources which are taken away from them.

Another point of serious concern is that rapid changes are undoubtedly overtaking most of the tribal societies consequent upon the advent of modern consumerist values and undergoing transformation aspirations of people even in the isolated communities in the remotest N-E highlands. The infusion of information technology, especially the electronic media and television, is widespread. In fact, these societies have been experiencing the effect of market forces. And necessarily, rural communities have been looking for opportunities for enhancing their cash flow. Hence, the community's ready acceptance of different income generation schemes introduced by different government and non-government bodies is widely observed[7]. But, for all practical purposes, all these efforts met with limited success. The result is economic insecurity brought about precisely due to increased dependence on external sources, the shift in land use pattern and gradual erosion of traditional management system, change in consumption pattern (traditional customs have been compromised), gradual transformation in the value systems (catalyzed by the increasing influences of market forces), migration of rural people to the urban localities looking for opportunities for capacity building (this robs the rural populace of able-bodied labour leading to labour shortage in jhum or traditional cultivation, further leading to further depletion of productivity and hence fall in purchasing power).

Cultural homogenization model does not fit the Third World countries like India, mainly for economic reasons. Economy and culture are intimately interrelated. Our age of *cultural realism* is tied to the current stage of *market capitalism*. Monopoly capitalism links cultural modernism; and post-modern cultural

---

7. The dominance of global capital has not been curbed; rather global capital has been systematically responding to changes through a process of evolution by adapting its strategy, tactics and even its culture. It is pertinent to note that the World Bank has invested quite a lot in the construction of large dams and interestingly, is active also at the same time in rehabilitation programmes (Basu, 2008).

phenomena constitute the denominator of managerial capitalism. Thus capitalist hegemony continues. Those who promote globalization conceal question of economic particularism and domination behind their programmes of global culture.

The values, beliefs, ideas, ethics and artefacts of the Occidental culture sneak into the territory of India through different media and thereby produce cultural hybridization. Youths are generally socialized into a set of sub-cultural ambiences rather than a single cultural environment. For this, Coke, Pop CDs, denims - the ingredients of the imported culture- are prestigious commodities.

Western-dominated globalization has helped to transform India into a cultural Chernolry and socio-economic Disneyland (Dasgupta, 2007). With it has come anxiety over the loss of cultural identity and clash between local and overseas tribals. The tribal areas like north-east India has become a mosaic of the old and the new. The cultural inputs have undoubtedly improved tribal style and quality of life. The influence of global culture on the local cultures has created marginality. This has now raised questions about cultural exclusion. In contemporary tribal community, the forces of globalization and its opposite, localization–between homogeneity and heterogeneity are exerting tremendous pressure on individuals.

In addition to dilemmas posed by local-global values and norms, people are now forced to choose between adoption and rejection of foreign innovations and consumer items. The institutionalization of corporate capitalism and domination of its political economy by the MNCs have created a peculiar type of universalism. Cumulatively, these assaults amount to "cultural genocide."[8]

---

8. Cultural globalization is malignant in the form of the ever expanding electronic culture and ever proliferating fast food outlets. A binary cultural fusion arises from this imposition. "...during the 1999 student demonstrations against the NATO bombing of the Chinese Embassy in Belgrade ...many young protestors were drinking Coca Cola as they chanted down with American imperialism in front of the US embassy in Beijing. The irony goes further, when some young activists sent messages over.

IV

By Way of Conclusion

Indian society holds the pride of bearing unity in great diversities of cultural ethos and the united common concern of all varying cultural wings for the committed support to the national ethos of mutual appreciation, mutual trust, mutual support, tolerance and common goal of building a vibrant and progressive society. Indian national culture is represented by the supreme value systems and life styles finding expression in diversified forms. Liberty and freedom of choice constitute the central theme in Indian culture.

Modern development process (through the globalization system) not only physically displaces increasing number of tribal people from their territorial survival resources and thereby destroy their traditional socio-economic structures but also tend to mutilate their very identity, social reproduction, culture art forms, language skills and the just limited autonomy. They get marginalized. They are forced to enter into the dehumanized cheap labour market. They invariably face re-colonization and general economic subjugation, socio-cultural stigmatization and various degrees of ethnocide. Their customary holistic and anticipatory conception of nature, generic and corporate character of land, community oriented values and collective identities, self-management systems, cognitive heritage, unique socio-cultural framework and consensual decision making process are derecognized. The cultural hegemony of the dominant global and national society has eroded the reproducibility of their collective existence - an indication of irreversible ethnocide.

Change is generally regarded as marks of progress and modernization, but in reference to tribal population, it has given rise to many contradictions and tensions which are often problematic. As it appears that the tribals are passing through a transitional phase in which the old generation is still associated

---

The Internet calling for a resistance movement to the invasion of western culture....Others went to eat at a KFC outlet immediately after parting anti-McDonald's slogans on the street." (Yunxiang, 2002).

with traditional behaviour patterns, while the new generation is found to be prepared to adapt and insist on modern value. And in the wake of massive social change, the tribals are witnessing differentiation within their own social structure. The protective discrimination resulted in a conspicuous tribal social stratification. The state as an agent of implementing development programmes determines the direction of social change and it has accelerated the process of class formation among the tribals. In the context of present day tribal development, there is an intensive interplay between the tribal ethnicity, state and class. In the process of their integration with national and international ethos, it is difficult to retain the core of their ethnic identity. Even there is a probability of class antagonism to emerge.

Globalization is progressing at an unprecedented pace and intensity. The pervasiveness and depth of local identities have resurfaced. The ideal type of 'global village' which was created with the imagination of an open discourse of integration, interaction and harmony has failed to triumph over discord, difference, demarcation, discrimination and dissonance of local villages. However, people in the Third World have been misled into believing that the world has changed and globalization means homogenization. The hegemonies and domination of the globalists indicate the blackhole of exclusion. Under these circumstances, a key question is whether globalization is bringing people new freedom to act or it portends an uninvited, unwanted and cruel fate for the majority of the world's population, more particularly the tribals. The tragedy of the globalization is that it began with the aim of restructuring and rebuilding civilizations; yet the mission has produced discord and identity crisis.

Commercialization and urbanization are symbols of modernization and globalization. The forces of all these are difficult to stop. In the process, ultimately all these result in increased dependence on external sources of the communities which have hitherto been self-dependent. The increased exogenous nature of market–driven economies ultimately ensures the gradual erosion of traditional management system.

Globalization has brought about a change in different spheres, e.g. in social, economic and cultural areas. It has shaped even the thinking process in decision-making. This is revealed through the behaviour of the tribals, commoditization and then differentiation which eventually provide freedom of choice of the economic variables. For example, commoditization confers autonomy of agricultural labour in the form of dissolution of social bindings. In fact, the major problems generally faced by the tribals are, among others, land alienation, restrictions on their use of forest resources, displacement by dams and many other large development projects and cultural change. The tribal people are at a critical point in their history. They are losing command over resources at a very fast rate. They are facing social disintegration. Development would depend upon a system of self development based on their creative force, corporate productive resources and cognitive structures where the terms of dynamics are to be determined by the concerned people themselves.

Development should be looked upon as a process of increase in 'creativity' and 'decline in entropy' which is possible only when a 'holistic and symbiotic process' of social transformation could be ensured. With regard to such process of development, the issue is not merely that of creating abundance or prosperity as an alternative to the removal of poverty. Development is not a simple bi-polar or linear process of change from the levels of scarcity to that of abundance. Many problems concerning tribal development like displacement, poverty alleviation, health and disease, land alienation, indebtedness, etc. in fact are the resultant effects of such a development model with its econocentric perspective. These are sometimes supposed to be nothing more than cosmetics or administering pain-killers instead of providing a genuine remedy to the ailments.

All human societies, at all times, possess a 'creative capacity' for development in accordance with their own internal laws and necessities, as well as flexible adaptation-innovation complexes corresponding to the changing local circumstances.

Unfortunately, policy on commercialization, export orientation and market development in agriculture and industry has meant that acquisition of land has become a priority state concern with little efforts being made to prevent tribal land alienation or ensure food security in the state by economic exploitation legitimized by political superstructure.

Centralized mega projects of irrigation or power generation have shown more their inhuman face of displacing the poor tribals than harnessing the creative potentials of the human lots that self reliant, eco-friendly and job-oriented smaller projects could have done. This kind of modernization model of development has some features as well as failures. As regards features, it is to be noted that, firstly, the paradigm of development has treated the rest of the bio-spheres as an enemy to be defeated and tortured for immediate maximization of exchange value. This anthropocentric and essentially reductionism perspective of the natural world has eroded the ecological resource base of the humanity and destroyed the customary tribal matrix of harmonious, holistic and anticipatory equilibrium between nature and culture. Secondly, the doctrines of individualism and static ideology, being crucial, the collective identities are severely impaired and stigmatized. Thirdly, the dominant notion of development is a gradual triumph of reason, rationality and value neutrality. It has consistently cultivated contempt for conscientiousness, values, ethics and traditions, and thereby institutionalized the belief that abandoning the traditional, cultural and institutional elements is the *sine qua non* of development. And finally, the motive force of development of the backward people is through the external infusion of capital, technology and institutions, an alibi for neo-colonial hegemony.

The sustainable and enduring development, therefore, is always a self-generative, self-reliant, need-based and not greed-based and an emancipatory process of social transformation which lead a society to become a self-reliant and creative society. The emphasis should be on evolving a civil society rather than an affluent society - a society which is responsible to itself and its environment and responsive to the needs of its members, rich or poor (Joshi, 2004).

The co-operation, transcendental interaction, co-existence and synthesis of love and aid can lead to a true globalization. Secondly, the policy makers, planners and initiators should have it in mind that aid should not go with trade, but with universal love. Third, we should start with what the people belonging to the tribal communities have, not with what they lack.

REFERENCES

Basu, P. K. (2008): *Globalization: An Anti-text -A Local View. AAKAR*, Delhi.

Choudhury, D. (1998) : "Conservation by local communities in north east India". In Kothari, Ashish; Neema Pathak; R. V. Anuradha and Bansuri Taneja, 1998: *Communities and Conservation-Natural Resource Management in South and Central Asia*. New Delhi: Sage.

Dasgupta, A. ed. (2007) : *Constellations of the Transnational: Modernity, Culture, Critique*. Amsterdam and New York: Rodopi.

Dasgupta, Samir. 2004. *The Changing Face of Globalization*. New Delhi: Sage.

Ghosh, M. (2004) : "The Tribal World" View. In S. Miri (ed) *Rationality and Tribal Thought*. New Delhi : Mittal Publications.

Guha, Ramachandra (2007) : "Adivasis, Naxalites and Indian Democracy". In *Economic and Political Weekly*, August 11.

Jyoshi Vidyut (2003) : *Tribal Situation in India*. Rawat, New Delhi.

Maharatna Arup (2005) : *Demographic Perspectives on India's Tribes*. Oxford University Press.

McLuhan, Marshall,1962. *The Gutenberg Galaxy: The Making of Typographic Man*. Toronto, Ontario: *University of Toronto Press*.

McLuhan, Marshall.1964/2003. *Understanding Media*. Berkeley/ Hamburg: Gingko Press.

Mukherjee, A. (2004) : "Worldview about the Tribals vs. Tribal World-view –Some moral Issues". In S. Miri (ed) *Rationality and Tribal Thought*. New Delhi: Mittal Publications.

Nair, Sukumaran (1987) : *Tribal Economy in Transition*, Inter-India Publications, New Delhi.

Oza, Nandini (1997) : "Marginalization, Protests and Political Action–Tribals and Sardar Sarobar Project". In *Economic and Political Weekly*, July 19.

Ramaswamy, A. S. (1992) : "Community Organisation for Development", In *The Hindu* 19th February.

Rao, N. and K. Rana (1997) : "Women's Labour and Migration : the Case of the Santhals". *In Economic and Political Weekly*, December 13.

Salam, M. A. (2006) : *Agricultural Transformation in North–East India*.

Mittal Publications, New Delhi.

Thakur, Ashutosh (2007) : *Tribal Development and its Paradoxes.* Author's Press, New Delhi.

Tiwari, B.K., Barik, S. K. and Tripathi, R. S. (1995) : "Sacred Groves of Meghalaya Status and strategies for their conservation". *Report submitted to the North-Eastern Council,* Shillong.

UNDP, 2002. *Human Development Report.* New York/Oxford : Oxford University Press.

Yunxiang, Yan (2002) : "Managed Globalization: State Power and Cultural Transition in China", in P. L. Berger and Huntington (eds) *Many Globalizations : Cultural Diversity in the Contemporary World,* Oxford University Press, New York.

7

The Potentiality and Challenges of Developing Ecotourism in Arunachal Pradesh : An Empirical Study

Amitava Mitra and Maila Lama

Introduction

The term ecotourism emerged in the late 1980s as a direct result of the world's acknowledgement and reaction to sustainable practices and global ecological practices. A variety of definition exists for the term ecotourism. However, the earliest and the most widely used definition of ecotourism was given by Ceballos-Lascurain in 1987. According to Ceballos-Lascurain tourism "involves travelling to relatively undisturbed or uncontaminated natural areas with the specific objective of studying, admiring and enjoying the scenery and its wild plants and animals as well as any existing cultural manifestations (both past and present) found in these areas" (Boo, 1990: 20).

The Ecotourism Society in 1991 defined ecotourism as "purposeful travel to natural areas to understand the culture and natural history of the environment, taking care not to alter the integrity of ecosystem while producing economic opportunities that make the conservation of natural resources beneficial to local people". The society, later, shortened this definition of ecotourism to "responsible travel to natural areas which conserves the environment and improves the welfare of local people" (Western, 1993: 8).

Ecotourism is the fastest growing segment of the tourism industry and its market is growing at an annual rate of 30 per cent (Whelan, 1991). Ecotourism has come to be recognized as a powerful instrument for promoting sustainable development because of its potential to conserve environment and promote environmental education. Moreover, ecotourism is based on the use of natural resources for non-consumptive purposes that may be as profitable as any other type of exploitation. Successfully managed ecotourism can provide additional revenues to public and private land managers as well as offer additional justifications for managing the resource base for sustainable use. Ecotourism can contribute to economic development of its destination especially in its role of earning foreign exchange, diversifying regional economies, infrastructure improvements and in providing income and employment directly to local people. Its development can also promote the preservation of cultural and social values, including historical places of interest that might otherwise be lost. This is true because ecotourism promotes culturally and ecologically sensitive travel.

Since ecotourism is based on non-consumptive use of natural resources, it can be developed well in areas rich in such resources. Arunachal Pradesh, the easternmost State of India, is rich in biodiversity and forest resources. As per the data based on satellite imagery, the forest area consists of around 82 per cent of the total area of the State which is one of the highest among the States of India. It is also a home of various species of plants, animals and orchids. There are two national parks, eight wild life sanctuaries, one biodiversity reserve and one orchid sanctuary in the State. In addition, the State has a number of historical and archaeological sites, beautiful natural areas such as, snow capped mountains, peaks, passes, lakes, water falls, voluminous rivers, etc. Despite being rich in natural resources the State is one of the most underdeveloped States in India.

The state, due to its richness in natural resources, has an enormous potential for the development of ecotourism and adventure tourism which can contribute substantially to its economic development and provide enough justification for conservation and proper management of its resources. The present paper makes an attempt to identify the resource base of Arunachal Pradesh for promotion of ecotourism and assess the main challenges and obstacles for its promotion in the State. The paper also presents the results from the survey. It finally suggests some measures for proper development of ecotourism in the State because it can emerge as an effective instrument of sustainable economic development for this underdeveloped and ecologically fragile part of our country. This paper consists of four sections. Section I discusses the potentiality of tourism in Arunachal Pradesh. Section II identifies the major challenges for the development of tourism in Arunachal Pradesh. In section III, the results from the survey have been discussed. The last section deals with conclusion and policy implications.

SECTION - I

Potentiality of Tourism

Arunachal Pradesh has an enormous potential for development of tourism. The tourists can enjoy its picturesque hills, dales, seasonal climate, meet its people with beautiful arts, crafts and colourful festivals. There are eleven identified tourist spots in the State which can be grouped into different types of tourism as shown in Table 1.

Table 1
Identified Tourist Spots in Arunachal Pradesh

Name of the Tourist Spot	*District*	*Distance from the State Capital (in km)*
Itanagar	Papum Pare	0
Tawang	Tawang	540
Bomdila	West Kameng	360
Dirang	West Kameng	403
Tipi	West Kameng	210
Ziro	Lower Subansiri	168
Malinithan	West Siang	162
Along	West Siang	335
Pasighat	East Siang	280
Parasuram Kund	Lohit	795
Namdapha National Park	Changlang	640

Source: North East India Data Bank – Tourism, 2003, pp. 5-6.

(a) Heritage Tourism: Tawang, Bhismarknagar and Itanagar are historical and heritage tourist spots. Tawang has more than 350 year-old Buddhist Monastry which is one of the oldest monastries in Asia. There is also a Stupa called 'Gorsam Chorten' at Gorsam village of Zemithang Circle which is one of the largest Stupas in Asia. So, Tawang can be developed as a Buddhist tourist centre which can attract Buddhist tourists from Thailand, Japan, Korea, Sri Lanka, Nepal, Bhutan, etc. The Itafort of Itanagar was built in the 14th century A.D. and is a historical site as also Bhismarknagar in Dibang Valley district.

(b) Pilgrimage Tourism: Malinathan and Parasuram Kund are pilgrim centres of Arunachal Pradesh. Malinathan is a unique site developed between the 10th and 12th centuries A.D. It has an ancient temple housing sculptures of Gods and Goddesses. Parasuram Kund is a place where Parasuram is believed to have washed away his sin of matricide. During Makar Sankrati thousands of pilgrims from all over the country come here for a holy dip.

(c) Cultural Tourism: Arunachal Pradesh is a home of twenty-six major and numerous minor tribes with rich cultural traditions. The added attractions are the colourful festivals which form essential aspects of the socio-cultural life of the people of the State. Thus, Arunachal Pradesh is a wonderful destination for the cultural tourists.

(d) Nature-based Tourism and Ecotourism: Arunachal Pradesh is rich in forest resources and biodiversity. Therefore, the areas of the State which are rich in forest resources and biodiversity can be developed as destinations of nature-based tourism and ecotourism. So the tourist spots like Bomdila, Bhalukpong, Dirang, Tawang, Ziro, Along, etc. which comprise natural beauty like valleys, snow-clad mountains, plateaus, green forests, orchids, etc. can be developed as major destinations of tourists. Tawang and Bomdila can be regarded as mountain resorts for the tourists in Arunachal Pradesh.

(e) Adventure Tourism: Arunachal Pradesh has a huge potential to develop adventure tourism which is also a type of ecotourism. There are numerous voluminous rivers such as, Kameng River, Siang River, Lohit River, and Subansiri River, etc. It also has a number of mountain peaks such as Kangte peak in West Kameng district and Gorichen peak in Tawang district. There are numerous passes in the State such as, Bomdila pass, Sela pass, Bumla pass, Lumla pass, etc. The State also has a number of Lakes such as Sela Lake, Bangachanga Lake and Sangester Lake in Tawang district and Ganga Lake in Itanagar. So, the Tourists activities like mountaineering, trekking, boating and river rafting and angling can be made available of and developed in most of the tourist spots at the foothill regions of the State.

(f) Wildlife-based Tourism: Wildlife tourism is also a type ecotourism which promotes sustainable tourism and significantly contributes to sustainable development. In Arunachal Pradesh, there are two national Parks, viz. Namdapha National Park and Mouling National Park, eight Wildlife Sanctuaries and one Biosphere Reserve which house diverse species of animals. Viewing wild animals can be a satisfying experience for the tourists in the State. This fact clearly reveals the State's potential to develop wildlife-based tourism.

SECTION – II

Challenges for Ecotourism Development

Though the State has an enormous potential for the development of ecotourism, there are many challenges in the way for its proper development. The major challenges for the promotion of ecotourism in the State are identified as follows:

1. Poor Infrastructural Facilities: The State is one of the most backward States of India in terms of infrastructural facilities. The remoteness and inaccessibility of most of the tourist spots due to a lack of proper infrastructural facilities has hindered the development of ecotourism in the State. Among the North Eastern States, Arunachal Pradesh appears to be the most backward State in terms of infrastructural facilities. Even after more than sixty years of country's independence, the State does not have a functional airport. The status of railways in the State is also dismal. The State capital is also not connected with railways not to mention of the other parts of the State. The State is having only 12 km meter gauge railways line that is also not functional. Thus, the principal mode of transport and communication in the State is the road. However, the density of road in the State is one of the lowest in the country. In 2004 the State had road density of 18 km per 100 sq. km against the national average of 75 km per 100 sq. km and North Eastern average of 52 km per 100 sq. km. It has been observed that the condition of roads becomes unsuitable for plying of vehicles during rainy season due to landslides and floods resulting in cut off for number of days. Although road is the basic means of transport but the public means of transport is not adequate in the State.

2. Lack of Proper Accommodation Facilities: Availability of proper accommodation facilities near the tourist spots is also an important determinant of development of ecotourism. Ecotourists are nature lover and they basically want to have a close association with nature. So they prefer accommodation facilities located near the tourist spots. However, in Arunachal Pradesh it has been found that accommodation facilities in the identified tourist spots are not well developed accept some tourist spots like, Bomdila, Tawang, Itanagar and Ziro. The servicing facilities in the tourist lodges are also found to be sub-standard and below the satisfaction of the tourists.

3. Institutional Constraints: There are certain institutional constraints which also hinder the development of ecotourism in Arunachal Pradesh. The main institutional constraints are the provisions of Inner Line Permit (ILP) and Restricted Area Permit (RAP). All the domestic tourists are required to obtain ILP for visiting Arunachal Pradesh which can be obtained from limited places like, Delhi, Kolkotta, Shillong, Guahati, Dibrugarh, etc.

All the foreign tourists intending to visit Arunachal Pradesh are required to obtain RAP from the Ministry of Home Affairs, Government of India. However, the Central Government has recently delegated power to the State Government to issue Protected Area Permit (PAP) to foreign tourists visiting in a group of three or more persons for a maximum period of thirty days.

It has been observed that the procedure for obtaining ILP and RAP is very complex and time consuming. This is likely to serve as a disincentive for the potential tourists intending to visit the State (Mitra, 1998).

4. Marketing Constraints: Lack of proper marketing strategy of tourism products is also a major constraint for the promotion of ecotourism in Arunachal Pradesh. Arunachal's tourism industry is poorly developed because of lack of coordination by the Government agencies and virtually absence of information and marketing of the State's attractions. It is to be noted that success of Singapore and China in tourism industry would suggest that the marketing of tourism product is just as important as its nature and quality for promoting the tourism industry (Mitra, 2003).

5. Other Constraints: Other major constraints for the successful promotion of ecotourism in Arunachal Pradesh include; growing insurgent activities as well as 'Bandhs and Strike' in the neighbouring States. These have disrupted the development of tourism in the entire North-East India in general and Arunachal Pradesh in particular. Tourism as an industry is highly sensitive to potential disturbances. The growing insurgent activities in the region act as a psychological barrier to the potential tourists.

SECTION - III

Results from the Survey

The State has no doubt an enormous potential to attract tourists but the number tourist arrival has been limited as compared to the other States of India. However, in the recent years the total tourist arrival in the State has been increasing. It is clear from the Table 2.

Since there is growing number of visitors recently, an attempt was made to study the nature and structure of tourist demand in Arunachal Pradesh in relation to the tourist income, occupation, level and pattern of expenditure, purpose of visit and demographic characteristics such as age, based on the field survey which was undertaken in 2002-03 *(ibid).*

From the surveyed tourists it was found that around 88.49 per cent of the tourists of Arunachal Pradesh were between ages 20 to 50. The average age of domestic tourist was calculated at 35 years and that of foreign tourist was found to be 36 years. This fact emphasizes the need to organize more and more challenging, adventures and thrilling activities for the energetic and youthful tourist population. This would mean greater investment in activities like mountaineering, trekking, hiking, river rafting and allied sports along with fascinating cultural activities (Mitra, 2008).

Table 2
Tourist Arrivals in Arunachal Pradesh, 1999 to 2007

Year	*Foreign*	*Domestic*	*Total*
1999	86	2092	2178
2000	49	3126	3175
2001	78	4644	4722
2002	137	6878	7015
2003	404	3632	4036
2004	360	3242	3602
2005	364	3980	4344
2006	656	10854	11510
2007	1939	61100	63039

Source : Directorate of Tourism, Government of Arunachal Pradesh, 2008.

An attempt was also made to identify the different heads under which the tourist's expenditures were made especially in the selected tourist spots of Arunachal Pradesh. It was found that 39.92 per cent of the total expenditure was made on accommodation, followed by food and beverage (30.06%) and shopping (15.84%). Relatively less percentage (12.90) was spent on local transport which reflects the fact that tourists hired transport from outside the State since the local transport system was not much developed and relatively more costly. This is supported by the fact that around 77.87 per cent of the surveyed tourists was of the opinion that there is a need to improve the mode of transportation for developing tourism in Arunachal Pradesh (Mitra, 2008).

The propensity to enjoy natural beauty was highly pronounced in case of both domestic and foreign tourists. As high as 75.72 per cent of the surveyed tourists came to Arunachal Pradesh with a view to enjoy natural beauty and recreation. While some (15.15%) came to know more about the people and their culture yet enjoyment of natural beauty was also high on their agenda. Only 7.10 per cent came for educational and other purposes. The operational significance is that greater emphasis should be laid upon the creation and motivation of the tourism product to suit the needs and tastes of those tourists whose purpose of visit is recreation and enjoying natural beauty but not at the expenses of other purposes of tourist visit.

Furthermore, it was revealed that viewing natural beauty was a satisfying experience and most of the respondents (98.11%) wanted to return to Arunachal Pradesh provided transportation facilities and institutional facilities were improved. At the same time a high proportion of respondents (98.75%) informed that they would talk to their friends and relatives about their experience in Arunachal Pradesh and presumably advice a visit to these places. This was also supported by the fact that the recommendations of friends and relatives have induced 79.4 per cent of the tourists to visit the State as against the other factors such as publicity in newspapers, TV, Internet, etc.

These factors demonstrate the existence of a large market, particularly for ecotourism in the State and also strengthen the case for further expansion and development.

SECTION - IV

Policy Implications and Conclusion

On the basis of thrust areas of tourism the following policies as well as action plan may be suggested for maintaining sustainable tourism in Arunachal Pradesh.

1. A tourism master plan and identification of more circuits may be prepared. The circuits should be developed in terms of two primary categories. The first category circuits should cover some of the locally important attractions. The second category circuits should cover those attractions which have more local importance and which can be linked to tourist centres of North-Eastern region. Detailed circuit routes and location specific recommendations should be drawn with a phased approach. Commercial viability and competitive advantage of each route should be found out.
2. Public-private partnership should be treated as an essential ingredient of the policy for the development of tourism in

Arunachal Pradesh. The Government can build up the infrastructural facilities for tourism like, helipads, short landing run-ups for small aircrafts, tourist lodges and huts, etc. The private sector is best suited for the management and delivering of services. The tourist lodges are few in numbers and also scattered in different parts of the State. Hence, it is proposed to construct tourist lodges in the remaining Eleventh Five Year Plan in the selected places like Itanagar, Ziro, Malinithan, Sela Pass, Tipi, Yingkiong, Pasighat, Tuting, Anini, Daporijo, Hayuliang, etc.

3. The Government should also encourage adventure tourism by building necessary infrastructure for angling, river rafting, winter sports, etc. The angling and river rafting can be developed in West Kameng, Lower Subansiri, West Siang and East Siang districts of Arunachal Pradesh. The winter sports can be developed in Tawang, West Kameng and Upper Siang districts.
4. The participation of local people should be encouraged. The local management and skills must be built so that local people can maintain their culture and also improve sites. For example, the tourist destination will be developed in consonance with the local communities. It may be possible to provide a unique experience to tourists by building low cost infrastructure in the villages adjoining district headquarters by using local materials and local design inputs. This will create employment opportunity.
5. Relaxation and simplification of entry formalities can lead to more tourist inflow throughout the year in the State. This is expected to generate sufficient economic benefits to the local people and much needed revenue to the State Exchequer.

Conclusion

It is evident that Arunachal Pradesh is blessed with abundant resources for the development of ecotourism but the State has not been successful in attracting sufficient number of tourists. This is mainly because of various challenges and constraints which hinder the growth of its tourism sector. However, there is good prospect for the development of tourism in the State if the infrastructural facilities and institutional mechanisms are improved. The study shows that sustainable policies and guidelines for tourism could make Arunachal Pradesh one of the most frequently visited tourist States in the entire north-east India. This could provide a very significant and much needed revenue and employment source for Arunachal Pradesh in future. At the same time, the development of ecotourism to the full extent can help this ecologically fragile State to conserve and maintain its rich biodiversity while deriving economic opportunities. However, the tourism development of the State must be integrated with that of the North Eastern Region.

REFERENCES

Boo, E. (1990), *'Ecotourism : The Potential and Pitfalls'*, World Wildlife Fund.

Chirgwin, S. and K. Hughes (1997), 'Ecotourism: the Participants' Perceptions,' *The Journal of Tourism Studies,* Vol. 5, No. 2, pp. 2-7.

Data Bank of North - East India, 2003.

Mitra, A. (1998), 'Tourism Development in Hilly Regions of North-East India – A Study in Arunachal Pradesh.,' in Roy, K. C. and C.A. Tisdell (eds.), *Tourism in India,* Nova Science Publishers, New York, pp. 175-86.

Mitra, A. *et al.* (2003), *Environment and Nature-Based Tourism – An Endeavour at Sustainability*, Kanishka Publishers, New Delhi.

Mitra, A. (2008), Tourism Development, Chapter 18, in: *State Development Report of Arunachal Pradesh (Draft),* Planning Commission, Government of India.

Western, D. (1993), Defining Ecotourism. In K. Lindberg and D. E. Hawkins (Eds.), *Ecotourism: A Guide for Planners and Managers* (pp. 7-11). North Bennington, VT: The Ecotourism Society.

Whelan, T. (1991), *Nature Tourism: Managing for the Environment*, Island Press, New York.

Wight, P. A. (1993), 'Sustainable Ecotourism: Balancing Economic, Environment and Social Goals within an Ethical Framework,' *The Journal of Tourism Studies*, Vol. 4, No. 2, pp. 54-66.

8

Emerging Issues in Tribal Communities of Tripura : An Overview

Kashinath Jena and Rajesh Chatterjee

Over the last twenty to twenty-five years, the international tribal communities have been incessantly trying to draw the attention of the world's leading power blocks to save them from perennial miseries. Currently there are about 300 millions of tribal and indigenous people living in over 70 countries. They have come together to seek help from the UN to put an end to their poverty as well as to social discrimination against them. In response, the UN has taken some decisive steps. Among them is a series of programmes under the 'Declaration of the International Decade of the World's Indigenous People's, aimed at strengthening international cooperation on redressal of crises in the areas of human rights, environment, development, education and health.'

Long before this international effort, India had already made attempts to improve the condition of its tribal populations. Consisting of 461 groups (according to the people of India Project), they constitute 8.8 per cent of the total population of the country, making for a total tribal population of 83,580,634 in the 2001 census. Among them about 80 per cent live in the 'central belt', extending from Gujarat and Rajasthan in the West, and across the state of Maharashtra, Madhya Pradesh,

Chhattisgarh, Bihar, Jharkhand and Orissa to West Bengal and Tripura in the east. Most of the remaining 20 per cent live in NE states and in the UTs. A few of them live in the southern states. Since the inception of 1st Five Year Plan, the Indian government has formulated a series of development policies pertaining to the welfare of tribes.

After implementation of ten five-year plans, the scheme under the tribal development programmes have ranged from infrastructure building to empowerment, from collective welfare to family and beneficiary oriented development schemes, and from solitary area development to integrated area development. Though the thrust areas have undergone changes from one plan to another, some of the important issues like providing food security and nutrition, improving health services and checking morbidity, and education have been given priority during the all planning periods.

We now live in an era of globalization. The 'New World Order' has made the LPG model of development almost irreversible with no escape for any country or region at least in the present context. Globalization is a buzzword in the World, making people to think in new ways and work on new methods. World has become a global village in the sense that whatever happens in a village is easily known all over the World. Globalization means many things to many people. India is part and parcel of this Globalization process. India has the capacity to convert negative characteristics into positive force. This has been proved by extra-ordinary growth path India has entered into since the economic reforms were implemented in the country.

India is home to a tribal population of about 70 million, distributed over 500 communities, the size on which varies from 31persons to 7 million. Tribe-inhabited areas were not high on income generation until the arrival of the market economy and the advanced technology needed to exploit these regions, which contain about 70 per cent of India's mineral resources. The entry of the technology and the agents of the modern market economy interfered with the tribal way of life and made it degenerated. Almost a century ago, the tribal populations of central India witnessed the penetration of global capitalists and colonialists. British rulers suppressed many tribal movements - both violent and peaceful ways. Tribal lands were alienated *vis-à-vis* the capitalist economy despite several protective measures for the tribal land and its resources in post-independent India. The North East comprising several tribal states did not face the problem of land alienation, since most non-tribals are mostly concentrated in the urban areas, controlling trade and business. Still, the urge for greater freedom and control has endangered a number of political autonomy movements in the region.

There is now a growing awareness throughout the world about the role of women in economic development. In India too, many attempts have been made for highlighting and recognising the contribution of women to the economy of the country.

Women's studies and Tribal studies have been identified as important areas of research in the social sciences by the Indian Council of Social Science Research (ICCR). Indeed, tribe-specific and gender-specific studies are as important as region specific and area specific studies if we look at the problems from the angle of human development. This is particularly true of the North-Eastern Region where one must make a distinction between an area and development of its disadvantaged people.

The tribals of Tripura are endowed with values and sentiments which give them an identity, solidarity and commitment. According to 2001 census 993426 of the total tribal population 967997 tribal people live in rural areas of Tripura. That is, 97.44 per cent of the total tribal population of the state live in rural areas and only 2.56 per cent live in urban areas (see Table 1).

The study of tribal development is essentially an exercise in comprehending and combating with the problem of inequality. The tribal as a disadvantaged social group suffer from many crippling problems that retard their development keeping them relatively backward and marginalised in a growing economy. Tribal economy of Tripura, although characterised by its relative backwardness is undergoing some changes. Tribal people have been coming out of their traditional *jhum* economy to participate in a number of works which they did not do before. Keeping these facts in mind, an attempt has been made to study the different aspects of status of rural women in the tribal society of Tripura.

Status of women is affected by certain macro-forces as economic development, political participation, and ideological overtones. There have been infinite variations of the status of women, differing according to the cultural milieu, family structures, caste, class, property rights, etc. It is also shaped by the norms and values. Society lies down with regard to women's behaviour.

Women play a pivotal role in local agriculture. They attend to various field operations like transplanting of paddy, weeding of crops, *jhuming*, scaring away birds, sowing of seeds, and harvesting, etc. In the families of small and marginal farmers the women are involved in all stages of agriculture except ploughing. It is beyond any doubt that women have been making significant contribution to real income and welfare of their families almost everywhere at the cost of their labour in household activities.

Table 1
Distribution of Rural-Urban Tribal Population in Tripura as per 1951, 1961, 1971, 1981, 1991 and 2001 Census Records

Year	*Total Population*	*Rural Population*	*Urban Population*	*% of Rural to Total*	*% of Urban to Total*
1951	2,37,953	2,36,436	1,517	99.36	0.64
1961	3,60,070	3,56,372	3,698	98.97	1.03
1971	4,50,544	4,45,059	5,485	98.78	1.22
1981	5,83,920	5,76,252	7,668	98.68	1.32
1991	8,53,345	8,39,264	14,081	98.35	1.65
2001	9,93,426	9,67,997	25,429	97.44	2.56

Source: Various Census Report (1951, 1961, 1971, 1981, 1991, 2001).

Tribal people usually reside in hilly and rural areas. A few tribal people are living in the urban areas. It appears from Table 1 that the percentage of urban tribal population is microscopic although it has been increasing slowly. According to 2001 Census only 2.56 per cent of tribal people are living in the urban areas and the rest are in the rural. This makes a great comparison between tribal women and non-tribal women in many different ways.

A serious weakness of the traditional tribal society is the denial of opportunity to the women to take part in the decision making process at the village and community levels. This is, however, changing with the passing of time. Now, even tribal women who are educated are coming forward in every field to take part in different activities in many tribal areas.

It goes without saying that the best way of understanding the status of rural tribal women is to examine the nature and extent of its socio-economic participation along with education.

Tribes of Tripura

Speaking about the hill people, particularly the Tripuris, the Political Agent wrote in 1873: "The people were very simple, truthful, and honest until corrupted by the evil influence arising from closer intercourse with the inhabitants of the plains, and also by bad government, whereby they were left at the mercy of grasping subordinates. Every advantage was taken of their ignorance and credulity, till meet deceit with its own weapons" (Hunter, pp. 438). According to the 1961 census of India, the following Nineteen Scheduled Tribes reside in Tripura:

1. Bhil 2. Bhatia 3. Chaimal 4. Chakma 5. Garo 6. Halam 7. Jamatia 8. Khasi 9. Kuki 10. Lepcha 11. Lushai 12. Mog 13. Munda 14. Noatia 15. Orang 16. Reang 17. Santal 18. Tripuri 19. Uchoi

An interesting point to be noted here is that out of the total nineteen listed scheduled tribes of Tripura only eight tribes, Chaimal, Halam, Jamatia, Kuki, Noatia, Reang, Tripuri and Uchoi are the local tribes of Tripura. Other tribes like Bhil, Munda, Orang and Santal have come from central India groups of their respective stocks; Bhutias and Lepchas have hailed from the northern frontier tribes (Bhutan, Sikkim and north Bengal); Garo, Khasi, and Lushai are said to be from the neighbouring state of Meghalaya; and the Chakmas and the Mogs have come from Chittagong hill tracts and the Arakans.

It is evident from the given table that Tripuris constitute the largest tribal group followed by the Reangs in Tripura. According to the 2001 census, out of the total tribal population of 993426 persons, the populations of these two tribal groups in Tripura constitute 54.47 per cent and 16.62 per cent respectively.

This is to further mention that the census has identified some unspecified tribal groups with a population of 7098 persons as per the 2001 census.

Material and Method

Study has been made to find out the status of tribals especially the women in the context of globalisation by adopting the following field methods for survey:

1. Focus Group Discussion
2. PRA Method
3. Semi Structured Interview (SSI)

Tribal Women of Tripura

Among the tribal people of Tripura *jhuming* is still an important source of living and the tribal women constitute a significant part of this subsistence mode of production. Apart from the field work, they involve in different activities like gathering forest products, fuel collection, fishing, carding cotton, spinning yarn, weaving cloth, making basket and brewing rice-beer and liquor, etc. But these role performances of women in the subsistence activities are ignored and over looked by the Census estimation.

It is beyond any doubt that women have been making 'non-visible' contribution to welfare of their families almost everywhere at the cost of their labour in household activities. In tribal communities women devote longer hours of work compared to their men. In many cases *jhum* cultivation is entirely left to women. Tribal women are participating in all operations except in ploughing. A significant proportion of rural tribal women are working as agricultural labourers and only very few women are engaged in other than agricultural employment.

The position of women in tribal societies can be analysed by describing their condition or state, social standing in the family and community. A commonly held view among social scientists is that women in tribal societies enjoy a higher status than their non-tribal counterparts or even their men-folk mainly because of the leading role they play in their economy.

The status of any woman in general is largely associated with the family she hails from. Status of tribal women is neither so free nor so conservative. It is neither so extremely orthodox nor rigid like the Muslim type. Their status is quite flexible and simple. The women are not allowed to take an active participation in any religious ceremonies except in some few rites in very few religious ceremonies like the *randak mwtai*. The predominance of customary laws has debarred the tribal women to participate in religious ceremonies in few rites. However, in tribal society a girl child is not considered so much unwanted or inauspicious or liability as in many non-tribal societies.

In the tribal society *jhum* is not simply an economy but also a culture which help the growth of lots of traditional institutions and customary practices. Women are the main participants in this system and play a significant role.

The position in respect of indicators of social status like right to own or control land, involvement in different agricultural fields, house work, decision making, literacy rate, prevalence of bride-price, male-female wage rate which have been tested through household schedules in this surveyed village may unfold the real picture.

In tribal societies, the system of marriage can be seen in four types. They are: marriage by negotiation, marriage by service, exchange marriage, and marriage by elopement. Earlier, the most common practice happened to be marriage by service which is known as *chamari kamani*. In this system of marriage, the girl's status is placed at top position because a man usually requires to live in his in-law's house according to the customary practices.

The fast growing social evil which is widely prevailing now in the tribal society is the dowry system. It is actually influenced from the non-tribal societies where a girl is asked or demanded or even forced to give the dowry in huge sum. It is a curse in the society in the life of women as a whole.

Along with the exogenous forces, indigenous factors are also changing tribal society constantly. For example, tribal groups are changing their marriage system, occupation, place and type of residence, family bonds, community organisations, etc. There is a secular trend of change in the taste and preference of the tribes. In Tripura's tribal societies, spinning lost its importance. This deprived many tribal women of their work opportunity.

Rural tribal women are now working in many fields. They actively participate in self-help group organisations to earn an income and develop themselves. Many rural tribal women are involving in politics, even in some rural villages women are elected as the chairman or member of the Village Council. This is really a changing pattern in the status of rural tribal villages of Tripura.

Many rural women have been participating even in trade and commerce, petty business and so many business transactions which show a sign of improvement in the lives of tribal women of Tripura.

The Changing Scenario

Agriculture is still the predominant activity for the tribal women of Tripura. Of the existing tribal female workers of Tripura, there has been a sharp fall in the share of the cultivators between the periods of 1961 and 1991. The available data on tribal female participation rate in agriculture indicates a sharply rising proportion of agricultural labourers over the period. In 1961, it was only 2.81 per cent but if we seen in 1991, it has increased to 36.65 per cent. The increasing proportion of agricultural labourers among the tribal women workers in Tripura may be linked to the large-scale land alienation in tribal areas.

The household industry workers among the tribal women have been declining over the decades. It is a fact that the tribal household industry has been dying out under the impact of market forces, changing taste and preferences of the people and of course, increasing price of yarns. In 1961, it was 10.96 per cent female workers involved in household industry, but it has declined to 0.52 per cent in 1991, according to the Census records.

In tribal villages it is observed that one person is engaged in more than one occupation. Usually one form of activity is not sufficient to guarantee the survival but a combination of several is required. For example, *jhumming* and wage labour, or settled cultivation and wage labour, etc. are combined.

Exhibit-I
Types of Work done by Men and Women

Work done exclusively By men	*Work done exclusively By women*	*Work done by both Men and women*
1. Contract agricultural labour	1. Collecting fuel	1. Wet cultivation
2. Making and repairing Agricultural implements	2. Taking care of children	2. *Jhum* cultivation
3. Mat-making	3. Kitchen garden	3. Ravi cropping
4. Carpentry	4. Gathering forest products	4. Share cropping
5. Saw-work	5. Rice beer brewing and liquor making	5. Agricultural/wage labour
6. House-building	6. Cloth-making	6. Exchange labour
7. Working as drivers and assistant	7. Husking	7. Pasturing/ Fodder collection
8. Sub-contractor	8. Sewing	8. Collection of fuel
9. *Kabiraji* practice		9. Fishing
10. Business		10. Carrying products to the market
		11. Selling products in the Market
		12. Private tuition
		13. Cutting Bamboo for sale
		14. Basket weaving
		15. Selling milk
		16. Milking cow
		17. Extracting latex from market
		18. Pettty Garden
		19. Service
		20. *Agarbadi* stick making

Women are no longer tied up to their traditional activities only; they are found involved even in politics, seminars, meetings, etc. The village where this study was conducted is under the chairmanship of a female person. Further, there are three female members in the village council organisation. The women were also found playing an important role in the Self Help Groups (SHGs) organisation which has helped them to communicate with the modern world.

Literacy also influences the pattern of socio-economic participation as it enables the workers to move from the primary sector to the secondary sector and ultimately to tertiary sectors of the economy. In tribal villages it is observed that women's participation in socio-economic activities is not positively correlated with literacy because the main avenue of employment is unskilled labour in agriculture.

The fact reveals that the increasing access to education makes women's participation in economic activities, especially in agriculture, lower. It is true that in the villages under study the education system is neglected. There is no high school in the village and for this students are compelled to move to other places where higher education facilities are available. No regular class, lack of teacher, etc. are the other reasons as observed under study. Therefore, due to all these reasons, the rate of illiteracy among women workers is high and the female enrolment is less in higher classes.

There was a time when *jhuming* was universally practised in Tripura. But today this practice is declining. It is being replaced by settled cultivation. It is observed that in tribal village land is the principal source of livelihood for majority of the tribal people in the surveyed households. Although they are involved in different economic activities/works, yet they are very poor socially and economically. But it is interesting that among the tribal communities women's economic participation has not changed to any perceptible degree. Their income from different sources is quite observable. It is observed that during the field survey some women of the surveyed household earned greater income than the respective male members in the family. To a certain extent it can be stated that the status of women in the tribal society is relatively higher than non-tribal women due to the economic role they play in the family. Their earning by hard toil in the field or in any other works gives them a relatively higher status. But will this status continue in the context of globalisation?

REFERENCES

Bardhan, P. K. (1984), *Political Economy of India's Development*. New Delhi: Allied Publishers.

Rath, G.C. (2007), *Tribal Development of India: The Contemporary Debate*. New Delhi: Sage Publication

Majumder, D. N. and Madan, T.N. (2004), *An Introduction to Social Anthropology*, Mayoor Paperbacks, Noida.

Ross, M.G. (1967), *Community Organisation*, Harper and Row Publishers, New York.

Midgley, J. (1986), *Community Participation, Social Development and the State*, (London:Methuen).

Inbanathan, (1991): Profile and Participation of Women ZP and Mandal Member, *Journal of Rural Development*,Vol. 10(6).

Jain , L.C., (1994): "Panchayat: Women will win", *Kurukshetra,* June.

Jain, Devaki, (1992): *Women: New Vision of Leadership*, A presentation at Global forum, Dublin, July 9-12. http;//tripura.nic.in

GOI, (2000): *Women in India: Women in Partnership with Men*, (Social Development and Women's Programme Division), Chart by the Planning Commission.

Bose, Ashish, Singha. U.P., Tyagi. R.P. (1990): *Demography of Tribal Development*, Delhi, B.R. Publishing Corporation.

Das Gupta, Malbika (1993): *Status of tribal women in Tripura*, New Delhi, Vikas Publishing House Pvt. Ltd.

1. Khubchandani, Lachman, M. (1992): *Tribal identity: A language and communication perspective*, New Delhi, Indus publishing Company.
2. http;//tripurainfo.nic.in

III

Managing Development

9

Managing Natural Resources by Traditional Communities : The Case of Apatani Tribe for Sustainable Development in Arunachal Pradesh, North East India

Mihin Dollo and Prasanna K. Samal

Introduction

Contemporary interest in the indigenous knowledge systems across the globe has brought new opportunities to explore concepts, contexts and ethical use of such knowledge in national and international policy research. It is important to consult local knowledge to understand wilderness ecosystems and it functioning (Warren and Rajasekaran, 1993). Contemporary approaches regarding complex ecosystem management of any kind tend to look to conventional scientific processes of inquiry to answer questions about how nature works (Hudson, 1979). However, science is limited when it begins to address dynamic ecosystems, changing with natural resource tapping by the communities and other ecological interactions (Crowfoot and Wondelleck, 1990; Dollo *et. al.*, 2005). Because of the subtle and complex nature of normal ecological interrelationships and the compound random variables that influence any of them over time, contemporary scientific approaches by their design are limited and deficient in their ability to quantify these interactions. It needs to employ traditional ecological knowledge that gives insight into the realm beyond the confines of the scientific approach (Parker, 2000).

India is a land of diversity, varied cultural and ecological landscapes being embedded in rich traditional wisdom (Mishra, 1998). Over 450 tribal communities are distributed throughout the country, forming about 8.8 per cent of India's total population. These communities have been caught up in the process of modernisation, and much of their traditional rural-based empirical knowledge base developed over a long period through trial and error is getting depleted very rapidly (Ramakrishnan, 1998). Both biophysical and socio-economic factors were found to underlie these changes. Further, there are rapid changes in the belief systems. The breakdown of traditional beliefs and associated taboos, which underpin traditional natural resources management practices were found to be the greatest threat to the sustainability of these practices (Sarfo-Mensah and Oduro, 2007). However, a few traditional societies, including tribals, living in the forested uplands, have so far been able to conserve their traditional wisdom in the face of the onslaught of the modernisation process (Regenvanu, 1999), though they are also facing the transition and challenges.

After 2,000 years of almost universal belief in scientific progress, we are now seeing the price of this progress. The natural environment is being destroyed by the contradiction between technical and social advancement. We risk planetary destruction through the use of new technologies by countries that are philosophically or technically incapable of handling them (WCED, 1987). Populations are mushrooming, state agencies and free market players are becoming interdependent, and science and technologies are taking giant strides. The challenge is great, and conflicts are many. One of the great challenges of the 21st century is the task of protection of minority cultures against the powerful forces of standardisation and integration (MDGR, 2007). These forces - economic, linguistic, and technological - tend to dilute, homogenise and regulate cultures throughout the modern world. The preservation of cultural diversity is no less than biological diversity, which is crucial for the future of humankind (Nabhan, 1997; Apte, 2006).

A number of intergovernmental organisations and agencies are now taking steps to address issues relating to the recognition and the protection of the knowledge and innovations derived from traditional knowledge systems and traditional knowledge (Warren and Rajasekaran, 1993). The United Nations Food and Agriculture Organisation (FAO) is addressing this issue through Commission on Genetic Resources for Food and Agriculture which is negotiating the Revision of the International Undertaking on Plant Genetic Resources. The Convention on Biological Diversity (CBD) is addressing the issue through the Open-ended *Ad hoc* Intersessional Working Group on Article 8(j) and related Provisions (CBD, 2000). The World Intellectual Property Organisation (WIPO) is addressing this through the Intergovernmental Committee on Intellectual Property and Genetic Resources, Traditional Knowledge and Folklore. The World Trade Organisation (WTO) could address this issue through the Agreement on Trade Related Aspects of Intellectual Property Rights (TRIPS) (Das, 1998).

There are gaps in existing legal and non-legal techniques and mechanisms with regard to the recognition and the protection of the knowledge and innovations derived from traditional knowledge systems (RAFI, 1997; Twarog and Kapoor, 2004). Now, considerable effort is focused on evaluating the potential of existing Intellectual Property Rights (IPR) regimes to provide protection for traditional knowledge systems and indigenous innovations (Florez, 1998; Singh, 1998; Crouch, 2006). Land use for agriculture, fisheries and forestry, which forms the basis for the sustainable livelihood of traditional societies, is often based on traditional knowledge and technology, developed in a given ecological, socio-economic and cultural setting (ICSU, 2002; Farooquee, 2007). Not only is this knowledge base being threatened now, but very often we have failed to provide an alternative viable technology as a replacement for what is being eroded (Gadgil and Berkes, 1991). The reasons for this are varied and complex. Yet, in the context of the sustainable management of land resources, there is an increasing realisation of the value of this rich heritage, and therefore a renewed interest in traditional knowledge and technology (Posey and Dutfield, 1996). It is in this context that this paper examines a variety of situations to trace the linkage between traditional ecological knowledge and natural resources management, which is crucial for the sustainable development of the Apatani community of Arunachal Pradesh, North East India as case study.

Study Area

North-East India comprises seven states, namely, Arunachal Pradesh, Assam, Maghalaya, Manipur, Mizoram, Nagaland and Tripura, which is known for high ethnic and biological diversity (Ramakrishnan, 1984), and is often referred to as "Biological Hotspot" (Rao 1999; Myers *et. al.* 2000). Presently, Sikkim has been included in North-East India for developmental reasons. Arunachal Pradesh has an area of 83,743 km^2 with an elevation ranging between 100-7090 m msl and population of 1091117. The Lower Subansiri district, in which the community studied is located, lies between 26° 55' to 28°21' N and 92° 40' to 94° 21' E.

Ziro is the home of the Apatani tribe whose unique land use pattern, resource management and culture of conservation have made them a focal point of attraction (Haimendrof 1962; Kumar and Ramakrishnan, 1990). It is the district headquarters of the Lower Subansiri. It has 35 villages, with a population of 24,650 and a density of 23 people per km^2. The decadal (1991-2001) growth rate of 8.62 is much lower than the state (26.21%). The valley has an area of more than 1058 km^2, of which 33 km^2 is cultivated land while the rest is under forest, plantations and settlement (http://lowersubansiri.nic.in /html/forestpractice. htm). The valley lies between Panior and Kamla (Kuru) river at an altitude that ranges from 1525 m msl in valley to 2900 m msl in hilltops (Figure 1). The region is bounded with the areas traditionally belonging to the neighbouring Nyishi tribe except south-eastern region which is bounded by Assam.

It has a humid subtropical to temperate types of climate with 235 cm of annual rainfall and a temperature ranging from 6.3 to 28.1°C and 1.9 to 18.4°C during summer and winter, respectively. The soils of the valley are humid black and reddish in colour, developed from genesis and schist overlaid on a wide area with older alluvial deposits. The top soils are sandy loam to clay loam in texture, soil pH ranges from 5.10 to 5.64, organic carbon from 1.25-2.87 per cent, available phosphorus from 19 to 32 $kgha^{-1}$ and exchangeable potassium from 300 to 365 gha^{-1}.

Table 1
Demographic Profile of Apatani Tribe in Arunachal Pradesh

Year	*Population*		*% to state*
	Apatani	*Arunachal Pradesh*	
1961	10,793	3,36,588	3.21
1971	12,888	4,68,511	2.75
1981	16,580	6,31,839	2.62
1991	22,526	8,64,558	2.61
2001	24,650	10,91,117	2.26

Source: Census reports.

People and their Culture

Apatanis originally belong to the Tibeto-Mongoloid stock (Haimendorf, 1962). They trace their descent from one legendary ancestor, Abotani. Apatanis have migrated to this magnificent Valley from northern areas beyond Kuru and Kime rivers. This is revealed from finding of three neolithic celts at Parsiparlo and Raga circle, and historical remains at Talle Valley by Archaeological Survey of India (1992). It is, therefore, apparent that they followed the path of Kuru (Kamla), Kime and Tsangpo rivers. They settled at Talle Valley for few decades and ultimately migrated to Ziro valley. Apatanis live in fairly large villages, which are compact and permanent, although during recent years they are dispersed to avoid damage by fire accidents. Housing patterns are long and made of bamboo and timber.

They believe in indigenous religion 'Donyi-poloism', and are patriarchal in social system. Earlier, they had prominent tattoo marks on the face, which, however, has been discouraged in recent past, and almost abolished now. The community is sub-divided into numerous clans but all the clans are believed to have descended from same ancestor. The clan is the main social unit, which acts in solidarity. Like many other tribes of Arunachal Pradesh, they are highly co-operative and mutually linked up by kinship, ritualistic and by friendship ties through *Binee Aajing*. The tribe practises clan exogamy and community endogamy, and believes in monogamy. The community has diverse types of ritual ceremonies and dances. Among them *Daminda* and *Pakhu-Ittu* are popular dances while *Dree, Yapung, Myoko* and *Murung* are major ritual ceremonies. *Myoko*, the most important festival is celebrated each year in the month of March in cycle manner by forming three groups, each comprising one or numerous villages. The festivals are celebrated mainly to ensure better crop harvest, protect grain from hailstone, insect, pest, disease and wild animals, and also for the well being of individuals or community as a whole. There is Traditional Village Council to regulate the administration, which is of three tiers, according to age gradation, namely *Akha Buliyang, Yapha Buliyang* and *Ajang Buliyang*. In each tier of council, one or two persons represent from each clan. *Akha Buliyang* hold the highest authority on any decision making body while the role of *Yapha Buliyang* is mediator and interpreter in nature and *Ajang Buliyang* acts as messenger. The position of *Buliyang* is hereditary or selected through democratic means. They are arbiters of tribal law and upholders of tribal justice. However, the individual *Buliyang* are primarily the spokesman of their own clan or village.

Apatanis are agriculturists in nature and have immense traditional ecological knowledge on sustainable management of their limited resources. The exact date and time of origin and evolution of wet rice cultivation is still untraceable but through mythology, it is believed that it might have been started at *Pega-Sarang* (name of place). Apatani oral narratives suggest that *Hinkun Yari* carrying rice crops from mythological place called *Hinkun Lembyan* met *Ato Pussan* and *Ayo Tane* at *Miido Pyagan*. There, she offered varieties of rice seeds to *Ato Pussan* and *Ayo Tane* for cultivation and till now, through several generations, the crops are successfully cultivated. Once upon a time, Apatani Valley was believed to be having sporadic mountains, hills and marshy land. It was the sincere and hard work of their ancestors that made it suitable for wet rice cultivation.

The Apatani farmers practise rice-cum-fish cultivation with finger millet on the bund (risers) over an area of 3297 ha, while

1003 ha is under rain-fed upland farming. The wet rice fields are irrigated through traditionally well-managed canal systems. It is managed by diverting numerous streams originated in the forest into single canal and through canal each agriculture field is connected with bamboo or pinewood pipe. Socio-economy of the community is mainly based upon agriculture, fishery and bamboo resources, though majority of its land area is under primary and well managed secondary forests, which more appropriately can be termed as sacred groves. The blue pine and bamboo plantations on the fringes of a wide mosaic of wet rice fields surrounded by thickly forested mountains on all sides form a picturesque landscape. Though Apatanis are famed for their agricultural practices, high rice yields and forest and bamboo plantations, quantification of this land and plantation based economy have received little attention. Besides agriculture, they rear Mithun (*Bos forntalis)*, cattle, pig and poultry.

Forest Resources and Management

Forests are important repositories of bio-resource and play a key role in safeguarding the natural, climatic and cultural processes on which life depends (Herrmann, 2006). Forest ecosystems are also home to numerous traditional societies and represent a vital part in their daily life (Adamowicz *et. al.*, 1998). However, population growth and poverty have in many places led to the over-exploitation and destruction of bio-resource in forest areas. The estimated net annual loss in global forest area in the 1990s was 9.4 million ha (FAO, 2001). In view of the continuing loss and fragmentation of the world's forests, and the declaration about forests and biodiversity made during the 1992 Earth Summit in Rio de Janeiro, resource managers are looking for an enabling environment and the removal of disincentives that hinder sustainable forest management in several parts of the world. It is in this context that both ecological and the cultural significance of forests and contribution of culture in biodiversity need to be analysed (Dasmann, 1991; Bharuch, 1999).

Species diversity in the forest is profoundly influenced by cultural belief and traditional management (Laird, 1999). Traditional societies around the world have developed a sophisticated understanding of their biophysical environment.

Their practices and knowledge are grounded in ethical, spiritual and cultural values that significantly contribute to conservation, and in some cases enhancing, local biodiversity (Posey, 1985; Gagdil *et. al.*, 1993). The importance of ritual and belief system as a resource to the global community and their role in protection were highlighted in the Brundtland Report - *Our Common Future* (WCED, 1987) and the Convention of Biological Diversity (UNEP, 1992). Recently, anthropologists concerned with conservation have studied indigenous cultures, searching for knowledge and norms on which to premise ecologically sustainable relationships between people and the natural world (Nabhan, 1997; Kimmerer, 2002; Laird, 2002). Gadgil and Berkes (1991) reviewed numerous traditional resource management practices and systems that sustain biodiversity and ecosystems and build social capital. Traditional knowledge in the form of beliefs and rituals can be an information base for a society, facilitating communication and decision making, and serving as a foundation for local institutions (Warren and Rajasekaran, 1993). There are many cases showing that indigenous peoples have norms and TEK that conserve and enhance tropical forests or other natural resources (Chernala, 1989; Becker and Ostrom, 1995; Nabhan, 1997; Becker and Leon 2000), making it an important focus for conservation. During the past decade progress has been made in understanding the complementarity of cultural diversity and biodiversity, and there is an increasing appreciation of local perspectives and contributions in ecology and conservation (Berkes, 2004).

The Apatani community has distinct socio-cultural practices and rich traditional ecological knowledge of natural resources conservation and management acquired over centuries. Richness of forest is maintained through traditional ecological knowledge by means of selective harvesting, as well as by conserving the potential, ritualistic and socio-culturally valued species. They are settled cultivators and they do not practise shifting cultivation, which made them unique in sustainable management and conservation of forest around their settlements. The forests of Apatani Valley comprise four well-defined zones. In recent past these zones are slightly disturbed because less effort is being given on management and successional takeover of *P. wallichiana* forest. However, it is still

Table 2
Bamboo and Cane Resources being Used by Apatani Community

Species	*Local name*	*Availability*	*Uses*
Bamboo			
Phyllostachys bambusoides	*Bije*	Cultivated	Edible shoot, handicraft, fuelwood, fencing, timber
Dendrocalamus hamiltonii	*Yahi*	Cultivated	Edible shoot, fuel wood, timber
Chimonobambusa callosa	*Tabyo*	Natural	Handicraft, fuel wood, fencing, timber
Chimonobambusa sp.-1	*Beehe*	Natural	Fuelwood, fencing, timber
Cephallostachium capitatum	*Yabing*	Natural	Edible shoot, handicraft and medicine
Chimonobambusa sp.-2	*Rijang*	Natural	Handicraft, fencing and timber
Pleioblastus simoni	*Hebing*	Natural	Edible shoot, handicraft, fuelwood and fencing
Arundinaria sp.	*Tador*	Natural	Edible shoot, handicraft and fencing
Unidentified-1	*Tajor*	Natural	Ritualistic value
Schizostachyum sp.	*Taping*	Natural	Handicraft
Cane			
Calamus acanthospathus	*Tasser*	Natural/Cultis vated	Edible (Young apical portion), handicraft and fencing
Calamus khasianus	*Takhe*	Natural	Edible (fruit), handicraft and fencing
Calamus sp.	*Sarlang*	Natural	Handicraft and fencing
Plectocomia himalayana	*Tarpi*	Natural	Handicraft and fencing
Unidentified	*Rashing*	Natural	Fencing

Source: Field study.

maintained well, which is one of the sustainable systems of forest management and is better than government regulated protected forest. The first zone is just above the rainfed or wet rice cultivation, which is monoculture of bamboo or mixed vegetation with bamboo, pine and *Castanopsis* spp. The second zone consists of *P. wallichiana* plantations followed by third zone, which is a monoculture of *Castanopsis* spp., and or mixed vegetation of *Castanopsis* spp. with *Quercus* spp. etc. The fourth zone is the subtropical broad mixed vegetation that consists of *Quercus lanata, Castanopsis* spp. *etc.*, and temperate vegetation such as *Taxus wallichiana, Cephalotaxus* sp. etc. These forests are maintained not only to meet the fuelwood, fodder, food, and timber needs of the community but also for socio-cultural and ritualistic purposes. Though all forest types are important for the community, there is a high dependency on bamboo and *Castanopsis* dominated forests.

The common species thrive in these temperate forests are *Pinus wallichiana, Abies densa, Quercus* spp., *Michilus vilosa, Schima wallichii, Cinnamomum cecidephne, Prunus cornata, Taxus wallichiana, Cephalotaxus* sp., etc. in the top storey under which *Acer* spp., *Rhododendron, Pieris ovalifolia, Gaultheria, Rubus niveus, Prinsepia utilis, Indigofera* spp., and many species of ferns and orchids are also present. *P. wallichiana* is found in comparatively narrow belt of more or less pure crop of different age gradation at the lower slopes around the periphery of the cultivated land. The traditional afforestation practice is prevalent in Apatani plateau since time immemorial. It is believed amongst the Apatanis that afforestation technique such as *Sale/ Piisa/Sansu/Bije Gonnii* starts with their migration, which the younger generation inherited from their fore-fathers in the form of *Sadi-Sapa* (pine plantation) and *Bidu-Bikan* (Bamboo groves). Besides, pine tree and bamboo they also managed plant species like *Alnus nepalensis* (*Rime*), *Prunus* spp., *Pyrus* spp., etc. These species are traditionally managed by the Apatani for varieties of reasons; for example, the pine tree is managed not only for normal household requirements but also for ritual ceremonies like *Myoko/Murung/Subu*. In addition, resin is used in traditional medicine for joint pain and crack heel, and in olden days, the heart wood of pine tree (*Satti*) was used for lighting of the street in night by holding it on hand

and for ignition of fire wood by burning the split pieces at fire place. Roofing of the house is also made by *Santha* - splitting wood in fine thin layers.

To meet the fuelwood demand, lopping of pine tree branch is done after third year onwards of plantation and it is believed that proper lopping enhances growth and straightness of plants. Besides, *Castanopsis* spp., *Alnus nepalensis, Prunus* spp., *Pyrus* spp. *Quercus* spp. etc. are managed through cutting at the height of 3-8 m. This helps to promote large scale emergence of branches (coppices) and is believed that such type of management gives faster growth of plant in comparison to seedling plantation. Besides, the community have well-managed bamboo garden (*Bidu-Bikan*) in the periphery of settlement. This meets the demand of bamboo for house construction, fencing, handicrafts, rituals, etc. The bamboo species managed in the garden is *Phyllostachys bambusoides*, which is unique in Arunachal Pradesh. Besides, there are 9 bamboo and 5 cane species in natural stands, which are judiciously harvested for diverse uses (Table 2). Apatanis have huge knowledge of plant base ethnomedicine. Rawat and Choudhury (1998) have reported 65 species and Kala (2005) has recorded highest of 158 species. The community have initiated for conservation of 49 species (Dollo and Buker, 2007). They have also extracted nearly 34 species of wild edible plant from the natural forest, bamboo garden and cultivation fields (Table 3).

Table 3
Apatani Use of Wild Plant for Nutritional and Medicinal Purpose

Local (Scientific) name	*Fruit*	*Vegetable*	*Medicine*
1	*2*	*3*	*4*
Baching (*Myrica esculenta*)	√	√	√
Salyo (*Michelia champaca*)	√	√	√
Taro (*Ficus* sp.)	√		
Henchi (*Rubus ellipticus*)	√		
Samboo (*Prunus cerecedioes*)	√		
Piita (*Pyrus pashia*)	√		
Pecha (*Pyrus* sp.)	√		

1	*2*	*3*	*4*
Belling Komo (*Spondias axillaries*)	√		
Hari-ahi (*Actinidia callosa*)	√		
Yorkung (*Zanthoxylum armatum*)	√	√	√
Santhu Tero (*Litsea cubeba*)	√	√	√
Byako (*Solanum indicum*)	√	√	√
Thamo (*Rhus chinesis*)	√		
Lukhu (*Fagopyrium* sp.)		√	
Mapi (*Plantago major*)		√	√
Poto (*Clerodendrum glandulosum*)		√	√
Harro (*Solanum nigrum)*		√	
Hiika (*Diplangium esculentum*)		√	
Rharee (*Piper brachystachyum*)		√	√
Hailyang-hamang (*Crassocephalum crepidiodes*)		√	√
Yokho (*Spilanthes paniculata*)		√	√
Kochi-hamang (*Sonchus brachyotus*)		√	√
Ricco (*Dioscorea antidysentrica*)			√
Yabing (*Cephallostachium capitatum*)		√	√
Kaletolyo (*Acorus calamus*)			√
Kukulyu (*Artimesia indica*)			√
Lobe-tare (*Berberis wallichiana*)			√
Pasho (*Ageratum conyzoides*)			√
Sia (*Houtuynia cordata*)		√	√
Glangkhako (*Centalla asiatica*)		√	
Oihek (*Pouzolzia* sp.)		√	
Tashe (*Wallichia densiflora*)*		√	
Tache (*Cyathea gigantia*)*		√	
Tabe (*Angiopteris evecta*)*		√	

* Starch rich solid food is extracted from stem and processed before use.

Source : Computed on the basis of data collected from the filed.

It has been clearly observed in the Apatani plateau that the region has more intact forest cover compared to other neighbouring communities. The Apatanis have devised unique customary norms and guidelines, for example, *Kera Dapo, Yasoo Dapo, Moree Dapo,* etc. to conserve biodiversity. The *Dapo* traditionally used to penalize a person or a group of persons for violating traditional customary norms adopted orally through Traditional Village Council (*Bulyang*). A cross mark of bamboo and wooden pole is erected in the entry point of forest footpath, which indicates that the forest is well protected under the Apatani's traditional *Dapo* norms and guidelines. The practices are given more emphasis in modern time by using traditional symbol or modern means by erection of notice boards with description of the nature and gravity of penalty. For example, *Kera Dapo* is a means to protect socio-culturally valued *Castanopsis* spp. and *Yasoo Dapo* for canes.

As in the other parts of the globe, sacred groves are common in the Apatani valley, which directly or indirectly contribute significantly to biodiversity conservation, and sometimes act as depository of seeds for regeneration. The concept of the sacred groves is interwoven with indigenous religious and belief systems of Apatani community. Locally sacred grove is called as *Rantee,* which has diverse plants, and animals in large forest patch. Every village in Apatani valley has a sacred grove, for example Tajang *Rantee* and Bamin *Rantee* of Tajang and Bamin-Michi villages respectively. This kind of biodiversity conservation may be used as management tool for bio-resources or may be used to stabilize the declining of threatened species.

Traditional Management of Land Resource

Available case studies highlight, for example, that there is a complex relationship between human population and landuse practices (Lambin *et. al.,* 2001). Therefore, in-depth understanding of traditional landuse classification and management practices is utmost important to know the sustainable extraction of natural resources. In this context, Apatanis have classified their landuse in a systematic manner, which helps in efficient management and sustainable extraction of natural resources (Farooquee *et. al.,* 2007). The Apatani system of landuse management is organized and regulated by traditional cultural institutions. This may be the main reason for peace and harmony within the community. The landuse management is based on a traditional land regulation system, in which land is owned by an individual, clan or village through inheritance or by purchase. The land of the Apatani villages is classified into 10 major categories (Kala *et. al.*, 2008), which are as follows:

(i) *Ude Nechang* (residential land);

(ii) *Neshu Nechang* (grainary land);

(iii) *Sima-Liko* (burial land);

(iv) *Polang* (grazing land);

(v) *Morey* (forestland);

(vi) *Balu* (kitchen garden);

(vii) *Jebi Aji* (wet-rice cultivation land);

(viii) *Yorlu* (rain-fed cultivation land);

(ix) *Pirro* (land for traditional salt making); and

(x) *Uhi-Miko* (religious land).

Each village also has one or two sacred groves (*Rantee*) from which extraction of natural resources is prohibited. Indigenous land use classification was evolved out of centuries old experimentation on resource management and their effective utilizations. Categorization of lands by upland farming community of Apatani was largely based on their perception of most appropriate and sustainable use of their limited land resources. It has been well classified and regulated under the traditional customary norms. The major indicators of traditional classification of lands are available today in the forms of widely known landuse practices having ecological significance, such as forest, sacred groves, agricultural, grassland, etc.

Water Resources and Traditional Management

The Apatani system of irrigation is very old. The practice has evolved and perfected through community involvement and equitable sharing of water resources. In this system, water is tapped near the forest in the foothills of the valley and is channelled through major canals on either side of the valley to supply the agricultural land. The water is distributed via numerous small canals so that every plot of land is well supplied with irrigated water for rice cultivation and presently for fish culture. This also ensures that any surplus water is drained back to the main canal without the loss of any organic matter or soil.

Terraces made along the gradient are connected using bamboo pipes of small circumference (10–15 cm) at the higher elevations where water intake is lower. In the lower valley where the volume of water is greater, pine pipes of larger circumference (15-25 cm) are used. These pipes are made from pine trunks split vertically, hollowed out and then the two parts put back together. Water from the bamboo and pine pipes is not allowed to cascade from one plot to another; bamboo barriers are fixed on the upper elevations where the volume of water is smaller, with pine blocks at lower elevations where the volume of water is greater. Further, to contain losses of organic matter or fish from the plots, bamboo traps or straw bedding have been introduced into all plots. In addition, the outflow pipes are placed 5–8 inches above the surface of the lower plots so that water from lower plots cannot flow back to the upper plots. The dimensions of the dykes or *bunds* change from higher elevations towards the valley floor. At higher elevations, the plots are wider, whereas at lower levels the bunds are narrower.

To curtail soil erosion from the main canal, bio-fencing measures such as planting with *Phragmites* sp., *Ligustrum* sp., etc. have been carried out and wooden barriers of *Pinus wallichiana* A. B. Jacks, *Castanopsis* spp. or bamboo species have been installed to limit the flow of water. Weeding of *Houttuynia cordata* Thunb. is not done, as it is considered good for soil binding and stabilization of the bunds. Bamboo is also used to support the wider bunds. The bunds are repaired every year before rice planting. Ploughing is not done in the rice plots so as to avoid soil loss, but spades may be used to till the land before irrigation.

The Apatani community has evolved diverse traditional management tactics. For example, they have an informal organisation called *Bogo*, which is seen as the most important group as there are limited water sources for irrigation in the Apatani valley and good water management is essential for efficient production in the rice-fish system. These irrigation systems are managed by the traditional farmers' group led by *Bogo Ahtoh*. The *Bogo Ahtoh* is mainly headed by a male member as it requires heavy work. The post of *Bogo Ahtoh* can be held for 1-3 years and he is selected from among the members within the group. The number of households which form a *Bogo* can range between as low as three and as high as 600 households depending on the size of the village and length of irrigation canal. The main task of the organisation is construction and maintenance of the water supply system and regulation of the efficient sharing of water among the members of the group. The vision of this group is reflected in the management and sharing of water in the community, which recognises that water is the common concern, which binds the group. The farmers know that traditional practices are very important for maintaining sustainable production systems and that farmers' associations are the foundations of these practices. Apatani farmers recognise the importance of organisations and their participation in strengthening agroecosystem management and preserving the technical ecological knowledge from eroding away quickly. There are also 7 more informal traditional organisations to manage diverse natural resource that are described in Table 4.

Since water is most important for rice cultivation, the entire community has a stake in it, and its equal distribution ensures collective survival and social cohesiveness within the community. The proper distribution of water is regulated by a few nominated members of the community who ensure its equitable distribution and are empowered to resolve any conflicts that arise. Each year, repairing of the canal is carried out by collective participation, whereby one person from each household provides his labour. Some villages within the community have a small grant for the upkeep and maintenance of the canals. Each plot owner is bound to provide equal supplies of water to the neighbouring plots and violation of such regulations is dealt with by the community institution called *Buliyang*. The division of labour is such that men repair the bunds and canals, whilst women manage the plantations and weeding through harvest. Harvesting is done jointly by both, with women cutting the spikes and men doing the threshing.

The canal draining the village wastewater carries organic material, particularly the biodegradable wastes from the

Table 4
Types and Working Nature of Traditional Farmer Groups of the Apatani Tribe

Local name of farmer groups	*Description*	*Group Manager*	*Task*
1	2	3	4
Bogo	A farmer group sharing the common water sources. The group manager leads all the activities. Posts can be held for 1-3 year(s) and are selected/ elected from within the group. Group size is between 3-600 households depending on village size.	*Bogo Ahtoh* (male)	Construction and maintenance of water supply system and regulation of the efficient sharing of water among the group
Aji Lenda	A group which has their fields in the same area. The group manager leads all the activities. Tenure is normally for one year only. Group size is 50-350 households.	*Lenda Kagenee* (male/female)	Construction and maintenance of foot-paths to allow access to and from fields.
Sulu-sikhii	A group, which has their fields in the same area. The group manager leads all the activities. Tenure is normally for one year only. Group size is 50-350 households.	*Sulu Kagenee* (male)	Construction and maintenance of fencing to protect the agricultural fields from domestic and wild animals.

Table 4 ***(contd. . . .)***

1	2	3	4
Tanser Patang	Groups organised during field preparation and weeding. Group size is 5-15 households.	*Patang Ahtoh* (female)	Field and nursery preparation, seed sowing, and weeding.
Konchi Patang	This group works in the morning between 5 am to 8 am. Group size is 5-10 households.	*Patang Ahtoh* (female)	Field preparation, transplantation and weeding.
Halying Patang	This group shares labour during seedling transplantation. Group size is 5-15 households.	*Patang Ahtoh* (female)	Transplantation of seedlings, particularly paddy and millet.
Enthee Patang	This group forms to share labour during crop harvesting. Group size is 8-12 households	*Patang Ahtoh* (male/female)	Harvesting and carrying of harvests.
Bijee Lenda	A group having bamboo garden at same locality. Here also group manager leads all the activities. Tenure is normally for one year only. Group size is 70-300 households.	*Lenda Kagenee* (male)	Construction and maintenance of foot-path, a way for carrying bamboo, timber and fuelwood.

Source: Dollo 2007

homesteads- comprising vegetable waste, poultry and piggery manure and is a good source of fertiliser. It is also connected to the irrigation canal, which further drains into the agricultural fields. In addition, the organic material (decomposed leave litters) leaching from the forest floor is collected in separate pipes connected to the main canal so that whenever the additional forest run-off reaches the canal, it goes on to the plots. Plots not connected to the main canal collect any organic material from the forest through the normal bamboo pipe connected to the plots above them. The extra organic material accumulating near the inlet pipe is spread by hand on other parts of the plot. The traditional perception is that the run-off from forest with trees such as *Ficus* spp. are more fertile compared to forest with *Quercus* spp., *Castanopsis* spp. etc. This traditional perception may be correlated with the decomposition of leaf litters; the litter of *Ficus* spp. decomposes faster than that of *Quercus* spp. and *Castanopsis* spp.

Traditional irrigation systems are now in a transitional period, mainly due to outside intervention. It has been quite evident that the traditional check dam and irrigation canal are slowly and steadily transformed by the use of concrete and iron materials from outside sources. This transition not only endangers Apatani's ecological knowledge but also risks the future survival of the fish population, as the concrete reduces the movement of fishes from down to upstream and it also lacks a breeding centre. In the traditional system there is enough space for breeding as the channels are made of wood and bamboo, which is not common in concrete construction. Though the Apatanis are believed to be a very conservative community, now some of the traditional irrigation management systems are on the verge of extinction due to the integration of non-viable outside technologies. It is common for the youth to leave the communities in search of jobs, which creates shortages of traditional labour. In addition, outsider labour forces are increasingly coming to the area for timber sawing, quarrying and collection of non-timber forest products. Due to socio-cultural, climatic and physiographic differences, these outside people have different management techniques which often dilute the Apatani traditional practices. There is no doubt that the Apatanis have to depend on outside labour force in the context of changing socio-economic life. But what is important is that they have realised the importance of preservation of their efficient yet delicate systems of eco-management. So, they are trying to cope with the emerging situation and to preserve their time-tested knowledge by documenting it for future generations.

Except for financial support, particularly for erosion control, fencing and drainage maintenance, the farmers do not receive or seek any technological interventions or other help from any outside agencies. Outside experts have highlighted the Apatani rice-fish culture system as one of the most efficient crop production systems, encouraging the Apatani farmers to continue their traditional practices. The ingenuity of the Apatani community is well reflected in its traditional water management systems and in the sharing of resources for optimum utilization. The traditional system of wet-rice cultivation, which is a purely organic farming system, is functional even today and is modified by the community as and when required. There is optimum utilization of available natural resources such as bamboo, cane, pine, *Phragmites* sp., *Ligustrum* sp. and *Castanopsis* sp. apart from checking soil erosion, conserve soil fertility and raise fish in an integrated manner along with the cultivation of the many available rice varieties (Dollo, 2008). Valuing of Apatani irrigation system may offer ample of strategies environmentally suitable in sustainable resources management and may be replicated in similar micro-ecological conditions.

Traditional Agriculture (*Jibe Aji*)

Apatanis are agriculturists in nature and have good numbers of traditional ecological knowledge on sustainable management of their limited resources. The exact date and time of origin and evolution of wet rice cultivation is still untraceable but through mythology, it is believed that it might have started at *Pega-Sarang*. Apatani oral narratives suggest that *Hinkun Yari* carrying rice crops from mythological place called *Hinkun Lembyan* met *Ato Pussan* and *Ayo Tane* at *Miido Pyagan*. There, she offered varieties of rice seeds to *Ato Pussan* and *Ayo Tane* for cultivation and till now, through several generations Apatanis have been practising it. (Pussang, 1999). However, the practice of Apatani cultivation was first discovered in 1890 by H.M. Crowe and he has expressed, "the sight is one I shall never forget, as all suddenly emerged on a magnificent plateau, some 10 miles in length laid out in highly cultivated and artificial irrigated terraces, well watered by the Kale river, a sluggish stream some 45-60 feet in breadth with low alluvial banks. The valley was dotted with isolated hillocks and low pine clad spurs ran here and there into the valley".

Apatani villages have a monthly calendar of agricultural activities for maintaining optimum agricultural productivity (Table 5). Rice is the main crop cultivated on the wet terrace land where natural and artificial water supply is available. The arable land of Apatani valley is enough and full of natural fertile soil, which result in yielding of good crop every year. They have also developed the channel for irrigation and watering the fields where natural water may not be available. The principal crops grown by the Apatanis are rice, millet and maize besides few vegetables like pumpkin, bottle gourd, cucumber, beans, potato, ginger and few other leafy vegetables. Except rice all others are cultivated on the rainfed field. There are 16 varieties of rice grown in the wet rice cultivation field. These rice varieties are

Table 5
Chronological Order of Agricultural Activities

S.N.	*Description of activity*	*Period*
1.	Maintenance of channel for raising fish	November
2.	Burning of crop residue (straw) and weeding	December
3.	Sowing of seeds in nursery bed	January
4.	Repairing of bund and putting of domestic waste	February
5.	Maintenance of irrigation canal	March
6.	Filed preparation, weeding and putting water followed by fish in the field	April
7.	Seedling transplantation of paddy and millet (in bund)	April-June
8.	Weeding and first harvesting of fish	July-August
9.	Weeding and second harvesting of fish, draining out water from the field	September
10.	Harvesting	October

Source: Field Study.

classified according to the early and late harvesting varieties. The *Pyare* rice is an early variety which is harvested during the last part of July, and the *Emmo* variety is harvested in the month of October and the first part of November. The terrace rice field is also classified as *Jebi, Ditor/Pitang* and *Miding* based on the water requirement. *Jebi* (the marshy agricultural field that is normally kept without water during the fallow period) field is endowed with fine clay soil and water retention capacity is more than *Ditor/Pitang* (land under water for three months during fallow period otherwise there is high weed infestation) which is sandy in nature and water retention capacity is less. *Miding* (rice nursery), is the most fertile land with high water retention capacity. Millet is separately cultivated on the rainfed land called *Lyapyo* and on the bunds (*Agher*) of wet rice plots.

The Apatanis use local baskets of different sizes, such as *Giida Pata, Pai Pacha, Disinanii, Puhe Yagii, Paro Yagii, Pachu Yagii, Yopo* and *Liiha* as measuring cans at the time of bartering the surplus produce of crops. The pounded rice and millet are measured by *Kiiche* – bamboo made cup. Similarly, there is no unit to measure any type of land in order to know how many acres one possesses. All types of land are measured in term of yielding capacity of crops in case of agriculture plots. Extraction capacity of bamboo and pine are the measurement for bamboo and pine grooves. The price of all kinds of lands depends upon the location, size, distance, fertility of soil and yielding capacity of crop. The storage of agricultural produce mainly rice, maize and millet is done in a well designed traditional granary. These granaries are usually located away from the main settlement area of the village, and are located in a row for a clan. Like the houses, the granaries are also made up of bamboo and timber, and the storage of grains in the granary is usually 4-5 ft above the ground. Millet is stored in a box, where as rice is directly put in the granary.

Conclusion

Traditional communities, particularly tribals, living along the forest periphery have diverse beliefs and mechanism to manage the natural resources. Amongst the Apatanis, and indeed amongst other ethnic groups and tribes in North East India, local concepts and interpretations of nature link it inextricably with the social, material and spiritual life of the people. It is important to note that the Apatanis make a clear distinction between natural resource abundant forested area (*Morey*) and the settlement (*Lemba*). This distinction rather helps in regulating and sustainably extracting natural resources, which encompasses vegetation and all other natural resources including wild animals (*Acho-amio*), sand (*Sikee*) and stone (*Yalang*). The ingenuity of the Apatani community is well reflected in its traditional forest, land and water resources management systems and in the sharing of resources for optimum utilization of water, land and labour. The Apatanis are believed to have migrated from regions well provided with resources for wet-rice cultivation, and they have further modified their production systems to suit the prevailing local conditions and growing demands of the community. The traditional system of wet-rice cultivation, which is a purely organic farming system, is functional even today and is modified by the community as and when required. There is optimum utilization of available natural resources such as bamboo, cane, pine, *Phragmites* sp., *Ligustrum* sp. and *Castanopsis* sp. in order to check soil erosion, conserve soil fertility and raise fish in an integrated manner along with the cultivation of the many available rice varieties.

In the era of globalisation, traditional ecological knowledge of resource management provides a useful rationale for designing new technologies for sustainable management of valuable natural resources and efficient ways of resource conservation. The ecological traditional technologies of Apatani community, such as fish-cum-paddy cultivation, bamboo and forest resources management are found to be highly effective in resource conservation and management, which are unique in nature and economically and environmentally sustainable as well. A prerequisite, however, is proper documentation, appreciation and understanding of these ecological practices, which will help to harness the traditional knowledge to develop strategies for sustainable development of the fragile Himalayas. Although few of indigenous knowledge practices of Apatani community have been assessed by scientific world, nevertheless the need of the hour is proper documentation, analysis and in-depth understanding. Besides, sufficient credits need to be given to traditional ecological technologies and the practitioners. The integration of fish-cum-rice culture is unique in nature, and economically and environmentally sustainable. The choice of blending such knowledge with modern scientific technologies for the well being of the local people in particular and north eastern region in general, lies with the scientific communities, policy planners and administrators. However, undermining of the efficient traditional ecological knowledge of resources management and conservation will create disturbance in social as well as ecological setting.

Acknowledgements

The authors are thankful to Director, G.B. Pant Institute of Himalayan Environment and Development (GBPIHED), Almora for providing facilities, and all the respondents and villagers of Apatani plateau for providing information. Thanks are also due to members of Nature Care and Disaster Management Society, Ziro for their help during data collection.

REFERENCES

Adamowicz, W., T. Beckley and W. Phillips (1998). "In Search of Forest Resource Values on Indigenous peoples: Are Nonmarket Valuation Techniques Applicable?". *Society and Natural Resources* 11(1) : 51-66.

Apte, T. (2006). *A Simple Guide to Intellectual Property Rights, Biodiversity and Traditional Knowledge.* Kalpavriksh, GRAIN, and IIED, Pune/Delhi.

Becker, C. D. and R. Leon (2000). "Indigenous institutions and forest condition: lessons from the Yuracare" *in* C. Gibson, M. McKean, and E. Ostrom, editors. *People and forests: communities, institutions, and the governance.* MIT Press, Cambridge, Massachusetts, USA, pp. 163–191.

Berkes, F. (2004). "Rethinking community-based conservation". *Conservation Biology.* 18, 621–630.

Becker, C. Dustin, and E. Ostrom (1995). "Human ecology and resource sustainability: the importance of institutional diversity". *Annual Review of Ecology and Systematics* 26:113–133.

Bharuch, E. (1999). "Cultural and spiritual values related to the conservation of biodiversity in the sacred groves of the Western Ghats in Maharashtra". In: *Cultural and Spiritual Values of Biodiversity. A Complementary Contribution to the Global Biodiversity Assessment.* ed. D.A. Posey. Nairobi, Kenya: United Nations Environment Programme, pp. 382–385.

Chernala, J. M. (1989). "Managing rivers of hunger: the Tukano of Brazil". *Advances in Economic Botanty* 7 : 238–248.

Convention on Biological Diversity (2000). *Legal and other appropriate forms for protection for the knowledge, innovations and practices of indigenous and local communities embodying traditional lifestyles relevant for the conservation and sustainable use of biological diversity*, (UNEP/CBD/WG8J/1/2).

Crouch, Neil R. (2006). *Sustaining livelihoods—arresting the erosion of ethnobotanical knowledge and related plant resources*. SANBI Biodiversity Series 1.

Crowfoot, J. E. and J. M. Wondelleck (1990). *Environmental disputes: Community involvement in conflict resolution*. Washington D.C.: Island Press. 278 p.

Dasmann, Raymond F. (1991). "The Importance of Cultural and Biological Diversity". In: *Biodiversity: Culture, Conservation, and Ecodevelopment*, Margery L. Oldfield and Janis B. Alcorn, eds. pp. 7-15. Boulder: Westview Press.

Das, L. B. (1998). *An Introduction to the WTO Agreements*. Third World Network.

Dollo, Mihin (2007). "Traditional farmers groups supporting sustainable farming". *LEISA*. 23(1) : 22-24.

Dollo, Mihin (2008). "Apatani traditions revisited". *People in Conservation*. 1(3) : 10-11.

Dollo, M., Singh, K.I, Saha, D. Chaudhury, S. and R.C. Sundriyal (2005). "Livelihood and natural resources utilization pattern in an ethnically diverse area in Arunachal Pradesh". In: *Agroforestry in north east India: opportunities and challenges*. (eds. B.P. Bhatt and K.M. Bujarbaruah), ICAR Research Complex for NEH Region, Meghalaya, India. 55-70.

Dollo, Mihin and Rubu Buker (2007). "Ethno-medicinal knowledge of Apatani and its conservation initiatives in Arunachal Himalayas, North East India". In: *Regional seminar on Traditional Knowledge Systems and Community Development in North East India*. (ed. A. Arunachalam), 18-19th August, 2007. NERIST, Nirjuli, Arunachal Pradesh. pp.33-34.

FAO (2001). *State of the World's Forests 2001*. Food and Agriculture Organization of the United Nations, Rome Italy. [online] URL: *www.fao.org/ DOCREP/ 003/ Y0900E/ Y0900E00.HTM*.

Farooquee, N. A., M. Dollo and C.P. (2007). Kala. "Traditional Wisdom of Apatani Community in the management and sharing of natural resources in North Eastern India". In: Misra Kamal K. (ed.),

Traditional Knowledge in Contemporary Societies: Challenges and Opportunities, Pratibha Prakashan, Shakti Nagar, Delhi, India, pp. 110-126.

Florez, M. (1998). "Treatment of Biological and Cultural Diversity: Regulations, Domains, Actors and Dilemmas". In: *Beyond the Law* Vol. 6, Issues 18 and19: Biological and Cultural Diversity: Challenges and Proposals from Latin America.

Gadgil, M. and F. Berkes (1991). "Traditional resources management systems". *Resource Management and Optimization* 8(3-4):127–141.

Gagdil M., F. Berkes and C. Folke (1993). "Indigenous knowledge for biodiversity conservation". *AMBIO*. 22 : 151-156.

Haimendorf, C. V. F. (1962). *The Apatanis and their neighbours*, Oxford University Press, London.

Herrmann, Thora (2006). "Indigenous Knowledge and Management of *Araucaria Araucana* Forest in the Chilean Andes: Implications for Native Forest Conservation". *Biodiversity and Conservation*, 15(2) : 647-662.

Hudson, B. M. (1979). "Comparison of current planning theories: Counterparts and contradictions". *Journal of the American Planning Association*. 387-398.

ICSU (2002). *Science, Traditional Knowledge and Sustainable Development*. ICSU Series on Science for Sustainable Development No. 4. International Council for Science, Paris.

Kala, C. P., M. Dollo, N. A. Farooquee and D. Choudhury (2008). "Land-use management and wet-rice cultivation (*Jebi Aji*) by the Apatani people in Arunachal Pradesh, India: Traditional knowledge and practices". *Outlook on Agriculture*. 37(2) : 125–129.

Kimmerer, R.W. (2002). "Weaving traditional ecological knowledge into biological education: a call to action". *Bioscience* 52(5), pp. 432-438.

Kothari, Ashish (2007). *Traditional Knowledge and Sustainable Development*. International Institute for Sustainable Development, Manitoba, Canada. 11 pp. [online at http://www.iisd. org/pdf/2007/ igsd_traditional_knowledge.pdf].

Kumar A. and P. S. Ramakrishnan (1990). "Energy flow through an Apatani village ecosystem of Arunachal Pradesh in north-east India". *Human Ecology*, 18(3):315-336.

Laird, Sarah A. (2002). *Biodiversity and Traditional Knowledge*. WWF 2002.

Lambin, E.F., Turner II B.L., Geist H.J., Agbola S., Angelsen A., Bruce J.W., Coomes O., Dirzo R., Fischer G., Folke C., George P.S., Homewood K., Imbernon J., Leemans R., Li X., Moran E.F. Mortimore M., Ramakrishnan P.S., Richards J.F., Skånes H., Steffen W., Stone G.D., Svedin U., Veldkamp T., Vogel C., Xu J., (2001). "The Causes of Land-use and Land-cover Change: Moving Beyond the Myths". *Global Environmental Change*. 11(4):261–269.

MDGR (2007). *The Millennium Development Goals Report*. UNITED NATIONS, New York.

Mishra, A. S. (1998). "Traditional Knowledge and Management of Natural Resources". In: *The cultural dimension of ecology*, (Baidyanath Saraswati ed.) IGNCA and D. K. Printworld Pvt. Ltd., New Delhi. 185pp.

Myers, N., R. A. Mittermeier, C. G. Mittermeier, G. A. B. da Fronseca and J. Kent 2000. "Biodiversity hotspots for conservation priorities'. *Nature*, 403: 853-858.

Nabhan, G. P. (1997). *Cultures of habitat: on nature, culture, and story.* Counterpoint, Washington, D.C., USA.

Parker, Tom (2000). *Beyond Science*. USDA Forest Service Proceedings RMRS, Vol.-2: 304-305.

Posey, D.A. (1985). "Indigenous management of tropical forest ecosystems: the case of the Kayapo Indians of the Brazilian Amazon". *Agroforestry System* 3: 139-158.

Posey, D. and G. Dutfield (1996). *Beyond Intellectual Property: Towards Traditional Resource Rights for Indigenous Peoples and Local Communities*. International Development Research Centre, Ottawa.

Pussang, N. (1999). "Paddy-cum-fish culture at Ziro". *Popiriscope*, I(1):12-13.

RAFI (1997). *Conserving Indigenous Knowledge: Integrating Two System of Innovations*. The Rural Advancement Foundation International.

Ramakrishnan P. S. (1984). :Problems and prospects of conservation of north-eastern hill region of India". In Jain S.K. and Mehra K.L. (eds.), *Conservation of plant resources* Botanical Survey of India, Howrah, pp. 172-180.

Ramakrishnan, P. S. (1998). "Ecology and Traditional Wisdom". In: *The Cultural Dimension of Ecology*, (Baidyanath Saraswati ed.) IGNCA and D. K. Printworld Pvt. Ltd., New Delhi. 185 pp.

Rao R. R. (1999). "Biodiversity conservation in north-east India:

Priorities and strategies". In Sundriyal R.C., Shankar Uma and Upreti T.C. (eds.), *Perspectives for planning and development in north east India,* HIMAVIKAS Occasional Publication No. 11, GBPIHED, Almora, India, pp. 91-98.

Rawat, M. S. and S. Choudhury (1998). *Ethnomedicobotany of Arunachal Pradesh (Nishi and Apatani tribes).* New Delhi: Bishen Singh Mahendra Pal Singh

Regenvanu, R. (1999). "The Vanuatu Cultural Centres' efforts towards protecting indigenous knowledge and cultural expressions inn Vanuatu". In: *Symposium on the protection of traditional knowledge and expressions of indigenous cultures in the Pacific Islands*, Noumea, Feb. 1999.

Sarfo-Mensah, P. and W. Oduro (2007). *Traditional Natural Resources Management Practices and Biodiversity Conservation in Ghana: A Review of Local Concepts and Issues on Change and Sustainability.* [online at copy available at: http://ssrn.com].

Singh, G. N. (1998). Community intellectual rights protect indigenous knowledge. *Biotechnology and Development Monitor*, 36:11-12.

Twarog, S. and P. Kapoor (eds), (2004). *Protecting and Promoting Traditional Knowledge: Systems, National Experiences and International Dimensions.* United Nations Conference on Trade and Development. Document No, United Nations, Geneva. UNCTAD/DITC/TED/10.

UNEP (1992). Convention on Biological Diversity. UNEP Document no. NA. 92-7807. United Nations Environment Programme, Nairobi. http:// www.biodiv.org /convention/articles.asp.

Warren, D. M. and B. Rajasekaran (1993). "Putting local knowledge to good use". *International Agricultural Development* 13(4):8–10.

WCED (1987). *Our Common Future.* World Commission on Environment and Development. Oxford University Press.

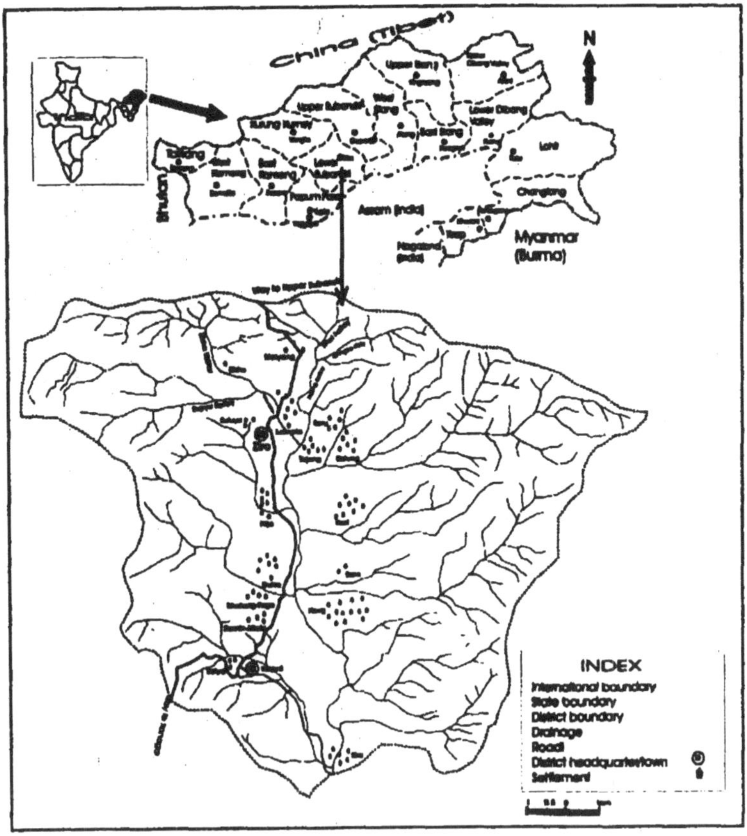

Fig. 1. Location map of Apatani Valley or Ziro Valley (cultivated and settlement land only).

10

Intervening Programmes and Schemes for Development in Mayurbhanj District of Orissa

P.K. Kar and S.K. Panda

Orissa is one of the most fascinating ethnographic states of India which has been the house of as many as sixty two different tribal groups. As per census 2001 the tribal population constitutes 22.13 per cent of the total population in the state. The mountainous and forest regions of Mayurbhanj, spreading over 4,500 sq. kms., have been ideally suited to the tribal habitations for centuries. According to census 2001, tribal population inhabiting Mayurbhanj district is recorded 12,86,938 persons. Mayurbhanj finds its place among the eight tribal dominated districts of Orissa with 45 ethnic communities, dominant among them being the Santals.

A major source of the intervention for tribal development has been the Scheduled Districts Act of 1874, Government of India Acts, 1919 and 1935 which have classified the hill areas as excluded and partially excluded areas. In these areas the provincial legislature had no jurisdiction. Later the Vth and VIth Schedules were included in the Constitution with provision for self-administration. The Constitution of India embodies about 20 articles for ameliorating the condition of the tribes through policies of positive discrimination and affirmative action. Article 14 bestows equal rights and opportunities to all, Article15 prohibits discrimination, Article 15(4) provides for special provisions for advancement of socially and educationally backward classes and Article 16(4), provides for reservation in appointments. Article 46 accords promotion of educational and economic interests of the weaker sections, particularly the STs, Article 275 (1) endows with grants-in-aid for raising the level of administration in the scheduled areas. Article 330, 332 and 335 stipulate reservation of seats for STs in the Lok Sabha and the State Legislative Assemblies. Article 342 provides for a Commission to investigate the condition of the socially and economically backward communities. The 73rd Amendment to the Constitution has provided 1/3 of the total seats reserved for tribals to tribal women. Apart from these provisions there are a number of legislations for mainstreaming their socio-cultural life and economic development.

Ever since the launching of the Five Year Plans, attempts have been made for developmental interventions. The First Five-Year Plan made special provisions for the development of the tribal population in our country. In the second plan 43 Special Multi-purpose Tribal Blocks were opened, in the fourth plan six pilot projects were opened with a separate Tribal Development Agency for each project. In the fifth plan Tribal Sub-Plan (TSP) was launched. The thrust areas in the sub-plan were promotion of development activities, protection of tribal interests through legal and administrative supports, allocation of funds and fixing accountability for non-disbursal of funds. In the sixth plan the fund allocation to the TSP was enhanced. The seventh plan emphasized on educational development in addition to the economic development. During the plan period two national level institutions namely Tribal Cooperative Marketing Development Federation (TRIFED) and National Scheduled Castes and Scheduled Tribes Finance and Development Commission (NSFDC) were set up. The eighth plan provided for bridging the gap between the development levels in the tribal and non-tribals. The tenth plan detailed about social and economic empowerment of the tribal people. It is to be mentioned that all the plans were not gender specific. The tenth plan continued with the policy of empowerment. The 73rd Constitutional Amendment has an edge over all the policies as it drew tribal women to the process of local governance. The tribals included in the study enjoy all the rights and have been included in most of the programmes initiated during the five-year plans.

However, a close look at the development programmes during different plan periods reveals that those have not been successful in ameliorating the socio-economic situation of the tribals. Some of the reasons are lack of education and awareness, stronghold of tradition, inadequacy of representation in government and non-government services, increased landlessness, steady decline in fund allocation since the late eighties, allocation mismatching the need of the target group, rigid attitude among the tribes to change their occupation, lack of risk taking capacity and asset accumulation culture, etc.

As regards other tribal development programmes operative in the state of Orissa, special programmes for the KBK (Kalahandi, Bolangir and Koraput) districts deserve mention. There are also several government schemes like PMRY, NREGS, REGP, RHA. In my Land - My Homestead campaign, ITDA, Indira Awas, IWDP, Jeebika, LAMPS, Mission Shakti Schemes which were introduced in tribal areas including in the district of Mayurbhanj. There are women's self help groups. More than fifty per cent of the people inhabiting the villages surveyed for the study have received government loans under the available loan schemes.

Employment Schemes

The PMRY programme is in progress since 1993 in the Mayurbhanj District and providing employment to the educated and unemployed youths through bank linkages. It gives special facilities to the STs and SCs, particularly to the women. Table 1 depicts the progress of the programme in the district during the financial years 2005-06, 2006-07 and 2007-08.

Table 1

P.M.R.Y. at a Glance in Mayurbhanj District (in Rs./mandays)

Sl. No.	*Year*	*Progress*		
		Number	*Investment in lakhs*	*Employment*
1.	2005-06	640	368.08	1040
2.	2006-07	585	342.54	1114
3.	2007-08	437	341.54	865

Source : DRDA, Mayurbhanj, Orissa.

The National Rural Employment Guarantee Scheme (Act) was implemented in 200 districts of the country including 150 districts which were earlier under National Food for Work Programme and Grameen Swarojgar Yojana. It was initiated in nineteen districts of the state which include the area of study. Four more districts were included in the scheme during the current year to provide livelihood to millions of people in rural households for a period 100 days annually or compensation instead otherwise. State governments, Panchayati Raj Institutions and non-government organizations have been involved in the implementation process. Classification has been made on skilled and non-skilled basis and minimum daily wage has been fixed accordingly. The basic objectives are to enhance livelihood security in rural areas, by providing at least 100 days of guaranteed wage employment in a financial year to every household whose adult members volunteer to do unskilled manual work. This work guarantee can serve other objectives: generating productive assets, protecting the environment, empowering rural women, reducing rural urban migration and fostering social equity. This is a centrally sponsored scheme on cost sharing basis between the centre and the states. Its basic implementation principle envisages collaborative partnership between the central government, the state government, the panchayat and the local community. Implementation of the scheme is at the village and block levels and coordination activities at the block and district levels. It envisages community participation through local beneficiary committees, self help groups and user groups. Panchayat and other grassroots structure are the principal authorities for planning and implementation. Key agencies involved in the process are the gram sabha, gram panchayat, intermediate panchayat at the block level and the district panchayat. A state level employment guarantee council coordinates and monitors the schemes which are operational. The state government formulates REGS and the rules and regulations for its implementation. The act confers entitlement on the people and puts their demand at centre stage. It requires a competent information sharing process so that the beneficiaries know their rights and obligations. Under the scheme all adult members of a household who register get job cards issued by the Gram panchayat. They apply for work and the GP provides work within fifteen days of receipt of the application. If not, they are entitled to unemployment allowance. Normally, work is provided within five kms but in case it is not available then they may be included in the inter gram panchayat works. The work entitlement of 100 days per year may be shared between different adult members of the same registered household. The act recognizes the right to work and in many ways an improvisation of earlier schemes involving enhanced allocation of funds.

After a year of its implementation allegations of exploitation, underpayment, irregularity, non issue of job cards, etc. have been reported though the state government has taken steps to ameliorate some of the grievances by depositing the wage in the bank account.

Table 2 explains the NREGS picture in the Mayurbhanj District in details. The progress is quite satisfactory as it has got the best District National Award in the year 2008-09. It shows that 374268 families have been registered under the scheme and 368017 job cards have been issued whereas 129019 families have been provided works and 6385 numbers of families have been provided 100 days works respectively.

In this district another programme named Rural Employment Guarantee Programme (REGP) aims to establish employment related industry in the village level by the financial assistance of the National Khadi Commission. It is found that 32 numbers of persons invested Rs. 31.22 lakhs and 221 nos. of persons got employment in the financial year of 2005-06, whereas in the financial year 2006-07, 24 persons invested Rs. 34.20 lakhs and 518 persons got employment. Table 3 shows the above achievements.

Table 2
NREGS at a Glance in Mayurbhanj District

Total No. of Registered Family	374268
Total No. of Issued of Job Cards	368017
Total No. of family provided works	129019
Total No. of Adults provided works	255770
Total No. of family provided 100 days works	6385

Total No. of working days	4242 (lakhs)
Total No. of Annual average working days provided to family	33%
Total available fund (in lakhs)	6076.89
Total utilities of fund (in lakhs)	4949.19
Total percentage of utilization of results	74%
Total No. of farm ponds for Irrigation purpose	3335
Total No. of savings Accounts for labour payment in banks and Post office	149131
Total No. of wage paid through banks and post office (in lakhs)	1729.90

Source: Same as Table 1.

Table 3

R.E.G.P. at a Glance in Mayurbhanj District (in Rs./mandays)

Sl. No.	*Year*	*Progress*		
		Number	*Investment in lakhs*	*Employment*
1.	2005-06	32	31.22	221
2.	2006-07	24	34.20	518

Source: Same as Table 1.

Table 4

M.S.M.E. in Mayurbhanj (in Rs./mandays)

Sl. No.	*Particulars*	*Progress*		
		Number	*Investment in lakhs*	*Employment*
(a)	2006-07			
	1. Industry already in operation	255	738.82	1218
	2. Primary registered industry	460	—	—
	3. Permanent registered industry	105	—	—
(b)	2007-08 (till date)	250	800	450
	1. Industry already in operation			
	2. Primary registered industry	460	—	—
	3. Permanent registered industry	105	—	—

Source : District Industrial Centre, Mayurbhanj.

In another programme named M.S.M.E., the main objective is to build minor industries, small scale industries and medium industrial centres by imparting technical training to the industrialists. Apart from this, a district industrial centre (DIC) disseminates information regarding the rules and regulations of the state government and the schemes particularly to the interested persons who want to undertake industrial activities. So ultimately it provides employment to the inhabitants of the district as shown in Table 4.

In Mayurbhanj District under the Scheme of Rastriya Sam Vikash Yojana (R.S.V.Y.) 473 schools at the cost of Rs.736 lakhs have been provided with toilets, water supply and hostels; Rs. 29.11 lakhs for sericulture development; Rs. 264 lakhs for construction of 113 Water Harvesting Structure (WHS) through soil conservation department; Rs. 50 lakhs to 100 households for dug wells; Rs. 4.21 lakhs for the construction of one Krishi Vigyan Kendra and poultry firm; Rs. 52.20 lakhs for cultivation of rubber plants and Rs. 17.07 lakhs for fisheries development. On the other hand, in backward areas under grants-in-aid fund scheme (BRGF), 127 concrete roads have been constructed at the cost of Rs. 317.50 lakhs, 112 Anganwadi Kendra buildings at the cost of Rs. 280 lakhs, 85 high schools at the cost of Rs. 212.50 lakhs, 6 hospitals at the cost of Rs. 30 lakhs, 16 residential high schools at the cost of Rs.240 lakhs.

Table 5
R.H.A. Scheme in Mayurbhanj District (in Rs./mandays)

Sl. No.	*Year*	*Progress*		
		Number	*Sanction in lakhs*	*Employee*
1.	2005-06	10	0.50	20
2.	2006-07	11	0.55	22

Source : Same as Table 4.

Under the scheme of RHA there are provisions for skilled artisans to get a maximum subsidy up to Rs. 5000 through the state directorate of handicrafts and district industrial centre. The sanctioned amounts given to the artisans in the year 2005-06 and 2006-07 have been shown in Table 5. On the scheme *my land – my homestead campaign* has been launched during the period from September, 2007 to October, 2007. The progress in Mayurbhanj district is shown in Table 6.

Table 6
My Land – My Homestead Scheme

Particulars	*No. of Beneficiaries*
Ceiling excluded land	2451
Distributed of lands for homestead	27037
Distributed lands for Agronomy	462
Distributed lands under Regulation – 2 – 1956	840
Bhu-sanskar law act – 23	517
Total	31,307

Source: Same as Table 1.

Table 7
Integrated Waste Land Development Programme Implemented by Soil Conservation Dept. under Watershed Project, Mayurbhanj

1.	Sanctioned Project	6
2.	No. of Blocks	9
3.	Project Period	2004-05 to 2008-09, 2005-06 to 2009-10
4.	Treatable area	11,000 Ha
5.	Total outlay	660.00 lakhs
6.	Up to date expenditure	189.89 lakhs
7.	Area treated	2922.18 Ha
8.	Total number of GP	13
9.	Total No. of village	87
10.	Total No. of Farm ponds	478
11.	Total No. of Gulli control structure	32
12.	Total area of land development	103.31 Ha
13.	Total No. of Run - off management structure	26
14.	Total area of plantation	62.11 Ha
15.	Total No. of Self Help Groups (SHG)	472
16.	Total amount of savings of SHG	43.38 lakhs
17.	No. of SHG to Bank linkage	142
18.	No. of user groups	233
19.	Total amount of watershed development fund	14.30 lakhs

Source: Soil Conservation Department, Baripada.

Table 7.1

Sl. No.		*No. of Assistance given to landless and marginal farmers*
1.	Poultry Sectors	30
2.	Fishery	61
3.	Sabai Grass	700
4.	Vegetable	1550
5.	Small entrepreneurship group	69
6.	Crop demonstration	213
7.	Horticulture plants distribution	2388

Source: Same as Table 7.

As another development intervention, the government has launched an ambitious scheme, Integrated Wasteland Development Project (IWDP), which seeks to develop wasteland, especially in non-forest areas for sustainable use. It is people's own programme which aims at giving them actual decision-making power in terms of project implementation and fund disbursement. The integrated wasteland developmental programme has been implemented since 1st April, 1995 on the basis of new guidelines for watershed development recommended by the Hanumantha Rao Committee, which envisages the bottom up approach whereby the Users Group themselves decide their work programme in the tribal zones in general. In the Mayurbhanj district 6 sanctioned projects (IWDP - II) have been in operation in 9 blocks for last 10 years. The details of the IWDP schemes are shown in Table 7 and Table 7.1.

Apart from the above, newly launched *Jeebika* project called *Watershed Plus* has been launched in the district of Mayurbhanj.

The Indian economy has been passing through liberalization on globalised norms since July 1991. The Indian Cooperative Movement is one of the biggest in the world, consisting of more than 488158 cooperatives (as per the report in the year 2000) with a membership of more than 207.577 million. The rural market becomes the main target market for cooperative business. The fields to be explored by cooperatives societies in the rural sectors are: economic deregulation, tax and tariff concession, trade liberalization, revitalisation of sick cooperative units and rural market exploration. In Mayurbhanj district, 52 LAMPCS – (Large Sized Agricultural Multi Purpose Cooperative Society) are in operation. This is shown in Table 8.

Table 8

Large Sized Agriculture Multi Purpose Co-operative Society

	Total Number	*No. of ST*
Total No. of LAMPCS	52	—
Total No. of Household (as per 1991 census)	285231	158774
Total No. of enrolment as on January 2009	267045	153052
Total issue of Kishan Credit Card (KCC)	138775	66580
Total No. of Credit linkage with LAMPCS	34188	13937
Total No. of defaulted members	12640	5730
Total loan outstanding	4779.96 lakhs	1968.09 lakhs

Source: District Co-operative Society, Mayurbhanj, Orissa).

Women Self Help Groups in Mayurbhanj District

Women represent half of the human resources in all societies. The strength of the nation lies in the strength of its people, especially the womenfolk. In this connection, self help groups of women are becoming one of the important means for the empowerment of poor women in almost all the developing countries including India. Orissa is no exception as regards the role played by women's collectivity, known by different names for empowerment of poor women. Self Help Groups or SHGs represent a unique approach to financial intermediation. Government of Orissa under the Department of Women and Child Development established Mission Shakti in 2002, an umbrella body for empowerment of women through formation and strengthening of Self Help Groups (SHGs). The total number of SHGs in Orissa is estimated to be around 3,00,000 with reported saving of Rs. 160.52 crores. On the other hand in Mayurbhanj District SHGs in 26 Blocks have been estimated 17048 with 199366 members. The total amount of money deposited by the SHGs in this district is Rs. 1387.37 lakhs. The detail information of the Mission Shakti is presented in Table 9.

Apart from this, different programmes have been operating through the District Social Welfare Office, namely National Old Age Pension Scheme, Madhubabu Pension Scheme, ICDS, KSY, National Family Assistance Scheme, MDM, Women and Child Welfare Programme, prevention of domestic violence, etc. successfully in the tribal zone. These are shown in Table 10.

Table 9
Details of WSHGS and Women's Empowerment in Mayurbhanj District

Sl. No.	*Information about SHG*	*Total Number/Total amounts*
1.	SHG in the District	17048 Nos.
2.	Members	199366 Nos.
3.	Savings amount	1387.37 (in lakhs)
4.	Bank linkage	5776.86 lakhs
5.	Loan amount	5776.86 lakhs
6.	SHG received revolving fund from WDCS	1505 Nos.
	SHG received total amount	Rs 752500.00
7.	SHG received revolving fund from DRDA in SGSY	1720 Nos.
8.	SHG received revolving fund from DRDA	3036 Nos.
9.	SHG trained in capacity building	5020 Nos.
10.	SHG trained in skilled up gradation	110 Nos
11.	SHG federations (Mahasangha)	411
12.	SHG covered Beema Yojana	3022

Source : District Social Welfare Office, Mayurbhanj.

Programmes Relating to Health Development

NRHM, AYUSH, ASHA, Water and Sanitation Mission are construed as the specific and comprehensive approaches for health development of the tribes. The tribals of Mayurbhanj have been immensely benefited by such schemes. Prior to the launching of the rural health mission there has been

Table 10
Programmes Operating through the District Welfare Office

Year	*Different Programme*	*No. of beneficiaries so far*
	National Old Age Pension Scheme	19532
1994	Integrated Child Development Scheme (ICDS)	307260
1995	Mid Day Meal (MDM)	336981
2005	Domestic Violence Act	61
2007-08	National Family Assistance Scheme	1253
2008	Madhubabu Pension Scheme	63084
	Kishori Shakti Yojana (KSY)	123600
	Women and Child Welfare Programme (ORPHAN AGE)	89

Source : Same as TableNo : 9.

infrastructure development by instituting public health centres and community health centres. These were staffed with ANMs, male health workers, lady health visitors, health assistants and doctors. But the health situation did not improve substantially due to the apathy of the service providers and recipients. In April, 2005, the Government of India has launched the National Rural Health Mission and Orissa being the high focus state all the villages of the state are included in the scheme. Its objectives are to reduce infant and maternal mortality rate; provide for universal access to integrated and comprehensive public health services, child health, water, sanitation and hygiene; and to strive for prevention and control of communicable and non communicable diseases including endemic diseases, population stabilization and gender and demographic balance. Further, the objectives are to revitalize local health traditions and mainstream Ayurvedic, Yoga, Unani, Siddha and Homeopathy system of health (AYUSH), and to promote a healthy life style. These objectives are to be achieved by capacity enhancement of panchayati raj institutions to own, control and manage public health services and by formation of village health plan by the village health plan committee of the panchayat. A untied fund has been created with the provision of depositing Rs.10,000 per year in a joint bank account of the ANM and Sarpanch. The account is operated by the ANM in consultation with the village health committee. The scheme provides for round the hour service through mainstreaming AYUSH human resource, preparation of district health plan by the district health mission and integrating vertical health and family welfare programmes at the national, state, block and district levels. This plan will continue up to 2012. The Accredited Social Health Activists (ASHA) are trained to serve as link between the health centres and the villages. They perform multiple advisory functions in the field of hygiene, sanitation, contraception, and immunization to provide primary health care for communicable diseases, and escort the patients to the medical centres.

Nevertheless, higher budgetary allocation does not automatically improve health service unless there is improved communication facility between the village and health centre and setting up of health centres as per the needs of the people rather than on political considerations. ASHA is similar to the voluntary health guide scheme introduced in 1977 which was defunct due to several reasons. As per the present training programme of the ASHA, a lot of time is consumed in training them in all facets of their responsibility with little time left for performance. Availing of the facilities provided under the scheme depends on the positive attitude of the people. In many cases there were complaints that the payment to the beneficiary is not handled properly. Such practices need to be discouraged. In the Mayurbhanj district 2986 ASHA employees are working to accelerate the NRHM programme. The progress and result of the NRHM is encouraging in the tribal zones of the district. A total of 5202 numbers of TB patients are being treated and 85 per cent of total patients have already recovered out of the disease. For malaria eradication programme, 410 numbers of ASHA employees have been trained. As a result, in the year 2006, a total of 17906 malaria positive patients had been identified whereas the numbers decreased in the year 2007 unexpectedly (14020 numbers).

The water and sanitation mission project has been in operation in the district since 2005. The main objectives of the project are to build home latrine and create consciousness among the public. Secondly, it aims at providing toilet in every school and Anganwadi Kendra for creating a habit with school children in connection with sanitation. Also it helps to decrease the water and sanitation related contaminated diseases and to check the infant and maternal mortality rates. Water and sanitation mission has played a major role providing 39 water supply projects in the rural areas and the beneficiaries are the inhabitants of 5668 villages in 241 Panchayats under 14 blocks of Baripada and Kaptipada sub-divisions. A total of 10328 tube wells are in operation providing safe drinking water. The water and sanitation project has also undertaken programmes as shown in Table 11.

Table 11
Water and Sanitation Mission Project

Programme	*Target*	*Achievement*
Home Latrine	464663	1,01,033
School Toilet	3585	1,146
Anganwadi Toilet	1698	1552

Source : ITDA, Baripada.

Development of Education among the Tribals in Mayurbhanj District

A major aim of developmental intervention, within the sub plans and outside, have always been the specific provision for educating the tribals, with residential schools, stipend, relaxation in age at entry in to higher educational institutions, free travel to appear in interview and write examinations. But these provisions have not motivated the tribals to educate themselves or their children. Language is the main problem for the new entrants. Non availability of teachers from among the particular tribal community is another hurdle. The rate of dropout is heavy. Whatever education they get in the primary school is soon forgotten and many lapse into illiteracy. To educate tribals some voluntary organisations have taken up literacy programmes under the National Literacy Mission, but the result is not very encouraging. The National Literacy Mission envisages a comprehensive programme for educating people within the age group of 15-35 years and achieving a sustainable threshold level of 75 per cent by the year 2007. This goal has to be achieved by imparting functional literacy to non literates in the said age group so that the group which is in the productive and reproductive periods of their life would be literate and get a chance to educate themselves if they have missed it during their childhood. The total literacy campaign aims at educating children in the age group of 9-14 years in areas covered by non formal education programme. The mission has both a quantitative and qualitative approach; the former aiming to impart functional literacy and the latter to enable them reading, writing and acquiring arithmetic skills. It also aims to educate the people about their environment, hygiene and health; to educate them to fight against discrimination, create an environment where the people themselves would demand information and knowledge, inculcate in them self confidence, fight oppression and to create awareness among parents to educate children. Very few in the area have utilised the opportunity to become literate. The values prescribed in the mission like social solidarity, collective action, entrepreneurship, confidence, etc. are in the village culture which could have been strengthened by further education. But due to the timing and economic reasons coupled with the value system of the tribals the response to the programmes is almost nil.

In Mayurbhanj district in Orissa DPEP project and Sarva Shikshya Abhiyan (SSA) project tell the success story which started in 2002-03 and 2003-04 respectively with the objective of universalising primary education in this district. The reports say that 3647 schools are embalmed and the percentage of total literacy rate of the district is 51.91 per cent whereas 35.42 per cent is for the tribals. Teachers and Shikshya Sahayak (SS) have been trained for pedagogical improvement. School improvement grant, teaching learning material and repair and maintenance grants are provided to Primary/Upper Primary Schools. Free text books are also distributed every year. Early Childhood Care and Education (ECCE) has been implemented through Anganwadi Centres. A total of 17 Kasturba Gandhi Balika Vidyalays (KGBV) have been established. Hostels have been opened in the existing upper primary schools in educationally backward blocks to retain dropout girls of class–VI to enable them to complete their studies up to class–VII. Education is implemented for mobilization of SC/ST community for their full participation in primary education. Management Information

System (MIS) is maintaining Computer Aided Education by providing computers to 50 schools through APTECH, EDUCOM and Azim Premji Foundation. Table 12 portrays the details of the status of primary education in the district.

Table 12
DPEP/SSA, Mayurbhanj

	Total Number	*No. of SC*	*No. of ST*
Total No. of Schools	3647	—	—
Total No. of child population (6-14 yrs)	232598 (Boys)	17830	151858
	215676 (Girls)	17111	137676
Total No. of enrolment (6-14 yrs)	215933 (Boys)	16511	138540
	199322 (Girls)	15771	124503
Total No. of out of school children (6-14 yrs)	8440 (Boys)	900	6118
	7970 (Girls)	713	6054
Dropout Rate	3.15		
% Total of literacy	51.91 65.76 (Male) 37.84 (Female)		
% Tribal literacy	35.42 49.59 (Male) 21.14 (Female)		
Total teachers position	9638 5803 (Tch) 3835 (SS)		
Total No. of Olchiki Schools	100		
Total No. of Olchiki Teachers	100		
Pupil Teacher Ratio (PTR)	39		

Sources : District Project Office, DPEP / SSA Mayurbhanj.

Some of the educated tribals of the district have entered state government services and other professions availing the reservation facilities. Reserved seats in the Lok Sabha, State Assembly and Panchyat Raj institutions have provided opportunity to represent the constituencies and further the interest of the tribals. Provision for reservation of 33 per cent of seats in the rural local government has benefited tribal men and women to represent the local government institutions at the panchayat and block levels.

Rather a quite interesting development in the study area is the inclusion of "OLCHIKI" script of the Santals at the primary school level mobilizing the tribal communities for their full participation in primary education. A total of 100 Olchiki Schools have been opened and Olchiki Text Books for class–I have been developed to introduce the mother tongue of SANTALI. However, two trends have been noticed in respect of incorporation of OLCHIKI at the school level. Whereas the old generation is in favour of spread of OLCHIKI, young generation appears to show interest in inclusion of the script gradually.

Impact of Development Interventions

1. Due to developmental interventions the tribals of Mayurbhanj are getting better life chances and life opportunities.
2. The socio-economic condition of the tribals of the district has improved a lot.
3. The water crises and sanitation related diseases decrease day by day.
4. The literacy rate improves due to the systematic educational policy.
5. Tribals are getting work regularly for their livelihood support.
6. The scope widens to develop and spread their languages.
7. The productivity increases due to irrigations facilities, watershed activities and introduction of new agricultural methods and techniques.
8. Decision making power is visible due to the operation of different government schemes.
9. Tribal women enjoy freedom due to the impact of Mission Shakti. They have also become economically empowered through WSHGs.
10. The standard of living and food culture have been immensely changed due to the impact of different developmental projects.

11. The rural marketing system obtains connectivity with the urban areas, resulting in the stability of financial status of the tribes.
12. Recognition of Forest Rights Act, 2006 provides the right of ownership access to the tribals to collect, use and dispose of minor forest produce.

Suggestions

1. Literacy programme should be taken up at a line suitable to the people with a missionary zeal involving local literate people.
2. Attention is required to be given to educate tribal women so that they can be aware of the health and hygiene and sensitise their family members as well as the villagers about nutrition, cleanliness, use of medicine, etc.
3. Community involvement should be encouraged to identify programmes for their local development.
4. Bank loan should be given to the married tribal couple, not exclusively to men.
5. Local markets need to be created to enhance their financial status.
6. Industrialization as well as displacement issue should be carried out by organizing peaceful meetings among the concerned villagers.
7. An exhaustive social impact assessment should be conducted before initiating a development project in the tribal areas
8. Irrigation facility with real and equal distribution of water should be maintained.
9. Proper training should be imparted for instant protection against natural disaster.
10. Last but not the least free insurance scheme should cover the poverty stricken tribal cultivators with immediate effect.

REFERENCES

Basu, D.D. 2002 : *Introduction to the Constitution of India*, Agra, Nagpur, New Delhi, Wadhwa and Company, Vol. 1, No. 1, 2002.

DRDA, 2008 : *Mayurgatha,* Vol. 1, No. 1, Mayurbhanj, DRDA, April 2008.

DRDA, 2008a : *Mayuri,* 3rd Edition, Mayurbhanj, DRDA, April, 2008.

GoO, 2005 : "District Statistical Hand Book", Mayurbhanj, Directorate of Economics and Statistics, Bhubaneswar.

GoO, 2007-08 : *Information Guard File,* District Social Welfare Office, Baripada, Mayurbhanj.

Hota, S.K. 2000 : "Cooperatives in Rural Economy", *Kurukshetra,* Vol. 48, No. 11.

Kar, P.K. 2001: "Social Transformation of the Tribes of Orissa" in *Backward Communities: Identity Development and Transformation,* Gyan, New Delhi.

Mishra, P.K. 2005 : "Mayurbhanj : A Socio Economic Profile", *Satabdi,* Baripada Municipality, Mayurbhanj.

Panda, S. 2007 : "Socio- Economic Profile and Development of Tribes in Orissa", *Kurukshetra,* Vol. 55, No. 10.

Rajora, Rajesh 1992: *Integrated Watershed Management,* Rawat Publications, Jaipur.

11

Fighting Drought in the Era of Globalisation : Programmes and Schemes in Anantapur District of Andhra Pradesh

Eswarappa Kasi

Prologue

The word 'development' has became a buzzword in majority of the welfare States of the world and more so especially in the contemporary era, wherein non-State actors are playing a crucial role in fulfilling the dreams and aspirations of the needy or oppressed. While discussing about the development, one must think, for whom the development we are all talking about? Or for what sake? Or why do we stress so much on it? Answers to these questions pave the way to address the term 'development' and its relevance in the present context. Here, I must refer Andrea Cornwell's observation of the term 'development': he says the term itself has become a 'modern shibboleth, an unavoidable password', which comes to be used 'to convey the idea that tomorrow things will be better, or more is necessarily better' (2007). It conveys us that there is no harm in expecting something better tomorrow. This hope leads us further to think and answer the questions which we raised earlier. Before going further to search for the answers, first let us discuss the word 'development' and its related terms here for our general usage of these terms.

For some, development is a word which means to enlarge the lives of the people and for others, the term refers to just a growth. If we see the disciplinary explanations, the term 'development' has different meanings and connotations. For sociologists the term development is just about improving the standards of living of the people. For economists, the term indicates the growth and its concomitant notions. For anthropologists, it is beyond both growth and standards of living. Further, it is made up of the everyday experiences of the needy and the efforts they put in differ from person to person, place to place, or region to region.

The discussion in this paper is based on the data gathered from official reports and records, Census records, published as well as unpublished research reports, papers, etc., with reference to India. Besides, it also draws its inferences from the studies made by the authors and other scholars in Andhra Pradesh, India. It also takes into account the studies made in other parts of South Asia.

For convenience of presentation the paper is organised into four sections: first section, introduces the links between Globalization and livelihoods of marginal and rural communities. The second section briefly explains the existing literature on development discourse and its analogy of intervention mechanisms catering to the needs of these communities. The third section gaudily explains the livelihood security and sustainability of resources. Finally, the last section sums up the discussion with relevant findings and broad conclusions of the paper.

I

Globalization *per se*

There are quite a number of studies, which highlight the impact of globalization on marginalized communities in Europe, America, Africa and Asia (Mills, 2008). There are also studies which have addressed the problems of the oppressed and socially excluded due to the relocation of development processes across the continents (Eswarappa, 2008). But there are a few studies available which have looked into the issues of the marginalised people/communities through anthropological lense. The present attempt is directed to fill that research gap while addressing the anthropological discourse on globalization and its impact on the marginalized communities.

Globalization *per se* has many connotations across the countries. There are quite a number of cases explaining the pros and cons of the globalization across the countries or continents. Globalization for me is a positive force which does not discriminate on the ground of sex or class. For instance, an illiterate can use the mobile phone to get his things done in the countryside and an IT graduate can transfer the money to his friends through internet banking system, and research scholars may send the messages or mails and chat with the professor sitting in USA or UK and can organize an international conference by calling for papers using Orkut network in the Google. There are many instances, which highlight the benefits of the globalization and it is even more helpful to educate youths who can use the networks well for their betterment. There is the other side of the globalization, where, in the name of development, depressed or marginal people's lands have been forcefully taken over by the project managers -be it a MNC or a government undertaking. We have noticed that farmers and labourers have agitated to get back their lands, for instance, Nano Project struggle at Singur, West Bengal. Issues relating to Special Economic Zones in Andhra Pradesh, Dams and Projects in Andhra Pradesh and Gujarat also point to such conflicts. Critics of globalization have argued that it accentuates inequality both within and between countries (cited in Mills, 2008).

Globalization represents a set of economic, political, social and cultural processes that operate simultaneously (cited in Mills, 2008). Further Mills (2008) defined globalization as four interrelated structural shifts that roughly occurred since the 1980s. These shifts are (i) internationalization of markets and declining importance of borders for economic transactions, (ii) tougher tax competition between countries, (iii) rising worldwide interconnectedness through new information and communication technologies, and (iv) the growing relevance and volatility of markets (Mills and Blossfeld, 2005). These changes have been clearly noticed in Indian scenario during the post globalization era of our society.

Globalisation can be defined simply as the accelerated movement of goods, services, capital, people and ideas across national borders. It is not an entirely new phenomenon since the internationalization of markets and cultures (*e.g.*, the spread of global religions) has been occurring for millennia, but the latest phase of globalisation is qualitatively distinct.

Smith (2001) identifies three main assumptions of past globalization discourses (Hofmeister and Bretenstein, 2008). The first assumption is that globalization is an inevitable process whereby free markets and western-style capitalism are unquestionably gaining in dominance and is argued to bring positive social change to all the people of the world (Mittleman, 1996 and 2000). Second, global inequalities are rising as a result of the processes of globalization that have been witnessed thus far, with a particular tension between 'the haves' largely in the northern hemisphere and 'the have nots' largely in the southern hemisphere (Faundez *et. al.,* 2000; Petras and Veltmeyer, 2001). Finally, the accelerated transnational flow of information, money, goods and people has been made possible by communication technology advances (Harvey, 1990) with profound effects.

'Globalization is not neutral, but neither is it exclusively the domain of the powerful' (Aronin, 2008). Further, Applebaum and Robinson (2005) suggest that globalization studies should take a mission of building 'bridges between the academic study of globalization and the policy makers, social justice activists, and advocacy movements that are directly engaged with the processes of globalization.

II

Development Interventions

The developmental debates are progressively attempting to look at the grassroots systems of ideas, knowledge and discourses which alter the main body of knowledge. Thus, there are many theories which discuss the idea of development and its discourse (see Eswarappa, 2009 : xxxix). As we know, the Development Dictionary, as explained by Andrea Cornwell, brought together critical genealogies of the key concepts of the age to write the obituary of development. It is a sign of how far, and how fast, things have changed that there is so little overlap between the words that feature there and here. But many of the entries in The Development Dictionary appear in today's development discourse in new guises: state as fragile states and good governance; environment as sustainability; planning (development institutions' preoccupation of that age) as harmonisation (their preoccupation in this one). Equality is as much of a concern as ever, but has come to be used in development more often with gender in front of it. Capacity building transforms helping into a technical fix, generating its own entourage of 'experts'. International NGOs have made much of a shift from needs to rights. And progress continues to be regularly invoked, even as the hopes once associated with it quietly slip away (Cornwell, 2007 : 473).

In this particular case, Gilbert Rist (2007:488) explains that the difficulty lies in the a priori positive meaning of the word 'development', which derives both from its supposedly 'natural' existence and from its inclusion in a cluster of unquestionable shared beliefs. This is why those who are ready to recognise that 'development' has not really kept its promises are also loath to discard the notion altogether. Failures, they would say, do not result from 'development' itself, but rather from erroneous interpretation or ill-considered implementation. Even in the most dramatic situations it is always possible to appeal to the presumed existence of a 'good development'. After all, God himself may not answer all our prayers or grant all our requests, but his righteousness remains beyond doubt. . . So, to formulate a proper, sociological, definition of 'development', one has to put aside its emotional and normative connotations and also to incorporate all the external characteristics – which anyone can observe – that are related to the subject matter. In other words, the definition of 'development' should not be based on what one thinks it is or what one wishes it to be, but on actual social practices and their consequences, *i.e.* things that anyone can identify. What needs to be highlighted is an historical process that concerns not only the countries of the 'South', or only operations conducted under the umbrella of 'development co-operation'. These arguments take us to local discourses on development, which are further segregated into developmental failures. Hence, an attempt is made here to represent the State response towards the drought mitigation in Andhra Pradesh.

Drought is a normal, recurrent feature of climate. It occurs in virtually all climatic zones, but its characteristics vary significantly from one region to another highlighting the need for specialized studies in the diverse eco zones. Drought is a temporary aberration; it differs from aridity, which is restricted to low rainfall regions and is a permanent feature of climate (World Bank, 2005:19). Drought is an insidious hazard of nature that is also relatively difficult to predict meteorologically. It originates from a deficiency of precipitation that persists long enough to produce a serious hydrologic imbalance. Drought should be considered relative to some long-term average condition of balance between precipitation and evapo-transpiration (*i.e.*, evaporation and transpiration) in a particular area. Drought differs in three essential characteristics: intensity, duration and spatial coverage. Intensity refers to the degree of the precipitation shortfall and/or the severity of impacts associated with the shortfalls (*ibid*: 20-21).

Intensity is generally measured by the departure of some climatic index from normal and is closely linked to the duration in the determination of impact. Impacts are, in turn, related to the timing (e.g., delays in the start of the rainy season, occurrence of rains in relation to growing stage of principal crop) and effectiveness of rainfall (e.g. number of rainfall events). Other climatic factors such as temperature, wind and humidity can significantly aggravate its severity. Droughts are categorized as meteorological, hydrological, agricultural and socio-economic phenomena (Nagarajan, 2003).

Agricultural drought links various characteristics of meteorological and hydrological droughts to agricultural impacts. It is related to precipitation shortages, differences between actual and potential evapo-transpiration, soil water deficits, etc. Plant water requirements depend on prevailing weather conditions, biological characteristics of the specific plant, its stage of growth, and the physical and geo-biological properties of the soil. Agricultural drought should be able to account for the variable susceptibility of crops during different stages of crop development, from emergence to maturity. Deficient topsoil moisture during planting may hinder germination, leading to low plant populations per hectare and a reduction of final yield (World Bank, 2005:22).

Socio-economic drought is associated with the supply of and demand for economic goods such as water, forage, foodgrains, fish, hydroelectric power, etc. Socio-economic drought occurs when the demand for an economic good exceeds supply as a result of a water-related shortfall in water supply (*ibid*: 22).

Drought Programmes

In order to address the problems of drought in Andhra Pradesh, the government has evolved certain strategies to minimize the risk and tried to support the affected people to certain extent. We present a succinct picture of the programmes which are undertaken by the government in Andhra Pradesh for our discussion.

(a) Risk Financing Programmes in Andhra Pradesh

(i) Crop Insurance: The National Agriculture Insurance Scheme (NAIS) has been implemented in Andhra Pradesh since 1999-2000. The schemes are a mix of voluntary and compulsory participation. They are voluntary at the State level in terms of specific areas and crops. Once the specific area-crop combinations have been notified, participation is compulsory for farmers in those areas cultivating the specific crops and taking agricultural loans. In the case of loanee farmers, the sum insured may be at least equal to the crop loan advanced. All farmers can insure to the value of the threshold yield of the insured crop.

Eighteen crops are currently insurable under NAIS during the Kharif season (e.g., rice, maize, sunflower, groundnut, sugarcane and cotton) and ten crops during the Rabi season (e.g., rice, maize, sunflower and groundnut). The standard area yield insurance scheme has recently been extended to farm income insurance and rainfall insurance.

The XI Finance Commission noted the need to strengthen the crop insurance scheme as a supplementary measure to what is done by the government for providing relief at the time of natural calamity.

(ii) Calamity Relief Fund (CRF): This fund was established separately for each State on the basis of recommendations of the IX Finance Commission and has since been approved for continuation by the X and XI Finance Commissions. This fund should be used for meeting the expenditure for providing immediate relief to the victims of cyclone, drought, earthquake, fire, flood and hailstorm. Table 1 describes the financial status of this fund over the last 5 years.

Table 1
Calamity Relief Fund for Andhra Pradesh, 2000 -2005, (Rs. lakhs)

Share of	*2000-01*	*2001-02*	*2002-03*	*2003-04*	*2004-05*	*Total*
Centre	14854	15597	16377	17196	18056	82080
State	4951	5199	5459	5732	6019	27360
Total	19806	20796	21836	22928	24074	109440

Source: World Bank, 2005.

(iii) National Calamity Contingency Fund (NCCF): This fund came into effect in 2000-01 and continued to be in operation till the end of financial year 2004-05. Natural calamities like cyclone, drought, earthquake, fire, flood and hailstorm considered to be of severe nature requiring expenditure by the State government in excess of the balance available in its own CRF qualify for relief assistance under NCCF scheme. The initial corpus of the National Fund is Rs. 500 crores provided by the Government of India. National Centre for Calamity Management (NCCM) is constituted by the Ministry of Home Affairs, Government of India, to monitor the occurrence of natural calamities relating to the above calamities on a regular basis and assess their impact on area and population. The assistance from NCCF is only for immediate relief and rehabilitation. Any reconstruction of assets or restoration of damages is financed through Plan funds. The unspent balance of NCCF at the end of the financial year 2004-05 becomes a resource for the next Plan of Central Government.

(b) Drought Proofing Programmes in Andhra Pradesh and in Anantapur District

(i) Drought Prone Areas Programme (DPAP). DPAP, a centrally sponsored scheme, in operation since 1973, aims at restoring ecological balance in the drought prone areas and mitigation of the adverse effects of drought on crops and livestock through integrated development of natural resources by adoption of appropriate technologies. However, the programme fell short of its initial objectives despite large expenditure.

DPAP is aimed at developing the drought prone area with an objective of drought proofing by taking up of soil-land moisture conservation, water harvesting structures, afforestation and horticulture programmes on a comprehensive micro-watershed basis. During 1994-95 the programme was implemented in 69 blocks of 8 districts. From 1995-96 the programme is extended further to 11 districts with 94 blocks. In Anantapur district it covers 16 blocks. So far, 3518 watersheds were taken up covering 110 blocks in 12 districts covering an area of 17.6 lakh hectares. Almost 30 per cent of the total watersheds in the country are located in Andhra Pradesh. A total sum of Rs. 507.57 crores has been spent towards implementation of the programme from 1995-96 to 2002-03. The expenditure for this programme is shared by the central and state governments in the ratio of 75:25.

(ii) Joint Forest Management/Community Forest Management: The Government of Andhra Pradesh adopted the Joint Forest Management Programme (JFM) in 1992 which envisages a strategy for production, improvement and development of forest with the involvement of local communities by forming them into Vana Samrakshana Samithis (VSS).

There are 7090 VSS actively involved in protection and development of forests. So far 8.71 lakh hectares have been treated out of 17.40 lakh hectares of forest area under VSS. The JFM Programme is being supported by the World Bank funded A.P. Community Forest Management Project, NABARD assisted RIDF schemes and Government of India funded Forest Development agencies.

(iii) Water Harvesting Structures : The Forest Department has taken up large-scale water conservation structures in forest areas under Neeru-Meeru (Water and You) Programme. The structures, such as continuous Contour Trenches, Check-dams, Rock-fill dams, Percolation tanks and sunken gully pits, etc., have been completed. So far, water storage capacity of 1566 lakh Cubic Meters has been created in forest areas incurring an amount of Rs. 309.72 crores in execution of the water conservation structures in forest areas.

(iv) Micro Irrigation Project: The State of Andhra Pradesh has been experiencing severe water stress due to continuous drought situation over the last 3 years. There is, therefore, an imperative need to promote judicious use of water, particularly

in-respect to agricultural activities. With this in view the Government has launched a massive Micro Irrigation Project in 2003-04 throughout the State, with special emphasis on water stress *mandals*. The project envisages installation of sprinklers, drip irrigation and rain guns to use the irrigation water available underground in the most efficient manner while improving productivity. The farmers would be given 50 per cent State Government subsidy on the unit cost.

(v) Andhra Pradesh Rural Livelihood Project (APRLP): The Andhra Pradesh Rural Livelihoods Project provides critical support to the on-going watershed movement in five drought prone districts in Andhra Pradesh. The mandate is to position livelihood concerns strategically in watersheds for the inclusion of women, the poor and the landless. The project advocates innovation, lesson learning, convergent actions and policy influence. APRLP invests in a new stream of approaches and ideas for bringing about a positive change in the well-being of the rural populace.

APRLP has initiated a paradigm shift in watershed development programme by adopting sustainable livelihoods approach. This site is to share the saga of promoting the poor and women into mainstream development through conscious policies, effective implementation and sustainable management. Moreover, this platform is to inform, educate and inspire all concerned stakeholders in the project.

The development of semi arid and rainfed drought prone areas is one of the priority areas of Government of Andhra Pradesh and it is also established that development of natural resources in these areas has led to sustainable rural livelihoods. Participation of the committee of resource poor and landless as primary stakeholders is precondition of sustainable rural livelihoods. Therefore, the Government of Andhra Pradesh has entered into an agreement with Department for International Development (DFID, UK), who shares this vision, for implementing AP Rural Livelihoods Project (APRLP) in Anantapur, Kurnool, Mahaboobnagar, Nalgonda and Prakasam districts. The APRLP facilitates the objective of people centred development and provides input to the ongoing watershed Programme of government including 500 new innovative watersheds, sustainable rural livelihood initiatives in 2000 ongoing watersheds, capacity building of various stakeholders, research and lesson learning for policy initiatives, and infrastructure support.

(vi) Watershed Development: National Bank for Agriculture and Rural Development (NABARD) finances a watershed development fund. Due to watershed development programme, the proportion of area under irrigation has increased by 19 to 129 per cent among all households. Total employment has risen up by 11 to 29 per cent. Yield rates have also shot up for irrigated as well as un-irrigated crops. Only 50 per cent of the watersheds studied are economically viable in terms of incremental returns. The equity effect is not clearly known, though the impact on rich and medium households possessing lands seems to be higher. Drinking water situation has improved substantially. Ground water levels also have improved to a limited extent. Migration of labour decreased during execution period. But in majority of cases, this is not sustained after the execution period. Household's preference for education increased and the role of women in financial matters has improved substantially.

(vii) Integrated Wastelands Development Programme (IWDP) : Rapid depletion of green cover and vast stretches of marginal lands lying fallow, found to be causing enormous ecological imbalance that had a multiplier effect. Productivity is also negligent on account of soil erosion and marginalization of lands. To arrest this, massive integrated wasteland development project was undertaken during 1991 with 100 per cent central assistance. The project has been implemented in 17 districts in Andhra Pradesh; in total 38 projects have covered an area of 3,62,985 ha with an outlay of Rs. 17,784.28 lakhs.

(viii) Rural Infrastructure Development : A fiscal package has been developed for the purpose of rural infrastructure development. In Andhra Pradesh the Department of Rural Development, Forest, Panchayat Raj, Minor Irrigation have availed this scheme. In this programme, each district has selected certain villages for treatment. The implementation at village level is through user groups who are formed on the basis of drainage line. These groups decide on the treatment of drainage

line or common lands. One of the features of this scheme is that it excludes private land treatment.

(ix) Sampoorna Grameen Rozgar Yojana (SGRY): The primary objective of the Sampoorna Grameen Rozgar Yojana (SGRY) Scheme is to provide additional wage employment in all rural areas and thereby provide food security and improve nutritional levels. The secondary objective is the creation of durable community-social and economic-assets and infrastructural development in rural areas.

The programme is self-targeting in nature with special emphasis to provide wage employment to women, scheduled castes, scheduled tribes and parents of children withdrawn from hazardous occupations. The works to be taken up must be labour intensive, leading to the creation of additional wage employment, durable assets and infrastructure, particularly those which would assist in drought proofing such as soil and moisture conservation works, watershed development, afforestation, etc.

(x) Employment Programmes: There are many other self employment programmes, based on income generation, to improve the livelihood of the affected population. These programmes are based on people's participatory approach. The government of Andhra Pradesh has created various employment generation programmes to eradicate poverty. While considering self employment schemes the government has given priority for mini and micro enterprises. These programmes can be considered as mitigation measures at the time of drought.

(xi) Mission Based Approach to Employment Generation : The Government of Andhra Pradesh has established Employment Generation Mission to coordinate activities of all the concerned departments in employment generation and manpower planning. The Mission has prepared a time bound action plan for implementation. The Government acts as facilitator, and identifies and prioritizes key sectors with employment potential.

(xii) Empowerment of Poor Women: Self Help Groups of Women (thrift groups) Programme has mobilized and organized 48 lakh poor women in the rural areas into 3.7 lakh groups across the state. These women groups have built up a corpus fund of

Rs. 750 crores consisting of their savings, borrowings from banks and Development of Women and Children in Rural Areas (DWCRA) and revolving fund from government. The empowerment process has enabled the DWCRA and thrift group members in addressing different dimensions of poverty. DWCRA movement has contributed to the augmentation of incomes, improvement of nutrition, better child care of the poor women, and has enhanced the status of women in rural households.

(xiii) Food for Work Programmes (FFW): India has launched an ambitious food-for-work programme aimed at helping millions of the rural poor stave off hunger and unemployment. The basic principle of FFW is to provide employment to the poor during hard times, to create community assets through labour-intensive work and to pay the labourers in foodgrains or other food items.

(xiv) Chief Minister's Empowerment of Youth (CMEY) Programme : CMEY Programme had the main objective of economic development of youth by empowering them with sufficient skills and infrastructure. This was to be achieved by extending financial assistance to the eligible youth associations by way of subsidy and margin money loans besides group savings for taking up economic activity of their choice.

III

Livelihood Security and Sustainability of Resources

Governments both at the Centre and in different States have initiated certain schemes with the emphasis of providing livelihoods security. The main purpose of these schemes is to enhance their livelihoods by affording their securities and also to enhance the sustainability of their resources. Schemes such as National Rural Employment Guarantee, DWCRA and Watersheds, are meant to maintain the sustainability of their resources and intern resulted the decline of migration and concentration of livelihood security in their own localities.

(i) National Rural Employment Guarantee Scheme: The UPA (United Progressive Alliance) Government enacted the National Rural Employment Guarantee Act on August 25, 2005. The NREGA provides a legal guarantee for one hundred days of employment in every financial year to adult members of any rural household willing to do unskilled manual work at the statutory minimum wage. Central Government meets the cost

towards the payment of wage, 3/4th of material cost and certain percentage of administrative cost. State Government meets the cost towards unemployment allowance, 1/4th of material cost and administrative cost of State council.

Adult members of rural households submit their name, age and address with photo to the Gram Panchayat. The Gram Panchayat registers households after making enquiry and issues a job card. The job card contains the details of adult member enrolled and his/her photo. Registered person can submit an application for work in writing (for at least fourteen days of continuous work) either to Panchayat or to Programme Officer.

The Panchayat/Programme Officer accepts the valid application and issue dated receipt of application, letter providing work is sent to the applicant and also displayed at Panchayat office. The employment is provided within a radius of 5 km: if it is above 5 km extra wage is paid. If employment under the scheme is not provided within fifteen days of receipt of the application daily unemployment allowance is paid to the applicant. The scheme has started from February 2, 2006 in 200 districts (out of a total of 593 in the country). Anantapur District is also included under this scheme. The government announced the addition of another 130 districts in the financial year 2007-08.

In Adadakulapalle settlement NREGA was started during the summer of 2006. Works that are sanctioned and intimated to the village Panchayat, Para-worker and the wage seekers are executed on dates fixed and coordinated by the Para-worker. Para-worker and wage seekers congregate at the work site and carry out the work as per standards and guideline already propagated. A wage seeker willing to work comes to work site and performs the work allocated. Once a week, the Para-worker prepares the Work Progress Report and submits the report along with the Muster Roll at the Mandal MCC. Para-worker also gives an acknowledgement slip to each wage seeker duly mentioning the weekly work details for the week. At the MCC, attendance is captured from the submitted Muster Roll. The data is validated and stored in database. Based on the reported progress of work and the number of person-days spent, payment to the workers is computed and a Wage List is generated. The generated work list is then sent to the village Panchayat and the paying agency can be either the village Panchayat or Post Office. The amount is remitted to PO savings account or Bank account whichever is convenient to the wage seeker. If the work is completed, the Para-worker reports the same to the executing department, which sends an official who prepares the Work Closure Report and submits the same to the Mandal MCC. Village Panchayat also endorses their remarks in the work closure report on the quality of work. Work closure report based on the previously reported progress of work and the number of person-days spent, payment to the workers is computed and a final Wage List is generated. The following picture shows the undergoing work under NREGA in Penukonda mandal of Anantapur District.

It promises Rs. 60 per day for 100 days of employment a year to one member of every rural unemployed family. The Central Government funds this scheme, with the State Government expected to contribute 10 per cent of the cost. The cost in the first year alone is expected to be around Rs. 15,000 crores (or approximately $3.3 billion.). From Adadakulapalle settlement there were 209 people who got the job cards and out of them 95 are Sugalis.

(ii) Development of Women and Children in Rural Areas (DWCRA) : The issues of women's empowerment were also included in the Integrated Rural Development Programme and Jawahar Rojgar Yojana, aiming to provide durable assets and employment generation during the lean periods. In practice, however, participation of women in all these schemes remained very low. Keeping this in view the government conceived of DWCRA programme. The long-term objective of this programme is to improve the survival of young children and women and the quality of their lives, and to achieve a significant growth in the income of poor women through appropriate interventions.

Besides the above, the government has been keen to bring development in the areas of education, health, economy, and political participation and so on through five-year plans implemented through various schemes and programmes. As detailed earlier, a primary school in the village and an upper primary school at a distance of 10 kms were established to bring the educational development among the Sugalis. Similarly, primary health centre was also established at the *mandal* headquarters and health functionaries were to periodically visit the Sugali Thandas to extend health facilities. Thus, the approach of government towards development has been comprehensive and holistic in nature.

DWCRA leaders said that approximately 80 per cent of the people are covered in this programme. Women members outrightly say that before the introduction of the DWCRA schemes in the village, they were not aware of outside activities of the village, except domestic and agricultural activities.

Because of the DWCRA programme, they (women) have a role in household decision making process, aware of cleanliness of surroundings and they are also contributing to the construction of school building, etc. They also said that their husbands are allowing them to attend the meetings. Whenever teacher does not come to the school, they complain to higher officials. As a result of their participation in DWCRA, now they are able to talk with officials without any hesitation and demand benefits/programme or schemes, etc. from the officials.

Some women faced problems while receiving the benefits. They had to run around the officials and offices for getting the sanction of grants and other funds. Women members have complained during field study that the Sarpanch delays sanctioning of funds by not signing the form.

(iii) Watershed Programme : People felt that before watershed programme their lands were not in good condition. Farmers felt that their yields also reduced drastically. Labourers were unable to get the wage works, so they used to migrate to other areas for works. Irrigated area acreage was less before watershed programme in the Adadakulapalle. Dairying people have felt that their milk yield was also very less before the watersheds in Adadakulapalle. Farmers used to go to distant places for grazing purposes. People felt that after watershed programme, bunding works were taken up in the lands. This was an action by which both farmers and labourers benefited-labourers by getting more wage works and farmers getting better yields due to soil enrichment.

Horticultural crops have been given to the farmers through which changes have come in the cropping pattern. Due to the watershed programme, ground water table has increased to 110 feet from 80 feet. According to Venkatesh Naik, who is practicing dairying, milk yield has improved drastically from 60 litres to 300 litres over a period of three years. People have also felt that forestland has increased. According to Ramanji Naik, crop yield has gone up from 5 to 6 bags per acre to 8 to 10 bags after watershed programme.

Non-farm activity has also increased after watershed programme in the village. There are 3 hotels, 3 petty business shops in the village which were not there before the programme. Some of the people have been maintaining autos and running between Adadakulapalle to Penukonda. According to them due to watershed programme, self employment has been improved.

Majority of respondents felt that wage rates have increased compared to the other areas. As a result of equity in wage rate in the watershed programme, women labourers felt happy.

Due to watershed programme, woman's position has improved and savings has increased drastically. Anasuya Bai, who is the chairman of the watershed committee, has said that watershed programme has brought changes in their livelihoods systems.

(iv) Future Livelihood Strategy: She said that she is already to face the problems and should manage the affairs to achieve the sustainable living. Anasuya Bai has said that she is now participating in all the developmental activities of the village and also attending all the Janmabhoomi and DWACRA meetings and able to speak/talk with officials without any hesitation or fear/shy. She said because of the DWACRA, now she is able to improve her livelihoods and also aware about all the developmental programmes.

Case Study : Ramanji Naik is the present Sarpanch of the Adadakulapalle Gram Panchayat who is 33 years old; he has not completed his graduation. His family consists of 14 males and 13 females, out of which men workers are 6 and female workers are 5. Now he is the member of women's watershed committee in Adadakulapalle settlement. He is also president of the Penukonda Mandal Sarpanch Association and also member of the Education Committee of the Government Degree College, Penukonda.

The main occupation of the Ramanji Naik is agriculture. Ramanji Nail has 30 acre of rainfed land and three acres of irrigated land. In the irrigated land he is growing paddy, ragi and mulberry, whereas in rainfed land, he was growing horticultural crops, through watershed programme. (Tamarind 6 acres and Mangoes 5 acres). He also said that major sources of his include cultivation (50%), tractor hiring (15%), dairying (15%) and flourmill.

Ramanji Naik has further said that 7 years back there are only 5 working population in the family. Major source of income was agriculture only. There was no other occupation at all according to him and thus no other sources of income. Ramanji Naik has narrated that 10 years back there are 3 male workers and 2 female workers in the family and major sources of income is from own cultivation only (65%) followed by leased in land (35%) cultivation. Ramanji Naik's father has said that 15 acres of land was leased in from the farmer in the Adadakulapalle village.

Change : Ramanji Naik has felt that the change is due to the cropping pattern because of the rainfed land and further he says that they were partially shifted from agricultural crops to horticultural crops and also to dairying activity.

Future : Ramanji Naik has felt that in future there would be scope for horticulture crops and to save the water, it is better to adopt the drip irrigation system, which is beneficial to the farmers as well as labourers of the village.

(v) Risk management (since 5 years): Due to droughts, his family faced severe financial problems and did not get the returns in the crop, not even seed cost/input cost. To overcome these financial problems, they have taken loan from the banks and also borrowed from relatives in the Adadakulapalle Settlement. He also believed that, to overcome these debts, they have preferred the change in the cropping pattern, but that way, they were slowly shifted to Mulberry, horticulture crops and to dairying activity. He also felt that watershed programme has changed their lives and livelihoods have been improved enormously. He has also narrated that after facing the severe financial problems, he has realized and shifted to horticultural crops. He also felt that frequent visits of officials to the

settlement made them to realize the importance of watershed programme and other programmes as well which is beneficial for our livelihood strategies.

IV

Findings and Conclusions

Earlier without wages people used to spend sleepless nights. They used to migrate to other areas for wage labour. Wages were also very less and working hours were also longer. They were not aware of their health, children's education, sanitation, savings, etc. Earlier they also felt that for women there was no role to play in the family or household decision-making process except to nod their heads to the mothers-in-law and the husband's opinion. Women were not aware of the programmes like *Balika Samriddi Yojana* (Girl Child Development Programme), mother and children's protection, etc. After the entry of SEDS, works such as pebble bunding and contour bundings have become regular. Another important feature is that there is no difference in wage rates for men and women. Women felt very happy that there was no gender discrimination in the rates of wages. Their saving levels, according to them, have improved enormously due to the efforts of the SEDS. Majority of the women are sending their children to schools as they have realised the significance of education. They also have plans to contest and win the elections in the village and thus participate in the village administration and policymaking process.

REFERENCES

Applebaum, Richard P., and William I. Robinson, (eds). (2005) : *Critical Globalization Studies*, New York and London: Routledge.

Aronin, Larissa. (2008) : Book Review: Richard Applebaum and William Robinson, eds, Critical Globalization Studies (2005), New York and London: Routledge, *International Sociology Review of Books*, 23 (5) pp. 773-777.

Cornwall, Andrea (2007), 'Buzzwords and fuzzwords: deconstructing development discourse', *Development in Practice*, 17:4, 471–484.

Eswarappa, Kasi (2007) : 'An Anthropological Study of Livelihoods: A Case of two Sugali Settlements in Anantapur District of Andhra Pradesh' (an un-published Ph.D. thesis submitted to the University of Hyderabad, India for the partial fulfilment of the Doctorate Degree).

Eswarappa, Kasi (2009) : 'Introduction: Anthropological Encounter of Development in Contemporary World', in Eswarappa Kasi (ed), *Rethinking Developmental Discourse in the 21st Century India*. New Delhi: Serials Publications.

Faundez, J., Footer M. And Norton, J. (2000) : *Governance, Development and Globalization*. London: Blackstone Press.

Harvey, D. (1990): *The Condition of Postmodernity : An Enquiry into the Origins of Cultural Change*. Cambridge, MA: Blackwell.

Hofmeister, Heather and Andre Pascal Breitenstein (2008): 'Contemporary Processes of Transnationalization and Globalization', *International Sociology* 23 (4): 480-87.

Mills, M. 2008: 'Globalization and Inequality' *European Sociological Review*, 1-8, downloaded from http://esr.oxfordjournals.org.

Mills, M. and Blossfeld, H.P. (2005): Globalization, uncertainty and the early life course: a theoretical framework. In Blossfeld, H.P., Klijzing, E., Mills, M. and Hurz, K. (eds), *Globalization, Uncertainty and Youth in Society*. London and New York: Routledge.

Mittelman, J., ed. (1996): *Globalization: Critical Reflections*. Boulder: Lynne Rienner.

Mittelman, J. (2000): *The Globalization Syndrome*. NJ: Princeton University Press.

Petras, J. and Veltmeyer, H. (2001): *Globalization Unmasked: Imperialism in the 21st Century*. Black Point, Nova Scotia: Fernwood.

Rist, Gilbert (2007): 'Development as a buzzword', *Development in Practice*, 17:4, 485-91.

Smith, D.A. (2001): 'Editor's Introduction: Globalization and Social Problems', *Social Problems* 48 (4): 429-34.

12

International Fund for Agricultural Development (IFAD) and Poverty Alleviation in Hilly Areas of Manipur

A. Rajmani Singh

Introduction

Manipur, one of the eight states of the north east India is nestled on nine hill ranges with a small and beautiful oval shaped valley at the centre. The state shares 352 kms long international border with Myanmar to the south east and 502 kms long border with Nagaland to the north, Cachar district of Assam to west, Chin Hills (Myanmar) and Mizoram to the south and the south west, and Surma tract and Upper Chindwin of Myanmar to the east.

Manipur has a geographical area of 22,327 sq. kms, which constitutes 0.7 per cent of the total land surface of India. Ninety per cent of the total geographical area of the state i.e, 20,089 sq. kms is covered with hills, remaining area is a small valley covering only 2,238 sq. kms and accounting for only one-tenth of the total area of the state. The hilly area of the state is divided into five districts and the valley area into four districts.

Despite massive efforts undertaken by the central as well as state governments for alleviation of poverty and uplift of socio-economic conditions of the poor through different centrally sponsored schemes, the progress of poverty alleviation and development in the state is found to be very slow. After sixty years of India's independence, still there are a number of villages which do not have such facilities as electricity, connecting road, drinking water, health and education.

However, in 2000, the International Fund for Agricultural Development (IFAD) gave a ray of hope to two hill districts of Manipur i.e, Senapati district and Ukhrul districts out of six districts of the region. The present paper focuses on three important aspects such as the socio-economic status of Senapati district of Manipur, the role of IFAD sponsoring projects in the development of remote parts of hilly districts of Manipur specially Senapati district, and finally on policy options for the development of the rural poor based on findings.

What is IFAD?

The International Fund for Agricultural Development (IFAD), a specialized agency of the United Nations, with its headquarters in Rome, was established as an international financial institution in 1977 in response to the provisions of the 1974 World Food Conference. The Conference was organized in response to the food crises of the early 1970s that primarily affected the Sahelian countries of Africa. IFAD is dedicated to eradicating rural poverty in developing countries. Seventy-five per cent of the world's poorest people - 1.05 billion women, children and men - live in rural areas and depend on agriculture and related activities for their livelihoods.

Working with rural poor, governments, donors, non-governmental organizations and many other partners, IFAD focuses on country-specific solutions, which can involve increasing rural poor's access to financial services, markets, technology, land and other natural resources.

IFAD in India

India receives more funding from IFAD than any other country in the world. Working in close partnership with the Government of India and donors, IFAD funds projects for rural development, tribal development, women's empowerment and natural resource management. Since 1979, the organization has financed 22 programmes and projects, approving loans for a total of approximately US $ 595.3 million.

IFAD's strategy in India centres on improving rural people's access to economic and social resources. In all operations, IFAD emphasizes the importance of strengthening people's capacities to establish and manage their own institutions. It supports self-help groups, community institutions and village development associations in tribal and non-tribal areas that work in synergy with local self-governments. These and similar groups participate directly in designing development initiatives and become progressively responsible for programme and project resources and management. Empowering women and other disadvantaged groups is a strategic priority.

IFAD has an important role in developing replicable models through project activities and it acts as a catalyst for far-reaching innovative change. In areas such as micro-finance and women's empowerment, IFAD-funded operations have tested institutional and technical innovations that have been scaled up by the government.

North Eastern Region Community Resource Management Project for Upland Areas [NERCORMP] (IFAD and GoI Assisted Livelihood Project)

The NERCORMP is a joint initiative of the Government of India and the IFAD. The North-Eastern Council (NEC), Ministry of Development of the North-Eastern Region (DONER) represent the Government of India. The United Nations Office for Project Services (UNOPS) works as the cooperating institution. Started in 1999, the project has been able to achieve its objectives to a great extent. The objective of the project was to improve the livelihood of vulnerable groups in a sustainable manner through improved management of their resource base in a way that contributes to protecting and restoring the environment. The project has two broad focus areas, viz. (a) social mobilization, organization and capacity building to tap and realize great potentials of the communities employing traditional value systems, and (b) intervention with economic and social activities through income generating activities to achieve economic transformation. The project has been successfully implemented in 860 villages covering 39,161 households. The project activities provide important clues for adoption of appropriate policy in natural resource management in three states of north-east India *i.e.* Assam, Manipur and Meghalaya. The specific objectives of NERCRMP/IFAD are :

- to promote a more sensitive approach to the design and implementation of development intervention;
- to enhance the capabilities of the local people to manage new technologies and institutions at the village level;
- to increase income through more sustainable farming system and establishment of non-farm enterprises;
- to make people more aware of the need to preserve and regenerate natural resources;
- to establish effective and appropriate delivery system for inputs and for the maintenance of assets and resources;
- to increase the participation of women in local institutions and decision making process within the community;
- to enhance savings capacity and habit of thrift and
- to increase access to basic services and infrastructure facilities.

Before discussing the role of IFAD in poverty alleviation in two districts of Manipur, let us know about the demographic status of Manipur for better analysis and evaluation.

Demographic Profile of Manipur

Population of a state is its most important asset and resource for all kinds of development. As recorded on the 1st March 2001, the population of Manipur was 22,93,896 consisting of 11,61,952 males and 11,31,944 females. Among the 35 different states and union territories of India, Manipur state is 23rd in rank in term of its population. Manipur is fourth largest state in the North Eastern Region of India which constitutes 5.88 per cent of the total population of eight north eastern states. The distribution of population in the nine districts of the state is very much heterogeneous in nature showing a heavy concentration of the population in one district and very thinly spreading population in other district. For example, Imphal West district shares 18.40 per cent of state's population while Tamenglong district 4.67 per cent.

Role of IFAD in Senapati District

NERCRMP/IFAD was commissioned in Senapati district of Manipur in June, 2000. Over the past several years, the District Project functionaries (NGOs) and NaRMGs & SHGs have collectively gained experience, learned from the past mistakes and earned expertise in the field of community mobilization, micro credit, marketing, extension and technology, project management, planning and implementation.

Towards this end, the District Project Management (DPM) has identified a few selected products and introduced new crops which have the potential of large scale production and marketability. Further, the district has been divided into various clusters and each cluster has been identified with one or two commodities or products (both farm and non-farm) based on villagers' preference, the soil type, agro-climatic zones, etc.

The principal thrust of the project is to secure the participation of communities in planning and management of all development interventions. The emphasis is on promoting self-reliant community institutions that are empowered to identify, analyze and seek solutions to the production constraints of their natural resources endowment. The project focuses its attention on changing attitudes and behaviour of the principal agents of the development in the region. The main beneficiaries of the project are the households who depended on Jhum agriculture.

Findings of the Study

Following are some of the significant achievements under IFAD projects in Senapati district of Manipur:

SHGs Bank Linkages

The district as a whole along with the project villages in particular has entered into a new era of economic development through SHGs bank linkages. Women participate in different economic development activities like animal husbandry, weaving, gardening, floriculture, piggery, etc. As a result of the synergy efforts of the DST, 350 SHGs received credit support with total amount of Rs. 87.5 lakhs sanctioned as on March 2007.

Table 1
District-wise Distribution of Population in Manipur

Districts	*Area Sq. km.*	*Population as per 2001*			*Literacy %*	*Den-sity*	*Sex Ratio*	*Sub-Div*	*Unemploy Ed as on 31st Oct'08*	*% to total*
		Total	*Male*	*Female*						
A:Valley Districts	2,238	1411766	706952	704814		630		14	456385	32.33
Imphal West	519	444382	221781	222601	80.2	847	1007	4	213828	48.12
Imphal East	709	394876	198371	196505	75.4	555	992	4	90347	22.88
Thoubal	514	364140	182250	181890	66.4	713	998	3	95165	26.13
Bishenpur	496	208368	104550	103818	67.6	415	1004	3	57045	27.38
B: Hills Districts	20,089	882130	455000	427130		44		24	170449	19.32
Churachandpur	4570	227905	117232	110673	70.6	50	993	5	57342	25.16
Ukhrul	4544	140778	73465	67313	73.1	31	920	5	25132	17.85
Senapati	3271	283621	146548	137073	59.8	116	928	6	46685	16.46
Chandel	3313	118327	59741	58586	56.2	37	986	4	18876	15.95
Tamenglong	4391	111499	58014	53485	59.2	25	922	4	22414	20.10
Total	22,327	2293896	1207388	1181296	70.5	103	974	38	634314	27.65

Sources :1. Census Publications of the Office of the Registrar General, India.

2. Directorate of Employment Service, Manipur. 2007.

Table 2
The Details of the NaRMGs and SHGs Under IFAD Project in Senapati

Sl.No.	*Information*	*Numbers*
	Village Information	
	Total number of Villages	106
	Old Villages	55
	New Villages	51
	NaRMG Information	
	Total number of NaRMG	150
	Old NaRMG	73
	New NaRMG	77
	Total Number of Households	7033
	SHG Information	
	Total number of SHG	417
	Old SHG	178
	New SHG	221
	Total number of SHG Members	6369

Source: NERCRMS/IFAD, Senapati.

Table 3
Fund Received from NERCRMS/IFAD as on 31-3-2007

Sl. No.	*Year*	*Amount (in Rs.)*
1.	2000-2001	20,08,000
2.	2001-2002	1,30,20,000
3.	2002-2003	1,64,73,000
4.	2003-2004	2,09,00,000
5.	2004-2005	5,00,00,000
6.	2005-2006	3,07,00,000
7.	2006-2007(up to March 2007)	4,08,00,000
	Total	17,39,01,000

Source: Same as Table 2.

Livelihood Sector

The project has promoted different livelihood activities for the NaRMGs and SHGs. One of the focus areas for improving livelihood of poor and vulnerable people is through income generation activities (IGA) taken up mostly by the SHGs. IGA fund is channelized directly through SHGs since 2004. The major component taken up by the groups are piggery, poultry, petty business, weaving, cattle rearing, agricultural crops, etc. NaRMGs and SHGs have also taken up different group activities like production of king chilly, potato, ginger, tomato, mushroom, etc. The major livelihood group activities by NaRMGs are: passion fruit, pineapple, banana, tree bean, forestry plantation, land reclamation, etc.

Alternatives to Jhum Cultivation

Jhum fallows are being converted into pineapple and banana orchards in Saikul cluster villages as permanent crop, which has reduced the jhum practices to some extent. The training on proper cultivation method has been imparted to the growers by the project. Cultivation of MAPs *i.e.* green economic can act as critical sources of livelihood for the poor and marginalized tribal communities of the state. It can provide viable economic and ecological alternatives to unsustainable forms of Jhum/Shifting cultivation, which is the predominant form of agricultural practices of the hill people in the state. It also has the potential to be the substantial sources of revenue to the government.

In view of the important position of MAPs occupy in both the national and international agri-business, SEDCORMS through NERCRMP has been taking up cultivation of some high value and high demand MAPs like Safed musli, Rauvolfia, Vanilla, Stevia, Aloe, etc. in the district on an experimental basis as future crops of the poor farmers of the district. The initial results of the experimental cultivation show a blend of success and failure. Crops like Safed, Aloe and Stevia grow and adapted well to the local agro-climatic conditions of the district. On the contrary, assessment on the growth performance of Rauvolfia and Vanilla shows not so satisfactory results. However venturing into this programme should not be taken as futile exercise but should be viewed as very positive step moving in the right perspective. Introduction of both exotic and locally available high market potential MAPs and scaling up to commercial level may take some years but will definitely help in accelerating the cause of income generation of the poor and marginalized farmers in the district in particular and the state in general.

Vermicompost Manure

Vermicompost is used in the paddy fields, home gardens, floriculture unit, passion fruit farms and king chilli gardens. Some NaRMGs are selling the excess products to the local market @ Rs. 8 per kg. The intervention is highly appreciated by villagers and gaining ground.

On the other hand, the project has intervened in increasing the production of staple food (rice) through construction of new terraces and reclamation of abandoned terraces. Altogether 237 acres of land has been so far reclaimed for wet rice cultivation. As a result around 248 MT of additional rice is produced from these new/reclaimed terraces. The respective NaRMGs are giving preference to the C groups (as per the wealth ranking results) to access these new areas for cultivation. As a result, landless farmers have been able to get ownership of terraces. In few areas where the poor have to buy rice from market throughout the year, the project intervention has improved the food security thereby enabling to sustain them for a few months.

Livestock Sector

Livestock production was given much emphasis through the project. It was mainly taken up as IGA through self-help groups and also promoted as a group enterprise. Livestock like cattle, piggery, duckery and poultry are being promoted in all the villages. For proper management of livestock, trainings were conducted in collaboration with line department for veterinary health workers from the village. Vaccination of the Livestock has been a common feature for project related IGA. The numbers of livestock units in the villages have been increased to a considerable extent.

Social Sector Activities

The project has so far introduced 7444 units of low cost latrine (LCL) in all the project villages, with total investment of Rs.1,50,36,510. With this small amount of support, some of the household could construct attached bathroom with the latrine from their contribution. The community has learnt the benefit of sanitary latrines and its contribution towards public health. Further, this has drastically reduced the incidents of water-borne diseases in the village especially for the children.

A pilot health project was implemented in Senapati district with an investment cost of Rs. 27,06,324 in the year 2001 to 2004 covering 40 project villages with 40 First Contact Cares (FCC). The project period expired on August 2004.

Village Infrastructure

The major infrastructures supported by the project are water supply system, Community Facility Centre (CFC), school building and suspension bridge. So far 9 CFCs have been completed and 10 CFCs are in the pipe line; the biggest water supply scheme is the water supply project of Maram Khullen. The villages have mobilized more than Rs. 6 lakhs apart from free labour contribution.

Fish Farm Development

As a new intervention, the project has promoted 74 fish ponds. The types of fishes grown are Carps (rahu, common carp, grass carp, etc.), and local fishes. The intervention had made a significant impact in terms of income generation. The SHGs/individuals have started selling the fish at the local market. More interested groups are coming up for this sector, as the demand for the local fish is quite high in the market.

Agri-Business and Marketing

Marketing of agricultural produce in the district has not been systematically organized. By and large the rural/village market is dominated by middlemen. Neither proper Market Regulation Act nor the Agriculture Produce Marketing Act has been enacted.

The primary markets in the district do not have required facilities. The market stalls even in the district headquarters were not properly laid. Temporary structure made of bamboo and plastic spread, not to speak of good market sheds, are common features in small towns/villages.

Common Facility Center (CFC)

Construction of Common marketing and Facility Centre at strategic location of each cluster are in progress. The main purpose is to create the logistic arrangement of grading and packaging (post harvest management), training and extension for better price for the farmers.

Market Linkage

The project has supported for training of SEBA members for various activities in all the clusters. The SEBA member Mr. Chungneithang, IRADA cluster has been facilitated for obtaining 62 hawkers license from the Imphal Town Municipality.

Natural Resource Management

One of the project objectives is conservation of natural resources to ensure sustainable livelihood of upland communities. These communities are heavily dependant on forest for their livelihood. In the recent years there has been alarming increasing pressure on forest and other natural resources. The traditional concept of "Food from Forest" has changed to "Money from Forest". This change in concept and practice has alienated people from forest.

The distortion in shifting cultivation, feudal land tenure system and unsustainable exploitation of forest resources have made the people marginalized and vulnerable. The approach of NRM is to make people aware of the harmful practices, proper and sustainable sharing of Natural Resources as a Developmental Tool.

Self-sufficiency and Poverty Alleviation

Widespread environmental degradation in the north-eastern region of India in general and Manipur in particular is aggravating poverty and food insecurity, and forcing rural and hilly people to exploit dwindling resources to meet subsistence requirements. An IFAD-supported project in Senapati and Ukhrul has introduced a new model for sustainable management of the resource base. Now communities care for the environment, and have learned to make use of natural resources to improve livelihoods and ensure that the land will continue to provide for future generations. The hills and highlands of Senapati and Ukhrul are covered in lush vegetation and inhabited by indigenous tribal peoples. The area is famed as a biodiversity 'hot spot'. Yet the inhabitants of this beautiful, remote region live in extreme poverty – isolated from markets and other services – and the resources they depend on are becoming increasingly degraded.

The project introduced more sustainable land management that preserves the ecological balance of the region and creates better livelihood options for poor farmers. Protected areas have been created, such as wildlife and fish sanctuaries, and timber and forest reserves. They are now owned and managed by the communities. Terracing has been introduced, allowing farmers to grow cash crops without the need for *jhum* cultivation or forest exploitation. Villagers have seen an improvement in productivity thanks to extension services and to training in better, more sustainable farming techniques for soil and water conservation and crop diversification. With available food crops, communities no longer need to strip the forests of their valuable resources.

The grass-roots organizations have fostered an entrepreneurial spirit. A range of on- and off-farm income-generating activities now exist, thanks to revolving funds for microcredit created within the NaRMGs and self-help groups (SHGs). These self help groups are for women only. They have helped promote credit and savings and various small enterprises, such as kitchen gardens, pig- and poultry-raising and, importantly, village grocery shops. By linking banks with the self help groups, the project has facilitated the availability of credit. Banks, in turn, have been keen to extend finance to rural communities as a result of the success of these groups.

To support these growing enterprises, NERCORMP has trained young men and women from the villages to become marketing professionals. These self-employed business agents store produce and transport it to larger towns, earning commissions from the villagers when they sell the produce to wholesalers. This innovation has allowed niche markets to evolve and has helped forge strong links between producers and wider markets. Processing and value chain development are beginning to take off. Local products such as honey, pickles and decorative candles are increasingly finding their way onto the shelves of some of the bigger stores in the region.

There have been considerable benefits for everyone in the project area. Maternal and infant mortality rates, once higher than the national average, have declined considerably. More children are enrolled in school. Women, in particular, benefit from their new empowerment – not just because they have better incomes, but because they have also acquired new status in their communities and are participating fully in decision-making at the group and village levels. With the extra income earned through project interventions, poor people are beginning to buy their own plots of land, securing food production for the future.

Conclusions

The IFAD-funded North Eastern Region Community Resource Management Project for Upland Areas (NERCORMP) helped reorganize land use and resource management in six districts across the states of Meghalaya, Manipur and Assam. It has improved productivity and ensured the sustainability of farming and harvesting practices, and more than 2,30,000 rural people in the project area have seen dramatic improvements in their living conditions. They now have substantially higher incomes, regular and more nutritious meals; and their children are healthier and better educated. The project closed in September 2008 but the benefits continue and will continue in future.

The income generated activities undertaken under the aegis of IFAD project have to go alone without care and support from the government and funding agencies like IFAD. At the stage more and more care is needed from the state government specially forward and backward integration of the existing ventures undertaken by the poor farmers in the remote and hilly areas of Senapati and Ukhrul districts. Further, the two IFAD projects have shown a vivid example for alleviation of poverty specially in the hilly areas of Manipur. State government, DONER and central government should consider similar type of projects in the other hilly areas as well as valley districts for eradication of rural poverty from Manipur.

REFERENCES

North Eastern Region: Vision 2020 Vol. 1.

Singha, Komol, (2009): *Village Development in North East India*, Concept Publishing House, New Delhi-2.

Stakeholders Workshop and Project Assessment of Ukhrul District UDCRMS at TTA Conference Hall, Hamleikhong, Ukhrul on 24th May, 2008.

Singh, Rajmani (2008) : Contract Farming: a forward and backward linkage to rural Agri-horticultural produce in Manipur. Paper presented in 2 days training programme on marketing practices in Agri-horti finished products for SEBA on 19th and 20th Feb., 2008 at Youth Centre, Khuman Lampak.

Singh, Rajmani (2008): Rural Marketing in Manipur: Its Problems and Remedial Measures, Workshop Organized by SEDCORMS (IFAD) Senapati, Manipur on 19th and 20th Feb., 2008 at Youth Centre, Khuman Lampak.

Progress Report of NERCORMP/SEDCORMS/Senapati (as on 31st March, 2007).

Statistical Abstract Manipur 2007: Directorate of Economics and Statistics, Government of Manipur, Imphal.

Economic Survey Manipur, 2007-08: Directorate of Economics and Statistics, Government of Manipur, Imphal.

10th State Level Banker's Committee Meeting, Manipur, March 2007.

Deb, Bimal J. and Ray B. Datta (2006): *Changing Agricultural Scenario in North East India*, Concept Publishing House, New Delhi-2.

Basu, Debashis *et. al.* (2006): *Agriculture Food Security Nutrition and Health in North East India*, Mittal Publication, New Delhi.

RBI, (1990): Report of the Agricultural Credit Review Committee on the Agricultural Credit System in India.

13

Decentralised Planning in Tripura

Jayanta Choudhury

Development is that strategy by which persons, families, communities or societies can take their own responsibility to change their own situation and to achieve this goal in a systematic way is called planning. Planning is usually designed to maximize welfare of the people. In our country there are two types of planning. One is centralized planning and the other is decentralized planning. Since independence in our country the strategy of planning was centralized one based on top-down approach where economic decisions are taken up by central planning authority. Experiment with top-down approach shows that planning could not prove effective because consulting with the people, understanding their needs, involving them for mobilization or corrective efforts to deal with the problem have been mostly neglected. India is a developing country and 70 per cent area of this country is rural area. There are certain specific characteristics of the developing countries such as regional imbalances and uneven distribution of resource, rural-urban disparity, high degree of inequality in income distribution, etc. and centralised planning has been proved ineffective to reduce these problems.

To develop the country equitable distribution of the benefit between different regions and also between sections of population is very important. It is for this reason the

Government of India is keen to modify the planning process in the country by introducing decentralised planning.

Decentralized planning is a system through which planning process is brought close to the people who are the ultimate target of development. It is a multi-level planning system in which planning is attempted at different political, administrative and executive levels so that there is greater integration between developmental needs of socio-economic classes with the regional, sub-national and national level development policies and goals. Decentralized planning is neither a substitute to centralized planning nor a bottom of process of planning. It is in fact a two way process which begins at both top level (national or state level) as well as at grassroots level (local level) simultaneously and merges with each other at the point below where centralized planning becomes irreverent and above which micro planning is meaningless.

Panchayat Raj Institutions: Foundation for Decentralisation

Development experiences tell us that development cannot be imposed from outside. It is the people themselves who have to come forward for development and to improve their socio-economic conditions.

Decentralization, interpreted in simple terms, would mean moving away from the centre or *deconcentration*. In the context of development, which is our concern here, decentralization means transfer of certain authority and power in the matter of formulation and implementation of development plans from the highest organization or institution at the national level or state level to organisations or institutions at the sub-state level and to people.

The lower level, which includes district, block and panchayat has a particular role in the planning exercise and is vested with the powers and the responsibilities associated with the role. In a truly decentralized situation such power includes the power to determine goals and targets and to raise resources locally.

Decentralized Planning can, thus, be defined as a type of planning where local organisations and institutions formulate, adopt, execute actions and supervise the plan without interference by the central body.

In Tripura, about 85 per cent of people live in the rural areas, and most of them are economically and socially backward. To improve the condition of these people is the major objective of the village development plan.

Panchayati Raj was first introduced in Tripura during 1959 by enacting Tripura Panchayat Raj Act, 1959 (adopted from U.P. Panchayat Raj Act with some modifications). In this Act, single tier (Gram Panchayat) was proposed. Tripura Panchayats Raj Rules was framed in 1961. Under the Tripura Panchayat Raj Rules, 1961 (which continued till 1978), the Gram Panchayats were constituted through open election by raising hands. The Rules were amended in 1978 to ensure the constitution of the Gram Panchayats under adult franchise by secret ballot with participation of political parties. At the block level, Block Development Committee (BDC), an advisory body, was constituted with the elected Pradhans of the Gram Panchayats and the MLAs from the block area. The BDCs were encouraged to act as *de facto* Panchayat samitis.

Following the 73rd Amendment of the Constitution in 1992, Tripura was one of the first states to enact Tripura Panchayats Act, 1993 with a provision for setting up of three tier Panchayat system - Gram Panchayat at Village level, Panchayat Samiti at Block level and Zilla Parishad at District level. During 1994, various functions of 12 departments were assigned to the Panchayat bodies. Again during 2000, some more functions were transferred to the Panchayats. The state Finance Commission was set up in 1994 which has submitted its report in 1996 and is accepted by the Government. The second SFC has already started functioning. Two elections of the PRIs have been held (1994 and 1999) so far. Similar reforms were done in the Nagar Panchayats following the 74th amendment.

The Tripura Tribal Areas Autonomous District Council was set up on 18th January, 1982 as an autonomous body in the state under the 7th Schedule of the Constitution. Later, with the objective of entrusting more responsibility and to give more power to the TTAADC, Provisions of the 6th Schedule to the Constitution of India were extended to Tripura from 1st April, 1985 by the 49th Amendment of the Constitution. The TTAADC covers an area of 7133 sq. km., which constitutes about 68 per cent of the state's total area. As per the 1991 Census, the total population in the District Council area is 8.87 lakh which is about one-third of State's population. Of this, 6.62 lakh are tribal, which is about 66 per cent of tribal population.

Before the 73rd Amendment, or more specifically, before the enactment of the Tripura Panchayats Act, 1993, the one tier Gram Panchayat used to just act as an implementing agency of the various labour intensive schemes and recommending the names of the beneficiaries. But the 73rd Amendment enabled the Panchayats to function as "Institutions of self-governance" by empowering the panchayats to have some original functions and some agency functions.

The original function of the Panchayats is the preparation of plans for economic development and social justice, while the agency function relates to the implementation of schemes for economic development and social justice as may be entrusted to them including those in relation to the matters listed in the Eleventh Schedule. It may be mentioned here that there can not be two sets of schemes, one for economic development and another for social justice, because any plan for economic development must automatically enhance and/or promote social justice. Active participation of the deprived masses in every stage of planning is the essential precondition in order to enhance/ promote social justice by developmental planning.

Earlier System of Planning

Notwithstanding wide differences of opinion among scholars regarding details, they agree that the centralized system of planning has been a failure in addressing fundamental problems of development faced by the country, such as eradication of mass poverty and unemployment. Even though it would be too simplistic to attribute the above failure exclusively to what may be referred to as 'centralization', there is growing consensus around the view that over-centralization had been a major debilitation feature of the Indian System.

Commonly identified evils, that are attributable more to centralization than to any other important feature of the system are:

- widespread apathy among people;

- lack of involvement of people in nation building activities;
- indifference to the development needs of the people;
- channelling of resources for wrongly perceived goals;
- disregard of local specificities even where it matters most;
- insensitive to local knowledge;
- lack of efforts at integration of isolated development interventions which often tend to work at cross purposes; and
- spiralling of corruption.

All the same, it would be unrealistic to assume that planning of everything is best done at the local level. While optimal solutions for many problems are to be found at the local level, there are also issues, which require to be addressed at higher levels. It is also important that development interventions are integrated both horizontally and vertically among various tiers of decision-making so that complementarities are maximized and conflicts are reduced to the minimum.

Obstacles to Decentralization

Desirability of a decentralized system of planning was never in doubt. The slogan 'gram raj' is as old as the freedom movement. During the post-independence period, the demand for making the country's governance more democratic through a meaningful process of decentralization of power continued to enjoy pride of place on the national agenda. In spite of such conviction and support, the process of decentralization could not make much headway in the country. The failure of earlier efforts is usually attributed to a variety of reasons, viz.,

- resistance offered by the vested interests nurtured by the centralized structure;
- lack of pressure from below due to the absence of representative governments at levels below the states; and
- paucity of expertise and preparedness at the local level, etc.

There were many efforts in the past to identify factors constraining the process of decentralization and to suggest concrete measures to overcome the hurdles. Not to be lost sight of are also some important experiments at the field level, including the efforts of states like Rajasthan, Karnataka and West Bengal and many micro-level interventions under the auspices of various agencies, which provided valuable insights for future attempts in the same direction. But the country had to wait till 1993, when the 73rd and 74th Constitutional Amendments were enacted, to see a comprehensive and determined effort to tackle the various factors that hinder the process of decentralization.

Nevertheless, the constitutional amendments, at their best, serve only as a favourable framework. As the inter-state variations in the responsibilities, powers, and resources devolved to the newly constituted Panchayat Raj Institutions would amply testify, the constitutional amendments leave many important parameters of the process of decentralization to be determined by the State legislatures even now. The State Governments can either make use of the constitutional provisions to establish true local self governments or misuse the loopholes to maintain the *status quo*.

It has been the experience in Tripura that success of government initiatives and legislations depend a lot on the environment in which such moves are made and the pressure exerted from below. This is more so because what is envisaged in the context of decentralized planning is a total restructuring of the planning and execution system.

The state government has already set a good example for the rest of the country with respect to division of responsibilities, devolution of power and resources, provision of facilitating services, and complementary changes in administrative procedures and practices.

Tripura was one of the first few states to frame its Panchayati Raj Act on the pattern envisaged in the 73rd amendment of the Constitution. It was again one of the first to set up the State Finance Commission and accept many of its recommendation. As per the recommendations of the State Finance Commission, funds and responsibilities are being devolved to the Panchayati Raj Institutions. Even though the 73rd Amendment to the Constitution and the recommendations of the State Finance Commission are not applicable to the ADC areas, the Government was conscious of the fact that these areas cannot be left behind as far as the devolutions are concerned. A separate arrangement was accordingly worked out to devolve funds and responsibilities to the ADC areas.

Devolution of powers, responsibilities, and resources and the complementary measures taken at the government level are necessary conditions, but not sufficient in themselves to ensure genuine democratization of the planning process. Hardly any tier of the Panchayati Raj Institution can claim to have prior experience in the art of development planning. Nor are they equipped with expertise, infrastructure or the required information base to take up the task of making development plans, all by themselves, for their respective regions. Further, many of them may not even be prepared to come out of the shell of inactivity with which they have been accustomed for long.

Development Challenges before the State

The development dialogue that follows is phenomenal in terms of widespread participation, range of issues raised, amount of details and insights generated, etc. For our purpose, it suffices to note the consensus in favour of a decentralized process of decision making and revival of the old legacy of collective intervention by the people in development activities.

The decline in the quality of services, especially of those supplied by the public sector, needs urgent remedial measures, for it has already started affecting the quality of life of people, especially, vulnerable sections of the society. The over centralized system of development planning and implementation is totally unsuitable to take on these challenges. This is especially so with respect to land and water management, development of agriculture and allied sectors, rural and cottage industries, drinking water, sanitation and many of the social service sectors. In view of the consensus in favour of a decentralized system, the state also witnessed some important moves to evolve a viable mode of decentralized system of administration and planning.

GRAMODAYA – A New Initiatives

Under the above background, 'Gramoday' is an effort to consolidate and articulate public opinion in favour of decentralized planning and thereby help the government to translate its commitment to concrete actions. 'Gramoday' is a system of multi-level planning, where the lowest unit is allowed to plan and implement everything that can be performed most effectively at that level and only the residual is left to the higher levels.

The primary objective of the 'Gramoday', is to motivate and empower the Panchayati Raj Institutions to take up the new challenge of development planning. It is sought to be achieved by mobilizing people regardless of their political affiliations, religion, caste, etc. to help the Panchayati Raj Institutions in all the stages of development planning from plan formulation and implementation to maintenance.

Enthusiasm of the masses and their wholehearted participation is the key to success of any effort at decentralization. Government orders and directions alone are no guarantee for informed and enthusiastic participation of the people. This is especially so in the context of the contemporary reality of near total alienation of people form development activities. Therefore, a mass awareness programme is found to be necessary to mobilise people and motivate them to take up different tasks related to planning from below.

The centralized system of planning is insensitive not only to local conditions but also to local knowledge on development problems with which people of each locality are richly endowed. In this respect, what 'Gramoday', has sought to do is to establish a system at the village level in which the villagers themselves harness such scattered information and knowledge to be used in evolving future development activities. But local experience and knowledge constitutes only one of the many pieces of information required for making development plan at the local level. The local knowledge needs to be blended with information on modem technological alternatives, alternative sources of funding, ongoing development programmes of line departments and other agencies, etc. In short, the Plan Campaign has to ensure that minimum necessary skills of development planning are imparted to the local people and the representative governments at that level. In other words, what is being sought through the Campaign is not just nominal participation but informed participation of the people.

Evolution, Structure and Process of GRAMODAY

The Tripura State Planning Board was reconstituted in early 1998. It held its first meeting on the 6th July 1998. During this meeting, 4 (four) sub-committees for the primary sector, secondary sector, tertiary sector and tribal welfare were formed for formulating sectoral plans. On the basis of recommendations of these sub-committees, "Approach to People's Plan in Tripura" was prepared which clearly identifies the areas of strengths and weaknesses, sets about the objectives of the State Government, chalks out the strategies for the development of each of the above four areas and lists the steps to be taken for this purpose. "Approach to People's Plan in Tripura was approved by the Council of Ministers on 27th January, 1999 and placed before the State Planning Board on the 25th February, 1999.

Among many other initiatives mentioned in the "Approach to People's Plan in Tripura", preparation of area-based plans taking into account local resources and with active participation of the people was adopted as a strategy of decentralized planning in the state. Three consecutive workshops (May 3-4, June 12-13, September 11, 1999) were organized at the state level to give a concrete shape to the idea of participatory planning and resource mapping. Experts from Kerala State Planning Board, Geological Survey of India (GSI), North-Eastern Regional Institute of Water and Land Management (NERIWALM), National Remote Sensing Agency (NRSA), Action Aid India, etc. were invited to share their experiences. After several rounds of discussions, the concept of 'Gramoday' got crystallized.

It was then decided to launch 'Gramoday' first in the West Tripura district and after learning from the experiences of West Tripura, to extend it subsequently to all the districts of the state. The district level training of Sector officers in West Tripura district was organized on January 18, 2000. 'Gramoday' was formally launched at Harishnagar J.B. School in Bishalgarh Block on 7th February, 2000 by His Excellency the Governor of Tripura. The work was reviewed and experiences of West Tripura district were shared in a workshop held on the 16th October, 2000. It was decided to expand 'Gramoday' to the entire state during 2000-01 for formulation of plan for 2001-02.

At the very begging a format was prepared and supplied to all the panchayats. The format devised for the 'Gramoday' has four parts as indicated below :

1. *Part - I–Village Profile*-It includes the basic data of the village.
2. *Part - II–Identification of Gaps*–On the basis of data collected and norms/requirements, the gaps in resources/ infrastructure existing in the village are to be identified in this part.
3. *Part - III–Perception of the People*–Views and observation of the local people on their developmental needs are to be recorded in this part.
4. *Part - IV–Village Development Plan*–This is the last part and is the plan for development of the village, prepared on the basis of perception of the people recorded in Part-III and with reference to information available in Part-I and II.

Series of workshops were held at the district level in all the four districts. At the end of workshop in each district, district level resource persons were identified and dates for the training of sector officers were fixed.

Within a block, for the purpose of 'Gramoday', all the villages are grouped into sectors. Each sector comprises about 5-6 villages. Generally, an officer (Sector Officer), not below the rank of an extension officer of a line department, called Sector Officer, be in-charge of the sector for imparting training, supervision and coordination of works.

In each village, a Village Planning Team had been constituted by the Sector Officer, in consultation with the Village Pradhan. The Village Planning team consists of 2-3 government officials and 2-3 volunteers from the concerned village, and essentially consists of Gram Pradhan, Panchayat Secretary and VLW of concerned village. Panchayat Secretary is the convenor of the Team. The volunteers preferably should have an educational background of Madhyamik and above. The number of members may vary either way (by 2-3 members), depending on the availability of good volunteers and the need of the area. To accommodate additional volunteers/experts, sector/subject wise task forces or sub-committees may be constituted.

The sector officer is mainly responsible for the training of the Planning Teams, supervision and co-ordination of the 'Gramoday', at the sector level. He also acts as moderator for the village level meetings.

The Village Planning Team is the most crucial and important component in the organizational hierarchy of the 'Gramoday'. This Team is primarily responsible for undertaking the works of:

- Awareness campaign.
- Collection of information.
- Understanding and recording the perception of people, and
- Preparation of the development plan at the village level.

At the block level, a Block Level Planning and Coordination Committee, consisting of officials from the major development departments and some non-officials, is formed for Sector Officers/VPTs, for examining the plan proposals (panchayat/ block), their technical viability, compilation of plan proposals form the panchayats, and supervision and co-ordination of the 'Gramoday' at the block level. The BDO acts as convenor of the Block Level Planning and Coordination.

The Objectives

In order to ensure maximum active participation of the people in the planning process, they must be assured that their suggestions/advices, derived from their knowledge and wisdom, are not going to be wasted. Active participation of people and formulation of plan proposal are the two essential components of any micro-level plan exercise. The unique feature of 'Gramoday' is that both these components are given maximum priority for the preparation of the village/panchayat development plan. Active participation of the people does not mean just giving importance to their advices in the formulation and implementation of schemes. It means the enhancement of the level of their consciousness and increase in their level of self-confidence in the process.

The primary objective of 'Gramoday' is to empower the local bodies so that they formulate their plan proposals with maximum participation of people. However, its real agenda has been much more challenging than the immediate objective of drawing the plan proposals.

Defined in the broad sense, 'Gramoday' is an attempt to conceptualize, operationalise and institutionalize a system of multi-level, people centred planning process suitable to the regional specifications of Tripura. As a corollary of the above objective, it also aims at bringing about a major transformation in the attitude of various participants in the development process, viz., officials, elected representatives, intelligentsia and the people at large. It is also an effort to make the local people aware of the locally available resources. What is needed is a new development culture itself. It is also of equal importance that the system of multi-level planning thus put in place helps the State to overcome its contemporary development crisis.

Needless to assert that the broad goals of 'Gramoday' identified above could be broken into a series of detailed objectives, *viz.*,

- an assessment of locally available resources;
- reconstructing the received ideas on decentralization and people's planning;
- enabling the State Government to translate its commitment to concrete actions by mobilizing people in support;
- harnessing popular opinion and will to overcome resistance offered by vested interests;
- correcting popular and well entrenched but wrong notions of development by initiating development dialogues and introducing plausible alternatives;
- involving mass organizations of the people in development activities;
- imparting knowledge and skills needed for local level planning; and
- evolving and institutionalizing a systematic procedure by which development needs of the people are articulated, suitable solutions arrived at, prioritized, integrated into

comprehensive development plans, implemented, and monitored with maximum people's participation at all levels.

Last but not the least is the objective of horizontal and vertical integration of planning between various tiers.

Importance and timeliness of 'Gramoday' is best understood in the light of the following :

- Prevailing criticism of centralized planning and administration in the country.
- Failure of past efforts at decentralization and the intimidating long list of obstacles that new attempt at genuine decentralization face.
- Contemporary development challenges of the State which by consensus demand a decentralized approach to planning as also a revival of the participatory spirit to protect the widely acclaimed gains of the past.

Grassroots Reality

For better understanding, about the actual process of Gramodaya, a micro level rapid appraisal was conducted with few necessary components of decentralized planning in two villages – one non-ADC village and another ADC village in West Tripura district. Rangutia village is a non-ADC village having seven wards while Sepaipara is an ADC village having four wards under Mohanpur R.D. Block.

(i) Planning Process

In each ward, meeting (Gram Sansad) is organized. In this meeting all adult members of that ward and Panchayat members are required to be present. In this meeting all people can express their needs and problems which are noted in the ward register copy.

Then after completion of all ward level meetings, one meeting takes place in the Panchayat office or other place where the elected Panchayat members, Panchayat Secretary, other Panchayat workers, Pradhan (Chairman of GP), Upa-Pradhan (Vice-Chiarman of GP), BDO and other related officials of the block are present. In the presence of above mentioned persons and with the help of register book of each ward the action plan of the following year is made.

After the preparation of the action plan, every person of each household of that village is invited formally to be present in the Gram Shabha. In this Gram Shabha, the BDO, Panchayat body and others officers of the block are present.

Gram Shaba starts when the one-third of the population is present. The action plan is read by someone in front of the whole population and after the reading of the action plan, if there is any objection and suggestion of the people, it is included in the action plan. Approved action plan is sent to the block for further approval and funding.

(ii) People's Participation

In this planning system villagers can participate. However, the Panchayat Secretary, Pradhan and Upa-Pradhan control the process. In Ward Sansad, people express their needs, but it totally depends on the members as to what will be registered in the list or not. Ultimately, only the Panchayat members and other officers determine the plan. Again, when the plan is ready it is read by someone for the village people and all the calculation of fund is also shown. Members present are asked to give their opinion if they have anything to say. But in such a big gathering hardly anyone gets chance to express his/her view. Sometime, one may not express his/her view due to hesitation. So ultimately people's view is not taken properly.

In ADC village the situation is more pathetic. In the Panchayat (VDC), all the members are tribals who are not so much educated and therefore totally dependent and guided by Panchayat Secretary who has very little knowledge about local needs and local language. For example, villagers wanted a health centre various times but it never got any importance in the village planning. The whole planning system is centred only. Some elite class people express their views and suggestions in favour of the tribal villagers.

(iii) Utilization of Local Resources

There is no village resource which can be used in implementation of plan without human resource. Human resources are used in the plan. Sometime it is seen that the human resource is not trained enough to utilise village resources and therefore trained manpower has to be brought from outside.

Again the work is not enough according to the human resources. So the problem arises regarding the distribution of work.

(iv) Implementation of Plan

The overall responsibility of implementation of the plan in each ward is given to the elected ward members and the people of that ward along with concerned officer. The labour is taken from the village and the Secretary, Pradhan and Upa-Prodhan allot the work. In implementation of plan one management committee is made. Generally, small works are given to the villagers; but when the scale of the work is large the responsibility is given to the contractor.

In A.D.C. Village the Pradhan, Upa-Pradhan and Panchayat Secretary are related with the implementation of plan.

Major Problems

1. The process of Gramoday is not followed properly. Only information format are filled up and sent to upper levels.
2. There is lack of active participation of the people in the grass root level planning. This is due to lack of awareness and lack of importance given by the authorities.
3. Elected Panchayat members are not trained properly for Panchayat activities and don't have the required skill for planning.
4. In the village level, hardly any VPT exists. Therefore, Panchayat Secretary is responsible for the village planning and as a result the quality of the planning widely varies from panchayat to panchayat.
5. Gram Sabha is full of different agendas. Planning hardly gets any importance both by the villagers as well as by the panchayat functionaries. Villagers are mostly interested on development schemes, from which they are 'personally' benefited.
6. There is some bias in the Panchayat activities. Therefore, some people think Gram Sabha is a political meeting rather than public meeting and become reluctant to attend and give their opinion.
7. The fund is neither available in time, nor up to the requirement. The fund is given quarterly. So sometimes, it

creates problems during implementation. Beside this, getting approval of various estimations is a long process which spoils the time. This causes delay in project implementation in the village.

8. The officers from line departments participate half-heartedly. They have their own departmental target and planning. This is the biggest obstacle towards success of this innovative planning system in Tripura. It became an isolated activity of Planning and Coordination department.

Steps Forward

To minimize the above problems and prepare meaningful and effective planning, following measures may be taken:

1. Gramodaya process needs to follow the preparation of not only village development plan but also preparation of block, district as well as state plan. Then only the objectives of decentralization of planning can be achieved.
2. Active people's participation is the heart of decentralized planning. Adequate attention should be given for ensuring people's participation in real sense.
3. Gram Sabha meetings are vital for the identification of the felt need at the time of preparing the plan. Quality meeting in Gram Sabha must be ensured. In such meeting people can't expresses their view and can't understand all about distribution of fund and work. Therefore to make understand the people about the fund and work another meeting would take place at the ward level after the preparation of plan.
4. Education level of the villagers, particularly among the tribals, should be improved by giving all the facilities of education. It will widen the meaningful participation in the development process.
5. Panchayat members should not ignore the involvement of local people during preparation of plan.
6. Political bias should be avoided because it has been disturbing the social harmony and for these people also think about Panchayat system as a part of political party which is controlled by political members.

7. Some specific and mandatory training programmes need to be organized for the elected members and panchayat functionaries.
8. For improving decentralised planning the Gram Panchayat must be equipped with necessary manpower and infrastructure.
9. Utilization of local resources in a proper way among the local people is very much necessary and for that an inventory of socio-economic information of each village is quite essential.
10. In Panchayat there should be co-ordination between Panchayat members and government functionaries, locally active NGOs, CBOs, clubs and other developmental agencies.
11. Panchayat should try to augment its income. For these, they should identify the under utilized and unutilized resources and make commercial uses of the available resources.
12. The Gram Sabha should be organized on holidays so that all people of the village can participate and can express their view.
13. Fund which is allotted to the Gram Panchayat is not enough. More funds are needed to meet the need of the people of the village.
14. Panchayat should give importance to the socially excluded classes of the village.

REFERENCES

Aziz, Abdul, 1995: *Decentralisation - Mandal Panchayat System in Karnataka*, National Institute of Rural Development, Hyderabad.

Ghosh, Arun, 1988: "Decentralized Planning, West Bengal Experience", *Economic and Political Weekly*, March 26.

Sanyal, B.M., 2001: *India: Decentralised Planning Themes and Issues*, Concept Publishing Company, New Delhi.

Cheema, G.S. and Rondineli, D.A. (eds.),1983: *Decentralization and Development: Policy Implementation in Developing Countries*, Sage, Beverley Hill.

Das Gupta, Ashim, 1994: "Panchayati Raj and Decentralized Planning in West Bengal in Decentralized Planning and Panchayati Raj". (Proceedings of the D.T. Lakdawala Memorial Symposium), Institute of Social Sciences, New Delhi, Concept Publishing Company, New Delhi.

Thimmaiah, G., 1998: "Democratic Decentralisation; Lessons from India", *Man and Development*, CRRID, Vol. XX No. 3, Chandigarh.

Palanithuran, G., 1999: *New Panchayati Raj System at work : An Evaluation*, Concept Publishing Company, New Delhi.

Govt. of India, 1993: "Microlevel Planning and involvement of people at grassroot level", *Report of NDC Committee*, Planning Commission, New Delhi, April.

Hazra, A. and Choudhury, J. (eds.), 2005: "Participatory Micro Planning for Village Eco-Development", in *Decentralized Planning and Participatory Rural Development,* Concept Publishing Company, New Delhi, pp. 92-105.

Institute of Social Sciences, 1994: *Decentralized Planning and Panchayati Raj* (Proceedings of the D.T. Lakdawala Memorial Symposium), Concept Publishing Company, New Delhi,.

Narain, Iqbal, 1960: "The idea of Democratic decentralization", *Indian Journal of Political Science*, Vol. XXI, No. 2, 184-92

Meenakshi Sundaram, S.S., 1994: *Decentralization in Developing Countries*, Concept Publishing Company, New Delhi.

Mishra, S.N., 1984: *Rural Development Planning - Design and Method*, Satvahan, New Delhi.

Misra, R.P. and Sundaram K.V., 1980: *Multi-level Planning and Integrated Rural Development in India*, Heritage Publishers, New Delhi.

Mukherjee, Amitava, 1991: *Methodology and Database for Decentralized Planning, Vol. 3 (Parts A, B and C)*, Heritage Publishers, New Delhi.

Reddy, Y. Venugopal, 1979: *Multilevel Planning in India*, Vikas Publishing House, New Delhi.

Ali, Shaikh Maqsood; Safiur, Muhammad and Das, Kshanada Mohan 1983: *Decentralization and People's Participation in Bangladesh*. National Institute of Public Administration, Dhaka.

Shalini, Rajneesh, 2002: *Rural Development through Democratic Decentralisation,* Deep and Deep Publications, New Delhi.

United Nation Development Programme, 2001: *Decentralisation in*

India Challenges and Opportunities, Discussion Paper Series I, New Delhi.

United Nations, 1962: *Decentralization for National and Local Development*, UN, New York.

United Nations, 1987: *Local Participation in Development Planning*, UN, New Delhi.

United Nations, 1975: Popular Participation and Decision-making for Development, UN, New York.

Vyas, V.S.; Bhatt, Snil and Shah, S.M.,1985: *Decentralized Planning in India*, Oxford and IBH Publishing, New Delhi.

Yadav, R.P. and Kafle, M.P., 1980: "Development Planning in Nepal", Paper to the *Expert Group Meeting on Development Planning at District Level*, Kathmandu, Nepal, Oct. 24-Nov. 1, (mimeographed).

Yugandhar, B.N.and Mukherjee, Amitava, 1991: *Readings in Decentralized Planning (with Special reference to District Planning, Vols. I and II,* Concept Publishing Company, New Delhi.

14

System of Land Management in Arunachal Pradesh

K. Haloi

Introduction

Arunachal Pradesh is the 24th state of the Union of Indian with 83,743 km^2 geographical area and 10.98 lakh population as per 2001 Census. It lies in the extreme North East corner of India and in the global grid, the state is situated between 26^0 28' N and 29^0 30' N Latitude and 91^0 34' E and 97^0 30' E Longitude. The state shares its boundary with Tibet to the north, with Myanmar to the north and north-east, with Bhutan to the west and with Assam to the South. Being part of the eastern Himalayas, the terrain of the state is extremely hilly. The plain lands are available in patches bordering the state of Assam and few valleys in between which constitute a small fraction of the total area. Administratively, the state is divided into 16 districts. To the India's total, the population constitutes a small fraction (0.11%) while in terms of geographical area, the state shares 2.55 per cent of India's total geographical land area.

According to Census, 2001, people in the state are housed in seventeen towns and 3863 inhabited villages. Towns except Itanagar, the capital of the state, are basically administrative headquarters and small in population size. Villages are tiny with 71.6 per cent having population less than 200 and 17.5 per cent having in the range of 200-500. Nearly 80 per cent of the people live in rural areas. On density count, the state is sparsely populated with 13 persons per km^2. The population with 26.21 per cent growth in the last decade maintained much higher rate than the national average while on sex ratio count, it registered low status with 901 female per thousand male. In the literacy front, the position of the state remained low (54.30%) as against the all India average (64.80%). The back bone of rural economy in the state is agriculture and thus land is an important asset attached to the livelihood of the people. It provides employment for about 62 per cent of the working population of which 58 per cent are self-employed and 4 per cent are wage earner in agriculture.

Arunachal Pradesh is the home of 25 major tribal groups of Mongoloid racial origin and is a tribal state. Tribal population constitutes 64.20 per cent of total population in the state. The habitations are located distantly over the vast mountainous territory. It is typical in the state that land belongs to the people of the villages as per the provision of the Constitution of India and it is governed by the customary laws. The state government in other words is not the controlling as well as management authority of land. The customary laws are such that these are oral and transferred from one generation to the next. The same is the case with the laws related to the land also. As such there is no verifiable written record. The state government is left with very little business to initiate any improved land management measures as it is not the custodian of the land. As part of government effort, there is survey and settlement only in the capital town of the state and administrative headquarters. The vast territory thus is under oral land record system of the people of the village.

Against this backdrop, the land management systems that are in practice among the people are important areas of understanding. It assumes importance not because that there are uniqueness to learn from the traditional systems, over the period of time there might have taken place various changes in the course of development causing varieties of issues necessitating appropriate measures for better management of land. It is in this light, the paper makes a presentation about the land system in the state along with the emerging issues with a view to outline some recommendations for needful action.

In order to assess the practices, available literature, government orders, ordinances and Acts and other available literature on the subject published in journals and newspapers were scanned. Secondary data available under various government sources have also been made use of. The data gathered by the National Institute of Rural Development from five sample villages (Yachuli of Nyishi tribe, Tamen of Nyishi tribe, Siro and Lempia of Apatani tribe and Dek Godak of Nyishi tribe) of Lower Subansiri District for a land reform related study in the state is the source of primary data used in the paper. This has been presented under six broad headings namely; (1) Introduction and Methodology, (2) Legal Provision and Official arrangement for Land Management, (3) An Account of Few Land Related Statistics, (4) Indigenous Land Management System, (5) Issues related to Land and management System and (6) Recommendations.

Legal Provision and Official Arrangement for Land Management

Legal Provision

As per the provision of the Constitution of India, land belongs to the people of the village. The Government of the state is not the custodian of the state land. By provision, land neither can be sold to the non-tribal nor can non-tribal buy land in the state. Inner Line System is still another provision. With this, the entry of countrymen other than the state is possible into the state only with due permission of the state authority.

The state is yet to have an Act dealing adequately the various issues related to effective management of land. There are three old regulations which are supposed to govern the land till today. These are:

Balipara Frontier Tract Jhum Regulation of 1947.
Sadiya Frontier Tract Jhum Regulation of 1947.
Tirup Frontier Tract Jhum Regulation, 1947.

Official Setup

For management and administration of land in the state, the state government has a Directorate located in the capital. Presently, the Directorate is manned by a Director, Deputy Director, Asst. Director, Office Surveyor, and Office

Superintendent along with 4 Assistants, 3 UDCs and 14 LDCs. Besides, there are the surveyors (6), Supervisor Kanango (26), Recorder Kanango (10), Mandal (49), Chainman (75), Draughtmen (3) and office assisting staff (12) to carry out the field activities of the Directorate. To equip and update the skill of surveyor, there is no training institute in the state. The surveyors are sent to other states for training.

For strengthening of revenue administration and updating land records, there is a scheme of central government. The office has received funds under the scheme and made use of the same. It however, could not undertake aerial survey work. Computerization of land records is another scheme of central government. Since there is cadastral survey only in small pockets, the implementation of the scheme did not take place. The activities that are performed by the Directorate in the state are presented below:

Land Survey, Settlement and Record

Conduct of survey and settlement is one of the activities of the Directorate. The activity however, is piecemeal in nature. The areas targeted under it are the government land in the capital complex and district, sub-divisions and circle headquarters. Land records are prepared and provided when sought for. Land revenue in the surveyed area however, is not collected. Instead of land revenue here in the urban area a kind of fee once for all is being fixed at a minimum rate in per square metre. Thus, it may be seen as an attempt to familiarize the tribal people with land revenue system on land and gradually to bring the state under the purview of formal land administration and land reforms policies initiated by the Government of India.

There is thus, no regular survey and settlement done till date in the state covering entire territory. The areas that belong to the people of the village and the area an individual family or any other social unit own are not known with verifiable document. Unlike some other states of north-east India, there is no tribal resistance to survey and settlement in Arunachal Pradesh. What is required is a time bound plan of action to undertake and accomplish the survey and settlement operation in the state.

Land Acquisition and Compensation

The need for land for undertaking various development activities keeps on rising. The government acting as the authority of the land usually keeps on meeting such need. In Arunachal Pradesh, the state government has no authority to acquire land from the people as land belongs to the people of the villages. The issue of land acquisition by government is related to the issue of paying compensation. Whenever there arises need for land for undertaking various development activities, government initiate the purchase process and make it available provided people of the concerned village or villages agree to do so. Necessary payment as agreed upon is made. Such purchase/transformation of land began with the establishment of district headquarters followed by establishment of capital complex at Itanagar, construction of hydro-electricity project in Lower Subansiri district, construction of National Highway, etc. People usual provide land free of cost for the purpose of establishment of schools, health facilities, drinking water, electricity line, etc.

Land Possession Certificate

Documentary proofs of land are required more often for undertaking various development activities and particularly where credit from formal banking institution is involved. Since such records are not available in the present system, the government of Arunachal Pradesh has introduced a system of issuing land possession certificate to the holder of the land to fulfill such necessity of the people. The Deputy Commissioner is the recommending authority and the state government is the approving authority of such land possession certificate. At the district level, the DC in this task is assisted by Assistant Commissioner and Circle Officer. The process to reach the top is very far from the bottom and is extremely difficult for people living in far flung areas. There is no end to such problem until there is cadastral survey and settlement operation in complete form.

An Account of Few Land Related Statistics

State Territory and Reporting Area

As per data available in government records, the territorial area of the state accounts for 83,743 km^2. As against this, the reporting area as figures in land use statistics of the government stands at 54,978 km^2. This means that the reporting area of the state is less by 34.35 per cent as compared to its total territorial area. There are as a matter of fact, many instances of the states where reporting area is lesser than the geographical area of the state. Such gap usually is found to be negligible or very small nearly for all cases. What is striking and different in the case of Arunachal Pradesh is that the gap is too high. Secondly, the phenomenon has continued for long period. The country (India) as it is known to all had its external boundary fixed along with its independence. With a definite territory and population, Arunachal Pradesh evolved in 1987 as the 24th state of the Indian Union. In other words, the country as a whole found 61 years and the state of Arunachal Pradesh 22 years for consolidation of its territorial area. Given the time factor in mind, the reporting area remaining short by more than one-third of the total area is an issue to ponder. With this, does it mean that the control and governance is confined only to the present reporting area of the state? And if it is to be understood so, then where lies the boundary line? If not, why then there is no statistical account over one-third of the total area of the state? The fundamental question is: should the gap in statistical account continue further? The change particularly after globalization in any matter has been very fast. There is immediate need for the state to exercise its control and governance over the full territory.

Cultivable and Cultivated Land

As mentioned earlier, the reporting area of the state is less by 34.35 per cent of its geographical area. Out of the reporting area, the use of land on cultivable and uncultivable account stands at 5.72 and 94.28 per cent respectively. On cultivated and uncultivated account, the corresponding area covers 3.54 per cent and 96.46 per cent. With cultivable land (5.72%) if the area put to non-agricultural use (0.08%) and the forest area under Anchal Reserve (0.64%), Village Reserve (0.58%) and day today use of villagers, say one or two per cent are added, the total area under human intervention remains around 8 per cent of the reporting area. Table 1 shows area under broad land use categories in the state.

Table 1
Broad Land Use Category, 2004-05

Particulars	*Area (km^2)*	*% to Geog. Area*	*% to Reporting Area*
Geographical Area	83743.00	100.00	
Reporting Area	54978.00	65.65	100.00
Total Cultivable land	314.27	3.75	5.72
Total Cultivated land	194.63	2.32	3.54
Total Uncultivable land	5183.49	61.90	94.28
Total Uncultivated land	5303.13	63.33	96.46
Nine Fold Categories of Use			
Forest area	51540	61.55	93.75
Land put to Non-Agri. Uses	4.59	0.05	0.08
Barren and unculturable Land	20.95	0.25	0.38
Pasture/Grazing Land	3.95	0.05	0.07
Misc. Tree Crops and groves	35.98	0.43	0.65
Culturable Waste	36.65	0.44	0.67
Old Fallow	47.02	0.56	0.86
Current Fallow	30.43	0.36	0.55
Net Area Sown (NAS)	164.19	1.96	2.99

Source: Statistical Hand Book.

Forest Land

Arunachal Pradesh is a tribal state and in consideration of its recorded forest area, it can be termed as a forest state. The land use statistics reflecting as high as 93.75 per cent of the total reporting area under forest makes the point evident. Tribal and forest thus are a coherent coexistence exhibited in the state. Few indicators about the forest of the state in comparison to the nation are highly encouraging. In terms of area, state's forest area shares 6.65 per cent of the country's total. In terms of forest cover, it shares 10.03 per cent of the country's total. A per capita count indicates that forest and tree cover in the state is 6.27 hectare per person. Such a high position is to be understood with total geographical area of the state sharing mere a 2.5 per cent of the country's total.

As per government account, the forest areas in the state fall under different legal status (Table 2). In number count, there are as many as seven. Similar legal status is not seen in most of the states of the Indian Union. Among the seven fold categories, 'unclassified state forest' category covers the largest area occupying 60.08 per cent of the total forest area. By nomenclature although the category looks as if it belongs to the state government, but operationally it is not so. A keen look at the constitutional provisions makes the point clear. The land according to the provision of the Constitution belongs to the people of the villages. The areas, which are accounted under 'unclassified state forest', are in fact under community control. On the other hand, there is no act or law of the government putting such area under the control of the state. In that light, the area account of the state under the category appears to be an unauthorized act. Secondly, the act is likely to cause denial of the tribal rights over land and forest in course of time. Serious consideration at the earliest is must. History is harsh. Otherwise, the tribal state Arunachal Pradesh will be an example of acting against the interest of the tribals.

Table 2
Forest Area by Legal Status

Sl. No.	*Legal Classification*	*Area (km²)*	*% of Recorded Forest*	*% of Geographical Area*
1.	Reserve Forests	9722.69	18.86	11.61
2.	Protected Forests	694.30	1.35	0.82
3.	Anchal Reserve Forest	329.38	0.64	0.39
4.	Village Reserve Forest	300.24	0.58	0.36
5.	National Parks	2468.24	4.79	2.94
6.	Wild Life Sanctuary	7059.75	13.70	8.43
7.	Unclassified State Forest	30965.39	60.08	36.90
	Total	51540.00	100.00	61.55

Source: Forest Statistics (Up to Year 2000-2001) Arunachal Pradesh.

In the remaining 40 per cent forest areas, there are six legal categories. They include reserve forests, wild life sanctuary, national parks, protected forests, anchal reserve and village forests. The area under the corresponding categories accounts for 18.86, 13.70, 4.79, 1.35, 0.64 and 0.58 per cent of the forest area. Among them, reserve forest, wild life sanctuary, protected forest and national park belong to the government. But as a matter of fact, even within much of the protected area and the reserve forests, communities are present and they are actively engaged in its management. Disputes here too are an inherent element. The categories that are free from disputes are anchal reserve and village reserve forest. The middle tier panchayat is the owner of Anchal reserve forest and village community is the owner of the village reserve.

What constitutes the natural habitat *i.e.* forest, there are accounts available in various reports. Such reports indicate that the forest area of the state holds lot of the importance for its rich bio-resource reserve. The fact cited is that the North Eastern Region wherein Arunachal Pradesh is an integral constituent is considered as one of the world's 18 biodiversity hotspots. The state while possesses nearly 2.5 per cent of India's total land area, the richness it holds in terms of faunal and floral diversity is enormous as it retains 20 per cent of the faunal diversity, including 85 species of terrestrial mammals, 500 species of birds, 4,500 species of angiosperms and 500 species of orchids. The worth forest holds in the state particularly in the context of the concern of global warming is of high order and dividends are due in course of time. The need is to retain and preserve these forests with utmost care. Towards such need, it is encouraging to see the forest density status in the state. The analysis based on satellite image indicates (Forest Statistics, 2000-01) that 13,907 km^2 is under dense forest, 39,604 km^2 under moderately dense forest and 14,508 km^2 under open forest. The corresponding area accounts for 20.44, 58.20 and 21.32 per cent of the total area under forest cover (68045 km^2). The above implies that the impact of human intervention has influenced very little over the forest cover of the state.

Wastelands

As per available wastelands data, 2003 (Wastelands Atlas, 2005), there are wastelands in the state measuring 28354.65 km^2 in total. This accounts 21.70 per cent of the total geographical area of the state and is a quite a large figure. In a state where human interventions have very little influence in the use of land, it is necessary to take note of the factors causing wasteland in the state. A keen look at development of wastelands by sources is made. This shows that the most dominant wastelands category in the state is the snow cover/ glacial areas (12.22%) followed by scrub (with or without) land (6.23%). The two categories put together account for 18.45 per cent out of 21.70 per cent and the forces that lie behind are natural. Barren/ rocky (0.89%) and waterlogged/marshy land (0.05%) similarly are the other two natural factors affecting another 0.94 per cent of the geographical area. Thus, natural forces causing wastelands in the state account for 19.39 per cent out of 21.70 per cent. Human intervention may be attributed as the factor responsible for development of wastelands accounting for 2.31 per cent of the total geographical area. To this shifting cultivation (current and abandoned) contributes 1.93 per cent, grazing /pasture land 0.36 per cent and degraded unclassified forest land 0.01 per cent. What matters here also is the concept about the shifting cultivation. It is a system of land use in the hilly areas of the state evolved through ages. The basis of the system lies with the forest which is cut-used-rebuilt in cyclic order and there is a school of thought which regards it as sustainable.

Operational Land Holdings

Though there is no land survey and settlement and verifiable land records (except urban centres) in the state, Agricultural Census operation has enumeration system and according to 2000-01 records, the number of operational holdings stands at 1.07 lakhs in the state. Across the holding categories, the marginal category accounts 14.02 per cent, small 18.69 per cent, semi-medium 33.64 per cent, medium- 28.04 per cent and large 5.61 per cent. The figures recorded can be questioned to any length given the status of land survey and settlement operation in the state. These are, however, enough to push home the fact that the access to land by the people in the state is not a critical issue to address as there is land in plenty compared to the population.

Indigenous Land Management System

Traditional Land Management Authority

As per the Constitutional provision, land in the state belongs to the people and it is governed by the customary laws.

Importantly, the customary laws of all tribes have sanction for a village authority at the apex level to which the authority of control of land and the management of access to are attached. In the overall socio-cultural fabric of the tribal people also, these traditional village authorities are of vital importance. These institutions in their traditionality have been subjected to number of changes and this took place particularly in the last two centuries. The first wave of change began with the introduction of the institutions of Gaon Burah (Village Headman) and Dobhasis (Interpreter) by the British rule. The second wave of change made its beginning with the introduction of the Panchayati Raj Institution (PRI) by the state government. Operationally, in the state now, two types of local governments exist and function at the grassroots level. The one that continues with the legacy of the tradition may be distinguished as traditional village government. PRI, the other one that exists and functions under an Act of law of the state government may be distinguished as modern.

Each tribe having distinctive culture and custom of its own has its own traditional village authority. The governing rule of the customary laws similarly has variation among the tribes. Intra tribe variation and even variation from one village to another are also discernable. Among the tribes, the traditional village authorities are known by different names: the *Kebang* of the Adis and Bokar, *Dolu Keba* of the Pailibo, Tagin and Galo, *Mele* of the Akas, *Buliang* of the Apatanis, *Nimiyang* of the Bugun, *Bang Nyele* of the Nyishis, *Khapong* of the Tangsa, *Wancho-Wangsa* of the Wanchos [Chieftainship], *Ngongthum* of the Noctes [Chieftainship], *Mukchum* or *Mukchum-Khai-Kham* of the Kamptis [Chieftainship], *Tra Tangoai* of the Singphos, *Abbala* of the Idu Mishimis, *Pharai* of the Kaman Mishmi, *Tso Tsorgan/Yui Tsorgan/Thumi* of the Monpas, *Jong* of the Sherdukpens, and so on. Institutional variety thus is one of the traditional hall marks of the state with all tribal groups having one institution of their own at the village level.

The village elders and clan/lineage heads usually constitute the traditional village government with one of them acting as head. The person who among the village elders and clan/lineage heads draws respect from all and is thorough about the customs usually become the head of the village government. The members have terms of office usually for life time unless incapacity, serious misconduct and voluntary relinquishment from the job compel villagers to seek replacement. The selection usually precedes intense consultation among the families.

Most of the systems function democratically and most importantly, decisions are based on the principle of consensus. The system of chieftainship and hereditary head also exist in the case of few tribes like the Noctes and Wangchos, Khamptis. These institutions are the custodian of customary laws and act as administrator, justice provider and decision makers. Control of land and forest and management of access to land and other natural resources are the most critical functions of these institutions.

PRI, the modern type, is a three-tier system in the state with Zilla Parished (ZP) at the top, Anchal Samittee (AS) at the middle and Gram Panchayat (GP) at the bottom. The terms of office of the panchayat are five years and its constitution is based on adult franchise of the local people. Non-local is not entitled to vote. In latest Panchayat election (2008), the three-tier system accounts for 16 ZPs, 94 ASs and 1779 GPs. In the state thus, the traditional village governments exist and function side by side the PRI. Development although is the functional domain of the panchayat, they are weakly empowered in the state. Only functions have been devolved (2008). The devolution of funds and functionaries are yet to take place. Significantly, land is not an item in the functional domain of the PRIs.

In the management of land, the role of the institution of village government is of two types. The land belongs to the chief in the case of Wangcho, Nocte and Khampti as Chieftainship is the form of village authority among them. The Chief is assisted by the elders and clan heads in the control of land and the management of access to it. In the case other tribes like the Adis, Nyishis, Tagins, Galos, Akas, Apatanis, Buguns, Tangsas, Singphos, Idu Mishimis, Kaman Mishmis, Monpas, Sherdukpens, etc. the village authorities are custodian of village land. They function democratically. The administration of justice in case there is violation of the rights over land takes place, there prevails the traditional authority. The matters that are not settled at village level are brought to the area level. The customary land tenure thus rules the roost of land holding pattern in the state.

Over the years, the powers of the traditional institutions have been diluted due to lack of faith in them by the younger generations and by the entry of Panchayati raj institutions. The traditional fabric of society has also been wounded with the increased monetization of the economy and the commercialization of the use of natural resources. The natural resources and the forests have suffered as a result of continuous exploitation and degradation and have been treated as a source of revenue.

Land Rights

The customary laws recognize land ownership at the level of different social units namely; individual family, lineage/clan and community level. The landed property held by the corresponding ownership units is called as private, clan/lineage and community property. Under each ownership category, land rights such as use right, possession right, inheritance right and sale/purchase right are defined. Among the tribal groups, all the ownership categories, however, do not exist. Private property enjoys all the rights. Clan/lineage property has number of formalities in enjoying the land rights. The clan/lineage head usually is the final decision maker of such land. For community land, village authority on behalf of the community is the custodian. If two elementary rights over community land *i.e.* the right to use and the right to occupy are enjoyed by any person undisturbed and continuously over a reasonably long period, the custom sanctions permanent right which in course of time become heritable and transferable.

Transfer of land by inheritance is common. The society is patriarchal among all the tribal groups and descent; inheritance and succession are traced through male line. The land held by a family thus goes in the name of male heir. The variation that has among the tribes is in the succession among the male. The transfer by sale is also common and not very new. Sale to any citizen other than the state is banned by the provision of the Constitution. Sale of land to person belonging to other tribe or other village is possible provided the village authority permits to do so. Within village, mere information is sufficient.

Common Land Categories

At the end user level, following five land categories are commonly found in the villages:

- Built up including Homestead land.
- Land under Wet Rice Cultivation.
- Land under various gardens, etc.
- Land under Jhum and forest.
- Forest land.

The characteristic features of each category with reference to use and land rights are provided below:

Land Rights and Dynamics of Use

Built up including Homestead Land

Built-up including homestead is a permanent use category of land. All tribes have sanctions of their custom to provide for land for house construction besides the area holding the common facilities. Homestead lands are endowed with the right to use and the right to possess among all the tribes. Usually, transferable right is also attached to homestead land. This accrues either on account of inheritance or on account of sale or purchase. The Adis, in case abandon the house site, enjoy the property right on it. It is so with the Apatanis also. On the other hand, among the Nyishis (Hill Miri group), once a homestead land is abandoned, the new occupier gets the full right over it so long it is occupied. The area held under homestead ranges from 0.04 to 1.50 acres with an average of 0.46 acres as recorded from the study of 50 sample households (Survey, 2008) belonging to five villages of Nishi, Apatani and Hill Miri (Nyishi) of Lower Subansiri district. Landlessness is an absentee phenomenon and there is no family having scarcity for homestead land. The traditional village authority is duty bound to allot land for homestead if so required.

Land under Wet Rice Cultivation

There are two methods of agriculture in the state. In one, land is used permanently for the production of rice. Locally, the category is known as Wet Rice Cultivation (WRC) land. The river valleys, the plain land between the hills and the terraces developed belong to WRC land category. The tilling of land is done by using plough or hoe. All wet lands for paddy production have irrigation facility. During 2004-05, irrigated area accounted for 42140 hectares from the government source in the state. Irrigation in most of the wet fields however is the creation of the farmer themselves.

The WRC lands are private property in the five sample villages. Being private property, an owner can sale and the buyer can obtain the property right in absolute form. Sale within village is allowed without permission from village authority. Selling outside the village but within the tribe and beyond requires permission from village authority.

The productivity of paddy per acre of WRC is considerably good (Survey, 2008) which ranges from 9.36 to 15.1 qnt. among the five villages with an average of 10.5 qnt. The area under WRC however, is scarce. The survey also indicates that out of 50 samples households, 33 (66.67%) have WRC lands. The average area is 0.60 acre per family which ranges from 0.02 to 6.00 acres across 50 samples.

In the state, Apatani and Khampti are the most known sedentary cultivators. The tendency to have cultivation in wet field has increased among the people and as a result there are more area now covered under terrace. This infact is a sign of shift from Jhum towards settled cultivation. Importantly, the shift toward settled cultivation is linked with privatization of landed property. This however is not a new process. The age old custom has the sanction to it. As a matter of fact, nearly all landed properties including the areas under shifting cultivation irrespective of social and cultural diversity among the tribes are private property in the state.

Land under Jhum and Forest

The other method of cultivation is the Jhum (shifting cultivation). Jhum is a cyclic use of land primarily practised in the sloppy lands of the hills. The land put under Jhum is a much larger area than the land put to WRC. The WRC being scarce, Jhum is the source of livelihood of majority of the farmers and therefore is the dominant production mode. The land under it is characterised by the practice of use and fallow in succession.

Use usually goes for two years at a stress at the most while fallow varies from 3 to 12 years across the tribes. The use is preceded by clearing of jungle/forest. The process not alone provides farmer a piece of cultivable land but also helps in the collection/gathering of fuel need as much as a family want. The land after use for two years is put usually under fallow to build forest and to regain fertility of the soil that got lost during use. In other words, jhum minus forest does not exist and is objectively unsound to understand both separately.

Jhum is most popular among the Nocte, Wancho, Tangsa, Mishmi, Adi and Nyishi communites. The tribes those practise both sedentary and Jhum are the Monpas, Sherdukpens, Singphos and presently Nyishis and Adis.

There prevail two ownership types over Jhum land. In one, the ownership right of the area where Jhum is practised belongs to village community. Only use and occupation rights for a maximum period of two years are valid for the user. There is on the part of the customary laws no restriction to the issue of access to Jhum land. The ability of the farmer defined by working hands of the family and the capital to invest on labour and other inputs determines the area that can be put to use under Jhum in a particular year.

Under Jhum system, every piece of land where Jhum is practiced is owned by the individual family. These Jhum lands in other words, are private property. There are families with less land and also families with more land. The ability of the farmer as explained above does not determine the issue of access to Jhum land. The area what farmer own matter most. Under this Jhum system, the land taken from others on lease has emerged as another norm governing the issue of access to lands.

Most of the agricultural crops that constitute the food basket of the rural household are grown in the Jhum field. Crops are raised in mix and in sequence spread over many months. There is no crop failure in totality and thus stands guarantee to food security. On productivity count, the measurement although is a complex one, the quantity produced per unit of land is no way lesser than the one under mono crop. The yield measure usually referred to is against paddy leaving aside the other crops grown in the same plot. The low productivity per unit of land is not an issue at all. The issue that matter most is the labour productivity; which under jhum is low. Saving of labour while is the utmost necessity for acquisition of education, skill and knowledge and also for socio-cultural development; the farmers practising Jhum along with the family member are left with no option to save labour. The issue needs serious consideration to be addressed effectively in the context of the state.

Land under Village Forest

A forest in a village is almost a common item in the state. Five sample villages of Lower Subansiri district (Survey, 2008) also exhibited the same fact. The area figure in the five villages as per the estimate of the villagers, ranged from about 20 to 50 per cent of the total village area. These forests are regarded as the abode of various spirits and a lot of beliefs, myths, tales, etc. are linked with the village forest. It is also regarded as means for managing water sources. Usually, forest area is located away from the settled area. The rights and ritual and also ceremonial functions whenever are organized at village level limited use the forest is made. Access to villagers to serve basic needs like bamboo and timber for housing and for observance of death ritual like cremation is allowed whenever sought. For minor forest products, access to the villagers is open. With such cultural and economic uses, it is a common property resource of the village community in true sense of the term. Access to outsiders is banned. The traditional village government is the custodian of the village forest and the authority of management.

Issues Related to Land and Management System

Arunachal Pradesh assumes special significance in the light of its international border with China (Tibet), Bhutan and Myanmar. In the consolidation of its territorial area, the country as a whole found 61 years and the state of Arunachal Pradesh 22 years. Despite the reporting area of the state remaining less by 34.35 per cent than its geographical area the government as the apex authority appears to be not in full control and exercise of governance over the state's total geographical area. The status has prolonged lot while the change in any matter particularly after globalization has been very fast.

As in other parts of northeast India, the status of unclassified state forestlands is both unclear and disputed. Unclassified state forest lands are claimed variously as private, clan, and communal property and have been traditionally under the control of the community. Though termed as forest and included in the statistics, unclassified state forest areas are not under the control of the forest department, as the land does not vest with the state. The confusion and dispute continues for want of boundary demarcation, survey and settlement operation under well-defined Land Regulation Act.

The beneficiaries or the interested investors of the state are required to obtain a land possession certificate to be eligible to obtain loans or credit for developing land. Such certificate is essential for getting financial assistance from formal credit institutions for other purposes too. The people face great difficulty in obtaining land possession certificates. The Deputy Commissioner is the recommending authority for the issue of land possession certificates in favour of land owners and tillers of the soil. S/h sends all such cases for the final consideration of the state government. The process is time consuming and cumbersome.

Absence of a formal land ownership document does not encourage farmers to invest in soil conservation and other important developmental activities on the land. The rural banking systems, consequently, cannot make loans to finance tribal farming improvements, as farmers have no legally validated land titles as collateral. Thus, capital formation in hill agriculture is effectively limited.

The rules of custom and availability of land around are not critical factors at all as of now imposing limitation to the issue of access to agricultural land for production purpose. The distribution follows egalitarian pattern and maintains by and large generational equity.

The lack of clear land ownership may result in greater conflicts between the government and villagers, especially in the context of forestry projects such as JFM (Melkania and Bisht 2000). The Forest Conservation Act (1980), dealing with the diversion of forest land for non-forestry purposes, is often at odds with traditional laws as regards to cultivation in the hill areas, especially for tea, coffee, rubber, or medicinal plants in the jhum areas and no-notified areas. The present effort of the Land Record Department is highly limited as it performs extremely meagre duties.

Recommendations

In the light of the above discussions, the following are recommended-

Settlement of the State Boundary

External security implications and governance within necessitate proper demarcation of the international boundaries and maintenance of boundary pillars. The issue can be resolved amicably by initiating appropriate dialogue with China, Bhutan and Myanmar.

Introduction of Land Reform Bill

The immediate need of the hour is introduction of the land reforms bill. The bill should retain the very ethos of the custom ensuring egalitarian character on the one hand and maintaining the generational equity on the other. This can be done by taking all the tribal groups into confidence and entering into dialogue for a common comprehensive land Act. Further, people should be socially educated to understand the benefit which may accrue when land Act comes into operations. The rules should be framed in such a way that Gram Panchayat and Gram Sabha are involved actively in the land reform activities. The land reform measure in the state must lead to the saving of labour in agriculture. Towards these incentives measures encouraging farmers towards settled cultivation are to be adopted. The scheme may be framed in the line of Land Bank Scheme of the state of Sikkim. A detailed scheme be prepared for the survey of the entire state. Additional technical and non-technical staff should be recruited and training may be imparted to them with the expert aid and advice of the Survey of India. Application of GIS and remote sensing techniques be used and reduced the time cost in the preparation of cadastral map and land records. Of course, the Central Government will have to play a major role in granting special financial assistance to Arunachal Pradesh.

Formal Recognition of Community Forestry Areas

State forest departments should review all unclassified state forestlands and re-classify those under community and local government jurisdiction as community forestlands. Communities should be assisted to map and demarcate their forest areas, using participatory mapping, cadastral surveys, or 3D mapping, depending on their preference. The mapping process should be supported by the forest departments.

Strengthen Community Land and Forest Management Rules

Traditional community resource management rules and regulations require review and updating to respond to changing land, forest and water needs. Documentation, combined with community awareness building will help to formalize regulatory frameworks and reassert their effectiveness in arbitrating forest protection and management. Indigenous community institutions need to give more consideration to gender balance as women are major stakeholders in natural resource management. Indigenous resource management institutions need to be encouraged to include women and low-income members as active participants in guiding village policies and practices.

Develop Community-based Land Use Planning

Communities need support to review their land, forest and water requirements to formulate forward-looking resource management strategies. Community resource planning capacity should be facilitated through training to allow members to identify and demarcate areas suitable for Jhum and maintain and enforce a sustainable Jhum cycle (the ideal being 12-15 years, with a minimum of 10 years).

As part of resource planning activities, communities also need to identify and develop alternative land use systems for areas not suitable for Jhum, enhance soil and water conservation, and adopt improved technology to increase productivity of Jhum systems and home gardens.

Policy, Legal and Judicial Change

Community perspectives and rights need greater representation and expression in the legal rights system. In past decades, these in respect of forest have generally not been well represented in judicial hearings or decisions. This needs to be reflected in court decisions. Secondly, there is need for sustainable management of productive Jhum, wet terrace and forest to retain and encourage the interest of the communities. To check continuous environmental impacts of the small-scale forestry enterprises, community based networks should be established or strengthened for self-monitoring and decision making.

Privatisation of Communal Lands

The forests owned by the village community and clan need to be mapped, demarcated and registered. Where privatization has taken place already as part of ongoing agricultural transitions, each village community should attempt to agree on land ceilings to land concentration and ensure that privatized land remains with community residents.

REFERENCES

Baruah,T.K.M., 1960: *The Idu Mishmis,* NEFA Administration, Shillong.

Bose, Manjula (ed.), 1981: *Land Reforms in Eastern India,* Planning Forum, Jadavpur University, Calcutta.

Das, J. N., 1989: *Land System of Arunachal Pradesh,* N.M.Tripathi, Bombay.

Elewin, Verrier, 1959: *India's North East Frontier in the 19th Century,* Oxford University Press, London.

Mibang, T. and M. C. Behera (eds.), 2004: *Dynamics of Tribal Villages in Arunachal Pradesh - Emerging Realities*, Mittal Publications, New Delhi.

Pandey, B.B.; D.K. Duarah and N. Sarkar (eds.), 1999: *Tribal Village Councils of Arunachal Pradesh,* Directorate of Research, Government of Arunachal Pradesh, Itanagar.

Patel, G.D., 1970: *The Land System of Union Territories of India,* Charotar Book Stall, Anand.

Poffenberger, Mark, Editor and S.K. Barik, Dhrupad Choudhury, Vincent Darlong, Vishal Gupta, S. Palit, Ivan Roy, Ibobi Singh, B.K. Tiwari and Sanjay Upadhyay, 2007: *Indigenous Stewards of Northeast India*, Community Forestry International, Inc. / Community Forestry Alliance for the Northeast, South Lake Tahoe/ Shillong.

Sharma, R.P.P., 1962/1981: *The Sherdukpens,* Directorate of Research, Government of Arunachal Pradesh, Itanagar.

Sinha, Raghuvir 1962/1988: *The Akas,* Directorate of Research, Government of Arunachal Pradesh, Itanagar.

Srivastava, L.R.N., 1962/1988: *The Gallongs*, Directorate of Research, Government of Arunachal Pradesh, Itanagar.

Reports, Acts and Regulations

Annual Report of Rural Areas and Employment, 1995-96.

Chin Hills Regulation, 1896.

Jhum Land Regulation III, IV and V of 1947.

NEFA Regulation, 1959.

North East Frontier Areas (Administration) Regulation, 1948.

IV

Mapping Development Dynamics

15

Growth of Services Sector in Arunachal Pradesh : A Post Reform Experience

A. Ibotombi Singh and Amitava Mitra

Introduction

An economy is generally divided into three sectors, namely agricultural (or primary), industrial (or secondary) and services (or tertiary) sectors. The agricultural sector consists of farming, forestry, animal husbandry and fishery. The industrial sector is composed of mining, construction and manufacturing. All other economic activities which are not covered by the agricultural and manufacturing sectors are broadly defined as services and hence belong to the services sector. They include services provided for the agricultural sector, activities associated with the supply of water, electricity and gas, transport and communications, wholesale and retail trade, finance and insurance, business and personal services, and community and social services. Services can be broadly grouped under old and new services. The old or traditional services include government, health, education, petty trading, domestic services, catering and hotel services. The new services are generally associated with information, communications and business, and so are called intangible services. Further these services are tradable internationally and hence are also called tradable.

Over the past decades, particularly since the beginning of economic reforms and acceleration in the rate of growth in 1990s, the Arunachal Economy has followed a growth pattern which is different from the historical as well as the conventional development processes. An attempt is made in the paper to analyse the process of transition in Arunachal Pradesh on the basis of empirical evidences and to examine the relationship between the growth of services sector and economic development of Arunachal Pradesh for its long-term development strategy and policy perspectives.

The rest of the paper is organized into five sections. Section-I briefly analyses the theoretical perspective of structural changes. Section - II deals with a brief review of the developments in the services sector of Arunachal Pradesh. Section - III discusses the sectoral contribution to NSDP and changes in the occupational structure in Arunachal Pradesh during the last three decades. Section – IV investigates the relationship between the District Domestic Product and its factors affecting the demand service like the level of education, urbanization and the per capita district income. The final section summarizes the findings and concludes.

SECTION - I

A Brief Theoretical Perspective on Structural Changes

Structural changes have, in fact, most often, been described as a process combining economic growth with changing share of different sectors in the economy and their labour force. The most common structural changes that have been observed historically followed a smooth sequence of shift from agriculture to industry and then to services. Hence, with development of an economy, predominance of agriculture and allied activities gradually gives way to growing importance of non-agricultural activities like manufacturing and services. In other words, an underdeveloped economy is characterized by predominant share of agriculture; with development, the share of industry increases and that of agriculture declines, and subsequently after reaching a reasonably high level of development, the services sector increases its importance and becomes a major component of the economy thereby having less share of agriculture. This is, however, not to suggest that agriculture and related sectors necessarily shrink in absolute terms in the process of economic development. On the other hand, productivity and production growth of agriculture acts to facilitate the process of development in early phase.

Structural changes do not only characterize economic development, they are also necessary for sustaining economic growth. The neoclassical view that sectoral composition is a relatively unimportant by-product of growth has been convincingly questioned by structural economists like Simon Kuznets, who have empirically demonstrated that growth is brought about by changes in sectoral composition. Kuznets' data (1966) indicate that economic growth is accompanied by a gradual increase in the relative share of industry and services sector in their total output and labour force. This is due to the difference in the spatial distribution, requirements for agricultural and non-agricultural activities - a movement away from agriculture to industry involves a movement of population from agricultural areas to the industrial centres. Such a transfer of labour from agriculture to industry is seen by economists like Arthur Lewis (1955, p.241) as a source of capital accumulation and relatively a costless process of economic growth. Colin Clark also argues in the same line: "A high average level of real income per head is always associated with a high proportion of the working population engaged in tertiary industries" (Clark, 1940: 182). Hence, there is a general agreement among the economists that the employment share of services rise in the phase following the first phase of shift to industry. But the reasons why this shift takes place are attributed to the changing demand pattern (Fisher, 1939; Clark, 1940 and Boumol, 1967).

At the same time, the growth of the services sector is determined by several factors such as production specialization, income level and urbanization (Mulder, 2001; Wolfl, 2005). These factors are interrelated. As an economy grows, productive activities become more specialized and urbanization accelerates due to the rising level of income. In the meantime, as a result of the increasing specialization of production, firms tend to outsource many service activities such as legal, accounting and security services. Some authors call this process the specialization splintering (Bhagwati, 1984). It is the main source of demand for services from the producers.

At the household level, Engel's law shows that, as income rises, consumption of food and durable goods in turn becomes saturated over time and demand for services such as healthcare, travel, communications and finance increases. In other words, with raising levels of income, the demand for agricultural products relatively declines and that for industrial goods increases and, after reaching a reasonably high level of income, demand for services increases sharply. Accordingly, the shares of different sectors in the national output get determined by the changes in the pattern of demand. Thus, growth in income also boosts demand for away-from-home consumption of food and services.

Furthermore, urbanization contributes to the growth of the services sector in two ways. Unlike farmers who to some extent can provide self-services, urban consumers rely on the market for the supply of services. They are also more likely to enter the urban informal sector for employment if there are no job opportunities in the formal sector. Services account for the lion's share of the informal sector. Thus, urban residents are both consumers as well as suppliers of services. It is expected that the services sector grows as the level of urbanization increases in a society.

SECTION - II

A Brief Review of the Development in Services Sector of Arunachal Pradesh

Arunachal Pradesh (earlier known as North East Frontier Agency) started the journey to economic development programme only after the Independence of the country. Prior to 1947, the modern development process was hardly initiated by the Colonial Government. For example, population census which was a rich source of information to the Colonial Government was not available or rather not conducted in the area. The indifference of the Colonial Government towards the area was mainly due to the non-availability of any readily exploitable resources. So, at the time of Independence, the area was basically mono-economy, which was based on subsistence agriculture and forests. Arunachal Pradesh got the Union Territory status in

1972 with five administrative districts and the statehood status in 1987 with nine administrative districts. At present the State has sixteen administrative districts. The State has made a very significant progress in literacy. With only a 7.12 per cent literacy rate in 1961, the State covered a long route in the course of four decades in achieving a 54.74 per cent literacy rate by 2001 Census. In case of the level of urbanization, data on urban population prior to 1981 Census was not available. In the 1981 Census, the state had 6.56 per cent of urban population. This figure, however, had reached to 20.41 per cent in 2001 Census by surpassing many states like Orissa, Assam, Meghalaya, Mizoram, Nagaland, Sikkim, Bihar and Himachal Pradesh.

Immediately after the Independence, the Government of India took steps to launch development programmes. At the time of Independence the present State had three jeepable roads with a total length of around 170 kilometers, three primary schools with an enrolment of around 30 students and thirteen primary health centres (NCAER, 1967). With this background, the North Eastern Frontier Agency (NEFA) in 1964 asked the National Council of Applied Economic Research (NCAER) to conduct a techno-economic survey of NEFA. The Council in its report published in 1967 recommended action in three areas on a priority basis: (i) transport access both to and within the territory, (ii) development of natural resources and (iii) improvement of social infrastructure. Based on the recommendations, it is found that the highest priority had been accorded to the infrastructural development particularly in road constructions in almost all the five-year plans. The approach and strategy adopted under the various plans is reflected in the distribution of the plan outlay under different plan periods of the State as shown in Table 1.

Table 1 shows that from the inception of the plan, the main priority has been accorded to the development of economic infrastructure viz., transport and communication sector. This is due to the centrally push-plan to accelerate the development process through the creation of infrastructural facilities and expansion of social services like education. However, the share of power and irrigation including energy showed an increasing trend from 6.87 per cent in the Fifth Five Year Plan to 20.93 per

Table 1
Sectoral Plan Outlay in Arunachal Pradesh since the Fifth Five Year Plan

(in per cent)

Sector	*V Plan (1974-79)*	*VI Plan (1980-85)*	*VII Plan (1985-90)*	*VIII Plan (1992-97)*	*IX Plan (1997-2002)*	*X Plan (2002-07)*
Agriculture and Allied Services	26.77	20	21.66	20.24	13.16	18.11
Industry and Mining	2.05	2.1	2.41	1.91	1.29	1.78
Power and Irrigation	6.87	17.9	15.92	19.59	20.93	18.55
Transport and Communication	33.03	31.6	32.19	28.12	26.04	25.10
Community Services	30.84	27.6	26.62	26.08	33.03	29.83
Economic Services	0.44	0.4	0.66	1.92	3.26	4.64
General Services	0	0.4	0.54	2.14	2.29	1.99
Total	100	100	100	100	100	100

Note: Although in 1953, the State was in the First Five Year Plan, but the planning process in Arunachal Pradesh was intensified only since the Fifth Five Plan onwards.

Sources:

1. Basic Statistics of North Eastern Region, 2002.
2. Government of Arunachal Pradesh Draft Tenth Five Year Plan, Department of Planning, Government of Arunachal Pradesh, Itanagar (www.arunachalpradesh.nic.in).

cent at the end of the Ninth Five Year Plan. But, in the Tenth Five Year Plan, it was reduced to 18.55 per cent.

SECTION – III

Sectoral Contribution to NSDP and Changes in Occupational Structure in Arunachal Pradesh

Selecting the growth of per capita Net State Domestic Product (NSDP) as a measure of economic performance, it was found that the per capita NSDP experienced an exponential average growth rate of 4.03 per cent in the 1970s and 4.69 per cent in the 1980s against the all India average of 1.10 per cent and 2.85 per cent respectively during the same periods. The high growth rate of income is due to the grants-in-aid of the centre, which constitute nearly 60 per cent of its NSDP. Table 2 shows a brief comparison between the exponential growth rate of Net National Product (NNP) and NSDP of Arunachal Pradesh.

Table 2
Growth Rate of NNP and NSDP

(in per cent)

Period	*Growth rate of*		*Growth rate of Per capita*	
	NNP	*NSDP*	*NNP*	*NSDP*
1971-80	3.36	7.07	1.10	4.03
1981-90	4.99	7.81	2.85	4.69
1991-2002	5.93	4.81	3.95	2.31

Note: NNP data are from Economic Survey, 2003-04, Government of India and NSDP data are from State Domestic Product of Arunachal Pradesh for different years published by the Directorate of Economics and Statistics, Government of Arunachal Pradesh, Itanagar.

Table 2 demonstrates that the economy of Arunachal Pradesh grew rapidly in both 1970s and 1980s, but lost some of its initial momentum in the 1990s. A comparison of the growth of the State with the national economy presents a mixed dimension. For example, the growth of NSDP was markedly higher than the growth of NNP in the 1970's as well as in the 1980's. However, in the post reform period, the national economy performed better than the State economy. The policy of economic reforms pursued by the Centre in the 1990s seems to have released forces propelling the national economy to a higher growth path, but in the same decade, the Arunachal Pradesh economy slid to a lower growth path.

With the persistently high income growth, Arunachal Pradesh economy has undergone some structural transformation. The relative importance of agriculture in NSDP has sharply declined. This relative decline of agriculture has, however, not been accompanied with the relative expansion of the secondary sector but with the rapid expansion of the tertiary sector. Even within the secondary sector, the contribution of the manufacturing sector was accounting for around 4 per cent of the State income. The details are shown in the Table 3.

Table 3
Percentage of Workforce and Sectoral Contribution to NSDP of Arunachal Pradesh

(in per cent)

Period	*Sector*		
	Primary	*Secondary*	*Tertiary*
1970-71	80.44 (59.19)	0.44 (20.33)	19.12 (20.48)
1980-81	75.28 (47.28)	8.92 (22.21)	15.80 (30.51)
1990-91	67.44 (46.19)	8.66 (21.56)	23.90 (32.25)
2001-02	62.29 (36.88)	0.86 (22.16)	36.85 (40.96)

Note: Figures in parenthesis indicate share in NSDP.

Source: Based on Estimates of different issues of State Domestic Product, Directorate of Economics and Statistics, Government of Arunachal Pradesh, Itanagar.

Table 4
Sectoral Growth in Arunachal Pradesh at 1998-99 Constant Prices

(rate of growth in per cent per annum)

Sectors	*1971-2002*	*1971-1980*	*1981-1990*	*1991-2002*
1	*2*	*3*	*4*	*5*
Agriculture	6.53	6.40	9.18	2.68
Forestry and logging	2.94	0.32	4.05	-6.27
Fishing	19.99	16.09	34.28	8.50
Mining and Quarrying	16.53	14.39	37.26	1.33
Primary Sector	**5.93**	**4.61**	**8.48**	**1.32**
Manufacturing	11.81	14.20	7.85	2.02
Construction	6.78	7.70	6.26	2.55
Electricity, Gas and Water Supply	0	0	0	0
Secondary Sector	**7.68**	**8.03**	**6.43**	**5.11**

1	*2*	*3*	*4*	*5*
Transport, Storage and Communication	12.91	9.61	21.84	26.92
Trade, Hotel and Restaurant	9.35	17.60	9.69	3.33
Banking and Insurance	17.16	27.96	20.77	8.35
Real Estate, Ownership of Dwellings and Business services	12.07	3.57	4.54	- 1.36
Public Administration	7.78	10.81	5.29	10.85
Other services	10.03	9.58	9.50	6.44
Tertiary Sector	**9.38**	**11.39**	**7.62**	**7.87**
NSDP	**7.34**	**7.07**	**7.81**	**4.54**

Source: Based on Estimates of different issues of State Domestic Product, Directorate of Economics and Statistics, Government of Arunachal Pradesh, Itanagar, 2002.

From Table 3 it is clear that the structural transformation of Arunachal economy appears very lopsided. For example, the growth of the service production has overtaken the growth of the material production. In fact, a dimensional change in both the sectoral shares and employment generation is regarded as progressive structural change while the reverse is viewed as structural retrogression. During early decades of economic development, India suffered a structural retrogression while India's sectoral share and workforce moved in opposite direction as noted by Shetty (1978). This may well be a point of interest even in the case of Arunachal economy.

Let us analyse the contribution of various components of services sector to NSDP of Arunachal Pradesh. This is shown in the Table 4.

It is found that from 1970-71 to 2001-02 the services sector recorded the highest growth among the three broad sectors where it grew at an annual average rate of 9.38 per cent and the primary and secondary sectors at 5.93 and 7.68 per cent respectively. However, in the post reform period all broad sectors experienced an overall slowdown in the State economy where the primary sector declined to 1.32 per cent, secondary sector to

5.11 per cent and the tertiary sector to 7.87 per cent per annum. In this period, the performance of NSDP growth rates declined from around 7.07 per cent during the period from 1971 to 1980 to 4.54 per cent per annum during the period between 1991-2002. But, within the tertiary sector the public administration grew at an annual rate of 10.85 per cent during this period. The steady increase in the share of public administration is due to a steady flow of grants from the Centre from time to time as being a special category State as well as strategically located State having international borders with Bhutan, China and Myanmar. It is this inflow of funds which provided the initial impulse to growth in the State. During post Independence period, these Central funds were used to set up the administrative machinery and create infrastructural facilities. The spending of this money quickly began to monetize the erstwhile barter economies. However, in recent years the importance of the inflow from the Centre has declined.

As far as the sectoral composition of the District Domestic Product (DDP) is concerned, it was found that some districts of the State were not so dependent on agriculture as a source of income though the State is considered to be largely agricultural based economy. Table 5 shows the structure of Average District Domestic Product in Arunachal Pradesh for the period of 1993-94 to 2001-02.

Table 5 shows that in the post reform period the district with a high dependence on primary sector is East Siang with an average of 51.64 per cent of the Net Domestic Product during this period while Papum Pare a very low dependence on primary sector with 20.34 per cent. The three districts where more than 50 per cent of the income comes from primary sectors are East Siang, Dibang Valley and Changlang. The secondary sector is still largely underdeveloped in Arunachal Pradesh. Its contribution to domestic product varies from 31.08 per cent in Tirap to 7.72 per cent in Tawang. The tertiary sector has emerged as an important sector of the economy. For example, in Papum Pare the tertiary sector's share of domestic product was 53.67 per cent and in Tawang it was 52.74 per cent. There were six districts where this sector contributes between 30 to 40 per cent of the domestic product.

Table 5
Structure of Average District Domestic Product in Arunachal Pradesh for the Period of 1993-94 to 2001-02

(in per cent)

District	*Primary*	*Secondary*	*Tertiary*
Tawang	39.54	7.72	52.74
West Kameng	41.58	23.11	35.31
East Kameng	46.36	24.73	28.97
Papum Pare	20.34	25.99	53.67
Lower Subansiri	43.47	23.95	32.58
Upper Subansiri	31.08	23.60	45.32
West Siang	41.36	20.98	38.41
East Siang	55.98	15.57	28.98
Upper Siang	49.26	27.51	23.23
Dibang Valley	51.88	17.64	30.48
Lohit	40.90	21.61	37.72
Changlang	54.64	19.37	25.99
Tirap	33.49	31.08	35.43
Arunachal Pradesh	41.50	22.43	36.07

Source: Same as Table 4.

SECTION – IV

District Domestic Product: An Empirical Analysis

To examine the determinants of growth in services sector, an econometric model is considered which can be expressed as follows

$$Y = \alpha + \Sigma\beta_j X_j + \varepsilon \qquad \ldots(1)$$

Where, Y represents demand for services and X_j a list of factors affecting service demand, α and β are coefficients to be estimated and e is the standard error term. The term Y is thus a measure of the District Domestic Product (DDP) share of services in Arunachal Pradesh in 2001-02. The choice of the variables X in the model is dictated by the availability of data. In the model, X includes per capita Net Domestic Product (I),

Urbanization (U) and the literacy rate (L). The estimated results are given as follows[1]:

$$Y = -8.903 + 0.0858U + 0.793\,L^{*} + 0.863\,P \qquad \ldots (2)$$

$$(-1.649)\ (0.842)\ (11.361)\ (1.734)$$

$$R = 0.987 \quad R^2 = 0.974 \quad AdjR^2 = 0.965 \quad S.E. = 3.5591$$

$$F = 111.444 \quad N = 13$$

It is evident from the analysis that constant term (α) is negative but statistically not significant. However, the estimator of literacy variable (L) is positive and statistically significant at 0.01 level. This implies that the rate of literacy is an important factor affecting the development of services sector in Arunachal Pradesh. It has been convincingly analyzed by scholars like Singh, who have empirically demonstrated that the State has made a very significant progress in literacy. With only a 7.12 per cent literacy rate in 1961, the State covered a long route in the course of four decades in achieving a 54.74 per cent literacy rate by 2001 Census. Hence, the average growth of literacy stood at 1.09 per cent per annum and in the process, it has overtaken some States like Bihar and Rajasthan, etc. (Singh, 2007:85).

Further, it is found that the urbanization variable (U) and the district per capita income (P) variables have a positive impact on service development but the estimated coefficients are statistically insignificant. Therefore, further investigation is needed. The findings here are, of course, subjected to qualifications due to the limitations of data.

Findings and Conclusion

This paper reviewed the services sector development in Arunachal Pradesh in general and the post reform experiences in particular. It is found that the ongoing pattern of growth of services sector in the State is mainly due to the transition of the state economy from a low growth trajectory to a high growth path for over one and half decades now but the poor performance of other sectors viz., agriculture and industry need to be studied

---

1. The figures in parentheses are t-values, 2. The asterisk symbol, *denote significant at 0.01 level.

in its various dimensions to examine its sustainability and other macroeconomic and distributive implications since the pattern of growth has been different from the historical as well as the contemporary experiences of development. It appears to be reasonable to argue that the economic growth in Arunachal Pradesh is mainly driven by the level of education. Producing services tends to require relatively less natural capital and more human capital than producing agricultural or industrial goods. As a result demand has grown for more educated workers promoting the State to invest more in education – an overall benefit to its people. Another benefit of the growing services sector is that by using fewer natural resources than agriculture or industry, it puts less pressure on the local environment. Conserving natural capital and building of human capital may help overall development which will be more environmentally and socially sustainable. However, growth of services sector will not be a miracle solution to the problem of sustainability without the support of agricultural as well as industrial growth as both are necessary to meet the needs of growing population of the State. Hence, increasing productivity in agriculture by using modern cultivation techniques, double cropping and increased irrigation should be given a priority. And after agriculture, the priority should be accorded to the three most promising sectors *i.e.*, horticulture-floriculture, plantation and tourism where Arunachal Pradesh has enormous potential. The State also should make an effort for tapping hydro-electricity for industrial growth as well since economic growth cannot be sustained without growth of manufacturing sector.

REFERENCES

Bhagwati, Jagdish (1984): "Splintering and Disembodiment of Services and Developing Nations", *World Economy* Vol. 7, No. 2, pp.133–43.

Baumol, W. J (1967): "Macroeconomics of Unbalanced Growth: An Anatomy of Urban Crises", *American Economic Review*, Vol. 57.

Chanda, Rupa (2002): *Globalization of Services: India's Opportunities and Constrains*, Oxford University Press, New Delhi.

Colin Clark (1940): *The Conditions of Economic Progress*, third edition, Macmillan, London.

Gordon, James and Poonam Gupta (2004): "Understanding India's Services Revolution", *IMF Working Paper WP/04/171*, International Monetary Fund, Washington DC.

Government of Arunachal Pradesh (1971): *Statistical Abstract*, Directorate of Economics and Statistics, Shillong.

——— (1987): *Statistical Abstract*, Directorate of Economics and Statistics, Shillong.

——— (1995): *Statistical Abstract of Arunachal Pradesh*, Directorate of Economics and Statistics Department, Itanagar.

——— (1998): *State Domestic Product of Arunachal Pradesh*, State Income Unit, Directorate of Economics and Statistics Department, Itanagar.

——— (2002): *Statistical Abstract of Arunachal Pradesh*, Directorate of Economics and Statistics Department, Itanagar.

——— (2005): *Arunachal Pradesh Human Development Report*, Chapter 4, Department of Planning, Itanagar.

——— (2006): *Statistical Abstract of Arunachal Pradesh*, Directorate of Economics and Statistics Department, Itanagar.

Kuznets, Simon (1966): *Modern Economic Growth: Rate, Structure and Spread*, Yale University Press, New Haven.

Lewis, W. Arthur (1955): *The Theory of Economic Growth*, Homewood, Richard Irwin.

Mitra, Amitava (2006): 'Transformation of Arunachal's Economy: Opportunities and Challenges for a Less Developed State', *Indian Development Review*, Vol. 4, No. 2, pp. 433.

Mulder, Nanno (2001): "The Economic Performance of the Service Sector in Brazil, Mexico and the United States", in Robert M. Stern (ed), *Services in the International Economy*, Ann Arbor: The University of Michigan Press, Chapter 8, pp.185-210.

NCAER (1967): *Techno-Economic Survey of NEFA*, New Delhi.

NEC (2002): *Basic Statistics of North Eastern Region*, Shillong.

Singh, A. I. (2007): *Forest Dependency and Common Property Forest Resources: An Empirical Study of Rural Households in Lohit and Anjaw Districts of Arunachal Pradesh*, an Unpublished Ph.D Dissertation, Rajiv Gandhi University, Itanagar.

Shetty, S.L. (1978): "Structural Retrogression in the Indian Economy since the Mid Sixties', *Economic and Political Weekly*, Annual Issue, April, pp. 1051-67.

Wirtz, Jochen (2000): "Growth of the Service Sector in Asia", *Singapore Management Review,* Vol. 22, No. 2, pp. 37-54.

Wolfl, Anita (2005): *The Service Economy in OECD Countries in Enhancing the Performance of the Service Sector, OECD*, Paris.

16

Economic Diversification in Selected Tribal Villages of Arunachal Pradesh and Livelihood Options[1]

Priyanka Priyadarshini and Millo Mamung

Before the introduction of plan programmes in Arunachal Pradesh, the tribal communities living here had limited livelihood options, ranging between foregoing and subsistence agriculture, mostly of shifting mode and little of the permanent cultivation in plains. In other words, primary sector activities like fishing, hunting, foraging, domestication of animals and agricultural activities constituted the domain of tribal people's livelihood options. But, after independence, development programmes and schemes pertaining to sectoral activities were introduced which enlarged their livelihood sources. In particular, the tribal communities got exposed to sources of livelihood in secondary and tertiary sector activities. Moreover, in primary sector there emerged new activities like mining, quarrying and collection of timber and non-timber products for commercial purposes.

1. This the revised version of the paper presented in the national seminar on *Development of Tribal People in Arunachal Pradesh,* 20-22 November, 2009, Dera Natung Government College, Itanagar.

The present paper focuses on emerging livelihood options in four villages - two from Apatani and two from Khampti communities, with reference to economic diversification and concomitant changes in workforce participation. The analysis is based on empirical data collected from field studies.

Methodology

The discussion in the present paper draws on primary data collected from field study by administering structured questionnaires. Besides, the investigators had also followed the observation and group discussion methods. A few community elders were also informally consulted. Two communities, namely the Apatani and the Khampti have been selected purposively. From each community again two villages have been selected purposively for comparison and understanding of the changing livelihood options consequent upon changing rural economy. The field study was conducted during the months of January and February in 2008 for a period of 20 days in Khampti villages. In Apatani villages, the field study was conducted for 25 days during the months of May and June in 2009.

From the Apatani community the two villages selected are Tajang and Dutta, and from Khampti community Nongtaw̃ and Nanam Khampti. Both Tajang and Dutta are of equal distance, about 2 kms, from Old Ziro. A casual observation shows that there are not perceptible differences between the villages in terms of their exposures to district headquarters and market places. But in case of Khampti villages, there are differences in terms of remoteness. Nangtaw is a remote village, 30 kms from Namsai sub-divisional headquarters. There is no all-weather road to the village. But Nanam Khampti is situated 5 kms away from Namsai by the side of National Highway (NH-52) between Namsai and Chowkham. The village is well communicated with Namsai. The villages have been selected purposively for the study of inter and intra community differences by making a comparison between two communities and also between two villages of the same community. Further, the comparison is made between two villages of Apatanis which are equally exposed to outside forces, and two villages of the Khamptis which differ in terms of remoteness.

In this paper attempt has been made to study the changing livelihood options in terms of changing occupational distribution in the sample villages. The present attempt is a preliminary investigation to understand the changing livelihood options consequent upon diversification of rural economy. That is why there is a difference in criteria of selecting two villages from two different communities. Nevertheless, the study provides an analytical insight to understand the issue of livelihood in the context of changing rural economy.

State Scenario

Enlargement of livelihood option is associated with economic diversification and is evident in occupational shifts. In Arunachal Pradesh, the domain of livelihood options was exclusively primary sector activities in the traditional economy. With the transformation of traditional economy, the sources of livelihood expanded beyond the primary sector activities. In other words, the domain of livelihood options included secondary and tertiary sector activities. This is evident, as shown in Table 1, in the shift of workforce from primary sector activities to secondary and tertiary sector activities in general and in rural areas in particular. The shift shows the growth of activities beyond primary sector. When emerging activities are compared with traditional primary sector activities, we get an idea of the nature and extent of occupational diversification. Table 1 also shows different activities under three sectors of the economy which provide sources of livelihood. The emerging livelihood options beyond primary sector activities include manufacturing, processing, servicing, and repairing other than in household industry, trade and commerce, transport, storage and communication, and other services. Even in primary sector, mining and quarrying is new to traditional tribal economy.

As reported in 1971 census, as many as 80.44 per cent of total main workers in the state had their livelihood options in primary sector activities. This dropped to 75.28 per cent in 1981 and to 67.44 per cent in 1991 and further to 62.29 per cent in 2001. During the period from 1971 to 1991, the livelihood options in terms of workforce participation extended in secondary and tertiary sector activities. In industrial sector, the rate of work participation has increased from 0.44 per cent in 1971 to 8.92

per cent in 1981 and with a slight decline in 1991, where it is recorded 8.66 per cent. In tertiary sector, the rate of workforce participation has increased from 19.12 per cent in 1971 to 23.90 per cent in 1991; there being a decline to 15.80 per cent in 1981.

Though, the comparative data are not available on work participation rate under primary, secondary and tertiary sector activities for 2001, a rough idea about the nature of economic diversification can be obtained from Table 2.

Table 1
Percentage Change in Sectoral Composition of Workers in Arunachal Pradesh: 1971-91*

Sectors	*Main Workers*		
	1971	1981	1991
PRIMARY(1+2+3+4)	**80.44**	**75.28**	**67.44**
1. Cultivators	78.34	71.26	60.36
2. Agricultural labourers	1.96	2.49	5.13
3. Live stock/forestry/fishing	0.14	1.51	1.77
4. Mining and Quarrying	0	0.02	0.18
SECONDARY(1+2+3)	**0.44**	**8.92**	**8.66**
1. Manufacturing, processing, servicing and repairing in household industry	0.31	0.32	0.19
2. Manufacturing, processing, servicing and Repairing other than in household industry	0.04	1.64	2.49
3. Construction	0.1	6.97	5.98
TERTIARY(1+2+3)	**19.12**	**15.80**	**23.90**
1. Trade and commerce	0.58	2.22	3.31
2. Transport, storage and communication	0	0.41	1.13
3. Other services	18.54	13.17	19.47
TOTAL	**100.00**	**100.00**	**100.00**

Source: HDR, 2005.

* Sector-wise comparable data are not available for 2001.

There is a decline in work participation in agriculture sector which includes cultivators and agricultural labourers. When

Table 2
Occupational Diversification in Arunachal Pradesh in 2001

Category	*Cultivators*			*Agricultural labourer*			*HH Industry*			*Other Workers*		
	M	*F*	*T*	*M*	*F*	*T*	*M*	*F*	*T*	*M*	*F*	*T*
T	46.77	76.61	58.44	3.44	4.49	3.85	0.73	1.05	0.86	49.06	17.85	36.85
R	57.7	82.7	68.26	3.99	4.65	4.27	0.73	1.05	0.86	37.75	11.72	26.75
U	3.44	15.44	6.13	1.24	2.93	1.62	1.39	2.26	1.59	93.93	79.37	90.66

Source : Census of India, Primary Census Abstracts: Arunachal Pradesh, 2001.

Table 3
Sectoral Distribution of Workers in Arunachal Pradesh during 1971-1991

Areas		*Primary*			*Secondary*			*Tertiary*		
		1971	*1981*	*1991*	*1971*	*1981*	*1991*	*1971*	*1981*	*1991*
Total	Male	68.78	63.21	54.60	0.65	13.13	12.34	30.56	23.66	33.06
	Female	97.12	95.11	89.93	0.14	2.00	2.21	2.74	2.89	7.87
	Total	80.44	75.28	67.44	0.44	8.92	8.66	19.12	15.80	23.90
Rural	Male	72.30	68.00	62.34	0.55	11.85	11.09	27.15	20.15	26.57
	Female	97.38	96.10	92.61	0.11	1.74	1.87	2.50	2.16	5.52
	Total	82.92	79.08	74.13	0.36	7.87	7.50	16.72	13.06	18.37
Urban	Male	5.39	6.75	6.72	2.58	28.25	20.10	92.03	65.00	73.18
	Female	45.99	30.60	22.46	5.75	18.93	10.69	48.26	50.47	66.85
	Total	8.01	9.25	8.86	2.78	27.27	18.82	89.21	63.47	72.32

Source: HRD, 2005.

added, it stands at 62.29 per cent in 2001 (Table 2) as against 65.49 per cent in 1991, 73.75 per cent in 1981 and 80.30 per cent in 1971 (Table-1). The workforce participation is also recorded under 'other workers' category which is indicative of expanding livelihood option beyond the domain of agriculture. The rural population recorded under 'other workers' category stands at 26.75 per cent with 37.75 per cent for male and 11.7 per cent for female workers respectively. To wit, 26.75 per cent of the rural workforce depends on activities other than agriculture for their livelihoods (Table 2).

The extent of distribution of workforce on the basis of sex in both rural and urban areas of Arunachal Pradesh has been presented in Table 3. The extent and trend of distribution, as expressed in percentage, mark the diversification of livelihood options over a period of 20 years. During the period between 1971 and 1991, the livelihood options of rural population in terms of workforce participation in primary sector activities has decreased whereas, the rates of workforce participation in secondary and tertiary sectors have significantly increased. This is evident from Table 3. In primary sector, the workforce participation has reduced from 82.92 per cent in 1971 to 79.08 per cent in 1981 and further to 74.13 per cent in 1991. In secondary sector, the rate of workforce participation has increased from 0.36 per cent in 1971 to 7.87 per cent in 1981, but a decline to 7.50 per cent in 1991. In tertiary sector, it has increased from 16.72 per cent in 1971 to 18.37 per cent in 1991; however there is a decline to 13.06 per cent in 1981. Further, it is to be noted that both in primary and secondary sectors, the livelihood options of male and female population have constantly increased. But in tertiary sector, the rate of workforce participation for male population has declined from 27.15 per cent in 1971 to 20.15 per cent in 1981 and further it has increased to 26.57 per cent in 1991. Similarly, female workforce participation has declined from 2.50 per cent in 1971 to 2.16 per cent in 1981 and again to 5.52 per cent in 1991. Interestingly, both in secondary and tertiary sectors, the livelihood options for female population have constantly increased during the period as is evident from Table 3.

Table 4
Statement Showing Occupational Distribution in Sample Villages of Apatanis

Activities	*Tajang*		*Dutta*		*Total*	
	Male	*Female*	*Male*	*Female*	*Male*	*Female*
Agriculture	18.64	35.85	9.84	64.42	15.64	45.25
Agriculture and household	0.85	25.94	3.28	12.50	1.68	21.52
Business	11.02	10.85	8.20	4.81	10.06	8.86
Government jobs	69.49	27.36	78.69	18.27	72.63	24.37
Total	100.00	100.00	100.00	100.00	100.00	100.00

Source : Computed from field data.

Note : (i) Total male population in Tajang and Dutta are 164 and 96 respectively. Out of them total male main workers are 118(65.92%) and 61(34.08%) respectively in two villages. Total female population in Tajang and Dutta are 224 and 111 respectively. Out of them total female main workers are 212(67.09%) and 104(32.91%) respectively in two villages. In two Apatani villages, the male and female main workers constitute 36.16% and 63.84% of total population in each category respectively.

Work Participation and Livelihood options in Study Villages

During pre-independence period, the livelihood options in Apatani and Khampti communities were limited to very few activities, such as agriculture, hunting, fishing, livestock rearing and collection of edible fruits like roots, leaves, etc. After independence, development interventions through plan programmes in the state in general and in the sample communities in particular have enhanced and diversified the scope of livelihood options. This is evident in occupational diversification as shown in Table 4 and Table 5 respectively. The workforce participation recorded under various activities points to presently existing livelihood options as compared to only primary sector activities during pre-independence period.

In sample villages of the Apatanis, it is found that there are changes in livelihood options in terms of occupational distribution. Table 4 reveals that both male and female population are moving out of agricultural sector with emerging new livelihood options, though a large portion of female population is found still engaged in agricultural sector. The workforce that moves out of agricultural sector is found engaged in non-agricultural activities. A simple calculation of the data presented in Table 4 in percentage shows the changing occupational distribution. In Tajang village 35.85 per cent of female and 18.64 per cent of male main workers and in Dutta 64.42 per cent of female and 9.84 per cent of male main workers still pursue agriculture as their main occupation. For two villages, the figures stand at 15.64 per cent for male and 45.25 per cent for female main workers who are engaged in agriculture. It is to be noted that especially woman and children are engaged in more than one activity as reported from the sample villages of Apatanis during field study. Women, who are engaged in household activities, are also engaged in agriculture. However, there is one exception where a male person has been found engaged in household activities. Moreover, 25.94 per cent of female population is reported engaged in the same occupation in Tajang village. Similarly, there are only 3.28 per cent of male and 12.50 per cent of female population reported from Dutta village in the above occupation. For two villages, in aggregate, the figures stand at 1.68 per cent for male population and 21.52 per cent for female population in household and agriculture activities simultaneously. In business sector, female participation is more than that of their male counterparts. There are 11.02 per cent of male and 10.85 per cent of female population from Tajang village and 8.20 per cent of male and 4.81 per cent of female from Dutta village who are engaged in business. It indicates that in both villages, the female workforce participation is less than male workforce participation in business activities. On an average, there are 10.06 per cent male and 8.86 per cent female main workers engaged in business activities.

Diversification of livelihood options in terms of traditional activities can be evinced from the incidence of work participation in government jobs. From the studied villages, the male participation in government jobs is found more than that of female. There are 69.49 per cent of male and 27.36 per cent of female main workers in Tajang village and 78.69 per cent of male and 18.27 per cent of female in Dutta village who depend on government jobs as main source of livelihood. The figure comes to 72.63 per cent of male population out of total male main workers and 24.37 per cent of female main workers from the two villages on an average in government jobs. It is to be noted that the male workforce participation in formal sector is more than that of female. But in case of rural informal activities such as agriculture, livestocks, households and other wage oriented labour works, the female workforce participation is more than male workforce participation in Apatani villages. In aggregate, total main workers engaged in different activities in two villages have been recorded at 36.16 per cent for male and 63.84 per cent for female.

Diversification of livelihood option is also noticed in sample Khampti villages. Table 5 shows that in Nanam village 73.85 per cent of male workers still pursue agriculture. It is to be noted that no female person is recorded pursuing agriculture as main occupation both in Nanam and Nongtaw villages. However, 73.17 per cent of male main workers have been recorded pursuing agriculture as main occupation in Nongtaw. In two villages 73.40 per cent of male main workers on an average are engaged in agricultural activities. No case of male person pursuing household activities as main occupation is reported in Khampti villages. However, 84.38 per cent and 96.58 per cent of female workers are reported from Nanam and Nongtaw villages respectively who pursue both household and agricultural activities. In two villages 92.27 per cent of female workers are recorded in combined agriculture and household activities.

Table 5
Statement Showing Occupational Distribution in Sample Villages of Khamptis

Activities	*Nanam*		*Nongtaw*		*Total*	
	Male	*Female*	*Male*	*Female*	*Male*	*Female*
Agriculture	73.85	—	73.17	—	73.40	—
Agriculture and household		84.38	—	96.58	—	92.27
Agriculture and business	9.23	—	16.26	—	13.83	—
Government jobs	16.92	15.62	10.57	3.42	12.77	7.73
Total	100.00	100.00	100.00	100.00	100.00	100.00

Source: Field data.

Notes: (i) Figures in the parentheses show total population in all age groups. Figures without parentheses in the row, 'total working population', show total working population within the age group 14-59 years under male and female category.

(ii) Total male population in Nanam and Nongtaw are 135 and 247 respectively. Out of them total male main workers are 65(34.57%) and 123(65.43%) respectively in two villages. Total female population in Nanam and Nongtaw are 121 and 244 respectively. Out of them total female main workers are 64 (35.36%) and 117(64.64%) respectively in two villages. In two Khampti villages, the male and female main workers constitute 50.95 % and 49.05% of total population in each category respectively.

In business sector, there is no female person recorded as main worker. However, 9.23 per cent and 16.26 per cent of male workers have been reported from Nanam and Nongtaw villages respectively who pursue both agriculture and business in combination. The involvement of female in the process of development could be noticed from their employment in government jobs. There are 16.57 per cent male and 15.62 per cent female main workers in Nanam village and 10.57 per cent of male and 3.42 per cent of female in Nongtaw village who depend on government jobs as their main source of livelihood. In two villages 12.77 per cent of male and 7.73 per cent of female main workers have been reported in government jobs. In aggregate, the total working population has been recorded at 50.95 per cent for male and 49.05 per cent for female from two sample villages of Khamptis.

From the studied villages, it is found that industrial activity does not constitute livelihood options for any family. Significantly, their traditional role still dominates their occupation. The village economy is predominantly an agricultural economy with nascent business activities. There are also emerging plantation and horticultural activities enumerated under agriculture and business heads.

It is to be noted that ladies working in offices nearer to the village or in Anganwadi share household responsibilities including agricultural works during peak season. The day-scholar girl students are found helping in household works during morning and evening hours. The hostellers during vacation learn weaving and render helping hand in household works. That is why persons above 14 years of age have been reported as workers in household or in agriculture or in both for girls even though they are students. The boys of the same age group have been reported under agricultural work even though they are students and do not have any tangible contribution like the female counterparts[2]. That the male folks on an average do not have tangible contribution to agricultural labour is evident from the demand for outside labour.

2. The boys are found enjoying more freedom than girls in sharing household responsibility. As a result the girls do not get enough time for study. The boys on the other hand enjoying more freedom develop intimate relationship indiscriminately with any one they take interest in the bazaar and in the village. Their friend circle includes more of anti-social characters and as a result they fall victim to drugs and other type of delinquent activities. They do not study even though they have more time with them. Drug and opium addiction is found a menace among youths in Khampti area because of this laxity given to male members. This is further facilitated by money income which does not find use in any productive or acceptable consumption purpose.

Changing Livelihood Options: An Inter-generational Analysis

Consequent upon economic diversification, the occupation of younger generation has changed from their older generations. The nature and extent of inter-generational change in occupation marks the changes in livelihood options. So, a study of inter-generational change in occupation is considered to be a measure of changing livelihood options which is attempted in this section.

There is a change in livelihood options among the Apatanis from the older to the younger generations. The major change has been recorded in business sector followed by government job and other services sector. Presently, 13.46 per cent of workers are recorded in business, whereas 2.85 per cent of their respective fathers had business. In other words, 97.14 per cent are new in the field as their respective fathers did not have business as occupation. Similarly, of 61.92 per cent main workers in government jobs and other services, only 20 per cent had their respective fathers in same business. To wit, 83.85 per cent of the workers in government jobs and other services are new to the occupation. In the field of agriculture, 21.5 per cent of male workers are found engaged, while, 88.39 per cent of their respective fathers had agriculture as main occupation; the change is above 60 per cent.

Table 6
Inter-generational Change in Livelihood Options among Apatanis

Activities	*% of male workers whose occupation is*	*% of workers whose father's occupation was*	*% of change*
Agriculture	21.54	88.39	62.5
Business	13.46	2.85	97.14
Govt. Jobs and Other services	61.92	20.00	83.85
Total	100.00	100.00	–

Source: Computed from field data.

The inter-generational occupational change is also spectacular among the Khamptis. The change is more visible in government jobs and other services (95.83%) followed by agriculture and business combine (88.46%) as can be seen from the table 7. The change is least *i.e.*, only 6.52 per cent in agriculture. The expansion of livelihood options is enhanced by the introduction of new economic activities, such as, construction works, manufacturing activities, business and service sector. From the studied village, it is found that there is cent per cent change in inter-generational livelihood options like artesian, contractor, private job, forest activities and NGO workers respectively.

Table 7
Inter-generational Change in Livelihood Options among Khamptis

Activities	*% of male workers whose occupation is*	*% of workers whose Father's occupation was*	*% of change*
Agriculture	73.40	97.0	6.52
Agriculture and Business	13.83	2.25	88.46
Govt. Jobs and Other Services	12.77	0.75	95.83
Total	100.00	100.00	-

Source: Same as Table 6.

Multiple Sources of Livelihood

Diversification of sources of livelihood in tribal societies can be appreciated by the new economic activities in tribal areas. From the studied villages, it is found that the livelihood options of Apatanis are more diversified than the Khamptis.

Table 8 shows that Apatanis pursue one or other activities from among 11 types while Khamptis from 4. It transpires from Table 8 that 99 per cent of the households among the Apatanis in sample villages have more than one source of earnings. There is only 1 per cent (only 2) of households that depends on one source, *i.e.* government job. This follows Boserup's U-Shaped curve.[3] (Quoted in HDR, 2005). More concentration of

3. At initial stage, it is easy to combine traditional domestic responsibilities with part-time productive endeavour. With movement to higher levels of development as the production structure gets more formalized, the scope of such informal work

Table 8
Range of Livelihood Options among Apatani Households

No. of activities (main and subsidiaries)	*No. of households*	*% of households*
1.	2	1.0
2.	12	6.0
3.	15	7.5
4.	11	5.5
5.	18	9.0
6.	26	13.0
7.	43	21.5
8.	40	20.0
9.	20	10.0
10.	8	4.0
11.	5	2.5
Total	200	100.0

Source: Same as Table 6.

households is found pursuing number of activities ranging between 6 and 9. When a household pursues more activities, it means that most of its working members are engaged in non-agricultural activities like government jobs, trading, weaving, etc.

Table 9 shows multiplicity of livelihood sources among the Khamptis. About 75 per cent of households are engaged in more than one source of livelihood. The livelihood sources are not more diversified as compared to the Apatanis. It can be deduced that the sources of livelihood pursued traditionally by the

shrinks. At second stage, greater consciousness of the need for learning rather than earnings in early years of life on the one hand and lowering of average exit age with the growth of organized sector on the other, contributes to the decline of work of both males and females. At an advanced stage, spread of education among women, skill-acquisition as well as rising levels of living enhances the employability of women in the economy, particularly in the service sector, leading to rising work participation rates among females.

Khamptis are sufficiently secured to the magnitude of requirements for which they have not diversified their activities in many direction. Mainly Khamptis are engaged in agriculture, timber business and a few, in Government jobs.

Table 9
Range of Livelihood Options among Khampti Households

No. of activities (main and subsidiaries)	*No. of Households*	*% of households*
1	32	24.24
2	57	43.18
3	34	25.76
4	64	4.55
5	3	2.27
Total	132	100.00

Source: Same as Table 6.

Concluding Remarks

The economic diversification is evident from occupational distribution across sectoral activities in comparison to traditional primary sector activities before independence. To put it alternatively, there is an enlargement of livelihood options in contemporary rural economy of Arunachal Pradesh. This enlargement of livelihood options is studied along three axes namely, occupational diversification beyond agriculture, inter-generational mobility of workforce to different activities and pursuits of more than one activity as sources of livelihood. The present study was conducted in four villages of two tribes. Nevertheless, the livelihood options which exist in four villages are not uniform though there are diverse sources of livelihood.

In two Apatani villages, the percentage of work participation varies between the villages across the gender in spite of the fact that two villages are not different in terms of access to modern facilities. Similarly, there is difference in Khampti villages. Between the communities there is striking difference in work participation. Khampti females are not recorded in business activities and Khampti male in household activities. The percentage of main workers in government jobs is comparatively less than those of the Apatanis. Similarly in agriculture, Khamptis have more participation. The most important point is that the number of activities in Khampti community is 4 as compared to 11 in Apatani community. It can be deduced that there happened to be more vulnerability in traditional economic life of Apatanis than the Khamptis. That is why the Khampti economy is not much diversed as the Apatani economy. This is evident from higher participation of Khamptis in agriculture and also less percentage of inter-generational mobility in agriculture.

REFERENCES

GoA P., 2002. "Economic Review", Itanagar: Directorate of Economics and Statistics.

_____, 2005. "Human Development Report", Itanagar: Department of Planning.

_____, 2006. "Statistical Abstract of Arunachal Pradesh", Itanagar: Directorate of Economics and Statistics.

Mishra, D.K., 2007. *Rural Non Farm Employment in Arunachal Pradesh-Growth, Composition, and Determinants*, Noida: V.V Giri National Labour Institute.

Mishra, A., 2005. "A Study of Economic Transformation, Environmental Degradation and Female Work Participation in Arunachal Pradesh", *Ph.D Thesis,* Department of Economics, Doimukh: Rajiv Gandhi University.

17

Local Governance in the Tribal Areas of North East

Sujit K. Dutta

Introduction

Local Government is otherwise termed as good governance that is sensitive to the needs and aspirations of the local people. Governance here is used in a broader notion than government. Law and order thus encompasses not only government laws but it includes as well many informal laws, understandings, norms and practices which are known as customary laws among the tribes of north-east India. This is in other words known as social values. Good governance depends on the upholding of these values through out the existence of their societies. Customary laws are also modes of keeping the members of a tribe together and are basic to their identity (Fernandes, 2006). Moreover, there are specific laws governing the resources of the tribal people of north-east India. However, the colonial regime tried to introduce formal law in the tribal dominated areas of northeast India and integrate their system but failed to do so due to variation from tribe to tribe even though they lived under the same niche[1]. These tribal councils, evolved as administrative mechanisms of a local variety for fulfilling purely the local needs, are informal

1. See for example in Arunachal Pradesh the Village Council is known differently in different tribes and differs considerably in its work from tribe to tribe (Mibang: 2002).

in nature and free from legal complications. As institutions of social evolution the tribal councils have great potentialities. They are the expression of genuine democracy representing the cooperation and communal temperament of the people. Metcalfe thus explains that these councils are little republic and the union of village communities; each one forming little state in itself is in a high degree conducive to their happiness and to enjoyment of a portion of freedom and independence. Hence, many tribes in north east India even today continue to live by their respective customary laws under their traditional structure. However, except in the areas where it is recognized, the state considers them only customs not accepted by the formal law. Thus, the interaction creates contradiction and as a result an adverse impact on their communities. Nevertheless, recognition of the system may not be the prerogative but survival may be a question. It is difficult to survive with contradiction forever. Probably, that is the reason why the tradition and modernity never is complementary. The customary laws are community control over land, forests and other natural resources. Land cannot be alienated without the consent of the village council, whose head has the authority to grant permission.

Governance is a process whereby the traditional and modern institutions of the tribals of north east India conduct public affairs, manage public resources and guarantee the realization of human rights. Good governance accomplishes this in a manner essentially free from abuse and corruption, and with due regard for the rule of law. This is delivered on the promise of human rights: civil, cultural, economic, political and social rights. With this brief prologue let us see some of the functioning of a few local governments in the tribal areas of northeast.

Local Government (Modern/New and Traditional) in Meghalaya Today

From the available recorded accounts of the functioning of Autonomous District Councils (ADCs) one might have an idea that District Council has been functioning as well as any other existing local government in the country. But this seems to me paradoxical as the empirical findings show that the existing District Council which is a modern/new local government in Meghalaya is not at all fulfilling the local needs; rather it seems to have been created to fulfill the interest of a few affluent people and not for the welfare or benefit of the masses as pointed out by a good number of traditional Khasi Chiefs (they are still existing under traditional system). In fact it is an institution (ADCs), which has created more factional conflicts and cleavages within the Khasi Society today. Hence, the creation of District Council is a controversial issue in Meghalaya (Dutta: 2002, Preface). The situation, as such, is a very complex one. The findings were supported with several case studies conducted at the chieftaincy[2] level, Commune (raid) level as well as Village Darbar level. The system was found to be quite coherent and integral. The existing customary laws have no doubt bound the society to a self-content republic. On the contrary survival of the traditional institutions of *Khasi* Hills of Meghalaya is the question of the day. The struggle is more to prove the strength of the modern system through fraudulent method. Further, there is a struggle by a section of *Khasi* elites who are desperately trying to crucify the traditional institutions in the name of so called reforms and progress. This is the general remark of most of the *Khasi* Chiefs. However, it has become imperative to understand the discontentment of these Chiefs first rather than to understand the local government's (modern/new) functional role.

In fact they wanted to establish a separate statuesque on one hand and to bind the society together with traditional values on the other. Properties were undivided and maintained by the community or individual, and the traditional heads such as *Syiem, Lyngdoh, Sirdar or Wahadadar* were the custodian of these lands and property of those people who lived under this jurisdiction. These bodies were apolitical as they feel, but for survival they formed Federation of *Khasi* States and the non-states, which were established in 1933.

---

2. There are total 24 Khasi States and one non-state (Jaintia Hills) in Meghalaya. The respective Chiefs administer these States. Whereas Khasi Hills is divided into 10 zones which are occupied by 4 Traditional Chiefs, namely Syiems, Lyngdohs, Wahadadar and Sirdar, the Jaintia Hills is divided into 6 zones and are occupied by Dollois (Traditional Chiefs) mainly.

Now the question arises whether this plank (based on Sixth Schedule) is a sufficient condition to sustain those traditional institutions or not? Thinkers, administrators, scholars have diverse opinions regarding the provision of Autonomous District Councils in the Constitution. Some of their views are:

> Whereas Kuladhar Chaliha, Rajeswar Prasad and Rohini Kumar Choudhury gave opinion against the formation of Autonomous District Councils but Rohini Kumar Choudhury is a staunch protagonist of the policy of assimilation. Hence, he advocates the assimilation of tribal and non-tribal (Constitution Assembly Debate, n.d:1008).

However, Nichols Ray, Gopinath Bordoloi, Lakshminarayan Sahu, A.V. Thakkar and Jaipal Singh supported the formation of District Councils and therefore supported the spirit of the Sixth Schedule. The only argument these people had is that this Sixth Schedule would not only safeguard the hill people, but would satisfy hill people in many ways and the hill people would be able to come closer to the rest of the country.

In fact those who are in favour of the assimilation want to assimilate the tribal people by force. Naturally, they hold an imperialist attitude and suffer from superiority complex. They failed to see the distinction between integration and assimilation. The sub-committee of the Constituent Assembly of India of North-East Frontier Tribal and Excluded Areas further felt that the assimilation of the people of these areas with the rest of the country would not take place by the sudden breaking up of tribal institutions; what was required was evolution *i.e.*, it should come as far as possible from the tribes themselves and it was equally clear that contact with outside institutions was necessary, though not in a compelling way. In fact assimilation involves total loss of cultural identity of the group as a result of its complete absorption into the dominant group. Instead of assimilation, integration must be encouraged.

The age-old rivalry between the traditional institutions[3] and the modern/new institutions (the Autonomous District Council) created under the Sixth Schedule is well known. Even today it is eluding a solution. At times distrust among them led to conflict. In such circumstances the autonomy of the tribal institutions is jeopardised and the struggle sustained. This is the turmoil within the *Khasi* society and their institutions today. Most of the Chiefs feel that they are now under the control of District Councils. By enquiry it has been found that all the Chiefs are now under the jurisdiction of District Councils. The District Councils under the Act of 1959 wholly regulate the succession and appointment of Chiefs and headmen (Appointment of Succession of Chief Act). The Supreme Court of India observed in 1960 that *Syiem (traditional chief)* was a functionary under the District Council. All the Chiefs were now presiding officers of the Additional Subordinate District Council Courts. But their decisions are subject to appellate jurisdiction of the Subordinate District Council Court at Shillong. As regards financial matters, the Chiefs pay one-eighth of the total income to the District Council. The Council has also certain control over the budget of the Chiefs. Overall it has been found that the Chiefs are today under hard pressure in many ways; even their status has become subordinate. In such a situation many of them have become aggressive and are preparing for a revolt (Dutta, *op.cit*).

About sixty years have passed since the time when the modern/new local government in the name of the autonomous district councils was established under the framework of the Sixth Schedule of the Constitution, but no sincere attempts have so far been made to have a full-ranged in-depth study of the traditional institutions. Much legislation has been enacted, but instead of improving them, these legislations seem to have come into direct confrontation with the well-established customary laws and practices which are attached to the existing traditional institutions. At present these institutions are in need of a positive dynamic leadership, who possesses a sense of balance and proportion coupled with a sense of direction. The need of the

3. Total Khasi states and non-states are as follows:

Khyrim	Mylliem	Cherra	Nongkhlaw	Bhowal
Langrin	Mawiang	Malaisohmat	Mawphang	Lyniong
Pamsanagnt	Mawdon	Dwara Nongtyrmen	Nobosohphoh	Nongspung
Jirang	Maharam	Mawsynram	Myriaw	Mawlong
Nonglwai	Nongstoin	Rambrai	Sohiong	Shella

hour, they feel, is wisdom and political sagacity to pave the way for the future generations. This is what some very aggrieved chiefs of the *Khasi* States have felt.

While dealing with the *Khasis* the British administration did not interfere in the tribal customs and laws. The judicial powers of the *Syiem* and traditional political authority were curtailed only to a limited extent. The overall impact of the British rule was that although the *Syiem* and his *Myntries* and other officials remained in their offices, they were divested of their real power, which was then vested in the Deputy Commissioner. Again this establishment of District Council court after independence has eroded the Chief's judicial powers to a considerable extent. The authority structure is now organised at the level of District Council, Deputy Commissioner (only in certain Khasi area of the city) and finally the High Court.

Despite the changes, the traditional *Khasi* political structure still prevails in Meghalaya, though with the advent of the British rule and the promulgation of the Constitution of India later it has undergone modification to a certain extent. But District Councils have weakened the function of tribal courts in Meghalaya so much so that the *Khasi* states have virtually come under the domination of the state officials as well as the District Councils. Naturally, the *Khasi* states have come to occupy the subordinate position.

However, the *Syiem* as the chief of the tribe is always respected. He still receives different forms of tributes from his people. Despite the erosion of his powers and rights, he still plays a vital role in the administrative affairs of the tribe. He supervises the conduct of his subordinate authorities at the *raid (commune)* and village level. If a village headman or a commune headman is found incompetent and charged with abusing his powers, the *Syiem* can order fresh elections in order to replace him. He still protects the rights of the people, administers justice and punishes the culprits. After the formation of District Councils all *Syiems* have been given the powers of Additional Magistrates in their respective *Syiemships*. Accordingly they are empowered to try civil and criminal cases except murder case.

The present study focuses mainly on the controversies/ differences of opinion regarding the retention of district council in Meghalaya. It is yet to be clarified. According to Baljied *Syiem* JJM Nichols Roy (one of the founding members of ADCs) did not go out to protect the rights of the *Khasi* people and for which there came out the Sixth Schedule. This was actually imposed without taking the public opinion or existing local institutions into consideration as he felt. District Council is a political institution, which, though meant to be the protector of traditions and customs of the *Khasis,* has actually been so much politicised that it only serves the interests of some elected members. Actually, people do not look to the council so much for protection of the traditions of the society as for some measly grants, which ultimately end up in a few pockets. It is the political leaders both from the district councils and the state government who have not really been sincere in their duties towards their community. He felt that most of the problems could be solved if district council was scrapped. It is the duty of the state government to see that a new legislation comes out to ensure that the traditional institutions are left unhindered to co-exist healthily. For him the traditional institutions have some limitations in modern society. Even they are open to changes, but they should have the right to choose the changes required. They are in need of a healthy tradition and good political leaders who are not selfish and who really work for the benefit and development of modern society (Syiem, 1988).

Khasi polity and democracy (Traditional local government) has a three-tier system with built-in-checks and balance. At the bottom there is a village (Village *Darbar*), in the middle a *Raid or Commune,* and at the apex, a *Hima (elaka).* At the village level democracy is direct; it is based on adult male franchise. Each village has its own General Assembly and an Executive Council with well-defined powers and functions. At the *Raid* and *Hima* levels, democracy is indirect and representative. At the village level an individual is a unit, at the *Raid* level, a clan is a unit, whereas at the *Hima* level both a clan and a village are a unit. Each *Raid* has its own General Assembly consisting of all adult male members of the *Raid,* and a *Raid* Council, which consists of representatives, elected by the major clans of the area under its jurisdiction and which perform administrative, executive and judicial functions. At the *Hima* level we find two institutions, one is the *Syiem* in Council which consists of the

Syiem and all the members of the *Raid* Council within the *Hima* which is the highest administrative, executive and judicial body. The other is the General Assembly of the *Hima* or *Darbar Hima*, which consists of all the members of the *Syiem*-in-Council and the representatives elected by the people of the villages within the *Hima*. This *Darbar* formulates policies and makes final decisions on all matters referred to it by the *Syiem*-in-Council.

The Sixth Schedule was designed to confer a considerable amount of autonomy on the tribal people by giving them protection to retain their identity according to their own genius politically, socially and economically through their elected representatives and nominated members. The Sixth Schedule provides a type of local governmental (modern/new) arrangement, which aims to better the life of the tribal people, keeping in view the ample opportunity to grow in their own roots (Jyrwa, n.d). The very purpose of the Sixth Schedule is to provide complete safeguards to the tribal communities in respect of land, forest, and system of justice and social customs. It was felt that the state and central government would help them in securing the benefits of a democratic, progressive and liberal administration. In order to achieve these aims the Constitution has given the power to make laws on various subjects applicable to the tribal people as enshrined in the Sixth Schedule (Bose, 1979:182–184).

Against this backdrop, the District Councils/Autonomous Local Government (modern/new) came into being in Tribal Areas of the North-Eastern Region.

Basic Functions of the Modern/New Local Government in Meghalaya: Khasi Hills Autonomous District Councils (KHADCs)

KHADCs cover three districts in Meghalaya, namely, East Khasi Hills, Ri-bhoi and West Khasi Hills. There are three basic functions of the ADCs. These are:

Legislative: The district council enacts laws and regulations as well as frames rules for implementing them as per the provisions of the Sixth Schedule to the Constitution. Such laws and regulations are placed before the council's session in the form of bills for consideration. After the Council passes the bills they are sent to the Governor of the state for his/her assent or approval. The existing list of subjects on which the District Council can legislate covers all the important social and personal aspects of tribal life.

Executive:. The executive functions of the District Council are vested in the executive committee. Each member of the Executive Committee is entrusted with specific subjects and the Chief Executive Member (CEM) makes the allocation of the subjects to the members. The Council can discharge some functions in exercise of its executive powers even before the relevant laws are passed provided these are within the purview of the Sixth Schedule. At the highest level, all executive functions of the District Council are vested in the Executive Committee headed by the CEM who is elected by the members of the council from among themselves. The executive committee disposes of all matters of administration of the district except those which involve any important change in the administrative system of the autonomous district.

The Executive Committee is collectively responsible to the council for all executive orders, policy matters and their exception. It frames the policies, prepares the budget, executes them and mostly initiates legislation in the council. The Executive Committee has a secretary who controls and supervises the various branches of the council and is in the immediate charge of the day-to-day administration. Thus, it has separate branches for general administration, land revenue, forests, civil works, education, rural development, transport, taxation, and relief and rehabilitation, besides the legislative and judicial branches.

Judiciary: Paragraph 4 of the Sixth Schedule empowers the District Council to constitute village courts for the trial of suits and cases in which both parties are members of the Schedule Tribes. It may appoint suitable persons as members of such village councils or presiding officers of such courts as may be necessary for the execution of laws made by the District Council. According to the amendments of the Sixth Schedule under the Act, the Governor is authorised to make rules for regulating the constitution of the village councils and courts and the power to be exercised by them.

All the three ADCs have constituted their courts of appeals. Each has a judge and a magistrate. The traditional courts of the chiefs have always been functioning as additional subordinate courts of the District Council with the traditional chiefs as presiding officers.

Entrusted Functions

Apart from the basic functions as mentioned, the ADCs have some entrusted functions. However, the state Government is not authorised to entrust any of its powers to the District Council. The Sixth Schedule was further amended whereby it is provided that the Governor may entrust either conditionally or unconditionally some more functions to the District Councils. The functions enumerated relate to agriculture, animal husbandry, community projects, cooperative societies, social welfare, village planning or any other matter, which the State extends. But the Governor of Meghalaya has entrusted none of these subjects to any of the District Councils. And the ADCs have felt that they are deliberately ignored of such responsibilities.

Sources of Fund of ADC

There are some major sources of fund of the ADC which are listed below:

(i) Land, which abounds in major minerals (coal, silimonites, lime stone etc.) and minor minerals (sand, pebbles, etc.). The ADC gets its share of income from these resources from the state government.

(ii) Income of the ADC from the taxes collected at the toll gates.

(iii) Share of income from trade and commerce.

(iv) Income from professional taxes.

(v) Revenue from forests.

Constraints of the District Councils Today

The Autonomous District Councils in Meghalaya are facing the following constraints:

- There is resource (financial) crunch. Moreover, the resources provided under the Sixth Schedule such as the power to collect taxes on land and building, and tolls on residents in the District could not be made use of on account of the tradition and customs prevailing in the District.

- ADC has been given powers to collect taxes but not for the collection of royalties and fees on subjects within its legislative and administrative competence (Supreme Court Judgment:1972).
- The share of royalty in respect of any area within the District Council between District Council and the State Government as agreed upon was in the ratio 60:40 (e.g., share of royalty on coal). A dispute arose later on and the case was referred to the Governor who determined the share as 25:75 between the District Council and the State Government.
- Assent or approval of the Governor to the Bills passed by the ADC is often accorded after a considerable period of time; say two years or even more. It defeats the very purpose of the Bills and the Council is not in a position to implement its intention to promote good administration on different subjects.
- Paragraph 14 empowers the Governor to appoint a commission to enquire into the administration of a District Council or any particular matters specified by him/her relating to the administration of the Autonomous District in the State.
- Shares on royalty on major and minor minerals, taxes on vehicles collected by the State Government constitute one of the major sources of revenue of the Council. The State Government instead of paying the share in full and in time adopted a policy to release the share in the form of advance, and sometimes to deduct from such share. The State incurs election expenses and other charges from time to time without the consent of the Council. Above all no account pertaining to the actual collection and the share due to the Council was ever made available to the Council.

- Fund for carrying out developmental activities as provided according to the present system are found to be inadequate as well as unworkable. Fund is also inadequate for executing the schemes, strengthening of staff and salary to the deputed staff. Hence, the funds released as grants-in-aid are far from being sufficient to meet the actual requirements of the Council.
- There is no provision in the Sixth Schedule for the State Police to act at the instance of District Council and therefore enforcement of the Council orders etc. has become a major handicap in its day-to-day administration. The Council has been given the power to constitute village or town police. However, in view of the meager resources of the council it is not possible to create such a force. It is also obligatory on the part of the ADC to organise and strengthen the traditional Institution, but for paucity of fund no significant improvement could be made so far.
- When Meghalaya was created, the Councils in Meghalaya were subjected to great financial constraints. This is due to the fact that funds provided earlier under article 275 are no longer available, with the result that the Management of Primary Education – as the first casualty– had to be taken over temporarily by the State government and it is continuing till date even after about 10 years.
- By the 73rd/74th Amendments to the Constitution in 1993, substantial administrative and financial powers have been devolved to local bodies constituted all over the country (where PR system is existing), but the Sixth Schedule does not provide for devolution of development powers to ADCs. As a result financial and administrative autonomy of local bodies in other parts of the country has become much stronger than that in schedule areas.

Traditional System in Arunachal Pradesh

Village Council in Arunachal Pradesh

In Arunachal Pradesh most of the tribal groups have their own traditional systems of administration. There are some common features and there are differences too. But every village council is unique in its own genius. They have their own traditional system of administration for maintenance of law and order in their respective community. Of course, many traditional institutions have disappeared but the indigenous institutions remain functional for the needs of the community. *Kebang* is one of such traditional institutions found among the *Adis* of Arunachal Pradesh which is a democratic institution consisting of all responsible members of a village or area. The people who show good knowledge, married man and person having command over the customary laws and traditional conventions were the most influential persons in the *Kebang*.

Composition and Functioning of Kebang

Kebang is composed of all the adult members of the village like that of VDB in Nagaland. There is no presiding officer. Women do not generally participate unless called for. Hence their participation is limited to the extent of filing any complains unlike the Khasi women who do not have right to enter into the Village *Darbar*. *Kebang Abu* who is an experienced, elderly and a good orator starts the proceeding with an introductory speech. The senior members speak on the issue followed by the junior members. Inter-village administration is controlled by another type of traditional council known as *Bango* which is composed of members drawn from a few villages. They generally settle inter-village disputes and at times impose fines as punishment; the collections are deposited in the *Bango* fund for the purpose of spending mainly for the welfare of the entire region. Above *Bango* there is a divisional council known as *Bogum Bokang* consisting of all the *Bangos* in the division. The main function of this council is to take important decision for the welfare of the entire population under their jurisdiction. It also settles the inter *Bango* disputes.

Functions of *Kebang*

- It settles the disputes within the village boundary.
- It administers justice and look after day-to-day administration of the village.
- It acts as a court and decides all types of cases and disputes arising within its jurisdiction according to the customary laws of the community.

- It runs the administration according to the traditions and customs of the Adis.
- Matters concerning the clan and village affairs are all discussed thoroughly so as to arrive at unanimous decisions.
- The council used to deal with development works like the maintenance of the roads and bridges, water supply and sanitation.
- Traditionally the council is in charge of maintenance of the natural resources like forests, rivers, lands in their administrative area.
- The Council also decides the time of the main agricultural operations, fixes the dates of communal hunting including fishing and festivals.

Village Councils vs. Panchayat Raj in Arunachal Pradesh

Now-a-days after acceptance of the Panchayati Raj system development activities in relation to projects sponsored by the government are carried out by the Panchayats. But the consent of *Kebang* to execute such works at times became mandatory. Even today the traditional village council system continues to function in every village (Talukdar, 2001). But due to the introduction of *Panchayats* the *Kebang* has undergone a tremendous change. Now the people apply the political dictum like 'one man one vote' and 'majority vote' etc. including numerous formalities required for the modern participatory democratic institutions. This in turn restricts the importance of customary practices and conventions. It is in this sense some one feels that the *Kebang* became more democratic. The hierarchy in the membership of *Kebang* on the basis of status, wealth, command over the customary laws and conventions disappeared leading to increase in participation of people, irrespective of status, wealth, sex, marital status, knowledge of customary laws and conventions in the process of decision making. Moreover, earlier only the married and head of the family used to become a member in this institution for deliberation and decision making but at present these traditions have undergone change and the young and new panchayat leaders dominate the decision-making and the deliberation in the *Kebang* (Maibang: *op.cit*). These neo-leaders started dominating the *Kebang* by replacing the old and elderly people who used to command over the customary laws and traditional conventions getting eroded gradually. Moreover, now every thing in the *Kebang* is under the control of these neo-leaders who permeates a culture that also undermines the age-old institutions. The decisions now in *Kebang* are more on the political lines, which have not only created rift but also a vertical division in the otherwise, homogenous, and cohesive village hierarchy. In spite of such a situation the *Kebang* is always referred whenever there are developmental activities related to the customary law and traditional conventions. The *Gams* (officially appointed as head of *Kebang*) and traditional leaders are always consulted and their decisions still prevail. In Arunachal Pradesh, the Traditional and Modern/New local government are working together without any conflict unlike Meghalaya. There is a mutual respect and trust among the leaders of both the system. Whereas the modern/new local government takes care of the development works the traditional institutions mostly take care of the traditional customary practices at large, mostly at the local level.

The Village Council and Village Development Board (VDB) in Nagaland

In Nagaland the situation is slightly different; they have both Village Council (VC) and Village Development Board (VDB). Whereas the VC, the premier local self government (Traditional) used to perform both legislative and judicial functions by interpreting customs and maintaining traditions, the VDB (modern/new) performs all the development related activities. The VC comprises the village elders who used to meet together to decide prominent issues of the village life. In the advent of modern time also it has been found fit to the tune with present societal needs (Maithani and Rizwana: 1992). The VC used manages common property resources and mobilizes village fund in common interest. But it has been reduced significantly after independence due to 'erudite administration' where the significance of the VC remained 'only as a lower court' of the village (Singh: 2004). The Government of Nagaland by setting up the DRDA allows the VC and VDB to be instrumental in dealing with the process of rural development. The separate organs of the VC, namely the Common Fund Committee and the Village Social Security Trust, were separated and allowed to carry out management of the village development under the supervision and guidance of the Government. Later on the idea was developed to constitute a separate agency assigned with the task and responsibility to manage the affairs of village development and the agency should comprise 'educated young enterprising persons under the overall guidance of the Village Council' (Maithani and Rizwana, *op.cit*). The first Agency of the type, which appeared in 1976, was called Village Common Fund Committee and it was this committee, which assumed the terminology as the Village Development Board, popularly known as VDB. The government by formulating two notifications namely the Village Development Model Rules, 1980 and Village Development Model Rules, 1989 has elaborated provisions for composition, scope, powers and functions of the VDB. Since then they have been functioning effectively till date under this statutory provisions. This act was enacted according to the Naga traditions and customary laws. However, the functioning of these institutions varies from tribe to tribe, as the different tribes possess different customary practices.

The members in the Council are chosen either 'clan-wise' or 'khel-wise' (hamlet). The Chairman and the Secretary of VDB are chosen from among the village council members. Only Konyak and Sema Nagas have the hereditary chieftainship. The rest are having chiefs who are selected by the villages. Only married person holds the office of a councillor without any remuneration. However, these institutions carry out all development works. Whereas village council has become the village court to settle all disputes, the VDB is functioning as development agent of village council. VDB is like Gram Sabha in Panchayati Raj System, which comprises 'all permanent residents of village' who form the 'general body of VDB' (VDB Model Rules: 1989). The meeting of the VDB is mandatory at least twice a year to discuss and deliberate issues regarding village development and approve the schemes chalked out by the Management Committee (MC), which is the most effective body of the VDB. The MC is constituted for a period of three years, has the minimum strength of five and maximum twenty five members who are chosen by the village council from outside of its own membership. The provision permits women also to be its members. A chairman is nonetheless other than the Deputy Commissioner or the Additional Deputy Commissioner of the concerned area (*ibid*: clause 4b). The members of the MC select one from among themselves as the secretary who must be literate person of the village. In case such person is not available, the government may appoint one Government employee as the secretary to serve the purpose. It is to be noted that 'No VC's Chairman or Head *Gaun Burah* (GB) or village administration head etc. shall be permitted to hold the post of secretary of the VDB Management Committee (*ibid*). The power and responsibility bestowed upon the secretary by the government has made the post very much influential and attractive. It is he who places before the general body 'all details regarding the VDB schemes, money drawn, loans issued against fixed deposit security, interest of fixed deposit, manner of utilization of interest amount and other issues (*ibid:* clause 4a). The secretary keeps close contact with the district authorities in connection to his business. His power to receive cheques issued by them to meet the expenditure incurred on development works definitely highlights the rank and position of the secretary not only among the villagers but also amidst the Government Officials related to the VDB activities. The utilization of community fund and other development fund is always under the guidance and supervision of VC. Hence, in many ways VC and VBD are integral and not mutually exclusive. Here also there is no conflict between the leaders of the traditional (VC) and modern/new local government (VDB).

Financial Resources of VDB

The funding condition of VDBs is quite good. Their sources are as follows:

- Public contribution.
- Earning from fixed deposits.
- Matching Grant from the State Government, which is equal to the amount of common fund raised by the villagers. However, the upper limit is rupees one lakhs only.
- Grants-in-aid from State Rural Development Department annually.
- Grant under some centrally sponsored schemes.

Further, VDB can also borrow money from the bank against its fixed deposits as and when required. Moreover, the labour component generally rose by the villagers as the development schemes are mostly labour free of cost. Since VBD is a recognized field agency, subsidy amount is directly released to it. And they in turn sanction and disperse subsidy to a few selected households to meet 50 per cent of the cost of the scheme taken up.

Execution of Funds by VDB

The clause 8 of the model rules of VDB insists on opening of bank accounts and their joint operation by the chairman and secretary of the MC. Moreover, 'No cheque shall be honoured unless it is accompanied by a copy of the MC's resolution authorizing such withdrawal signed in presence of the members of MC (*ibid:* clause 8). The amount received from the sources must be put in fixed deposit, which cannot be withdrawn except the interests. Otherwise the VDB would not be eligible for any funds like grants-in-aid, matching grants, funds available under numerous centrally sponsored schemes including other development funds from the state Rural Development Department (*ibid*: clause 10). The secretary of the MC has to maintain full records of the amount received in forms of grants-in-aid. He also maintains details of drawls of money and disbursals under the on-going development schemes. The village council still has supervisory power over the VDB. Both the secretaries of the MC and the VDB are responsible to the village council. There is also provisions for auditing of the accounts for which initiative should be taken from the VC.

Concluding Remarks with Suggestions

The study focuses on the existence and functioning of ADC in Meghalaya. The main purpose of the discussion was to find out the reason and justification of creation of Autonomous District Council in the State of Meghalaya, which is a modern/new local government. The very purpose of creating District Council was to protect the tribal people with their cultural heritage as well as their socio-economic life and living. But on the contrary the committee responsible for setting up such bodies failed to understand the sentiment of the local chiefs (leader of the traditional institutions) as a result of which the conflict between District Council, *i.e.* the functionaries of District Council and the Chiefs of the Twenty-five Khasi States and non-states (Jaintia Hills) started. However, this is yet to take a violent form but internal non-cooperation is very much prevalent. Naturally, the District Council does not get sufficient cooperation from the chiefs although the chiefs have been given magisterial powers to function with limited capacity. But the chiefs feel that their major powers have been snatched away and they are not at all involved in development programmes of government. After attaining statehood, the District Council is standing alone with all its functions, powers and privileges. Further, the Khasi states and the Autonomous District Council are unable to maintain cordial relations. To wither away District Council is not possible, as it is a statutory body under the provision of the Constitution. On the other hand, the state has been created on the choice of the people of Meghalaya. But the Chiefs of the Khasi states and non-states claim their major stake. Whatever the reasons may be the Khasi states and non-states stand on their traditional values, wherein people feel more comfortable. Someone may have wrong conception about Khasi Chiefs; in fact they are neither autocrat nor feudal. They do not control the means of production of the people. People are allowed to possess any amount of land in their individual name. Customary laws framed by the people through consensus control all community land, clan land, forestland or sacred lands. The Chiefs are just titular heads who enjoy some tributes according to the desire of the local people. Hence, they are just custodians.

What is important at this stage is to find out a solution to the problem. Instead of looking at the personal interest it would be wise to see the general interest, which might benefit everyone. Constitutional provision for creating a statutory local government is no doubt very much important but at the same time it should adhere to the needs and aspirations of local people. If this is not done, then there may be anomaly in the society, and we are afraid, this might lead to destruction.

The *Kebang* of the *Adis* of Arunachal Pradesh has undergone considerable change in its structure and function but there is an effort to strengthen and retain the same for the sake of the interests of the local people at large. Hence these councils continued to function as village government carrying along the maintenance of law and order situation according to the norms, rules and procedures laid down in tradition. It is therefore suggested that the statutory panchayat should take the advantage of involving such institutions to a large extent for systematic planning, management and implementation of development projects including monitoring and evaluation. But we need to have correct approach *i.e.*, not just to involve them as an agent but also to develop partnership to execute the works through participatory process. There is no denying the fact that if proper respect is shown to these councils they can be of great help and in that process they will be self-reliant. Only thing is to develop the capacity of this council to the tune of their involvement in respective tasks. Hence, this is the responsibility of the development administration to take care of.

In Nagaland the local institution, the VDB, is quite a strong body and they do respect their traditional institution *i.e.*, the village council. There is hardly any dispute between these two institutions. Apart from executive, administrative and judicial functions, they do numerous welfare activities for their people. Hence, they get more respect from among the people. Even they are totally involved in executing the centrally sponsored development schemes. It is almost functioning like *Gram Sabha* in Panchayati Raj system.

Financially also VDB is quite strong. Apart from government grants they raise their funds from public contribution, fixed deposits, etc.

Women's Position in Local Government

As regards Naga women, they get good support from VDB. In fact there are funds exclusively kept for the women scheme. Specifically, the women take decision on their schemes independently and the male members don't intervene.

But women are controlled in other ways too, for example, they cannot claim property right. They are even unable to claim immovable property of their parents. This goes to the male members only. If a male member is absent it goes to nearest male relations. They have a very low politico-religious status. As per the customary practices the priest is sitting on the helm of affairs that takes lot many decisions. Since the priest is always a male, naturally the women are deprived of such privilege. Moreover, in order to prevent the women getting into the politico-religious activities, the women involvement is termed as taboo.

Hence, they are bound with domestic and family oriented activities only. However, it is better among the worse situations as in the case of women in Meghalaya. At least in case of Naga women they enter VDB as member but not as overall decision maker. They definitely enjoy freedom but with numerous restrictions. This situation will continue unless they amend the customary practices and recognise the women as equal partner (Dutta, 2006).

Similarly, many customary laws, social rights and religious rituals undermine the status of women in Khasi society. If such discriminatory practices are allowed to continue in the name of customary practices and tradition, this would amount to putting obstacles for the women power and thereby women empowerment in specific. In Meghalaya, the women have law of inheritance under which the youngest daughter inherits the property; but they are reckoned through males alone. However, it is noticed that there are some changes in some part of the state where the women are allowed to enter into the *Darbar* at least as a member but not as decision maker. (*ibid.*)

REFERENCES

Bose, Manilal. *Historical and Constitutional Documents of North-East India,* Delhi: Concept Publishing Company, 1979, pp.182–184.

Constitution Assembly Debate, n.d: p. 1008.

Dutta, Sujit Kumar. *Functioning of Autonomous District Councils in Meghalaya,* New Delhi: Akansha Publishing House, 2002, preface, pp. 3-5.

Dutta, Sujit Kumar. 'Problems of Women Empowerment: The Experiences of North East', a seminar paper presented at the *National Seminar on Rural Development through Women's Empowerment: Special Reference to North-East* at B.H.College. Howly. Assam, February 11, 2006.

Fernandes,Walter. "Tribal Traditional Systems: Can They Survive the Modern Onslaught?", Seminar Paper Presented at *the National Seminar on Traditional Institutions and Development Interventions* at the National Institute of Rural Development, North Eastern Regional Centre, Guwahati during February 20 – 22, 2006.

Jyrwa, E. 'Financial Status of Local Institutions in the Khasi and Jaintia Hills', unpublished document. nd.

Maithani, B.P. and A. Rizwana. *Decentralised Development:A Study of the Functioning of VDBs in Nagaland,* National Institute of Rural Development, Hyderabad, 1992.

Mibang, Tabang. 'Impact of Panchayati Raj on Traditional Village Councils of Arunachal Pradesh with Special Reference to Kebang of Adis' seminar paper presented at *National Workshop on the Traditional Self-Governing Institutions in the Hill Areas of North-East and their Relevance in the Present day Context,* organized by OKDISCD. Guwahati, February 2004.

Syiem, Baljied. 'Syiemships district councils can't co-exist', covered by *Grass roots voices,* October 26 – November 1, 1988.

Singh, Chandrika. 'Village Development Board (VDB): A Model Innovation in Lieu of Village Panchayat for Rural Development in Nagaland', seminar paper presented at *National Workshop on the Traditional Self-Governing Institutions in the Hill Areas of North-East and their Relevance in the Present day Context, op.cit.*

Seventy Third and Seventy Fourth Act to the Constitution of India, 1972.

Supreme Court judgment in Civil Appeal Nos. 2069–70 of 1972, paragraph 3.

Talukdar, A.C. 'Traditional Self Governing Institutions among the Tribes of Arunachal Pradesh', in Atul Goswami (ed.) *Traditional Self Governing Institutions among the Hill Tribes of North-East. 2001.*

VDB Model Rules (revised 1989), Government notification dated Kohima, 21st, Government of Nagaland, November, 1989.

Related References

Appointment of Succession of Chiefs Act, 1959.

Administrative Report of Khasi and Jaintia Hills 1875–76.

District Council's Report to Vaghaiwalla Committee 1959–60.

Das, Mitra. "Kebang as an Institution for Development of the Adis in Arunachal Pradesh" Seminar Paper Presented at the *National Seminar on Traditional Institutions and Development Interventions* at the National Institute of Rural Development, North Eastern Regional Centre, and Guwahati during February 20–22, 2006.

Instrument of Accession of Khasi Hills States, August 7, 1948.

Roybarman, B.K. "73rd and 74th Amendments of the Constitution, Public Discourse and State Response", PRI, Occasional Paper No. I, PRIA, New Delhi, November 1997.

18

Panchayati Raj Institutions, Women Empowerment and Economic Development

Ram Krishna Mandal

Women are an integral part in every society. The status of women in society is directly linked with social and cultural traditions, level of economic development achieved, level of educational achievements, and attitude of the society towards women, women's own awareness and political attainments. The economic status of women is determined by the role played by them in carrying out economic and non-economic activities in the family and in the society. The nature and type of economic and non-economic roles played by women have undergone changes in accordance with the changes in socio-economic factors, educational levels and technological developments and with the changing concepts regarding the extent to which women's contribution is desirable and necessary. It is now recognized all over the world that the status of women in society, both in the developed and developing countries, continues to be inferior to men. Although women's role is crucial in the family and household economy, they have not been given equal rights in social, political as well as economic fields. The necessity of improvement of status of women has been recognized as an important aspect of national progress and development. It is also felt that the problem of poverty cannot be tackled without providing opportunities of productive employment to women. Productive employment to women would provide necessary economic base and improve their social status. But it is still a fact that women in many countries of the world are facing discriminatory attitude in varying degrees on ground of sex in employment and working conditions. From time immemorial, women have faced the challenges of coping with a male chauvinistic milieu. Even after several years of planned development in India, the status of women in our country is low and their socio-economic conditions are much more depressed than that of men.

The principle of gender equality is enshrined in the Indian Constitution, in its preamble, fundamental rights, fundamental duties and directive principles. The Indian Constitution guarantees equal rights to both women and men. But the representation of Indian women in politics at national level is lower than that of men. Although women constitute nearly half of the population, but politics has remained largely a monopoly of men because, power and authority mainly lies in the hands of this gender. At present, there is a controversy about the 33 per cent reservation for women in legislatures and in parliament. However, the failure of recent efforts is to secure reservation for women in Parliament and Legislatures, the government has appointed a committee for the empowerment of women. Through reservation, empowerment of women has a long way to go. The women's participation in politics has been very low in the past 61 years after gaining independence. It was found that year 1977 showed the lower representation of women in Lok Sabha, it was 3.3 per cent only. The year 2004 shows that 9.5 per cent women participated in Lok Sabha.

Amendment to Constitution in 1992 to strengthen the sharing of power by women at local level has opened a new chapter in the history of women's struggle for empowerment. The enactment of the 73rd Amendment to Constitution *i.e.*, Panchayati Raj in India is no doubt a landmark event in this regard. It is important because of revolutionary measure by reserving 33 per cent seats for women at all levels in the local governance. Local governance interpreted as the active involvement of the local population within the territorial boundaries in local government is ensuring improved quality of service and leadership at the local government level. This is a significant shift in the approach towards the well being of women from 'Welfare during Fifties' to 'Development during Seventies' and to "Empowerment during Nineties'.

Political empowerment at local level *i.e.*, Panchayati Raj assumes particular importance as a means of producing democratic functioning and decision making decentralized governmental power, thereby restructuring political institutions. This development *i.e.*, amendment in the Constitution has brought the question of competitiveness of Indian women to the centre stage of controversy. In view of the majority of Indian rural women being illiterate and new in this role, this question has attracted the attention of the large number of commentators and researchers.

Women Empowerment

Women empowerment has a global concern, which has gained momentum in recent decades. In India, besides ratification of international conventions, there are provisions in the Constitution and several Legislative Acts have been enacted to ensure women empowerment. It however, appears that on this front the situation on ground is far from being satisfactory. In this context, in order to provide a big push, institutional support is necessary to empower Indian women in general and rural women in particular. Women empowerment demands a "Life-cycle" approach where empowerment is viewed as a process and not as an event, which challenges traditional power equations and relations. Empowerment in its simplest form means redistribution of power that challenges the male dominance. This does not, however, mean that the empowerment process adopts an antagonists approach. It is only to enable women to supplement and coordinate with men. Empowerment is an active process of enabling women to realize their identity, potentiality and power in all spheres of their lives (Sharma: 1992).

There are several indicators of empowerment. At the individual level, participation in crucial decision-making process, ability to prevent violence, self-confidence and self esteem, improved health and nutrition conditions and at the community level, existence of women's organizations, increased number of women leaders, involvement of women in designing development tools and application of appropriate technology, etc. are very crucial. At national level the indicators are, for example, awareness of social and political rights, adequate representation in legislative bodies, and integration of women in particular in national development plans, etc.

Empowerment has several other dimensions like social empowerment, economic empowerment, besides, of course, political empowerment. Social empowerment implies promotion of social capabilities such as education, health, cultural aspects and women's honour. Economic empowerment implies entitlement of employment, income, property, productive resources and benefit of development irrespective of gender difference. Political empowerment, of course, implies equal role in decision making process in power structure from grass root level to national level. All these dimensions of empowerment are interred related with each other.

There is scope for corruption in every step of the society when there is concentration of authority. There is a need that decentralization and dispersal of decision-making power should be explored fully.

Self-confidence and self-esteem of women proceed simultaneously with their empowerment. In brief, all indicators can be classified into two broad categories namely visible and invisible indicators. Amongst visible indicators a mention could be made of women's representation in parliaments. Thirty per cent of total women parliamentarians in the world come from just seven countries. Their share in national parliaments of a few selected developed and developing countries is shown in Table 1.

It can be seen from Table 1 that both in developed and developing countries women hold less seats than the men. However, in developed countries their representation is relatively higher than in developing countries. In this context it can be said that increasing the number of women in parliaments and also raising women's visibility in positions of authority are quite necessary for their empowerment, politically and economically as well. Again, much of women's work never appears in the national statistics because it is seen as an extension of their

Table 1
Seats in Parliaments held by Women (As % of total) in Developing Countries

Developing Countries	*Per cent*	*Developed Countries*	*Per cent*
China	21.8	Sweden	45
Pakistan	21.6	Denmark	38
Morocco	10.8	Norway	36.4
India	8.8	Finland	36.1
Indonesia	8.0	Netherlands	36
Nepal	5.9	Iceland	34
Egypt	2.4	Austria	33
Bangladesh	2.0	New Zealand	29

Source: Human Development Report, 2003.

caring and nurturing functions rather than as materially rewarding activity. All of them are taken as unpaid family labour.

Empowerment of women involves many things - economic opportunity, property rights, political representation, social equality, personal rights and so on. The Indian society is a patriarchal system in which women's position within the structure and duties towards the family precede their rights as individuals. Many who argue for empowerment of women do so either with or without a full understanding of the conflicts between the historical and contemporary status of women in the patriarchy and the goals of empowerment. Certainly we may track a great many changes that have occurred in the direction of change in the status of women in India but women have yet to achieve or realize many of the ideal stages of social, psychological, economic and political empowerment. Hence, it is certainly more appropriate to define empowerment as a process rather than an end-point.

Participation of women in economic and non-economic activities has been universally recognized as an important element in the adoption of the small family norm, essential for the achievement of the twin goals of economic development and population planning.

Panchayati Raj in Arunachal Pradesh

The recommendations of the Ering Committee constituted in April 1964 by the Governor of Assam were accepted by the Government of India, and the President of India promulgated the North East Frontier Agency Panchayat Raj Regulation, 1967, with effect from the 2nd October, 1968. The Regulation provided for the constitution of Gram Panchayats at the village level, Anchal Samiti at the block level and Zilla Parishads at the district level. Panchayat Raj in NEFA generally followed the all India pattern. Till the 14th September, 1997 only Arunachal Pradesh had retained the three tier system of Panchayat Raj system among the North Eastern States. In Assam, the three tiers Panchayati Raj system was reduced to two tiers by jettisoning the middle tier. In Manipur and Tripura, only Gram Panchayats are functioning, and in Meghalaya, Nagaland and Mizoram, only tribal councils are working. The 1967 Panchayat Raj Regulation was subsequently amended in 1970, 1971, 1972, 1994 and 1997.

According to the 1967 Regulation, the term of all Panchayat bodies was to be three years. However, in Arunachal Pradesh, the Panchayat Raj Bill of 1994 has raised the term to five years, as per the 73rd Constitutional Amendment Act (1993). In Arunachal Pradesh (the then NEFA), the total number of Gram Panchayats in 1969, when Panchayat Raj was first introduced in the State, was 938 which came down to 837 in 1987 due to a change in the size of Gram Panchayats, but again increased to 2012 in 1992. Similarly, the total number of Anchal Samities in the beginning was only 38, which subsequently increased to 44 in 1972, 60 in 1987, and finally to 78 in 1992, when Panchayat elections were held last in the State. Likewise the number of Zilla Parishads also rose from 5 in 1969, to 12 in 1992. Thus, after the 1992 elections on an average, each Gram Panchayat had 3 members, Anchal Samiti 16, and Zilla Parishad 13 members (White Paper, 1998).

In the last three decades, since the introduction of the Panchayat Raj in Arunachal Pradesh, seven elections to Panchayat bodies were held from 1969 to 1992. Though there was no provision for party system in Panchayat Raj elections in Arunachal Pradesh, the influence of party politics could not be stopped on Panchayat Raj elections. It has been observed that political parties played a big role in the elections though the names and symbols of parties did not figure openly.

Although Panchayat Raj System, introduced in 1969, has proved to be a unique democratic institution and played a vital role in socio-political and economic development of the people in the last three decades, unfortunately this august institution was dissolved on the 14th September, 1997. The problem was that the 73rd Constitution Amendment Act, 1992, which provides for a uniform system of Panchayat throughout the country (except in a few scheduled areas) with provisions for reservation of seats for SC/ST and women within a stipulated time frame, was itself the reason for it. In pursuant of the said Act, the State Government promulgated an ordinance in conformity with the provisions of the Constitution Amendment Act and later replaced it by a Bill called The Arunachal Pradesh Panchayat Raj Bill, 1994 and passed in the Assembly on the 9th September, 1994.

The NEFA Panchayat Raj Regulation, 1967, which has been the basic and parent law on the subject governing the Panchayat Raj institutions in this State for nearly three decades had not proved for any reservation to any others and it was purely an institution from the grass root level managed, controlled and administered by the tribals themselves for their betterment and development (Modi, 2001).

In Arunachal Pradesh, various tribal communities are at different stages of development; as such the status of women differs from community to community. However, in general the position of women in Arunachal Pradesh is respectable but not very high. The prevalence of polygyny, practice of bride price, sex abuse and child marriage were quite common. It had no doubt lowered their position. They were generally devoid of equal political and property rights. Today, the position of tribal women has changed. The educated women are coming forward to shoulder the equal responsibility with the men for the socio-economic development of Arunachal Pradesh. But the realities of women in rural Arunachal Pradesh are difficult to comprehend. Women, most of the times, are even deprived of some of the fundamental human rights and this denial is justified often in the name of tradition. In rural areas, women are generally relegated mainly to household duties and cheap labour in agricultural activities.

Women in tribal society in Arunachal Pradesh are generally not allowed to participate in the tribal village councils. Thus the councils are male dominated institutions. Tribal people cannot easily think of women being a member in village council. Consequently, women are invariably discarded even today. But the introduction of Panchayat Raj at grass root and parliamentary democracy at upper layer has armed the women with political rights on the equal footing.

The statuary Panchayat Raj Institutions functioned from 1969 to 1997 in Arunachal Pradesh wherein there were some 24000 elected incumbents as Gram Panchayat Member (GPMs), Anchal Samiti Members (ASMs) and Zilla Parishad Members (ZPMs). Out of them there had been only 4 women Anchal Samiti Members or Gram Panchayat Members. In 1987, at Anchal Samiti level, there was 1 and in 1992 there were 3 elected female representatives. The ratio of nominated female representatives has remained almost the same. Almost similar condition prevails in the traditional village council institutions. At present there were total 8077 Gaon buras, 6731 Gaon buras and 1346 Head Gaon buras. In this traditional band of a huge number of so-called village authorities, a few women GBs started being appointed since 1998 onwards. The process of proliferation of Gaonburas since 1998 has facilitated to some 91 women to occupy this office of the GBs (Dubey, 2000).

Arunachal yet stands to be a male dominated society. The number of women legislators was altogether 9 only in all the Legislative Assemblies put together within the span of 25 years. The most educated among the women Legislators is Miss Komoli Mossang who has a postgraduate degree in Political Science. On the other hand, Mrs. Nyari Welly, another women legislator was the least educated having had no formal education. Ms. Komoli Mossang (1984–1990) became the first lady minister of the state (Minister, Industries).

Arunachallee tribal women are poorly represented in the ranks of power, policy and decision making. Women in Arunachal Pradesh are not just behind in the political and managerial spheres they are still far away from their actual sharing of power with their male counterparts.

Reservation of Seats for Women in Panchayat Bodies

Under the framework of the 73rd Constitution Amendment Act, the one-third of the seats in Panchayat bodies is being reserved for the women for the first time in India. This was a new message for the rural population. Though the tribal communities accord high status to the women, the women never enjoyed such status in the corporate decision-making forum. Thus, the message of reservation was received with mixed response in these communities.

The tribal communities of Arunachal Pradesh had their own system of local self governance. "Age old traditional system of self governance in Arunachal Pradesh was replaced by Panchayati Raj Institutions in 1968". With the coming into force of the Constitution (Seventy Third Amendment) Act, 1992 with effect from 24th April, 1993, it was vested upon the state government to enact the Arunachal Pradesh Panchayati Raj legislation.

The system ordained though the NEFA Panchayati Raj Regulation, 1967 continued with regular elections till 1992. The Constitution (73rd Amendment Act) 1992 paved the way for restoring Panchayati Raj System in the state. It would suffice to mention here that several interactions across various levels were held to ensure maintain the relevance and applicability of the act in the context of Arunachal Pradesh. The present strength of PRIs in the state is depicted in Table 2.

The figures show that women's direct participation in PRIs is much below in comparison to their male counterparts. The overall female participation is only 38.54 per cent.

However, the Panchayati Raj Institutions also played a very important role in bringing about a major socio-political change in the traditional tribal society of Arunachal Pradesh with the increasing growth in education and political awareness of rural people and their increasing interface with the outside world due to greater mobility.

Table 2
Present Strength of Elected Members of PRIs in Arunachal Pradesh(As on 29th August, 2003)

Sl. No.	*Level of PRIs*	*Nos.*	*Members*			*Chairpersons*	
			Male	*Female*	*Total*	*Male*	*Female*
1.	Gram Panchayats	1639	3924	2561	6485	1092	547
2.	Anchal Samities	136	1062	577	1639	86	50
3.	Zilla Parishad	14	91	45	136	8	6
Total		**1789**	**5077**	**3183**	**8260**	**1186**	**603**

Source : Department of Panchayat Raj, Govt. of Arunachal Pradesh, Itanagar.

Note : Above figures do not include the allotted strength of Tirap District as PR elections were not held in that time.

The Panchayati Raj Institutions serve as a training ground for rural people and equip them with both knowledge and experience about the democratic system of government in the country thereby enabling them to play more important and useful role in the state and as well as in the nation.

With the instruction of Panchayati Raj System in the state, a large number of elected panchayat members would be involved in all development initiatives in rural areas in accordance with their levels (Srivastava, 2006).

Conclusion

President *A.P.J. Abdul Kalaml* said "empowering women was a prerequisite for creating a good nation, when women are empowered, society with stability is assured. Empowerment of women is essential as their thoughts and their value systems lead the development of a good family, good society and ultimately a good nation". Women need to be empowered to become equal to men and thus have equal access to developmental resources and benefits. In order to empower women we need not only to give them more economic power but also bring changes in the entire social, political and legal systems of the countries because these are responsible for women's lower status in society and the main hindrance in their progress.

REFERENCES

Aggarwal, J.C. (2004): *Development and Planning of Modern Education*, Vikas Publishing House Pvt. Ltd., New Delhi, pp. 273-279.

Alam. K. (1987): "The Changing Role of Women in the Rural Economy of Assam, Conference Volume of the Indian Economic Association". *Seventieth Annual Conference*, Jaipur.

Anker, Richard (1981): "Demographic Change and the Role of Women" in Richard, Anker (ed) : *Role of Women in Developing Countries*, I.L.O. Publications, Geneva, p. 27.

Azu. T. (1998): "Women in Nishi Society – A Cause Study of Yachuli Circle in Lower Subansiri District, Arunachal Pradesh 1998" (*An Unpublished M. Phil Dissertation. Dept. of Tribal Studies, Arunachal University).*

Baruah, S.L. (1992): *Status of Women in Assam*, Omsons Publications, New Delhi.

Behera. M.C. and Roy. N.C. (1997) (edit.) *: Trends in Agrarian Structure in the Hills of North-East India* . Commonwealth Publishers, New Delhi.

Begum, Mustary (2006): "Women Entrepreneurship in India: Challenges and Strategies" *University News*, April 10-16, Vol. 44, No.15, pp. 13-15.

Bhorali. D. (1998) (editor): *Economic Development of the North Eastern Region*, Spectrum Publications, Guwahati.

Bhuyan, B.C. (ed) (1993): *The Tribal Women*, Omsons Publicatins, New Delhi.

Bora, M.M. and Bhattacharyya, A. (1996): "Raising the status of Plain Tribes Women through Income Generating Training" in Medhi, K. (ed): *Status of Women and Social Change*, Women's Studies Research Centre, Gauhati University, Gauhati, pp. 102-03.

Bora. D.K., Duarah. D.K. and Paul. B. (1997): *Impact of Urbanization in Arunachal Pradesh*, Director of Research, Government of Arunachal Pradesh, Itanagar.

Bose. M.L. (1997): *History of Arunachal Pradesh*, Publishing Company, New Delhi.

Boserup, Ester (1970): *Women's Role in Economic Development*, George Allen and Unwin, p.71.

Chetana, K. (1986) : *Social and Economic Dimensions of Women's Development*, Discovery Publishing House, New Delhi, pp. 6-9.

Choudhary, D.S. (1981): *Emerging Rural Leadership in an Indian State*, Manthan Publication, New Delhi, p. 45.

Dubey, S. (2000): "Tribal Women and their Political Empowerment: A case study of Arunachal Pradesh", *Resarun: Journal of the Directorate of Research*, Govt. of Arunachal Pradesh, Department of Cultural Affairs, Itanagar, Vol, XXVI, pp. 12–13.

Modi, Milorai (2001): "Panchayat Raj System in Arunachal Pradesh," *Arunachal University Research Journal*, pp.42-45.

19

Perspectives on Education and Development in Arunachal Pradesh

R.M Pant and Aditya Joshi

'If you find education expensive, try ignorance'. No country in this world can better understand the essence of this statement than India as the country has seen the best and the worst, as far as education or lack of education is concerned.

India, regarded as one of the oldest civilisations in the world, at one point of time, was the epitome of knowledge and learning. Knowledge Centres of excellence like Nalanda and Takhsashila were established and flourished as early as 4th century. These centres of great learning attracted scholars from far off places in search of knowledge. Knowledge disseminated in these centres not only helped develop India but also its neighbouring countries. India was then known as the 'Golden bird' and its developed knowledge centres were instrumental in ensuring this unique 'metaphor' to India. These centres offered a platform for the understanding of cultural diversity that existed within Indian states and in neighbouring countries. This was the beginning of 'Globalization' that originated from the Indian philosophy of '*Vasudhaiv Kutumbkam*'. Even in the midst of various constraints, globalization of cultures did take place that paved the way not only for the intellectual development but also the economic development.

Gurudev Rabindra Nath Tagore who founded *Shanti Niketan,* in 1929, used to assert that "India has an obligation to offer the hospitality of her best culture" and it has "the right to accept from others their best".

This broad vision that India gave to the world helped empowerment of economics both intellectually and materialistically, yet India succumbed to the 'Darkness of ignorance' as a consequence of continuous foreign aggressions and foreign rule, that not only usurped India's physical wealth but also proved detrimental for the learning environment that India was once known for. Cultural suppression for centuries relegated Indian economy to its nadir and the 'Golden Bird' was left bleeding un-nursed till India got the independence.

Education in Post Independence Scenario

Soon after achieving the independence, the government of India embarked upon developing the modern temple of India and a due importance was given to develop education at every level *i.e.* right from primary education to higher and technical education. As a result, literacy rate showed a consistent rise. (Table.1).

To give thrust to education, a separate ministry, subsequently named as the Ministry of Human Resource Development was brought to the existence with a view to ensure better human development environment in the country.

Soon the National Education Policy on Education (1986) was formulated to strengthen the knowledge base of the country. New policy on education aimed at improving the education scenario in the country, both from qualitative as well as from the quantitative points of view. The National Education Policy on Education (1986) provides a broad policy framework for eradication of literacy and 6 per cent of GDP was set aside for the development of this sector. However, in actual practice, much less resources were allocated for education sector, as 2002-03 figures suggest that the total expenditure by the state and the union governments in education sector was only 3 per cent of the GDP. This attitude of apathy and laxity has taken its toll in terms of poor quality of education and majority of the educational institutions are facing problem of poor infrastructure and lying in a highly dilapidated state.

Despite apathy and low priority for the education sector, some centres of excellence create oases in the educational landscape of the country and are producing high quality human resources in various fields. Presently 335 University level institutions (20 central Universities, 215 state universities, 100 deemed universities and 13 institutes of national importance) are operational in the country. At the beginning of the year 2005-06, the total number of students enrolled in the formal system of education and colleges has been 104.81 lakhs (13.88 lakhs in university departments and 90.93 in the affiliated colleges). In addition, there are 1,349 approved engineering colleges at the degree level, 1,030 colleges offering MCA programmes and 990 approved management institutes imparting management education (MBA).

Growth in education sector has facilitated India's economic growth by supplying proper human resources to various sectors and India's per capita NNP has grown from a paltry 1.8 per cent during first plan period (1951-56) to 7.1 per cent during 10th Five Year Plan (2003-04). India with its broad knowledge base is well equipped to face competition from developed nations in today's globalised environment.

Literacy and Population Growth

One of the major hindrances in India's development is India's large population. Population growth seems to have a close linkage with the educational level of the mothers. National Family Planning Health survey (1998-99) final report (Table 2) suggests that with better access to education, mothers tend to have positive attitude towards family planning and prefer smaller families.

Arunachal Pradesh : Education Scenario

Arunachal Pradesh, where the sunlight touches Indian land at the earliest is not yet enlightened with the light of knowledge fully and is lagging behind in education front. Needless to say, that this backwardness in this front has its repercussions on the economic development of the state. Arunachal is one of the least educated states in the North East of the country (Table 3) and at national level, Arunachal stands poor at 33rd position out of 35 states and UTs of India, (Manorama Year Book, 2008). However, attempt to give boost to literacy level in Arunachal

Pradesh in post independence period is commendable and this is to be pursued more vigorously, if the state wants to get into the orbit of developed states of the country.

At the time of independence, literacy rate in Arunachal was almost negligible which today stands at an impressive 54.74 per cent figure. Today's Arunachal boasts of one Central University, one professional deemed University, two polytechnics, and several other institutions at different levels catering to the needs and aspirations of the different sections of the society. Private partnership is also contributing in expanding education base in the state, which was almost non existent in the past and is a welcome thing for Arunachal (Table 4).

Some quality institutions imparting higher education in the state are setting new standards and providing new horizons to the state's developmental thrust. For the development of technical education in the state, Industrial Training Institutes (ITIs) did a pioneering work in the area of developing Human Resources (HRs) in various trades at technician level. Students passing out from these institutions are successfully self-employed or placed in various government and non government organizations. These institutions have not only helped provide a career to trainee but have also helped increase productivity in the state. It is ironic that today majority of these ITI's lie in a state of dilapidation and need a complete overhauling. Plight of other Institutions in Arunachal is no different and are facing the same fate due to resource crunch. Low literacy rate in the state is giving birth to many other socio-economic problems and population rise in unwanted manner is one such consequences of illiteracy that paves the way for poverty and lower living standard.

Arunachal Pradesh stands at the top among all the NE states in registering highest Total Fertility Rate (TFR) of 6.74 followed by Meghalaya (6.53), Nagaland (5.6), Tripura (4.91) and Manipur (3.91), confirming the literacy and population correlation in the region.

From Darkness to Light

'If you are planning for a year, plant rice,

If you are planning for ten years, plant trees,

And if you are planning for hundred years, educate people'.

—An old Chinese proverb.

This Chinese proverb very rightly highlights the importance of education in transforming a society. Role of education is crucial in light of today's changing world scenario and our survival depends largely on our level of education in this competitive environment.

Educating Arunachal was no easy task with just two primary schools at the time of independence. Yeomen efforts on the part of pioneers like Padamshree Miss Silverine Swer and her contemporaries (Box 1) broke the ice and set the ball rolling in the state.

Box 1
Education in the Society in Transition

To change the attitude and to make people understand the importance of education, many unsung heroes dedicated their lives for the people of Arunachal and the future of this state. One of such pioneers, Padmashree Miss Silverine Swer, who joined as Social Education Officer in the Community Project, Pasighat in the year 1953, reminisces, 'It was in Ledum, a village 35 kms from Pasighat that some people wanted a school. To genuinely encourage people for starting a school, we put some conditions -1. School building is to be constructed by people themselves.2.Sufficient number of children is to be encouraged to join school.' A father of a child after much thinking asked us how much we would pay him for enrolling his child in the school. At another place, Ms. Swer recalls, a father was so keen to send his son to school but his son would not come unless his father too sat with him in the class. It was an amusing scene when the child was asked to stand; his father too would stand up, as the boy would not allow him to sit by.

'At Ngopok, a very far and lovely village on the left bank of Siang river which I visited to meet the people', writes Ms. Swer, 'a Sub Area Officer, down with fever was lying on a 'chhang bed'. A tiger entered his camp. The officer panicked and jumped up to catch the ceiling poles but fell back on his bed with a tremendous thump. This made the big cat panic and rush out. The officer rushed to Pasighat with a request for an immediate transfer.' Ms. Swer's experiences narrate the tough tasks the pioneers had to go through to lay the foundation of modern Arunachal.

Trends were further strengthened by the first generation of students from Arunachal like Daying Ering, Matin Dai who later served as the role models for the future generation.

Arunachal, although has made a good progress in expanding its intellectual base in post independence scenario, but situation continues to be far from satisfactory even after six decades of Independence. Although Arunachal Government appears to be liberal in allocating resources to education sector, but still these Institutions are unable to meet their requirements as resource allocation reflects fluctuating trends (Table 5). If resources are provided in a planned and consistent manner, better and consistent planning in education sector is possible. A steady stream of fund for education sector is the prime need as this ensures education at grass root level, which in turn can catapult the state into a developed state's orbit. Expenditure in education sector must be viewed as an investment.

Education must be strengthened from the primary and secondary level as these levels serve as the feeder for the institutions of higher education. Annual budget of Arunachal shows inconsistencies as far as budget allocation for education sector is concerned.(Table 6). In the Annual budget of 2004-05, share of school education which is a pre-requisite for the development of any state, saw a considerable fall from the previous year's amount of Rs.182.80 crores to Rs.103.77 crores. Such fluctuations in the resource allocation create bottlenecks in the smooth functioning of institutions.

Box 2

Pioneers who Became the Role Models for the Future Generation

On *Situation of Higher Education before 1964*, Joram Begi writes in his book *Dynamics of Higher Education* (2008, Commonwealth Publishers, New Delhi) that students of the state after completing their matriculation, had to go to places like Guwahati, Shillong, etc. for higher education as the state did not offer higher education. Cotton College (1901), Guwahati and St. Admund College (1924) Shillong were the usual destinations. Many prominent personalities of Arunachal Pradesh like Daying Ering, Matin Dai, Oshong

Ering, Toi Dai, C. T. Manpong, Odang Lego, etc. are some pioneers of their field who had to go to Guwahati and Shillong for higher education against all hardships. These pioneers played an important role in the state's development later at different capacities.

Past trends show that educated persons of Arunachal are very much conscious of their hard earned privileged status and have never failed in discharging their social responsibilities. They have been instrumental in ushering Arunachal to its present state (Box 2).

It is heartening to note that this trend is continuing even with the present generation educated youth who are carrying forward the legacy of these pioneers (Box 3).

Education in Arunachal has not only helped increase economic standards in the state (per capita income Rs. 12,335 (1998-99) and per capita consumption Rs. 240.38 (urban) and 203.72 (rural)), it has also helped develop new generation of entrepreneurs both in business as well as social sector. (Box 4 and Box 5).

Box 3

Pressure Groups Shaping the Future of Arunachal

AAPSU to launch 'School Chalo Abhiyan' - Arunachal Front-Nov. 5, 2008-11-08. 'The All Arunachal Pradesh Students' Union (AAPSU) announces to launch a campaign to gauge the reality of the education process in the state through questionnaire based analysis. The AAPSU central executives will go to the remotest corners of the state to collect data about the physical infrastructure of school buildings, teacher student ratio, attendance, etc. to asses the dismal education scenario in the state.' Initiatives of this kind shall make people aware about the importance of education and will also put pressure on various state functionaries to promote education with utmost sincereity.

Box 4

Education and Social Entrepreneurship

'Minu's heart beats for the visually impaired', Arunachal Front, Nov. 1, 2009. News paper published a report about

Minu Tanyang, who did a diploma in special education for the visually impaired from the Tura in Meghalaya, wants to start a school for such children in Tawang. Minu after completing her class XII, served as a teacher before going for the diploma with a purpose to serve the society to care the uncared once. Minu is the second among her six siblings, who all are well educated and her younger sister is happily placed with Chennai based Taj Hotel whereas her elder sister is a trader. Societal concern is growing among educated youths of Arunachal.

Moji Riba , a journalism graduate who presently heads Rajive Gandhi University's Mass Communication department, is another example of Arunachalee youth playing a constructive role to empower people of Arunachal intellectually through his very innovative interventions. Moji besides making films himself, screens socially relevant films produced by other creative media people at the CCRD. To popularize this meaningful cinema, Moji screens these films at a city's popular Cafés regularly.

Binny Yanga, a pioneer social activist and founder of 'Oju Mission' continues to be a source of inspirations for younger generation. She is a fine example of what educated citizens can do for the state's development in different sectors.

Box 5

Education and New Generation Entrepreneurship

SKY Cyber Cafe: Nirjuli. Manna Nabum, the youngest in a Nyishi family of 5 sisters and 2 brothers, does not come from a 'business family'. In fact, her parents are involved in 'subsistence level farming'. Studying up to class 12 in Government Higher Secondary School, 'Doimukh', Manna always dreamt of a life that she did not inherit from her parents.

Either a top Government job or work independently, Manna always told herself. Lack of guidance at home took its toll in terms of average performance in class 12 exams, and Manna decided to follow the latter option, work independently. Six months course from NIIT and a course in computer basics at Itanagar, motivated her to start her own business in computer line. Her childhood friend Senia was also sharing her dream of being an entrepreneur. So together they applied for loan under PMRY. 'I was very lucky to get a loan of Rs. 1,00,000 without much problem', says Manna. Her family members encouraged her.

With a loan of Rs. 1 lakh Manna started 'Cyber Cafe'. Initially Manna invested Rs. 60,000 in procuring computers, scanner and a DeskJet printer. Arranging necessary furniture, interior decoration, internet connectivity, telephone and other accessories also involved some expenditure that caused nervousness to Manna occasionally. However, determined Manna went ahead with her plan and presently having 5 PCs, 2 printers, one scanner and four cabins for internet surfing. With a proper business acumen and strategy, Manna not only created a niche for herself in the fast growing IT market but also serves as a role model for other new generation of entrepreneurs who aspire for a career in technology based business.

Manna's cyber café is a success story reflecting the beginning of a new entrepreneurial society in Arunachal Pradesh. This is an indication how a traditional agricultural society is gradually transforming with the changing economic environment of 21st century.

Table 1
Literacy Rate in India

Year	*Persons*	*Male*	*Female*	*Male female gap in literacy rate*
1951	18.3	27.2	8.9	16.30
1961	28.3	40.4	15.3	25.05
1971	34.5	46.0	22.0	23.98
1981	41.4	53.4	28.5	26.62
1991	52.5	64.1	39.3	24.64
2001	65.4	75.8	52.1	21.69

Source: Census of India, 2001.

Table 2
Total Fertility and Women's Educational Level in India (1998-99)

Educational Level	*Total number of children*
Illiterate	3.47
Literate but < middle school educated	2.64
Middle level educated	2.26
High School and above	1.99

Source: National Family Health Survey (1998-99) Final Report All India.

Table 3
Literacy Rate in the States of NE Region

State	*Total*	*Male*	*Female*
Arunachal Pradesh	54.74	63.83	43.53
Nagaland	66.59	71.16	61.46
Manipur	70.53	80.33	60.53
Mizoram	88.80	90.72	86.75
Tripura	73.19	81.02	64.91
Meghalaya	63.31	66.14	60.41
Assam	62.56	65.43	59.61
Sikkim	68.81	76.04	60.40

Source: Manorama Year Book, 2008.

Table 4
Education Institutions in Arunachal Pradesh

Sl. No.	*Type of Institution*	*Government*	*Private aided/ Unaided*	*Total*
1.	Universities	1	-	1
2.	Arts and Science College	8	5	13
3.	Engineering and Technical Institution/University	1	-	1
4.	Polytechnics	2	-	2
5.	Higher Secondary Schools	57	14	71
6.	Secondary Schools	92	28	120
7.	Middle School	296	51	347
8.	Primary School	1240	75	1315

Source: Statistical abstract of Arunachal Pradesh/Directorate of Higher and Technical Education, Arunachal Pradesh.

Table 5
State Budget of Government of Arunachal Pradesh
(Rs. in Crores)

Financial Year	*Plan*	*Non-plan*	*Total*	*% under Education*
2001-02	885.36	677.92	1563.28	12.92
2002-03	935.93	713.25	1649.18	10.72
2003-04	1045.86	1141.48	2187.34	9.44
2004-05	1014.22	1094.63	2108.85	6.36
2005-06	1248.61	1146.49	2395.10	10.09

Source: Directorate of Planning, Government of Arunachal Pradesh.

Table 6
Budget Grant of Education Departments in Arunachal Pradesh (Rs. in Crores)

Financial Year	*Higher and Technical Education*				*School Education*	*Education Department Grant Total*
	DHE	*RGU*	*RG Poly*	*Total*		
2001-02	9.66	3.75	11.0	24.41	177.51	201.92
	(39.57)	(13.81)	(45.06)	(12.10)		
2002-03	9.21	4.0	11.0	24.21	152.63	176.84
	(38.04)	(16.52)	(45.44)	(13.70)		
2003-04	14.08	4.0	5.50	23.58	182.80	206.38
	(59.71)	(16.96)	(23.32)	(11.43)		
2004-05	10.72	8.59	11.00	30.31	103.77	134.08
	(35.37)	(28.34)	(36.29)	(22.60)		
2005-06	12.64	8.59	23.70	44.93	196.81	241.74
	(28.13)	(19.12)	(52.75)	(18.59)		

Source : Directorates of Higher and Technical Education and School Education, Government of Arunachal Pradesh.

Suggestions

Education is the starting point for the development of any economy. Education and development have shown a positive correlation; hence development of education sector is no more a question of choice. It is rather a necessity. Some possible interventions are suggested below to improve and strengthen education scenario in Arunachal Pradesh, which is aspiring to be in the league of developed states of the country.

- As educational infrastructure is still in the underdeveloped stage, more resources need to be allocated in the annual budgets of the state for education sector.
- Many institutions like ITIs, schools and colleges which were started with great enthusiasm are lying in dilapidated state for the want of adequate rescurces. Need of the hour is to revive these institutions with better management of resources.
- Schools are the important breeding grounds for future citizens and future citizens need to be provided direction from the young age. The British XI plus examination pattern can be adopted in India also, in which all those who qualify this test are admitted to academic oriented 'Grammar Schools' and those who fail, go to vocationally oriented 'Secondary Modern Schools'.
- Educational institutions engaged in offering primary education are important as they are the 'feeders' to 'Secondary schools'. These schools have formative effect on the value system of students. Hence, primary education must be given a high priority and 'Catch them young' policy may be adopted in education sector to motivate higher enrolment and reduced drop out rate.
- Education at Secondary and higher secondary levels in the state also needs to be revamped and concerted efforts are required to produce good quality students. Private participation may be encouraged, as especially at school levels private schools through out the country have shown an edge over government schools.
- Institutions offering higher education can also adopt feeder schools to ensure uninterrupted quality supply from these institutions of basic education. Catch them young approach can help identify the right talents at the right time.
- Options, like keeping doors of academic institutions open for lateral entrants for late developers, is also a welcome

idea. This will integrate a large population who missed the bus earlier due to some constraints with the present day demand. NERIST's modular pattern of technical education is recognized through out the country and is being emulated by other premier institutions. IGNOU and RG University have also opened new opportunities for learners through their distance learning programmes. These programmes need to be publicized and marketed aggressively to motivate people to shed their inhibitions about studying at higher age.

- Entrepreneurship and vocational training should be imparted at school and college levels to equip entrepreneurial aspirants with appropriate competencies and also to motivate more and more people to start their own ventures rather than working for 'somebody else'.

Conclusion

In the new global economic order, knowledge occupies a great significance. Economies that have strong knowledge base only will survive in this highly competitive environment. Technology is changing at a fast pace rendering our education system obsolete, which necessitates continuous up-gradation of courses with better academia-industry linkage. Academic institutions need to offer relevant and need based courses that fit the global requirement and obsolete programmes will have to be phased out.

Arunachal Pradesh has made a speedy progress in the direction of education in the post independence period, but it continues to languish with lowest literacy rate in the North East of the country, which does not augur well with state's aspirations to be a economically self sufficient. Education with academic and professional orientation can bring a 'turn around' in the state's economy, which in turn will have a snowballing effect on all the sectors. Role of education sector needs to be understood in light of global demands and Arunachal's potentialities. Need based education planning is required to develop human resources having compatibility with its natural resources and other strengths. Arunachal Pradesh needs to adopt an 'out worldly' approach and restructure its education policies keeping a global perspective in mind. Arunachal has the potential to become a

'Knowledge state', if due importance is given to education sector. In the new global economic order, it is said, 'He who knows, grows', and planners in Arunachal can not ignore this dictum.

With the matching of new global economic order and local strengths, education shall no more appear expensive in the state.

REFERENCES

Begi Joram, ed. (2008): *Dynamics of Higher Education*, Commonwealth Publishers, New Delhi.

NCAER (2004): *East India Human Development Report*, Oxford University Press, Delhi.

Manorama Year Book 2008.

'Minu's heart beats for visually impaired', *Arunachal Front* (Nov. 1, 2008).

'AAPSU to launch 'School Chalo Abhiyan' - *Arunachal Front* (Nov. 5, 2008).

Statistical Abstract of Arunachal Pradesh/Directorate of Higher and Technical Education, Arunachal Pradesh.

Datt Ruddar and Sundharam K. P. M., 2006: *Indian Economy*, S. Chand and Company, Delhi.

Census of India, 2001.

Directorates of Higher and Technical Education and School Education, Government of Arunachal Pradesh.

Department of Planning, Government of Arunachal Pradesh, Itanagar.

20

The Economy of Arunachal Pradesh : A Note on Transformation

M.A. Salam

Once the development process is scaled on the material acquisition and the tribal character of a community is construed as a state of development, then the history of homo-economics can be studied through the development process of material acquisition. With this basic assumption the paper moves on the basic postulate that nearly all of us value two things: (i) a longer life and (ii) a comfortable life when we are alive. We take the life as precondition but we make the life comfortable through the material acquisition. In other words, 'the agency of being' gets re-oriented for enhancement of 'well-being'. This dialectical process of interaction between 'the agency of being' and 'the well-being' of an individual operates *ad infinitum*. This is the economic motive which provides rock bottom explanation of economic forces.

Just as we take life as precondition, similarly for a member of community the level of development forms the precondition which provides the working conditions to appropriate the material requisites of 'well-being'. Hence the level of development provides the course for the movement of economic forces for the material acquisition. The paper distinguishes three such phases of development during the post-independence period of Arunachal Pradesh. It notes down the two turning points which have transformed the economy of Arunachal Pradesh.

The Conceptual Framework and Methodology

Quite often it happens that from our common cognition we conclude that we know certain realities but when we are asked what do we mean by such thing(s) we often fall in the problem of defining the reality and we take help of some concepts to define it. More often than not defining becomes problematique because definition (or the process of defining) has its moving in epistemology. Here also we are under the grip of the same problem. But since we want to have a workable definition we start from our intuitive understanding of the term(s) and just move toward a little more i.e., adequate scientific description. We take this description as the meaning of the term in the whole writing that follows.

We select here the two key terms of the paper namely (1) the economy and (2) the transformation.

The Economy: It is the experiential reality in the form of social organization for the provisioning of material needs to the members of society. It consists of the ways to dispose of the goods to the relevant aspirants, to pool up resources from their owners, to settle the claims of the resource owners. It legitimizes the nature and pattern of ownership. It provides domain to various institutions and gives meaning to the evolved network of relationships. It has both spatio and temporal dimensions and it is capable to reproduce, expand and grow.

Now putting prefix of Arunachal (a political boundary of an area situated in the Eastern Himalayas) to economy, we immediately focus on the experiential reality. that How the people(s) of this area receive the material requisites ? How they come together to pool-up the resources to provide these requisites? How they legitimize the resource ownership and so they settle the claims? What are the institutions which effectuate the economic variables? Further, does the economy reproduce, expand or grow? And how much it is integrated with larger Indian economy?

But as we start answering these queries, the dominance of non-economic forces appears. As a result, the logic of movement of economic forces takes own shape. Along with the development process as initiated through various schemes, some of such constraints get liquidated as the economy of Arunachal Pradesh has experienced it in previous decades. The economic forces take turn accordingly. Thus, we find that Arunachal economy not only reproduces itself but also changes the course of reproduction during the process of its growth and development.

Transformation: It is clear that an economy reproduces, grows and operates under a network of structured relationship and many economics are integrated with varying degrees. During its reproduction growth the network of relationship slowly and gradually goes on changing due to the influence of various agencies. The defined role of individual under the structured relationship goes on changing. In the beginning the social construct moulds and shapes the individual behaviour under the evolved institutional framework. But latter the attitudinal changes in individuals modify and reconstruct the existing social construct. Transformation takes place when social construct gets restructured and begins to shape the individuals trait and behaviour under the modified form with the help of improved existing institution or new institution after replacing the old ones or additional new institution.

In Arunachal Pradesh changes have taken place in all walks of life. The usual cause of change is that due to increasing integration with larger economies and societies, the attitude of individual has changed and this change latter brought the required change in economy and society. Finally, the improved economic and social construction begins to shape the individual behaviour. However, the paper does not focus the whole ambit of transformation rather it notes down one such transformation namely the transformation which is due to the changing course of economic forces.

Methodology

Keeping these constructs as definitions of economy and transformation in the back of mind we proceed to methodological question. Every enquiry (here the logic of economic force under specific course) has reference point which then moves either in backward direction if it tries to underline the causal explanation for generalization or in forward direction if it tries to focus upon the likelihood of begetting such events i.e. prediction. In both movements, there is logical foundation which justifies the causal connection of explanation. Look at the following figures:

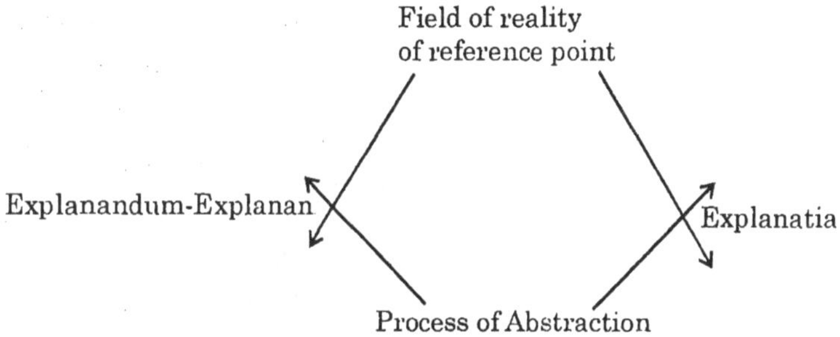

Starting from explanandum (area of enquiry namely the logic of movement of economic force under specific course) we come to explain the reality (of each such course) with the help of some abstract theoretical concepts which must have logical connection with field of reality and finally we reach to explanation where enquiry is explained. This is the common method used by the verificationists in the philosophy of economics (both Keynesian generalization philosophy and Friedman prediction philosophy).

At different stages of development when transformations occur, the conditions of the field of enquiry change. This causes corresponding change in the mode of enquiry (i.e. explanandum) and also the change in the use of abstraction (theoretical concept).

This paper highlights the three phases of development of Arunachal economy. In each specific phase of the economy the economic variables have specific course of movement. The paper tries to underline the logic of movement of economic forces and so finally notes down the quality of transformation which has taken place over the three phases of development.

As per design of the 'Philosophy for NEFA' (Elwin: 1964) it can be surmised that non-economic variables in Arunachal economy happen to be more cohesive and they provide a sub-servient domain to economic variables. On the way of progression, the economic forces do not negate the contextual audacity rather they formulate the path as per context – specific and also very subtly they bring changes in the attitude of individual through influencing on his economic motives. So, there has been an on-going interaction among individual (household), community and state. The paper notes down the transformation which emerges as a consequence of such interaction.

These three players namely the individual (household), the community, and the state have their roles to play in their domain. Given the geographical endowments and constraints the evolved social relations and knowledge base of the community provide the objective conditions. Households take these objective conditions as precondition to appropriate the material provisions for their 'well-being. State maintains the exogenous entity. It engineers and initiates the development process from above.

As the development process has started, the relative significance of their role has shifted. The objective conditions have changed and so behaviour of individual as homo-economics has also changed. This is because the economic forces have moulded and shaped their movement accordingly. Change in the course of economic forces has occurred. The post independence phase of Arunachal Pradesh has witnessed such two turns in the course of movement. Therefore, one can classify the post-independences experiences of Arunachal economy into three phases:

Phase I of the 1950s and the 1960s.

Phase II of the 1970s and the 1980s.

Phase III of the post 1990 period.

II

Phase-I: The 1950s and the 1960s

Let us first demarcate the domains of the three aforementioned players during this phase.

The State: The role of state was insignificant in controlling or designing the economy. The main concern was to develop the administrative network which could confirm the general administration of India. This phase may be termed as administrative integration. It was the phase of NEFT (North East Frontier Tracts) upto 1954 and then NEFA (North East Frontier Agency) from 1954 to 1972.

The Community: In this customary command economy there were two-way flow of customs namely from above and from below. The designer from above did not have free hand but a restricted one by the *kinds of conditions* acceptable from below. Similarly, the commons from below had to receive the limited due from above. These customs (coming down from above, and going-up from below) were sufficiently elaborated. The chief and the commons constituted the traditional structure which was integrated by a corpus of traditions. Accordingly, the economic variables were effectuated i.e. the structure of relationships which formed economy was deeply embedded in the structure of relationship that underlay the community. In other words non-economic factors were dominating and they were shaping the modus operandi of economic variables.

The Household: Other than this limited domain, the households managed all remaining activities themselves.

Now let us have a look on brief analysis of the economy during this phase. The Arunachal economy during this phase was remembered for food shortage, malnutrition, under consumption and low level of equilibrium and also the economy was reproducing itself without any substantial change.

Let us come to the question whether it was a subsistence economy or abundance economy? The argument in favour of abundance economy was that resources did not turn to be inadequate: whenever household pressed for more on the economy, they got more. The arguments for subsistence economy were: the production was oriented for household consumption and not for market; and the economy did not produce more than the survival limit i.e. (i) the size of production was limited, (ii) the range of production (variety of output) was limited, and (iii) the capacity to produce was also limited. It was essentially need-constrained economy where production was oriented for use-value only. Actual level of production was always less than the potential (maximum) production level. That is, the economy was operating at low level of equilibrium. It was due to leisure-work preference. Leisure-work preferences were high because (i) works inflicted more drudgery; (ii) surplus production could not be stored, (iii) production was not for market and exchange. So households involved minimum time for work and remaining time they devoted for leisure preferences such as music, dances, celebrations, etc. Hence, actual level of production had tendency to be minimum.

This was a need-constrained economy and the requirements of the people were constricted by the relative seclusion and by the local geographical endowments. The specificities of the region provided the opportunity to sustain the life. Accordingly, consumption pattern was shaped. That is to say consumption behaviour was patterned as per geographically determined availability of goods. So the perception of their needs was to cover the survival limit. It included the minimum physiological requirements, shelter and other social minima (in terms of cloth, utensils and social contributions).

These requirements were provisioned by a set of traditional economic activities and they were: (i) the traditional form of agriculture, (ii) the animal husbandry, (iii) the forest gatherings and (iv) the traditional cross-border trade. The traditional agriculture in the form of peasant family farm provided the main stay and all other activities were the supporting activities and almost every household engaged in all these activities simultaneously. Let us elaborate to each of these activities so as to understand their economic construct.

The traditional form of peasantry: Traditionally peasants had two methods of cultivation: the jhum cultivation and the permanent cultivation. These two methods were not mutually exclusive rather both of them were in practice. Flat lands nearby village settlement were used for permanent cultivation while high lands of interior were used for jhum. Family farm was the dominant form and production was mainly for household requirement. Mixed cropping pattern was in practices in order to meet variety of household requirements and also for averting the risk of crop failure. Non-recycling of surplus with stagnant indigenous technology caused to profess the fixed coefficient of production.

The animal Husbandry: Rich vegetation of the region has been the reason to emerge the animal husbandry as significant supporting economic activities. Invariably all tribes raised livestock which met many purposes: they provided rich source of food to the households; they were used as pre-cautionary measure to the family during the time of distress; they were also considered a form of wealth and status symbol of family e.g. Mithun. Further rearing the livestock did not involve and additional burden to the household.

The forest gathering: The traditional usufruct right on the variety of forest produce proved to be the last resort for the hill people. Forest products provided the base material support to the household. The construction material, firewood, material for carrying baskets and other belongings and above all rich source of a variety of local food (fruits, roots, nuts, leafy vegetables, fishing, etc.) sustained the life of the people. Various households, were knitted together mainly due to feuds. Feuds delimited the forest area of their activities.

The traditional cross-border trade: For the material provision of their people no region (above of specific tribe) was self-sufficient. To sustain their populace every tribe had link with outside world through trade but still exchange was not the dominant from of economic activities. There were two natural sets of geographical outlets for trade namely the La (natural passes) in the north and the Duars (gateways) in the south. There were 35 natural passes of which 8 passes were used for traditional trade; and there were 32 Duars connecting Assam plains in the south. Trades were carried out through Nyetzang institution (family friends and trading pastures). During the specified period the hillmen moved on the trade route for trade. They used to move in group usually belonging to the same household and clan and they used to stay with their specified Nyetzang household. During this time periodic bazaars were also instituted. The trade was mostly in barter mode and it was carried on conventionally determined equivalences (the specific quantity of specific item for bartering the goods). The trade was carried on surplus items. Production was not oriented for trade rather {production – (household annual requirements + social contribution i.e. Khrei and Chu in Monpa belt + material outlay for carrying production in coming season + inter-household transfers and loans)} was kept for trade. The trade had never regulated the other economic activities. Whatever surplus products were brought to market places during this period were bartered. Trade was not an event of self-regulating market system but a compensatory device for self-regulating.

This was the quasi-monetized phase of Arunachal Pradesh economy because the economy did not have any asset for which the liquidity premium was excess to its. Scale of liquidity was existing. The surplus was kept in grain-livestock-precious items in order of lower carrying cost. This typology of assets was used to meet the corresponding typology of transactions, for instance grains to defray day-to-day requirements; livestock to meet emergency and so they were used as pre-cautionary measure; precious items such as stones, beads, metallic items for prestige factor. So all-purpose money did not enter into the system and their use was limited even in cross-border trade.

These were no effective conversion of these assets across the categories. The different categories of assets corresponded to different types of social actions ranging from every day requirement of exchange to highly ceremonial presentation. Hence, whole transactions were broken in various circuits of exchange i.e. market was fragmented. So this phase saw that these were no convergence of money, market and trade.

This argument, however, does not amount to conclude that money has not entered into the system; rather money has failed to create adequate velocity within the local system of Arunachal economy. It was operating only in the uppermost ring of the economy. It was earned from outside the economy and was used to purchase those commodities in market places which were not available and produced within the local system of the economy.

Money per se did not have existence in the economy. So, other co-ordinates of money, for example savings, investment, capital formation, lending and borrowing and trade, were functioning without the use of money involving the social obligations.

The main argument is that even in this quasi-monetized primitive stage of Arunachal economy the natural incentive to produce the material requisites of life to meet the family requirements and to meet the community social obligations was evident. In such self-regulating traditional economy inward looking expectation (ILE) dominated the decision making of the household within the keep of social structuration.

Since agriculture was the main stay, most of the households were engaged in this activity in the form of family farm. Let us focus on how the production was carried out. What were the social obligations? And how the social relations were maintained? In this regard following facts have been documented:

The *agar publicus* (common land) belonged to the community but it was at the disposal of governing clan who performed the function of patron for all members of the community.

The commoners mainly used the family labour force to clear the land of modest size for cultivation. They helped each other on the basis of reciprocity in the works requiring more hands than that household provided.

The capacity to provide social loan and feast (in terms of stock of grain, livestock, etc.) determined the turn up of the commoners (villages) in the field which in turn determined the size of plot. This was positive correlates between the land holding structure of the economy and the kinship structure of the society.

Technology was stagnant and traditional in the form of dao, axes, digging sticks, split bamboo, etc. They were in common use for all.

P/W ratio (Population-Worker Ratio) was almost constant. Both birth rate and death rate were high. Workers (labours) were homogeneous because every one was doing all agricultural works.

There was non-monetization of the cost of production. Local seeds and organic manure were in use.

Therefore, considering all these facts we construct that production function was homogeneous and operated at constant return. But in jhum diminishing return operated so they were shifting the land. This was also a reason that household preferred permanent wet cultivation to the jhum cultivation.

Three things were obvious:

1. Households were not homogeneous in terms of land acquisition, livestock and other assets.
2. Hardly there was the desired coalescence between the household work force and the land requirement.
3. Agricultural works required the work force uneven over the season.

Therefore, three categories of households were noticed: Households with surplus production and collection; deficient households attached to the surplus producing household; self-sustaining households who were largely supplementing the survival from other sources like livestock, forest collection, etc.

The excess production and collection were saved in various portfolios e.g. grains, livestock and jewellery. Usually chiefs were able to save.

Stored grains and livestock were consumed profusely in feeding the persons working on reciprocity during the large works such as developing the land for cultivation, sometimes workers were paid in grain. This portion of savings functioned similar to that of working capital.

Prestige factor based on clan hierarchy was overwhelming. Contribution to the community feast or other social programme added to the family prestige. Prestige albeit immaterial added to the social strength of the household which household was utilizing in enhancing the physical productivity in the form of developing land (terracing, fencing, clearing, etc.), making house structure, etc. which was capital formation.

In such hierarchical society, lending and borrowing relationships interwove the social fabrics. Credit system was in practice. Credit relation was personal and involved interlocking of social relations between lender and borrower. It was in the line of kinship relationship and it was permanent in nature. It extended over many transactions. Stored grain, livestock, etc. were used to meet the obligation of social loan. Social loan was cleared either through repaying in the same goods or through rendering the services for lender.

Excess production and collection were also the source for cross-border trade. Hence the barter exchange, lending and borrowing, reciprocity, redistribution, presentation and periodic cross-border trade, etc. ensured the movement of goods and services in discrete circuit during this phase.

Let us collect the strands of our argument and sum up the phase-I

- The 1950s and the 1960s experienced administrative integration and gave free space for the local dynamics to operate as per their modus operandi.

- The *modus operandi* was the underplaying of economic forces within the super structuration of the two-way flow of customs.
- Consumption level and consumption items were as per locally available goods. So, it was under consumption economy.
- Agriculture was the main activity. Others like raising livestock, forest gathering and cross-border trade etc. were supporting economic activities.
- Actual level of production had tendency to be minimum because of drudgery in work, use value being organizing principle and lack of storage facilities.
- Scale of liquidity was in practice. So, money, market and trade did not coverage.
- The co-ordinates of the economy like consumption, production, trade, saving, investment, capital formation and trade relations were functioning under the customary design of social relations.
- Barter exchange, lending and borrowing, social loan, cross-border trade, reciprocity, presentation, etc. ensured the movement of goods and services in discrete circuits of the economy.
- It was not market regulating economy but 'self-regulating traditional economy'. So the economy was not capable to expand. Hence, it reproduced itself without much change ad infinitum.

III

Phase-II: The 1970s and the 1980s

The second phase began when government agency deliberately intervened into the on-going system. This phase coincided with the Union Territory phase of Arunachal Pradesh and it covered the decades of the 1970s and the 1980s. This phase may be termed as the phase of administered economic integration since government agencies came forward to initiate and shape the development process and they did it. So this phase had an embedded logic of dirigiste form of development.

Hitherto Arunachal economy reproduced itself and lacked conspicuously the capability of expanding or growing economy as elaborated in the previous section. This was due to four constraints namely (i) the indigenously evolved stagnant technical coalescence, (ii) the designed material flow shaped by interlocking social behaviour, (iii) the inadequate liquidity causing non-monetization of economic activities, (iv) the fragmented local market in the form of many circuits of exchange. This economy had unique experience that the process of socio-economic changes did not begin from the internal dynamics as such due to the above mentioned four constraints. The hard shell of these constraints could have been broken only by the determined efforts of government agencies to accelerate the development process in the region. Therefore, a turn in the course of economic forces has become obvious in this phase. This section focuses on this turn and thereafter the change in the course of economic forces.

The state agencies initiated the development process with a clear philosophy in their mind i.e. the process of development must be designed in such a way that would change the socio-economic system without fragmenting the inherent tribal character of the society. So the progress could depend upon the rapidity with which exogenous factors of change could be internalized in the tribal system. And it was possible (i) if new market opportunities could be made available to the local economic forces in the form of generating demand by various government establishments and (ii) if capital, technology and know-how from external sources could be provided.

The state therefore started the development process with a view of (i) bringing a gradual change in the life pattern of the people in such a way that hunger, diseases, ignorance and isolation could be overcome without fragmenting indigenous culture, (ii) investing to enhance the productive capacity of society in the form of communication and transportation facilities, and (iii) developing the human capital through education and medical facilities. This design of development process generated income and employment in the region which brought change in the then on-going system.

The infusion of liquidity through a series of development works and integration of local markets through developing the tertiary sector has brought spectacular change in the material acquisition of the people in the province. With this improvement in the material acquisition not only structural change (in terms of the sectoral contribution to the net state domestic product) has occurred but also institutional and attitudinal changes have become obvious.

This process of change has been accelerated through the network of modern banking system. Modern banking system has provided institutional credit through various schemes of rural development undertaken by DRDA (District Rural Development Agency). The benefit of these schemes, however, did not percolate down (as expected) but remained with the upper strata of the society (who happened to be mostly from the traditional elite section of population).

The governance has changed and all tribes were brought under one system of governance as patterned elsewhere in India. Administrative integration has been the hall mark of this phase. Government sector has emerged as the biggest employer and initiator of development process. The rate of absorption of workforce in government sector was significantly high. More specifically the employment elasticity of public investment in government sector was substantially large. This has led to the development of tertiary or service sector during this phase.

As a result of the rise of tertiary sector, this phase has experienced the development of domestic regular market. The emergence of regular market has caused the convergence of money, market and trade. Villages have been linked through markets where shops were full of the goods and commodities not produced in Arunachal Pradesh but from other pars of India. The market mechanism has replaced the interlocking of traditional social behaviour by the interlinkages of market oriented social behaviour of economic agents. Consequently demand for cash among individuals rose significantly.

Changes did not take place simultaneously and uniformly in all walks of life. Change in consumption pattern has appeared first while change in production pattern has become obvious latter after a time lag. During this phase generated demand

and requirements were not met by the local production; rather they depended on the supply coming from outside Arunachal Pradesh. This rise in demand fascinated the merchants and traders from outside to infiltrate but these have been checked from government on such inflow through inner line regulation of 1873. This caused supply to remain insensitive to the prices in Arunachal Pradesh. This was one of the factors for the emergence of price-cliff (huge price differential between the administratively regulated high price in the market price and the low price of under consumption village economy) during this phase.

Now let us collect the threads of economic forces of this phase - II.

- The 1970s and the 1980s experienced the state led economic integration where the state agency played dominant and decisive role in shaping and directing the economy.
- During this phase the dual character of the economy was conspicuous i.e. the small urban monetized economy emerged from vast mass under-consumption rural economy.
- The middle class in the form of government servant, contractors and local leaders emerged. The government sector provided the employment opportunity and the salaried section was dominant.
- Service sector due to the development of physical infrastructure in the form of roadways, electricity and soft infrastructure in the form of education, health and governance has developed while the commodity sector did not maintain the pace.
- Money has entered in the domain of economic activities. Monetization and commodification in product market have started taking place.
- Government spending and the timber business on the usufruct right of forest produce were the two main sources of cash inflow in the economy.
- Regular market was encouraged because cross-border trade ceased to operate and in regular market goods not produced in Arunachal Pradesh made available for sale.

- Consumption items and consumption pattern have changed and propensity to consume was high due to demonstration effect among the elite group (i.e. new middle class).
- Price cliff developed.
- Supply was insensitive to demand because of castel type of nature of the business in Arunachal Pradesh. Castel type of business was due to (i) Inner Line Permit and (ii) the absence of local supply.

IV

The Phase-III: The Post 1990 Period

This is the period of statehood. It is the phase of economic liberalization. During the dirigisme phase, threshold has been provided to the economy through public investment. The hard-shell of non-economic constraints have been broken and it is postulated that economic forces have been liberated from the traditional dictate of non-economic factors and economic development will orient as per market principle because economic forces will operate as per economic laws (as devised by the neo-classical school).

The phase-II began with the idea in mind that 'we should judge result not by statistics of the amount of money spent but by the quality of human character that is evolved (Nehru, 1959 : xiii). In contrast to phase-II, Phase-III ushered in an era when the on-going sources of cash inflow namely the government spending and the timber business have started declining. Government spending has declined partly because (i) expansion of government departments has reached to saturation, (ii) partly due to change in the status of province from the status of Union Territory to the statehood status, and (iii) also due to the wave of liberalization where withdrawal of government control on the economy with the disinvestment in government sector has been advocated. Timber business which was very lucrative and money fetching halted due to the ban on forest cutting by the Supreme Court in December,1996.

Hitherto availability of liquidity and events of monetization and commodification have changed the attitude of the people.

Commodity fetishism particularly of manufactured items gave them flavour of eliticism. Already exiting prestige factor added with prodigal tendency has made the middle class to depend heavily on market. Further the adoption of new wants (items of consumption) subsequently has turned into necessity because these new consumption items and pattern have turned into habits. Standard of living has raised.

Due to these two events (i) progressively increasing demand for cash (ii) drying up the on-going sources of cash flow, the economy has taken a new turn that it has become progressively market oriented. This change in psychological disposition and thereby the changes in the attitudes and motives of the middle class have brought changes in institutional arrangements and changes in follow up actions and practices. We will note here few changes in trend for our analysis.

High profitability partly due to the prodigal tendency of the middle class and partly due to the price-cliff has fascinated the inflow of capital in Arunachal Pradesh but the provision of Inner Line Permit has *blockaded* this inflow. Already entered capital got license to trade. This blockadedness on the free flow of capital has caused to confer the monopoly status of capital. Further the term of licensing and contract executing institution could not encourage the capital to be invested in developing the industries and industrial estate. So, they got invested only in trade i.e. the trade without industrial base. Shop culture has advanced and buildings for shops and commercial complexes have been in demand.

The capital formed within the state has got the outlet for investment in developing such commercial complexes which have been immediately rented out mostly to the traders who were waiting for such complexes to trade. Further licenses of trade have been prepared in the name of the domiciled who have rented them to the non-domiciled merchant class. In this way the capitalist has converted into the renter and capital has been diverted for rent collecting and rent seeking.

The massive potentialities of natural endowment of Arunachal Pradesh have been documented with appreciable note but their utilization for industrial purposes has ended with regrettable note. Resource industry linkage gap is very conspicuous. There are many reasons. Some of them are noted here:

> Usually the entrepreneurs take up the government sponsored schemes which sometimes hardly suit to the context of local Arunachal economy. Government agency stresses more on paper document and viability consideration in terms of actual delivery of output (not potential) receives less weight. The rational entrepreneurs calculate the pecuniary benefit in the form of subsidies and concessional loan which happen to be higher than the expected rate of profit from that project/scheme. As a result, industries as warranted by the natural resources of the state have not come up.

As we have seen, the capitalist has become the rentier. It means still we lack some institutional mechanism to divert the domestic savings for the investable fund which ought to be used by the local entrepreneurs.

Due to price-cliff the industrial entrepreneurs could not develop, for they could not have any share in the markets outside Arunachal Pradesh. Still they are unable to have any sizeable share in the markets within Arunachal Pradesh.

On the whole on industrial front, the capitalists and entrepreneurs have largely become petty profit earners and rent seekers.

Pressing requirements for cash because of increasing dependence on market shops and opportunity of earning cash due to remunerative price level have brought significant changes in village economy too. We can classify the two spates of such changes on the village economy:

(1) In the first spate there has come attitudinal change when commodification of surplus production has taken place. A portion of surplus produce has been diverted to market place to earn cash.

(2) In the second spate, the production is oriented for market sale. It has brought changes both in the pattern and method of production. Mixed cropping pattern with jhum (shifting) method of cultivation has changed into single commercial cropping pattern with permanent settled cultivation.

The reach of these two spates of changes to the villages depend on the distance of the village location from the township. That is to say villages near the district headquarters and connected with road have become relatively more commercialized than the villages of interior parts of Arunachal Pradesh.

This pressing need of cash and diversion of agricultural production to market place have many pronged fall out effect.

The first effect is on the labour relations of production. In patron-client interlocked labour relationship, the cliental households have found the short of customary loans and support from patron households due to diversion of surplus for market sale. They have to compensate this shortage from market purchase after earning money in working for wage. This has trade off effect in their time allocation i.e. either to go for presentation or reciprocity or wage earning. Natural economic incentive is that they prefer wage earning over traditional presentation or reciprocity engagements. Patron households on the other hand have gradually started hiring in labour on wage payment because of decreasing labour turn over rate. As a result, the patron household has become capitalist farmer and cliental household has become agricultural labour. It is economically not viable for capitalist farmer to produce traditional crops on wage payment. Hence commercial crops are raised with commercial method of production. It is therefore found that hire-in labour and marketed surplus are positively related.

The second effect is on the land tenure system. The excess lands used to lease out on moral ground to the poor land holders or sometime they were leased out for labour rent. Since cultivable land is scarce and production of commercial crops is remunerative, the leasing out land on rent or on moral ground has gone down particularly in commercialized villages connected with road. Because of the availability of labour on wage payment, labour rent is becoming redundant in such villages. Further the institution of private property from common village property has emerged. The logical corollary of all these developments is the emergence of capitalist farming with marginalization of land holding.

Another effect is on raising the cattle, sheep, yak and mithun. The livestock happened to be a measuring yard of family status. But this phase has experienced decline in this economic activity. This decline is mainly due to the irksomeness involved in such works and the shrinking of grazing land due to decrease in common village land.

Let us recollect the arguments of economic forces during phase-III.

- This is the phase of economic liberalization wherein economic forces have started operating as per market signal.
- Exchange value and its accumulation have become the organizing principle.
- Dependence on market has increased substantially and so cash requirement has increased.
- Industries as warranted by the availability of natural resources are yet to come up. Resource-industry linkage gap till persists.
- Capitalist has turned and become the rentier class, for capital is invested in developing the shopping complexes to rent them out.
- Shops are full of goods which are produced outside Arunachal Pradesh.
- Commercialization of agriculture is taking place. In market places local vegetables are being supplied.
- Commercialization of village economy depends on the village location and connection with road. .
- Market mechanism has disciplined all economic relations and economic activities in village such as land tenure relations, livestock activities, etc.

V

A Note on Transformation

Traditionally regulated subsistence economy provided the material support to their populace with a limited variety of output and low level of production. Geographical specificities in terms of opportunities and constraints designed and shaped to both production pattern and consumption trait. Lending, borrowing, barter trade, periodic cross-border trade were supplementing economic activities. Forest gatherings and livestock were the lost resort of survival. Savings, investment and capital formation were taking place instantly under static equilibrium. It was quasi-monetized economy where scale of liquidity existed to effectuate the material flow through discrete circuits of exchange. This was the course of movement of economic forces which Arunachal economy inherited.

During the 1970s and the 1980s, a turn has come when these subsistence economies were integrated through external state agency. They were integrated by both physical infrastructure like means of transportation and communication and soft infrastructure such as common governance, health facilities and education. Government sector is added into the hitherto two-sector economy. This sector assumed the leading role in designing, shaping and finally directing the economy. This sector has poled up the middle class from all sub-self-subsistence economics. Mostly the *chieftain* section of various tribal groups formed this class. During this phase-II the economy was just like the conical rectangular shape with small middle class on the top of a large base of poor masses. As government sector expanded, the middle salaried class was nourished and grew in size. In this phase the relationship between the newly emerged middle class and the vast masses was mechanistic because this middle class was not getting the material support in the form of expropriating the surplus from the base of vast poor masses but they were getting their wherewithal externally. Hence it was externally erected dual economy. The second phase therefore, gave altogether a different course for the movement of economic forces. This system more or less lasted with the Union Territory period.

A new turn has come during the 1990s when external support has started loosening and the economy has to develop own material support. This is the phase of liberalization and globalization. Now the relationship between the erected middle class and vast majority has become organical. This organic symbiotic relation of these two organs of the economy has given still another course for the movement of economic forces. Now the economy is becoming more and more sensitized and it is striving to develop the mechanism to more on the new path.

REFERENCES

Bhargava, Rajeev 1992, *Individualism in Social Science: Forms and Limits of a Methodology*, Clarendon, Oxford University Press, Oxford.

Elwin, Verrier 1964, *A Philosophy for NEFA*, Directorate of Research, Govt. of Arunachal Pradesh, Shillong (Itanagar).

Firth, Raymond and B.S.Yamey 1963, *Capital, Savings and Credits in Peasant Societies*, Aldine Publishing Company, Chicago.

Furer-Haimendorf, Christoph von 1980, *A Himalayan Tribe from Cattle to Cash*, Vikas Publishing House Pvt. Ltd., New Delhi.

Hicks, J. 1969, *A Theory of Economic History*, OUP Clarendon Press, New York.

Keynes, J.M. 1936, *The General Theory of Employment Interest and Money*, Macmillan & Co. Ltd., London.

Kurien, C.T. 1992, *The Economy: An Interpretative Introduction*, Sage Publications, New Delhi.

Lokanathan, P.S. 1976, *Techno-Economic Survey of NEFA*, National Council of Applied Economic Research, New Delhi.

Marx, Kasl 1964, *Pre-Capitalist Economic Formations*, Edt. By E.J. Hobsbawm, Translated by Jack Cohen, Lawrence and Wishart, London.

Mishra, Deepak, K. 1999, *The Political Economy of Agrarian Change: Locating the Role of State, Market and Community IInd* Annual Conference of NEFA, Margharita, Assam.

Patnaik, Prabhat 1999, *The Performance of the Indian Economy in the 1990s*, Social Scientist, Vol. 27, Nos. 5-6, May-June.

Polnyi, Karl *et. al.* 1957, *Trade and Market in Early Empires: Economics in History and Theory*, The Collier-Macmillan Limited, London.

Salam, M.A. 2006, *Agricultural Transformation in North-East India with Special Reference to Arunachal Pradesh*, Mittal , New Delhi.

———, 2007, *Impact of Globalization on Agrarian Transformation in Arunachal Pradesh*, Political Economy Journal of India, Vol.16, No. 2, July-December.

———, 2008, *Money, Market and Trade: Case of Lhou in Arunachal Pradesh in India in the Emerging Global Order* ed. By Amar

Mohanty, P.K. Nayak and M.G. Jomon, Tata McGraw Hill, New Delhi.

Sen, Amartya 1999, *Development as Freedom*, OUP, New Delhi.

Singh, K.S. 1995, *People of India, Arunachal Pradesh*, Vol. XIV, Anthropological Survey of India, Seagull Books, Calcutta.

50 Years Space of Development in Arunachal Pradesh (1947-97), Director of Economics and Statistics, Govt. of Arunachal Pradesh, Itanagar.

Index

A

B

Y

Z